ASIAN STUDIES ASSOCIATION OF AUSTRALIA
Southeast Asia Publications Series

No 17
NATION IN ARMS

ASIAN STUDIES ASSOCIATION OF AUSTRALIA
Southeast Asia Publications Series

Titles in print

4 Anthony Reid & David Marr
(eds)
*Perceptions of the Past in
Southeast Asia*

9 R E Elson
*Javanese Peasants and the
Colonial Sugar Industry*

10 Benjamin A Batson
*The End of the Absolute
Monarchy in Siam*

11 Patrick Guinness
*Harmony and Hierarchy in
a Javanese Kampung*

12 John Ingleson
*In Search of Justice:
Workers and Unions in
Colonial Java, 1908–1926*

13 Richard Robison
*Indonesia: The Rise of
Capital*

14 Norman G Owen (ed)
*Death and Disease in
Southeast Asia:
Explorations in Social,
Medical and Demographic
History*

15 Jennifer Alexander
*Trade, Traders and Trading
in Rural Java*

16 Anne Booth
*Agricultural Development
in Indonesia*

17 Greg Lockhart
*Nation in Arms:
The Origins of the
People's Army of Vietnam*

EDITORIAL COMMITTEE

David Chandler
Keith Foulcher
James Fox
John Ingleson (Chairman)
Anthony Milner

Monash University
Flinders University
Australian National University
University of New South Wales
Australian National University

C/-School of History
University of New South Wales
Kensington, AUSTRALIA

Nation in Arms

The Origins of the People's Army of Vietnam

GREG LOCKHART

Asian Studies Association of Australia
in association with
Sydney
ALLEN AND UNWIN
Wellington London Boston

© Greg Lockhart 1989

This book is copyright under the Berne Convention. No reproduction without permission.

First published in 1989

Allen & Unwin Australia Pty Ltd
An Unwin Hyman company
8 Napier Street, North Sydney, NSW 2059 Australia

Allen & Unwin New Zealand Limited
75 Ghuznee Street, Wellington, New Zealand

Unwin Hyman Limited
15-17 Broadwick Street, London W1V 1FP England

Unwin Hyman Inc.
8 Winchester Place, Winchester, Mass 01890 USA

National Library of Australia
Cataloguing-in-Publication entry:

Lockhart, Greg
    Nation in arms: the origins of the People's Army of Vietnam.

    Bibliography.
    Includes index.
    ISBN 0 04 301294 9.
    ISBN 0 04 324012 7 (pbk.)

    1. Vietnam, Quân dôi nhân dân. 2. Vietnam — Armed Forces
    — History. 3. Vietnam — History — 1858-1945. 4. Vietnam
    — History — 1945-1975. I. Asian Studies Association of
    Australia. II. Title. (Series: Southeast Asia publications
    series; no. 17).
    959.7
Library of Congress Catalog Card Number: 89-80237

Printed in Singapore by Kim Hup Lee Printing

This book is dedicated to my Parents

And ideally the chime of this
Will come to have the fascination of a remembered thing
Without avatars, or so remote, like a catastrophe
In some unheard-of-country, that our concern
Will be only another fact in a long list of important facts.

John Ashbery
Voyage in the Blue

I took out my dice for the ritual game of *Quatre Cent Vingt-et-un*.
How those figures and the sight of dice bring back to mind the
war-years in Indo-China. Anywhere in the world when I see two
men dicing I am back in the streets of Hanoi or Saigon or among
the blasted buildings of Phat Diem, I see the parachutists,
protected like caterpillars by their strange markings, patrolling by
the canals, I hear the sound of the mortars closing in, and perhaps
I see a dead child.

Graham Greene
The Quiet American

Contents

Abbreviations

Literary Abbreviations

BEFEO	*Bulletin de l'Ecole Française d'Extrême Orient*
CKCT	*Cuoc Khang Chien Than Thanh cua Nhan Dan Viet Nam* [The Sacred Resistance War of the Vietnamese People]
CMCD	*Tai Lieu Tham Khao Lich Su Cach Mang Can Dai Viet Nam* [Research Documents on the History of Vietnam's Modern Revolution]
CMTT	*Tai Lieu Tham Khao Cach Mang Thang Tham (Tong Khoi Nghia o Ha Noi va Cac Dia Phuong)* [Research Documents on the August Revolution (in the General Uprising in Hanoi and other Regions)]
JRAS	*Journal of the Royal Asiatic Society*
JSEAS	*Journal of Southeast Asian Studies*
JSEAH	*Journal of Southeast Asian History*
LSDC	*Lich Su Dang Cong San Viet Nam So Thao* [Draft History of the People's Army of Vietnam]
LSQD	*Lich Su Quan Doi Nhan Dan Viet Nam* [History of the People's Army of Vietnam]
NCLS	*Nghien Cuu Lich Suu* [Historical Studies]
VKD	*Van Kien Dang ve Khang Chien Chong Thuc Dan Phap* [Party Documents on the Resistance War against the French Colonialists]
VKQS	*Van Kien Quan Su cua Dang* [Military Documents of the Party]

Other Abbreviations

AOM	*Archives Nationales de France, Section Outre-Mer*
ARVN	Army of the Republic of Vietnam
CCP	Chinese Communist Party
CHEAM	*Centre de Hautes Etudes Administratives sur L'Afrique et L'Asie modernes*
DMH	*Viet Nam Cach Menh Dong Minh Hoi* [Vietnamese Revolutionary Nationalist Party]
DRV	Democratic Republic of Vietnam
FCP	French Communist Party
ICP	Indochinese Communist Party
NF	*Nouveau Fonds*
NLF	National Liberation Front (This term is itself an abbreviation of the term 'National Front for the Liberation of the Southern Region' or '*Mat Tran Dan Toc Giai Phong Mien Nam*'.)
NXB	*Nha Xuat Ban* [Publishing House]
PAVN	People's Army of Vietnam
PLAF	People's Liberation Armed Forces
SHAT	*Service Historique de l'Armée de Terre*
VNQDD	*Viet Nam Quoc Dan Dang* [Vietnamese Nationalist Party]

Maps

Preface and Acknowledgements

The subject of this book was first suggested to me by Dr Craig Reynolds who supervised my studies at the University of Sydney. I had been in the Australian Army for ten years, and gone to the Vietnam War. After leaving the Army in 1975 I had also studied some Vietnamese history for my undergraduate degree. A conspiracy of background and astute academic supervision then set the course of the doctoral thesis on which this work is largely based.

The inclination to write a work based on Vietnamese language sources naturally preceded Dr Reynolds' prompting. In 1972 I picked up some Vietnamese when I was an adviser with regional force units of the Army of the Republic of Vietnam. Later, I also read a passage in Bernard Fall's book, *Vietnam Witness*, which was published in 1966:

> As the Viet-Nam problem grew into its present magnitude, there developed among long-time observers a distinct feeling of *déjà vu*—the impression of once more going through a situation that already has been played or even replayed several times.
> There is the constant stream of high-level visitors to Saigon—which had its counterpart even in French days—who strenuously try to reach the realities of the situation by reducing the physical distance between themselves and the problem at hand. Apparently, they forget that the very officials who escort them around Viet-Nam are those who write (or wrote) the reports they read in Washington (or Paris).

I decided to tap Vietnamese sources because I did not want to replay yet again one of the great failures in modern history.

Soon after the French defeat at Dien Bien Phu in 1954, *Le Figaro* ran a story on 2 June which spoke of a 'turning back' of almost five

xi

centuries of world history in which the Western powers had extended their hegemony over the globe. In *Vietnam Witness* Bernard Fall then compared the fall of Dien Bien Phu to the fall of Constantinople in 1453. For the Americans and their English speaking allies, Western power in Asia did not necessarily seem to turn back at Dien Bien Phu. The falls of Singapore in 1942 and of Saigon in 1975 provided other Constantinoples. Yet President Kennedy's awesome inaugural address in 1961, which announced American 'globalism', certainly verified the Gallic analogy as it marked an intensification of the effort that failed to restore Western hegemony in a new form.

In this global context, aspects of the Vietnam War may certainly be illuminated on the basis of French and English language sources. Without access to libraries and archives in France and America which contain masses of primary and secondary sources, it is also true that I could not have written this book; the Vietnamese authorities left unanswered my request for a research visa in 1981. Yet no matter how far the shock waves of Dien Bien Phu have scattered papers all over the world, no attempt to make a statement about the nature of the Vietnam War which overlooks Vietnamese sources can make much sense. The result would be, and often is, something like trying to explain the nature of the First World War from the sole perspective of the German Army, something like *Mein Kampf*.

Once the decision to learn more Vietnamese was taken, the idea that I should write about the People's Army fell into place. As it grew from a guerrilla platoon in 1944 to an army with some 450,000 regular soldiers in 1954 and a million in 1975, the People's Army had clearly played an important role in defeating French and American power and creating an independent nation-state in Vietnam. The decision to write about 'the origins' of the Army, to take the story from its conception in the colonial period through the formation of the first guerrilla bases in 1943 to the landmark victory in 1954, was then imposed on me. The 'anti-French' period from 1945 to 1954 forms a distinctive one in the thirty year war. It is also the formative period of the army's development, when its social and political functions, its organisation, logistics, and strategy were shaped. An historical understanding of the 'anti-American' phases of the war is impossible without a grounding in this earlier period. Moreover, when I carried out my primary research between 1979 and 1981, much of the source material necessary for a full study of the People's Army between 1955 and 1975 was not accessible, and this would have prevented me from writing on the period even if the scale of the task had not.

While the subject thus defined itself, its execution was protracted. When I began work in 1979 there was no book published in English on the People's Army and, even now, there is only one other, published in 1986, by Douglas Pike. This gap in the literature may seem surprising when the People's Army has defeated successive Western attempts to change the course of Vietnamese history. Yet political-military interventions in other people's countries are not merely political-military affairs. They are rooted in assumptions of cultural superiority, and in phrases like the *mission civilisatrice*, the white man's burden, saving the world for democracy. When such deeply rooted assumptions are destroyed the culture is shaken, and the gaps that occur in our consciousness are difficult to fill. Between the destruction and gaps in my employment as an historian, this book took ten years to work itself out.

Many people have helped. Dr Reynolds is a fine scholar as well as a fine person. His rigorous readings of my first drafts were always accurate and did much to shape the product. Detailed readings of the manuscript by Dr David Marr and Professor Alexander Woodside then expanded my good fortune. They drew on a great depth and breadth of knowledge about Vietnam to help me. Dr Marr was also generous with his library. Three other scholars who gave the manuscript valuable readings were Mr Georges Boudarel, Ms Nola Cooke, and Dr David Chandler. All three prevented me from making further mistakes, and Dr Chandler helped to edit the manuscript for publication.

Mme Christiane Rageau at the Bibliothèque Nationale in Paris gave bibliographical assistance that was a big help. The staff of the Historical Service of the French Army at the Château de Vincennes were kind and helpful. Because of my long trip across the ocean, they gave me permission to use their archives even as they were being prepared for opening to the general public. While I was a Visiting Fellow at the Strategic and Defence Studies Centre at the Australian National University in 1987, the head of the Centre, Professor Desmond Ball, also approved the funds that were necessary to have the manuscript photo-scanned so that I could throw it around on the computer. To these people I am grateful.

Other people whose friendship and knowledge have been important to me are: Jim Gordon, Graham Jennison, Rollin Schlicht, Margaret Sankey, Rod Tiffen, Pham Van Minh, Graham Walker, Adriana Novelo, Esta Ungar, Ton That Phuong, Greg Pemberton, Frank Frost, Michael McDermott, Greg Dodds, Greg Gilbert and Bill Rolfe.

The contribution of my wife Monique overshadows all the others. She has done more than I could reasonably have asked to help this book come into print.

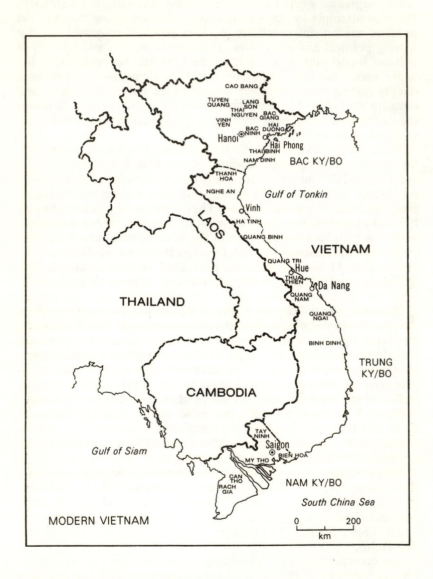

Introduction

According to Douglas Pike, the story of *PAVN*, the People's Army of Vietnam, begins in a 'cave' somewhere near the Sino-Vietnamese border in the dying stages of World War Two.[1] In this vague setting, a 'peculiar alchemy' of messianic leadership and martial spirit is said to have transformed a gang of thirty four outlaws from colonial society into what finally became an army of 'monstrous' size.

As the monster develops Pike speaks in brooding metaphors. These afflict his subject with 'mental blocks' and shroud it in 'dark clouds'. Some attempt at theory can be discerned in the chapters which use the Vietnamese notion of 'struggle', *dau tranh*, to try to explain why the communists won. However, after a not very promising venture into Vietnamese metaphysics these chapters fall away into incoherence—*dau tranh* 'is vague, amorphous, and given to endless interpretation'.[2] Aimless and eccentric, the first book length account of the People's Army in English ends on a garbled note about how history has warped, corrupted, and played to the worst instincts of its subject. *PAVN* is a case study of American and, more generally, Western confusion at the outcome of the Vietnam War.

With the exception of William Turley, who offered some preliminary findings on the mass mobilisation process in 1972,[3] no liberal

[1]Douglas Pike, *PAVN: People's Army of Vietnam*, Novato: Presido, 1986, p. 2.
[2]Ibid., p. 222. The two major kinds of *dau tranh*, military *dau tranh* and political *dau tranh*, which in Pike's view 'incidentally' explain 'Why the Communists Won', are delineated in Chapters 9–10.
[3]William S. Turley, 'Army, Party, and Society in the Democratic Republic of Vietnam: Civil and Military Relations in a Mass Mobilization System', PhD, University of Washington, 1972. Also see his other works listed in the bibliography.

1

writer to my knowledge has made a concerted attempt to understand the People's Army. Général Gras who has written something on the subject merely has the People's Army growing without internal momentum through the contradictions in French colonial policy.[4] And George Kahin, whose powerful critique of America's intervention in Vietnam justly dominates that field, does not even have an entry for the 'People's Army' in his index.[5] Although Kahin's is a political rather than a military history, his lack of focus on the nature of the armed forces that the Americans were intervening to repress, still suggests that Pike's *PAVN* is not alone in its inability to establish a conceptual foundation for the main force of the Vietnamese revolution.

The term 'People's Army' (*Quan Doi Nhan Dan*) is a generic one[6] which first came into general circulation to describe all the forces of the nation whose unity and independence had been established under the Democratic Republic of Vietnam in August-September 1945. Once French attempts to divide the nation had been defeated in 1954, but the explicit provisions of the Geneva Accords for re-unification elections in 1956 were not honoured, the term 'People's Army' continued to describe the forces of the Democratic Republic. However, with the existence of the Republic of Vietnam in the south from 1955, the term 'People's Liberation Armed Forces' (PLAF) was used to describe the army that came into existence in early 1961 under the National Front for the Liberation of the Southern Region or *Mat Tran Dan Toc Giai Phong Mien Nam* (NLF). Therefore, while the existence of the Republic of Vietnam makes it necessary to maintain the People's Army/PLAF distinction between 1961 and 1975, the PLAF are still correctly described as national forces because they were derived from a 'National' Front, and the nationalist ethos of PAVN still went back to its beginnings.

What I propose is that the origins of the People's Army of Vietnam can not be separated from the birth of the modern Vietnamese nation. Moreover, as a national army, the People's Army of Vietnam had origins that are part of a world historical process. After the new concept of 'nation' came into Vietnamese political philosophy in the

---

[4]There are some passages on the People's Army in Général Yves Gras, *Histoire de la guerre d'Indochine*, Paris: Plon, 1975.

[5]George McT. Kahin, *Intervention: How America Became Involved in Vietnam*, New York: Knopf, 1986.

[6]Most notably in Ban Nghien Cuu Lich Su Quan Doi Thuoc Cuc Chinh Tri [Board for the Historical Study of the Army in the Political Department], *Lich Su Quan Doi Nhan Dan Viet Nam* [History of the People's Army of Vietnam], Hanoi: NXB Quan Doi Nhan Dan, 1974.

1900s, it was first realised between 1945 and 1954, at a time when widespread resistance to Western imperialism gave birth to many other nations in Asia, Africa, and Latin America. Furthermore, the emergence of these nations does not provide the only set of parallels for the Vietnamese experience, for nations had already come into being in Europe a century before.

It was indeed in the wake of the French revolution, when the Napoleonic invasions began to stimulate the rise of modern nation states in Europe, that Clausewitz probably offered the first theoretical discussion of 'Arming the People' (*Volksbewaffnung*).[7] This discussion came in the context of the 'people's war' (*volkskrieg*) he perceived in various parts of Europe and Russia as a response to the invasions of Napoleon's grand armies. Clausewitz also used the term 'people's war' to describe the action of irregular militia and peasant bands. These could not fight the unprecedented power of the invader on his own terms, but they could 'gradually' threaten his 'lines of communication and his very existence'.[8] This was guerrilla war. And if we add a sense of the new political, economic, and cultural forces that were unleashed in the European resistance to Napoleon, we are reminded that the strategies of the *guerrilleros* in Spain, the unification of Germany, and the Italian Risorgimento prefigure the wars of 'national' liberation that erupted in Asia and Africa a century later.

Once the Second World War had destabilised the international order and led to a spate of wars in the Western colonies, these were usually fought by peasant armies against the technologically superior forces of Western imperialism. They tended to be protracted guerrilla wars because any idea of a rapid victory using massed attacks by lightly armed peasants was impractical. At the same time, however, the strength of the guerrilla armies tended to grow out of their weakness. As Mao saw in his influential military writings in 1937 and 1938,[9] the need to develop protracted strategies forced the guerrilla armies to formulate political, economic, and social programs that reflected the popular goals of national liberation, or those guerrilla forces could not survive for long. In other words, the guerrilla forces that survived to win nationalist victories in many countries after World War Two were necessarily a manifestation as well as an

---

[7]This is the title of Chapter 26, Book Six of Carl Von Clausewitz, *Vom Kriege*, Bonn: Ferd. Dümmlers Verlag, 1973, p. 799.

[8]Clausewitz, *Vom Kriege*, pp. 799–802. The quotations on the peasant bands largely follow Michael Howard and Peter Paret translation of *On War*, Princeton University Press, 1984, pp. 480–481.

[9]See Bibliography, Western Language Sources, under Mao Tse Tung. These works, *On Guerrilla War* and *On Protracted War* are discussed in Chapter 2.

instrument of the revolutions which propelled them. Their strength was their popular support.

The central idea of this book is that the People's Army of Vietnam grew from strength to strength in a protracted struggle because it was a manifestation of a new national consciousness that was stimulated by colonial rule. Chapter 1 will show how the main effect of the French conquest on Vietnamese political culture between 1859 and 1884 was to destroy the institution of the monarchy and remove the lynch pin of the ancient order. With no king there was chaos, and this made it possible for the French to 'divide and rule' the country until 1945. At the same time, however, the destruction of the monarchy caused a revolution in the way Vietnamese came to think about their polity.

In the 1900s new terms including *dan toc* and *quoc dan* came into the Vietnamese political vocabulary. These terms can be translated as 'people', as in 'the Vietnamese people', and *quoc dan* is more usually translated this way.[10] One of the main points of Chapter 2, therefore, is to show how, with the destruction of the monarchy, these terms were based on the new political category of 'the people' (*dan*). In other words, while people had certainly existed as subjects in ancient times, 'the people' as citizens with political and economic rights now came to be the category of fundamental importance which underpinned modern concepts of 'the nation' (*quoc gia*). Another point of Chapter 2 then stems from the fact that the unprecedented power of the French systematically repressed any concrete manifestation of Vietnamese nationalism.

It was not in terms of a purely nationalist or republican ideology that the Vietnamese people, or what Ho Chi Minh once described as the 'basic force' of the Vietnamese revolution, could be shaped conceptually into the armed force of the nation. As the Vietnamese 'Nationalist' Party found when it led an uprising in 1930 and never recovered from the French repression, purely nationalist and republican ideologies had their limitations. They had identified the people as the only possible force for nationalism, but they could not define an independent context for the nation in the face of French colonial power. In fact, under the specific circumstances of the Vietnamese revolution, the ideology of Marxist-Leninist internationalism was the only one to define successfully the force of the nation.

This was not because Marxist theory necessarily offered a convincing analysis of Vietnamese history. Indeed, Vietnamese Marxist-Leninists had to abandon the classical Marxist notion of class struggle by the 1940s in the interests of both common sense and national

---

[10]The ambiguities in these terms are discussed in Chapter 2.

solidarity against the French. But, after 1920, when Lenin's writings on imperialism demonstrated the connection between capitalism and colonialist exploitation, some radical Vietnamese nationalists were able to understand the dichotomy between the Vietnamese as 'one people' or 'nation' and the modern political category of 'imperialists' (*de quoc*).

In Dao Duy Anh's 1928 *History of Colonialism*,[11] for example, the author used the terms 'imperialism' (*de quoc chu nghia*), 'the soldiery' (*binh linh*), and 'the army' (*quan doi*) to describe the philosophy and force of the existing colonial order in Vietnam and other countries. These were old terms for describing the armed forces of any established order, and, although under the influence of Marxism-Leninism the term 'imperialism' had new connotations of greed and exploitation, all it literally meant was 'the doctrine of ruling the country'. But this old order terminology only highlighted the new order which writers like Dao Duy Anh were beginning to build. For both rooted in the old terms and opposed to them, was the implication of power for 'the people' and power for 'the nation', rather than power for 'ruling the country'.

Ben Anderson has argued that 'nationalism has to be understood, by aligning it not with self consciously held political ideologies, but with the large cultural systems that preceded it, out of which—as well as against which—it came into being.'[12] Yet, for all its importance, this formulation is only half right in the case of Vietnam. Vietnamese Marxist-Leninists frequently turned Marx on his head. But it was only through a highly self-conscious alignment with Marxist-Leninist internationalism that the Vietnamese proved able to align their revolution with the large culture system out of which—as well as against which—the Vietnamese nationalist movement finally realised the country's independence.

In pre-colonial times the independent monarchical state was always constituted within a larger Confucian world order because Vietnam was a small country located in the ambit of China. Tribute missions, the use of Chinese political and administrative models, and the use of Chinese military books reflected this relationship. For the Vietnamese, recognition by the Chinese court reinforced the monarch's internal power because of the harmonious inter-state relations it signified and the patina of high culture it provided. For the Chinese, the relationship helped to ensure that the southern border regions were in good hands. By reducing the possibility of Chinese

---

[11]Dao Duy Anh, *Thuc Dan Lich Su*, Hue, 1928.
[12]Benedict Anderson, *Imagined Communities: Reflections on the Origins and Spread of Nationalism*, London: Verso, 1983, p. 19.

interference or invasions the internal power of the Vietnamese monarch was reinforced further. One of the paradoxes in Vietnamese history was that, as in the first half of the nineteenth century, the unity and independence of the state tended to be most secure when kings adopted Chinese models of government and administration.[13]

In modern times this relationship changed and continued. By the mid-1920s it had become clear to many intellectuals that even though colonialism had ripped Vietnam out of the Chinese world order, the French would never permit the Vietnamese to enjoy modernity and independence within their imperial order. Some Vietnamese radicals thus began to look to the Soviet Union; to the Russian revolution and the Comintern to help them find an independent place in the modern world. The Comintern supported anti-colonial movements, and we will see that Marxist-Leninist internationalism provided Vietnamese radicals with the universalising creed that they needed to imagine an alternative to colonial rule.

One advantage of being able to imagine such an alternative was the vision splendid of electrification, abundant harvests, and political independence that went with it. In the 1930s when French power was unshakable, the sense of purpose this vision bolstered, and the belief it encouraged in 'world revolution', in a coming world crisis that would undermine the power of the French, also helped the Indochinese Communist Party (ICP), formed in 1930, to steel itself against the vicissitudes of the decade.

In keeping with these vicissitudes, William Duiker has shown how the ICP's commitment to Comintern models of 'class struggle' and urban revolution caused it many problems. When the vast majority of the population were in fact peasants and French repression was ruthless, the ICP could not have been more remote from local political realities than it was in the 1930s.[14] But, then, when the Second World War erupted and the Comintern connection was cut, the ICP found itself in a position that no other anti-colonial party found itself in as the Sino-Vietnamese relationship began to reassert itself. As they began to expand their power, Marxist-Leninist internationalists in China were now able to offer the ICP political-military

---

[13]It is well known that on the numerous occasions they have defeated Chinese armies of invasion one of the first actions of Vietnamese kings has been to re-establish tributary relations with the Chinese court and often to institute Chinese style reforms. Even after Nguyen Hue, who is remembered by Vietnamese historians for promoting populist Vietnamese culture and *Nom* literature, defeated a Qing army in 1789, he sought to re-establish good relations with China.

[14]William Duiker, *The Communist Road to Power in Vietnam*, Boulder, Colorado: Westview Press, 1981, Chapter 3.

and economic models that related Vietnam's revolutionary goals to ancient methods of statecraft. Indeed, Marxist-Leninist internationalism permitted the ICP to fuse old and new political-military methods which crystallised the armed force of the nation. This is the main theme of the book.

It will be recalled that the Vietnamese had always used Chinese military texts. Therefore, the past was surely present in 1938 when Vietnamese translations of parts of Mao's *On Guerrilla War*,[15] reached radical intellectuals in Vietnam. At the same time as the ideology of Marxist-Leninist internationalism was left intact, Chapters 2 and 3 will then show how the influence of Mao's writings on protracted guerrilla strategies and national liberation had an important bearing on ICP policy between 1939 and 1942. Indeed, while the Japanese invasion of China prefigured the Japanese occupation of Vietnam and the fall of the French colonial regime in March 1945, Mao's ideas helped to shape the ICP's decision to abandon its earlier emphasis on Comintern models for urban revolution. This was because Mao's guerrilla strategies suggested a more appropriate method of mobilising the mass of the peasant population. And, as the old Vietnamese practice of using Chinese political-military models brought the ICP's policies closer to local realities at a crucial time, there was a revival of other political-military traditions.

In the late 1930s and early 1940s a number of Vietnamese writers began to tap their people's ancient history of resistance to foreign invaders. Major studies in the late 1930s and early 1940s were devoted to Le Loi who defeated the Ming invaders and unified the country between 1416 and 1427, and to Nguyen Hue who led the Tay Son rebellion, defeated the Qing invasion of 1788–89, and unified the country for the first time in three centuries.[16] These works were well known in radical circles, and vigorous efforts were made to popularise their findings. By 1945, for example, one language primer that was used in the Viet Minh's literacy campaign to help mobilise the masses, made model sentences out of references to ancient resistance leaders: 'We must venerate our heroes' and 'Tran Quoc Tuan was a famous Vietnamese general who panicked the Mongol army many times'[17] in the thirteenth century.

[15]See Bibliography, All Other Books, Part 2, under Mao Tse Tung and Che Guevara.

[16]For example, Chu Thien (Hoang Minh Giam), *Le Thai To* [i.e. Le Loi], Hanoi: 1940; Hoa Bang (Hoang Thuc Tram), *Quang Trung* [i.e. Nguyen Hue's reign name], Hanoi: 1944. Between about 1500 and 1800 the country was divided between the Trinh family in the north and the Nguyen family in the south.

[17]Viet Nam Dan Chu Cong Hoa, *Van Quoc Ngu* [Learning the National Language], Hanoi: Bo Quoc Gia Giao Giup, 1945, lesson 30.

Chapters 3 and 4 show how the use of guerrilla strategies in the mass mobilisation process in late 1944 and 1945, must be related to pre-colonial practices as well as to international events that undermined the power of the French colonial regime during the Second World War. For example, when ICP cadres first raised the red flag with the yellow star during the Nam Ky uprising in 1940, and when they began consciously to use the very important political-military technique of 'armed propaganda' (*vu trang tuyen truyen*) to mobilise the society in 1944, they were doing what Le Loi had done when he raised the banner of a 'righteous uprising' or '*khoi nghia*' against the Ming in 1416. They were integrating demonstrations of armed strength with the political propaganda that promised good government and a better life. Under modern conditions the only difference was that 'armed propaganda' integrated the use of armed force with the generally accepted goals of the revolution—national unity, independence, and modernity. In fact, the moralistic idea of '*khoi nghia*', which modern scholars say was rooted in the Confucian right to revolt against corrupt or illegitimate authority, meshes with the modern technique of armed propaganda.

Chapter 5 also highlights the revival of an ancient tradition under modern conditions: the development of state unity in the face of foreign invasions. Once Ho Chi Minh declared the independence of the Democratic Republic of Vietnam in September 1945, the central government used armed propaganda to pump up its administration in the villages and expand the 'national army'. In the period to December 1946 when the Indochina War began, there were great regional variations in political-military development. These were accentuated by the presence of four foreign armies in the country—British and Chinese armies which came to disarm the Japanese army, and a French army which came to reclaim the colony. However, as hostilities immediately broke out in the south where the British facilitated the French re-entry, and the Hanoi government negotiated with the French to try to avert a full scale war, the central government's success in unifying the state reflects the universal hostility to the French reoccupation. Such was the historical impulse for the polity to unite in the face of foreign invasions, as it had done in the days of Tran Quoc Tuan, Le Loi, and Nguyen Hue.

Once Franco-Viet Minh negotiations broke down and full scale hostilities began in the north as well as the south, Chapter 6 will show how national unity was severely strained in 1947. The administration and military organisation that had developed in 1945–1946 collapsed. But, as the resistance forces creatively adapted Mao's model to the pressures of total war by 1949, it is remarkable that they were re-erected along pre-colonial lines. In Chapter 1 it will be seen that established pre-colonial armies had always been structured along regional lines using Chinese models of military organisation. At the state level, this meant that the army was composed of elite guard regiments, *linh ve*, recruited from the dynasty's home region and responsible for the close defence of the dynasty. At the regional level, it meant that locally recruited regiments, *linh co*, were responsible for regional defence. Chapters 6 and 7 will then show the emergence of the following force structure on the Maoist model between 1948 and 1954: Guerrilla Units (*Doi Du Kich*) at the village level, Regional Forces (*Dia Phuong Quan*) at the district and provincial levels, and Main Force Units (*Chu Luc*) at the national level. The only difference was that at a time of foreign invasion the army had to be re-established from the bottom up, or 'from small to big' as the Viet Minh literature puts it.

Irregular village guerrilla units using armed propaganda first rooted the army in its social base. On the Maoist model small scale hit-and-run tactics against the invaders were used primarily to demonstrate the power of the revolutionary party in the villages. As such demonstrations were linked with revolutionary political propaganda, and mass organisations were developed to mobilise people and resources. When enough guerrilla units had been mobilised in a region and the political and economic infrastructure was well developed, people and resources were channelled upwards into the formation of quasi-regular regional units of up to regimental strength. Chapter 7 demonstrates how from 1950 the main force divisions that defeated the French garrison at Dien Bien Phu in 1954 were finally formed at the national level.

At this level, internal mobilisation at the village and the regional levels was of fundamental importance. In view of the need to fight major French formations, however, international support from China and other socialist bloc countries was essential to arm the regular divisions. Nevertheless, as the volume of Chinese aid paled into insignificance compared with American aid to the French, the need for international support only highlights the primary importance of internal political-military development, because internal development was necessary to attract and apply the aid. In other words, while the French could not effectively utilise their aid because they did not have popular support, the Viet Minh fulfilled old and new needs when they established the independence of the Democratic Republic of Vietnam with the support of China and other Marxist-Leninist states.

While its success depended upon specific conditions, the ideology of Marxist-Leninist internationalism was therefore of tremendous importance in the Vietnamese revolution. It permitted the Vietnamese to integrate old political-military methods with the changes that had overcome them in the modern world. The People's Army then grew at the core of the new nation because it integrated the armed force of 'the people' with the ideals of unity, independence, and the promise of modernity.

From a technical point of view I have largely based my discussion on primary sources. This claim does not apply to the first chapter. In fact, to try to lay out the structure of eighty years of French colonial rule I have largely had to make my interpretations on the basis of turn of the century French studies, relatively recent Vietnamese works, and compilations of primary sources such as Taboulet's *La geste française en Indochine* that was not published in Paris until 1955–56. I must say, however, that I was particularly fortunate to have Nola Cooke point out the pitfalls in this literature which she knows far better than me.

There are two main limitations to the sources I have used in the rest of the book. One is that I have not always been able to use original editions of Vietnamese works. This is the case with Phan Boi Chau's turn of the century writings which I read in Vietnamese and not the original Chinese characters. It is also the case with Ho Chi Minh's 1927 publication, *The Road to Revolution* (*Duong Cach Menh*), which, although written in Vietnamese, was edited in unacknowledged ways before it was finally published in Hanoi in 1980.[18]

The second limitation is that the primary collections of Party Documents and resistance newspapers I have used are usually edited.[19] This means, for example, that details of the Party's political activities during its clandestine phase between late 1945 and early 1951 have been largely eliminated from these sources even though they provide a fulsome coverage of Party policy. While oblique references to Chinese aid to the People's Army can be found in the edited newspaper collections and Party Documents, it is also the case that details of this aid have been almost entirely expunged. However, none of these sources were written or collected in isolation, the collections are sufficiently voluminous to provide a strong foundation for independent interpretation, and all can be monitored to some extent.

It is possible to check different writings by Phan Boi Chau against each other and against the writings of his contemporaries. There are Vietnamese and English commentaries on Ho's *Road to Revolution*,

---

[18]For Phan Boi Chau's works see Bibliography, All Other Books, Part 1, under Phan Boi Chau and under Van Hoc. The edition of *The Road to Revolution* I have used is in Ho Chi Minh, *Tuyen Tap* [Collected Works], Vol. 1, Hanoi: Su That, 1980.
[19]These documents are listed in the Bibliography, Primary Sources, Part 2.

the 1980 edition can be checked to some extent against fragments published earlier, and a knowledge of available editions of other radical writings published around 1927 at least sharpens one's intuition. With respect to the voluminous compilations of Party Documents and resistance newspapers, there is so much other primary and secondary information now available to augment and monitor them that as long as they are read critically I do not think it matters much if they are edited.

Such is the basis on which I have tried to bring the People's Army of Vietnam out of the shadows in the Western literature. If I have been successful it will mean, above all, that I have clarified the way popular nationalism was focussed to both legitimise and augment the authority and power of the Democratic Republic of Vietnam. As a political and a military force the People's Army was central to the mass mobilisation process. It pumped up the power of the state with armed propaganda from 1945, and if this power had not been *legitimate* there is no way the People's Army could have grown from strength to strength through all the battles that lay before it. The large extent to which Western literature has overlooked the way the People's Army grew as a manifestation as well as an instrument of the *legitimate* power of the Vietnamese nation-state, is therefore the extent to which it has overlooked the central reason for the outcome of the Vietnam War.

1
French Conquest, 1859–1939

The French conquest of Vietnam was not a concentrated historical event. It began when French forces occupied the southern citadel at Saigon in 1859. They then took twenty five years to occupy the major central and northern citadels by 1884, and a further sixteen years to 'pacify' the northern regions. Even when the foundations for colonial government were established by 1900, the regime was always patchy; it had not surveyed vast tracts of the country by 1939, and its administrative systems tended to divide rather than unify the inherent regional interests. The French conquest of Cochinchina in the south, Annam in the centre, and Tonkin in the north was thus a piecemeal affair which developed along regional lines over many decades and only serves to emphasise the repeated failures of the old order to respond effectively to the challenge of modernity.

In the decades prior to the French conquest the Nguyen dynasty had been carrying out a program of Confucian reform designed to unify the country and to stabilise its imperial power after a long period of regional conflict. This program was reflected in the important field of military affairs where the precedence given to civil mandarins over military mandarins was emphasised to integrate the regional structure of the imperial army and to foster loyalty to the emperor. Such measures then enabled the dynasty to contain the widespread regional revolts to its authority that were exacerbated by agricultural, religious, and political problems in the first half of the nineteenth century. However, both the Confucian reforming zeal of the Nguyen and the regional structure of the army would compound the relative weakness of the dynasty as soon as it was attacked by the French.

From the 1860s the strong tendency of the majority of Confucian mandarins at court was to oppose an accommodation with Western influences.[1] This tendency became more pronounced as the court's existing unpopularity in the regions grew with its repeated failures to defend the country and with the progressive disintegration of the imperial army. With the exception of Ky Hoa in early 1861, the French hardly fought a battle against the forces of the Nguyen dynasty in the entire 'conquest'.[2] They largely occupied parts of the country when they were ready to, and campaigned most strenuously against local resistance groups which had almost no support from the court. And, in view of the profound political and cultural crisis which permitted French forces to 'divide and rule' Vietnam in the interests of economic exploitation, far more was at stake than the faint fall of the Nguyen dynasty.

At a time of great, irresistible change, the inability and unwillingness of the Nguyen to modernise doomed the institution of the monarchy. The ancient conceptions of moral order and righteous government on which the monarchy was based were destroyed by French fire power. As political and economic revolutions soon followed the French army in each region, the failure of the old order was such that Vietnamese troops complemented French forces at every stage of the conquest. From around 1900 it is accurate to describe the colonial army as a Franco-Vietnamese colonial army, for its complement of around 30,000 men was always about two-thirds Vietnamese. And when this small force had little difficulty in maintaining public order between 1900 and 1939, we have some idea of both the revolution and the political-military problem that the French conquest set up in modern Vietnamese history.

Last Views of the Army in Old Vietnam

When the Nguyen dynasty came to power under emperor Gia Long in 1802 it did so against a backdrop of long term regional divisions and decades of civil war. From the early sixteenth to the late eight-

[1]Nguyen The Anh, 'Traditionalisme et réformisme à la cour de Hue dans la seconde moitié du XIX ème siècle', in Pierre Brocheux, ed., *Histoire de l'Asie du Sud-Est: révoltes, réformes, révolutions*, Presses Universitaires de Lille, 1981, pp. 111–23 offers the best demonstration of this point.

[2]This word is used copiously in the French literature, and although its used with good reason to describe the invasion and forcible occupation of the country its does not adequately incorporate a sense of the Nguyen Dynasty's passive response to the French invasion. For an example of its use see A. Thomazi, *La Conquête de l'Indochine*, Paris: Payot, 1934. The battle for Ky Hoa is discussed in some detail below.

eenth centuries state power had been effectively divided by the Trinh family in the north and the Nguyen family in the south, although neither renounced its symbolic allegiance to the moribund Le dynasty which had first come to power in the fifteenth century. In the 1770s and 1780s, however, new tendencies towards the centralisation of state power began with the Tay Son rebellion against the Nguyen, the Trinh and, finally, the Le. The Siamese invasion of 1785, and the Qing invasion of 1788–9 also accentuated these tendencies. Under the leadership of the gifted Tay Son general, Nguyen Hue, (no relation of the southern dynasts), the old kings were overthrown and the invaders were defeated in brilliant campaigns so that the unity of the country was established for the first time in 300 years. However, with Nguyen Hue's death in 1792, the unity of the country proved to be fleeting. A period of renewed civil war broke out before the Nguyen dynasty finally came to power in 1802, and began a major program of political and social reform to stabilise its position throughout the country.[3]

In accordance with tradition this program included the use of Chinese models of government and administration. But it also included a highly conscious application of Confucian principles that probably had no parallel in Vietnamese history.[4] These were rooted in the idea that the monarch's god given virtue was the foundation for good order in the affairs of men and states, and in the universe. While catastrophes consequently called for kings to examine their moral character (*tu tinh*) in order to reform it and ensure the common good,[5] well regulated political and military affairs were a manifestation of a righteous moral order. Beginning with the reign of Gia Long (1802–1820), and developing strongly through the reign of Ming Mang (1821–1840) such measures as the revival of literature under the auspices of the Han Lam Academy, the establishment of the Imperial Cabinet and Inspectorate, and the development of the Privy Council were part of the Confucian program designed to enhance the

---

[3]The best general history of this early period is Le Thanh Khoi, *Histoire du Vietnam des origins à 1858*, Paris: Sudestasie, 1981, Chapters 6 and 7. For a colonial view see Charles Maybon, *Histoire Moderne des pays d'Annam, 1592–1820*, Paris: Plon, 1920. The standard work on the first half of the nineteenth century is Alexander Woodside, *Vietnam and the Chinese Model*, Harvard University Press, 1971.

[4]After the rise of the Le dynasty in 1427 there was a conscious attempt to apply Confucian principles to the law codes, the writing of history, and methods of government by scholars like Nguyen Trai and Ngo Si Lien. However, Esta Serne Ungar, 'Vietnamese Leadership and Order: Dai Viet Under the Le Dynasty', PhD, Cornell University, 1983 will show you how superficial these applications finally were. Woodside, *Vietnam and the Chinese Model*, provides the nineteenth century contrast.

[5]Nguyen The Anh, 'Traditionalisme et réformisme', p. 112.

moral prestige of the dynasty and articulate its centralised power
after a long period of division and strife.[6]

At the same time, however, it is clear that the 'supreme harmony'
(*thai hoa*)[7] which the institutions of the Nguyen dynasty were designed to radiate throughout the regions, was very much an idealisation of the political realities it had to contend with there. In the
south, which was the home of the Nguyen, the political situation was
generally stable in the first half of the nineteenth century, although
the dynasty still had to face the major revolt of Le Van Khoi and the
Catholic minorities around Gia Dinh between 1833 and 1835. Meanwhile, the dynasty's lack of popularity in the northern regions was
reflected in frequent revolts against its authority. Le and Trinh
loyalists often held out against the state with the support of highland
minority peoples, whose military skills and mountain habitats had
been used by dissident Vietnamese clans to challenge state power
since ancient times.[8] Frequent famines and epidemics also exacerbated the Nguyen dynasty's problems, and according to its own
chronicles there were some 405 revolts between 1802 and 1862.[9] If
the Nguyen court was thus forced to idealise its centralised state
power in the nineteenth century, it was also forced to realise it in a
variety of ways.

From the time Gia Long rose to power the Nguyen had to take
what Le Thanh Khoi has described as 'diverse measures'[10] to pacify
the regions. In the north these included the conferring of honorific
titles on the descendants of the old Le and Trinh royal families, the
granting of land for them to maintain their dynastic cults, and the
establishment of a northern Governor-General (*Tong Tran*) at Bac
Thanh whose local magistrates were very often Le loyalists. In the
south, local political interests were also recognised when a
Governor-General with a significant degree of autonomy was established at Gia Dinh (Saigon). It is true that Ming Mang moved to
curtail the excessive independence of the Governors-General as he

[6]Le Thanh Khoi, *Histoire du Vietnam*, p. 346.
[7]Quoted in Ibid., p. 345. The Hall of 'Supreme Harmony' was in fact in the palace
where Gia Long was proclaimed emperor in 1806.
[8]John T. McAlister Jr, 'Mountain Minorities and the Viet Minh: A Key to the
Indochina War', in Peter Kunstadter, ed., *Southeast Asian Tribes, Minorities and
Nations*, Vol. 2, Princeton University Press, 1967, p. 787 offers a sixteenth century
example. For an eighteenth century example see Nguyen Quang Ngoc va Phan Dai
Doan, 'Can Cu Dia Buoi Dau cua Cuoc Khoi Nghia Tay Son' [The First Base of the
Righteous Tay Son Uprising], *NCLS*, No. 1, January/February, 1979.
[9]Chu Thien, 'Ve Nhung Cuoc Nong Dan Khoi Nghia Trieu Nguyen' [On Righteous
Peasant Uprisings against the Nguyen Dynasty], *NCLS*, 1960, No. 19.
[10]Le Thanh Khoi, *Histoire du Vietnam*, p. 246.

strove for greater Confucianisation and centralisation after 1831, but there was still no change to the lower administration at province and district levels.[11] Also, in the 1840s, when the dynasty was well established, there were probably fewer than a thousand bureaucrats in the capital at Hue and another thousand in the provinces. This was not a large number for a population of perhaps eight million people in a country whose length and variations in regional conditions posed particular problems of administration.[12]

Despite its drive towards the centralisation of autocratic state power, therefore, the Nguyen dynasty tended paradoxically to tolerate a significant degree of regional political autonomy. As Ralph Smith has noted, its power was not absolute.[13] But as the Nguyen worked to institutionalise regional differences because they had no choice, there is also no doubt that without the strength to enforce a high degree of submission the dynasty's institutions would have been powerless to override and contain the myriad potentials for regional resistance. Military affairs were thus central to the life of the dynasty and, in keeping with the strong Confucian emphasis of the period, these were reformed in the first half of the nineteenth century.

The most important change from the military practices of preceding dynasties was a concerted attempt to give strict Confucian precedence to the civil mandarinate over the military one, which also had nine Chinese style grades in the state bureaucracy.[14] As in China, or

[11]Ibid., pp. 346–347.

[12]R.B. Smith, 'Politics and Society in Vietnam During the Early Nguyen Period (1802–1862)', *Journal of the Royal Asiatic Society*, 1974, pp. 153–169.

[13]Ibid.

[14]On the military bureaucracy see Le Thanh Khoi, *Le Vietnam: Histoire et Civilisation*, Paris, 1955, p. 139; Lieutenant Baulmont, 'Les Troupes du Dai Viet Quoc', *Revue Indochinoise*, Octobre 1905, pp. 1450–1451; Woodside, *Vietnam and the Chinese Model*, p. 68, p. 146. In China the primacy of civil affairs over military ones (*wen* over *wu*) was a long established principle of government. See the introductory essay in Frank A. Kierman and John F. Fairbank, *Chinese Ways in Warfare*, Harvard University Press, 1974. However, this principle often broke down. With the founding of the Qing dynasty, for example, the Manchu banners were founded to take charge of military activities, and civil officials were prohibited from overseeing these functions. By the mid-nineteenth century when the Manchus were weak and the Taiping rebellion broke out civil officials such as Tsing Kuo-fan were called in, and Han civil officials came to be in charge of regional armies. In Vietnam, it is unlikely that, except for short periods such as the 1430s when the Le dynasty tried to institute Confucian reforms, the principle of civil primacy had much force before the nineteenth century. The division of the country between the Nguyen and the Trinh from 1500 to 1800 rather suggests the rule of military houses. In any case, given the dominance of the banner system in Qing China until the mid-nineteenth century, the strict primacy of civil mandarins in Vietnam by the 1830s did not reflect contemporary developments in China.

any other pre-industrial society for that matter, there always tended to be an overlap in civil and military affairs in Vietnam, and as late as 1847 a military mandarin like Vo Van Giai could become so influential in the capital at Hue that he was a member of the group responsible for enthroning the emperor Tu Duc (1847–83).[15] The nineteenth century literature also refers to the military mandarins who came immediately beneath the Marshall of the Centre in the military hierarchy, the Marshalls of the Advance Guard, the Rear Guard, the Left, and the Right, as the 'four pillars' (*tu tru*)[16] of the empire. Nevertheless, in the first half of the nineteenth century the War Ministry was almost always in the hands of a civil mandarin like Truong Dang Que who passed the civil examinations in Quang Ngai in 1819 and remained in charge of the ministry for some years after 1835.[17] Both the civil-military overlap and the civil precedence thus came out in 1839 when the emperor Ming Mang said:

> All civil officials ideally should be forced to learn the military arts and all the military officials should be forced to learn civil business. That is why in the various provinces the governors-general alternate between civil and military business. Civil officials must not consider guns and cannon to be the sphere of responsibility of military bureaucrats.[18]

This Confucian trend in military affairs was reinforced in other ways. For example, in the field of military education civil mandarins dominated the examination bodies. After the series of concourses that could constitute a military mandarin's training—study of the Chinese military classics, drill with the lance on horseback, and the brandishing of weapons—a candidate's performance was adjudicated by civil mandarins who were merely assisted by military mandarins.[19] Another important example of the civil bureaucracy's precedence was that nineteenth century campaigns were not generally commanded by military mandarins. As we will see, overall command was usually given to civil mandarins, while the military mandarins led the fighting columns. Such unmistakable attempts to make the army loyal to the Confucian emperor and the unity of his state were then reinforced by the general use of Chinese models of military organiza-

[15]Smith, 'Politics and Society', pp. 153–169.
[16]Baulmont, 'Les Troupes du Dai Viet Quoc', p. 1443.
[17]Smith, 'Politics and Society', pp. 153–169.
[18]Quoted in Woodside, *Vietnam and the Chinese Model*, pp. 147–149.
[19]Nguyen Tuong Phuong, *Luoc Khao Binh Che Viet Nam qua Cac Thoi Dai* [A Short Examination of Vietnam's Military System over the Centuries], Hanoi, 1950, pp. 57–62; Le Thanh Khoi, *Histoire du Vietnam*, p. 347. Success in the military concourses led to the award of the title *Tao Si*, the martial arts equivalent of *Tien Si*, or Doctor of Letters.

tion and administration which tended paradoxically to institutionalise regionalism.

Since at least the eleventh century strong, Vietnamese dynasties had always divided their armies into two basic categories on Chinese models. These were the elite regiments responsible for the close protection of the dynasty and the regional regiments responsible for local defence. In the nineteenth century the regular elite 'guards' regiments (*linh ve*), whose nomenclature reflected the Ming Chinese model of 'guards' (*wei*) regiments, were only recruited between Quang Binh and Binh Thuan, the regions most loyal to the dynasty. The far northern region of Bac Ky and the far southern region around Gia Dinh only provided regional regiments (*linh co*), which did not serve in the capital.[20] Vietnamese regionalism thus tended to be institutionalised in the basic structure of the imperial army within an overarching use of Chinese organisational models.

The method of recruiting also tended to institutionalise regionalism within a Chinese framework. When the court wanted soldiers it calculated the relative capacities of the regions to supply them on the basis of population statistics, and left the responsibility for the selection of recruits to local village authorities who were usually advised at district level by a military secretary (*cai binh*). Under the Nguyen the number of soldiers required from a village depended on its population and location, but one soldier was generally recruited for every three names on the census lists.[21] According to military establishments that date from Gia Long's reign and appear to remain the same under Ming Mang's, the eight imperial guards divisions each of ten regiments, plus the elephantry, the artillery, and the naval squadrons were around 60,000 strong, while the regional regiments accounted for another 50,000 soldiers.[22] Chaigenau who lived

[20]A. Schreiner, *Les institutions annamites en Basse Cochinchine avant la conquête française*, 3 Vols., Saigon, 1901, Vol. 3, pp. 49–52 uses the terms '*ve*' and '*co*' for the nineteenth century. Baulmont, 'Les Troupes du', p. 1444 uses the same terms but also notes the existence of other nomenclatures for various regional units. Tran Trong Kim, *Viet Nam Su Luoc* [A Short History of Vietnam], 2 Vols, Saigon, 1971 reprint of the first 1928 edition, Vol. 2, p. 198 talks of '*kinh binh*' and '*co binh*'. Nguyen Luong Bich and Pham Ngoc Phung, *Tim Hieu Thien Tai Quan Su cua Nguyen Hue* [An Investigation into the Military Genius of Nguyen Hue], Hanoi: Quan Doi Nhan Dan, 1971, p. 340 gives other nomenclatures for the elite guards and regional regiments in other periods. Frank A. Kierman and John F. Fairbank, *Chinese Ways in Warfare*, Harvard University Press, 1974, p. 24 notes the existence of the '*wei*' regiments in China. Le Thanh Khoi, *Histoire*, p. 348 on recruiting.

[21]Schreiner, *Les institutions annamites*, Vol. 3, pp. 55–60; Le Thanh Khoi, *Le Vietnam*, p. 146.

[22]Schreiner, *Les institutions annamites*, Vol. 3, pp. 51–52; Baulmont, 'Les Troupes

in Hue for many years also says that in time of war these figures could be expanded rapidly and doubled easily.[23]

For a small agricultural society these establishments are impressive. In fact, they are so impressive one may well wonder about the extent to which they reflected reality, especially when Bissachère's first hand observation in 1812 suggested that the army was adept at 'small war'[24] in which enemy groups no bigger than forty or fifty men were attacked. However, while the absence of pitched battles does not necessarily mean the number of soldiers the court could call on was small, a long line of independent first hand observers from Alexandre de Rhodes in the seventeenth century to Chaigenau and other French scholar-administrators in the nineteenth century all suggest that the army's size was large.[25] And such evidence can not be dismissed lightly when the integration of military and agricultural work, and the blurring of soldier and peasant categories in Vietnam are taken into account.

In Vietnam as in China, one common method of compensating the society for the burden of supporting a standing army was the employment of military units in such tasks as repairing dikes, digging canals, collecting harvests, growing their own food, and working on palace and temple constructions.[26] On the other hand, it was quite common for soldiers to be raised straight out of the rice fields to suppress outbreaks of banditry and revolts if the need arose.[27] Moreover, such aphorisms as 'to be a soldier is to be a peasant' (*ngu binh u nong*) and 'plough the fields as you fight the enemy' (*vua cay ruong vua danh*

du', p. 1444; Maybon, *Histoire Moderne*, pp. 365–370. See also Tran Trong Kim, *Viet Nam Su Luoc*, Vol. 2, p. 198 for supporting information.

[23]Michel Duc Chaigenau, *Souvenirs de Hue*, Paris, 1867, pp. X–XI.

[24]M. De La Bissachère, *Etat actuel du Tunkin, de la Cochinchine, et les royaumes de Cambodge, Laos, et Lac-Tho*, 2 Vols., Paris: Galigani, 1812, Vol. 1, p. 309.

[25]Ibid., especially pp. 311–312 written around 1812 appears to have based his account on personal observations as well as a knowledge of contemporary Vietnamese military establishments. He was probably also aware of earlier sources such as De Rhodes and Tissanier which form the basis for the commentary on seventeenth and eighteenth century military affairs of more recent writers like Maybon, *Histoire Moderne*, pp. 17–18, and L. Bezacier, *L'Art Vietnamien*, Paris, 1954, p. 109, p. 117–118. Of course, the French were involved in training and arming Nguyen Phuc Anh's army in the early nineteenth century which accounts for their detailed knowledge for this period.

[26]Schreiner, *Les institutions annamites*, Vol. 3, pp. 57–60. Woodside, *Vietnam and the Chinese Model*, p. 129 says Ming Mang had 10,000 soldiers working on the Hall of Supreme Harmony in Hue in 1833.

[27]Tran Trong Kim, *Viet Nam Su Luoc*, Vol. 2, p. 55 offers an example. And in this context it might be added that there would have been a considerable number of men in the society who had gone back to their villages after a period of military service.

giac)[28] have roots that go back as far as the early fifteenth century when Le Loi was building up his imperial forces in the face of the Ming invasion. Given the strong tendency for soldier and peasant categories to be interchangeable and the large reservoir of people with military experience thus available in the society, there is a strong foundation for arguing that armies were relatively large in pre-colonial Vietnam even if the numbers of soldiers which both the Nguyen dynasty claimed and independent observers noted in the nineteenth century might have been inflated. The existence of another Chinese model of military organization in Vietnam, the 'military-agricultural colony' (*don dien*), also reinforces this argument.

Don dien had been introduced into the Red River Delta in the first century,[29] and as in China their role was to stabilise frontier areas and open up new land. In these colonies convicts, vagabonds, and landless peasants, were often sent out to the frontiers, organised into military units by mandarins, and given buffalos, ploughs, seed, and tax exemptions until the area was established.[30] Throughout the centuries the court also sent military mandarins to highland regions and to the Sino-Vietnamese border area to organise minority peoples for frontier defence,[31] and at such times as the Nguyen dynasty's rise to power from the late eighteenth century the military-agricultural colonies stand out as institutions of fundamental political-military importance.

The *don dien* which Gia Long set up around Gia Dinh in 1788[32] were in fact the institutional bases from which he marched north against the Tay Son and eventually reunified the country in 1802. In the 1830's, the Nguyen dynasty reactivated a number of these *don*

[28]Quoted in Hoang Minh, *Tim Hieu ve To Tien Ta Danh Giac* [An Investigation into the Wars of our Ancestors], Hanoi, 1977, p. 68.
[29]Keith Taylor, *The Birth of Vietnam*, University of California Press, 1983, pp. 45–46.
[30]E-Tu Zen Sun and J. DeFrancis, *Chinese Social History: Translations of Selected Studies*, Washington, 1956, p. 33; M. Coughlin, 'Vietnam in China's Shadow', *Journal of Southeast Asian History* (Hereafter *JSEAH*), Vol. 8, No. 2, 1967. Other readings on the *don dien* are E. Dechaseaux, 'Notes sur les anciens don dien annamites dans la Basse Cochinchine', *Excursions et Reconnaissances*, XIV, 1889; Georges Durrwell, 'Les colonies militaires dans la Basse-Cochinchine', *Bulletin de la Société des Etudes Indochinoises*, 1898; Phung Van Dan, 'La Formation Territorial du Vietnam', *Revue du Sud-Est Asiatique*, 1963; and Phan Quang *Cuoc Nam Tien cua Dan Toc Vietnam* [The Southern Advance of the Vietnamese People], Saigon, no date (1960s?), p. 387.
[31]For example, Nguyen Khac Vien, ed., *Vietnamese Studies, Number 55, Our Military Traditions*, Hanoi, no date, p. 10, pp. 14–15 gives one example from the Ly period at the time of the Sung invasions in the eleventh century.
[32]Le Thanh Khoi, *Histoire du Vietnam*, p. 334.

dien which spawned regional regiments for the war then being conducted in Cambodia. Similar levies were later used to bolster the imperial forces that were sent south in 1861 in an attemp to stop the French invasion at Ky Hoa. It was not until they were disbanded by a colonial decree of 1862 that these thriving military institutions ceased to function in the south.[33]

Such was the basis for the regionalised imperial army which Nguyen dynasty paradoxically required to centralise its power in the nineteenth century. And a good idea of how the tensions in the polity shaped the army's operations may be gained from a typical campaign to exterminate the rebel Nong Van Van, who led a revolt among Muong minority peoples in Tuyen Quang and Cao Bang provinces between 1833 and 1835.[34]

While it had no direct relationship with Le Van Khoi's southern uprising in the same period, Nong Van Van's revolt was part of a much wider disturbance in the northern provinces in the early 1830s where the Le loyalist, Le Duy Luong, built up a 'righteous army' (*nghia quan*) and military camps in numerous areas. Yet, if these revolts reflected the court's low prestige in many regions, there is also no doubt that the Nguyen court had multiple layers of defence available to it to defeat the multiple threats it faced, because of its regional structure.

Once the regional forces and their highland auxiliaries in Tuyen Quang were unable to manage Nong Van Van the court sent an imperial army. This army consisted of both elite guard regiments, including elephant and artillery units, and regional forces that were mustered from all over the country. The War Ministry set up a logistics office at Hue, but no high command. In keeping with the Confucian emphasis of the period provincial governors and district magistrates from the civil bureaucracy controlled the campaign in the regions to ensure political control of the forces, and the military

---

[33]Durrwell, 'Les colonies militaires', pp. 10–22 gives a fascinating description of how numerous regiments sprang from the southern *don dien* between the 1830s and 1860s. Nguyen The Anh, 'Traditionalisme et réformisme', p. 115 mentions Tu Duc's attempts to increase revenues by colonising and cultivating unoccupied territories in various northern provinces in the late 1860s, although these were called *nha doanh dien*.

[34]The following account draws on A.L.M Bonifacy, 'La Révolte de Nong Van Van', *Revue Indochinoise*, Juillet 1914, pp. 25–57. This source offers a rare contemporary account of a Vietnamese campaign in pre-colonial times. It consists of a French translation of a contemporary monograph of Tuyen Quang province by the magistrate Dang Xuan Bang, plus a commentary by Bonifacy. See also Nguyen Phan Quang, 'Khoi Nghia Le Duy Luong' [The Righteous Uprising of Le Duy Luong], *NCLS*, No. 5, 1985, pp. 64–70.

mandarins who actually commanded the fighting columns remained in subordinate positions.

Because these columns could consist of units from different parts of the country their command was very often shared by two or even three officers. However, this manifestation of regionalism was sufficiently well integrated into the imperial army to ensure its final victory after what must have been some fairly heavy fighting. Nine senior regimental officers or their equivalents were killed, one committed suicide, and one was captured. Although Ming Mang thought this campaign was of secondary importance to others he was waging against Le Duy Luong, he nevertheless demonstrated his satisfaction with its conduct by promoting some of the senior officers, issuing many certificates of merit, and distributing a thousand strings of cash among the other officers and soldiers. He was then able to reorganise his forces and create different combinations of elite and regional regiments to deal with other revolts elsewhere. By August 1835, for example, he was directing another combination of imperial-regional forces on Gia Dinh which exterminated the rebel Le Van Khoi and his supporters by the end of the year. In other words, the failure of regional forces in one particular area could be rectified eventually by any number of combinations of elite and regional regiments from other areas. It was this ability to integrate the power of the centre with the power of a substantial number of regions in various combinations that does much to explain the survival of the Nguyen state in the first half of the nineteenth century.

Yet, as this integration of political and military power held the empire together in the decades just prior to the French conquest, it would fail when the modern forces of French imperialism attacked the country from the late 1850s. To account for this failure some conservative historians such as Tran Trong Kim have pointed to the court's failure to develop the interest in Western military methods which Gia Long had shown at the beginning of the century.[35] Other

---

[35]Maybon, *Histoire Moderne*, p. 279 thought it was 'incontestable' that French military assistance 'contributed to a very large extent' to Gia Long's rise to power in 1802. Yet, especially when the same source also says that information on the 'handful' of French advisers who were involved with Gia Long did not permit a 'detailed definition' of their contribution to his rise, Maybon's untested assertion about the importance of French influence should not be accepted uncritically. On French military engineering in the two decades after Gia Long came to power see Le Thanh Khoi, *Histoire du Vietnam*, p. 349. Tran Trong Kim, *Viet Nam Su Luoc* [A Short History of Vietnam], Saigon, 1971 reprint of the 1928 edition, Vol. 2, p. 243 then complains that after the army's strength at the beginning of the nineteenth century general neglect had left it in a sorry state by the 1860s. For a similar approach see Phan Khoang, *Viet Nam Phap Thuoc Su* [A History of Vietnam under French Colonialism],

radical historians such as Dang Huy Van have attacked the courts's defeatism once the power of the French was revealed. When the emperor Tu Duc said that 'trying to fight the French is no different to grasshoppers kicking wagon wheels'[36] the radical historians think he was placing undue emphasis on the importance of weapons in war and not enough on the people. But the weakness in both these arguments is that they overlook the institutional weakness of the Vietnamese imperial army when compared to that of French imperial forces.

There had been a considerable infusion of Western weapons into Asia since the sixteenth century, and the Vietnamese imperial army was able to field large numbers of French firearms and cannons when they first confronted French forces. Yet huge armies were defeated all over Asia and Vietnam were defeated in the age of European expansion by tiny Western forces because of their highly rationalised organisation which was the necessary base for the application of their technology. Because Vietnamese did not have such an institutional base, but a highly complex one that was shaped by regional interests in a pre-industrial society, they did not understand how to use modern weapons to the same devastating effect as the French. When the French attacked, the court therefore had no idea of what an effective response might be, as the regional structure of its military forces and its political power soon began to disintegrate.

The French Conquest of the South

After the French admiral, Rigault de Genouilly, failed in a first attack on Da Nang in 1858, but successfully blasted his way up the Saigon river and occupied the Saigon citadel with a tiny Franco-Spanish force in February 1859,[37] the Vietnamese response was deeply defensive. The thrust of the memorials that began to come

Saigon, 1961, p. 129.

[36] Quoted in Dang Huy Van, 'Cuoc Dau Tranh giua Phai "Chu Chien" va Nhung Phai "Chu Hoa" trong Cuoc Khang Chien Chong Phap o Cuoi The Ky XIX' [The Struggle between the "War Faction" and the "Peace Factions" in the Resistance War Against the French at the End of the Nineteenth Century], NCLS, 94, Hanoi, 1962, p. 30. I have made a number of quotations from this source which come from memorials to the emperor Tu Duc in the period. These memorials were originally written in Chinese characters and have been translated into modern Vietnamese in Dang Huy Van's work.

[37] J.T. Cady, The Roots of French Imperialism in Eastern Asia, Ithaca, 1954, pp. 210–218. G. Taboulet, La geste française en Indochine, 2 Vols., Paris: A. Maison-neuve, 1955, 1956, Vol. 2, pp. 433–443.

into the emperor Tu Duc from his mandarins in the Privy Council in
Hue was that 'the enemy has strong ships and powerful guns' and that
'although we want their withdrawal we cannot yet see an opportunity
for victory, so the only thing to do is to prolong our defence and wait
for them to tire.'[38] The court thus decided on a policy of 'passive
defence' (giu de hoa)[39] in which it decided to sit out French raids
behind its fortifications. Consequently, once the Saigon citadel was
occupied 'the Vietnamese army did not', as one French dispatch
noted, 'try to employ its crushing numerical superiority to mount a
serious offensive'.[40] Commanded by Ton That Hiep, then by Nguyen
Tri Phuong, the Vietnamese army simply burnt the town, blockaded
the small French garrison, and set about constructing extensive
fortifications around Ky Hoa some distance to the southwest of Gia
Dinh.

These fortifications consisted of from twelve to sixteen kilometers
of entrenched positions protected by rows of bamboo stakes, studded
with numerous strong points, and manned by a large army of imperial
guard and regional units which may have been 20,000 strong.[41] The
troops were armed with an assortment of traditional weapons, but a
heavy sprinkling of French muzzle loading rifles and many cannons
meant that in terms of weaponry the Vietnamese army was by no
means grossly disadvantaged.[42] Yet the essentially defensive military
posture of the army still touched on the profound weaknesses in
military theory and practice that the French would soon exploit.

The Vietnamese had no adequate logistics system for modern war
and did not understand how to use the Western weapons they
possessed. Artillery pieces, deeply pitted with rust, were often rolled
into battle. There was little understanding of the trajectory of modern weapons which meant that the French could make use of dead
ground, and sometimes when approaches to forts were not adequately covered on all sides it was an easy matter for the French to
take them from the rear or a flank.[43] Also, while the fortifications

---

[38]Dang Huy Van, 'Cuoc Dau Tranh', pp. 29–30.
[39]Ibid., p. 30.
[40]Taboulet, La geste française, p. 461.
[41]On the basis of available figures this is a conservative estimate. Documents in
Taboulet, La geste française, p. 459 say the army at Ky Hoa consisted of 20,000
regulars and 10,000 local levies. Recent Vietnamese histories use French sources. For
example, Dao Dang Vy, Nguyen Tri Phuong [i.e. the general at Ky Hoa], Hanoi: Nha
Van Hoa, 1974, pp. 112–113 uses A. Thomazi, La Conquête.
[42]Taboulet, La geste française, p. 461. Baulmont, 'Les troupes du', p. 1455.
[43]These deficiencies can be gleaned from various sources. See for example, Baulmont, 'Les Troupes du Dai Viet Quoc', p. 1455, and Lt Baulmont, 'La Prise de
Tourane, (Septembre 1858 – 7 et 8 Mai 1859 – 15 Septembre 1859)', Revue Indochi-

around Ky Hoa were being constructed, the French had over a year to build up the modest force of around 4,000 men that would destroy them with the flexible tactics and coordinated fire power of a bureaucratically organised Western army on February 24–25.[44] In only two days the Vietnamese Imperial Army lost what was arguably the only significant battle it was to fight against the invaders. By the end of the year French positions in the hinterland were consolidated around Tay Ninh, My Tho, and Bien Hoa, while memorials such as those of the mandarin, Nguyen Ba Nghi, added further depth to the gloom in Hue:

> The enemy's ships are as fast as the wind, their guns can fire through stone walls, and have a range of over ten miles. Since the enemy has weapons like that fighting them is not feasible . . . during the last three or four years our soldiers have not been dependable, our guns not good, and our fortresses not strong . . . with the exception of a peace policy I am at a loss to say what we should do.[45]

Even though the court continued to send agents into the south to organise irregular war against the French until the end of 1862, it therefore ordered its mandarins in the region to withdraw from their posts and concluded the treaty of 5 June 1862 which ceded the southeastern provinces of Bien Hoa, Gia Dinh, and My Tho to the French.[46] In June 1863, Admiral La Grandière then occupied the three southwestern provinces of Vinh Long, Chau Doc, and Ha Tien when he had sufficient forces at his disposal. The region which the French called 'Lower Cochinchina' had fallen into their hands without virtually any resistance from the court.

However, this evaporation of the court's power did not mean the

noise, 1904, pp. 691–704, 1905, pp. 13–29 offers considerable detail on the state of the military art in mid-nineteenth century Vietnam.

[44]Taboulet, *La geste française*, p. 459, pp. 460–463. To salvage some national pride Dao Dang Vi, *Nguyen Tri Phuong*, p. 113 says that, although it is not possible to be sure the French could have had as many as 10,000 troops with auxiliaries they had recruited in China and Cambodia. But this figure of 10,000 is a gross exaggeration and Dao Dang Vi probably does not mean it to include the Vietnamese auxiliaries that accompanied the French forces at Ky Hoa. Baulmont, 'Nos Premières Troupes', p. 189 indicates that at least one combat company composed of Vietnamese Christians joined in the attack. On the impact of bureaucratic Western armies on Asia in general in the age of imperialism see Gayl D. Ness, 'Western Imperialist Armies in Asia', *Comparative Studies in Society and History*, 19, 1977, pp. 2–29, especially p. 13. Carlo M. Cipolla's brilliant study, *Guns and Sails in the Early Phase of European Expansion 1400–1700*, London, 1965 should also be consulted.

[45]Quoted in Dang Huy Van, 'Cuoc Dau Tranh', p. 30.

[46]Taboulet, *La geste française*, p. 473.

end of localised resistance in the south to the French. As numerous writers have discussed in detail,[47] resistance was led by men like Truong Cong Dinh, Nguyen Trung Truc, and Nguyen Huu Huan who had participated in the battle of Ky Hoa and returned to their home villages to organise local guerrilla resistance once the imperial army broke up. The motivation for this resistance was the widespread fear of 'extermination at the hands of "the Westerners"' and the belief that those who gave up the struggle were people who 'sell out their heritage'.[48] Small scale harassment of the French thus continued. Leaflets circulated around the Mekong Delta calling on the 'righteous armies' of the various regions to unite in their resistance to the invaders in 1863, and as late as 1866 the French still had to mount some sizeable operations against regional strongholds.

If the Nguyen dynasty had not left its fortunes to a few secret agents and ordered mandarins out amongst the population to focus a generalised guerrilla resistance instead of withdrawing them and leaving the population leaderless, it is possible to imagine a protracted struggle that could have forced a French withdrawal. There was considerable opposition to colonial adventures in France in the 1860s and 1870s,[49] and stronger resistance to French forces in southern Vietnam could have bolstered it significantly. But when the Nguyen dynasty abdicated responsibility for the region by 1863 there is no way the southern resistance could have avoided increasing division, isolation, and final extinction in the face of French power. As modern French military power blocked off the possibility of a royal restoration in the south it had begun to do far more than paralyse the Nguyen dynasty's capacity for action there. It had begun to destroy the foundations for the monarchy in Vietnamese society.

Truong Buu Lam has argued that since the idea of 'king' (*vua*) did not necessarily mean the incumbent in Hue but a ruler worthy of the title the monarchy was 'an idealised institution not tarnished by any accidental deviation from the ideal'.[50] Yet, in Cochinchina by the mid-1860s, the Nguyen dynasty's failure could hardly be described as

[47]David G. Marr, *Vietnamese Anticolonialism*, University of California Press, 1971, Chapter 2 is the best reading in English.

[48]Quoted in Ibid., p. 32, p. 38. The second quote comes from a poem by Phan Van Tri.

[49]Philippe Franchini, *Les Guerres d'Indochine*, 2 Vols., Paris: Editions Pygmalion, 1988, Vol. 1, pp. 87–88. See also Raoul Girardet, *L'idée coloniale en France de 1871 à 1862*, Paris: La Table Ronde, 1972, Chapter 3.

[50]Truong Buu Lam, *Patterns of Vietnamese Response to Foreign Intervention 1858–1900*, New Haven, Southeast Asia Studies, Yale University Monograph Series 11, 1967, p. 10.

an 'accidental deviation'. No matter what monarchist sentiment smouldered on in the villages for some decades to come, any idealisation of the institution of the monarchy was already an extremely weak foundation for effective political action,[51] as the military conquest was reinforced immeasurably by the political and economic conquests that went with it.

As soon as the French arrived in the south a new class of people came into positions of power that overturned the old values of the Confucian state.[52] By the early 1860s Christians, and others with grievances against the old regime acted as interpreters and general intermediaries between the French and the local population, while Vietnamese forces frequently supported French attempts to break up the old empire. Vietnamese combat companies had been attached to Genouilly's forces since their first attacks on the country, and a Civil Guard, recruited as Vietnamese regional forces had always been by canton chiefs, was set up to police the colony by the early 1860s.[53] And, while the son of a persecuted Catholic like Tran Ba Loc is remembered for his effective repression of various anti-French revolts, the French Inspectors of Indigenous Affairs constituted a new administrative echelon that could not have been more remote from any lingering monarchist sentiment that was still alive in the villages. Although the Inspectors worked above the system of village councils of notables that went unchanged from the past, they were modern men, and their job was to open Cochinchina up for the markets of international capitalism, to set the country up for long term economic exploitation. Indeed, between the 1860's and 1880's, huge quantities of rice were already being extracted for international markets, and Saigon was being set up as an urban entrepot which the French could use to rival the British at Singapore.

By the late 1860s some awareness of the modern industrial base which had propelled French forces into Indochina and stimulated these changes was dawning at court. In 1860 a brilliant graduate of the Confucian examinations from Nghe An Province, Nguyen Truong To, had gone to France with Bishop Gautier to study the

[51]Truong Buu Lam's idealisation of the monarchy, which is also entrenched in the French colonial literature leads one to the conclusion that it retained considerable power under the French. However, as David Marr and Nola Cook emphasised to me when I suggested this conclusion myself, there is clearly no foundation for it. The monarchy had no effective political power in the south by 1863 and none in the rest of the country after the Protectorate Treaty of 1883.

[52]Alexander B. Woodside, *Community and Revolution in Modern Vietnam*, Boston: Houghton and Mifflin, 1976, pp. 8–14.

[53]Baulmont, 'Nos Premières Troupes', offers the fullest account.

French political system, literature, and industry. Between his return in 1863 and 1871 he informed the court of his findings in many memorials. In 1867, for example, he was explaining the 'truly great' engineering capacity of one French arms factory he visited, where 'up to ten thousand cartridges are produced each day; and the number of people working in the factory exceeds 300'. After a visit to one large steel works 'as far from Paris as Nghe An is from Hue' he was also able to explain how he 'came to understand clearly how the power and prosperity of their country is far greater than of our country'.[54] But, as such information was accompanied by schemes for extensive Western style reforms in areas as diverse as poetry, irrigation, clocks, and military affairs,[55] none of them came to anything, if only because the court was never in any position to implement them.

It is too simplistic to suggest, as some historians have done, that the Nguyen emperors were opposed to all reform and lapsed into abject defeatism in the 1860s and early 1870s.[56] Between 1861 and 1875 there is no doubt that Tu Duc had been examining his conscience. Dozens of royal edicts reflected a serious attempt to respond to the internal and external calamities that had overtaken his empire. These dealt with the need to promote talented mandarins who knew about military, technical, customs, agricultural, and medical matters. An agreement the court made under the treaty of 1874, in which the French would supply it with two steam ships, 100 cannons, 500 rifles, and technical advisers in return for various concessions, also suggests that Tu Duc was not entirely opposed to modern innovations. However, as Nguyen The Anh has shown,[57] these attempts at reform were still carried out within the old Confucian intellectual context, and in many respects they represented a reaction against Western influences which posed the fundamental threat to the survival of the dynasty. At a time when the dynasty's internal problems with famines, epidemics, and regional revolts were exacerbated by the loss of the southern provinces and unprecedented external pressures, the overwhelming

[54]Quoted in Nguyen Lan, *Nguyen Truong To* [i.e. the reformer], Hanoi, 1942, second edition, pp. 22–23.

[55]*Ibid.*, offers a full discussion of these proposed reforms and many others in several chapters. Also on Nguyen Truong To see Dang Huy Van, 'Cuoc Dau Tranh', Nguyen The Anh, 'Traditionalisme et réformisme'; and Philippe Langlet, 'Point de vue sur Nguyen Truong To et le réformisme vietnamien au milieu du XIXème siècle', *Etudes Interdisciplinaire sur le Viet-nam*, Saigon, Vol. 1, 1974, pp. 179–195.

[56]Writers like Dang Huy Van in 'Cuoc Dau Tranh', p. 30 convey abject defeatism. But see Tu Duc's fighting memorial of November 1860 translated in Patrick J.N. Tuck, *French Catholic Missionaries and the Politics of Imperialism in Vietnam, 1857–1914: A Documentary Survey*, Liverpool University Press, 1987, pp. 63–64.

[57]Nguyen The Anh, 'Traditionalisme et réformisme', especially pp. 114–120.

reaction of the mandarins at court was to cling tenaciously to old ways, to resist ideas of modernisation, and to reject the contacts with the French that such modernisation would have required. Given the depth of old traditions and the problems posed by Vietnamese regionalism, the court in Hue would have needed what Nguyen The Anh has described as 'more calm and serenity'[58] to embark on a well considered program that would have had any chance of success, and if it had had the calm there would have been no need to embark on reforms in the first place. Therefore, when the French conquest of the north eventually proceeded with almost no opposition from the Imperial Army, the fate of the monarchy was sealed.

The French Conquest of the North

From the early 1860s there had been persistent, widespread disturbances in the northern regions as a range of pirates and former Le dynasty pretenders tried to take advantage of the court's difficulties in the south. An example of a serious and typical challenge to court authority that arose at this time was that of the Le pretender, Le Hung, who thought he might further his claims to the throne if he offered his services to the French. But even though the French did not accept this offer he was still able to raise an army, defeat a royal fleet sent to eliminate him, and gain control of several northern provinces with the result that after late 1861 Tu Duc never controlled much more than the citadels in large areas of the north.[59] Moreover, in many provinces, the repugnance of local scholars at the French occupation of Cochinchina was such that they began to ignore the court and take matters into their own hands. As Monsignor Theurel, the Vicar Apostolic of West Tonkin, reported to his superiors in Paris in early 1868:

> I have already mentioned how little sympathy the scholars have for association with the French or for religious liberty. This repugnance has merely grown since the occupation of the three provinces of Lower Cochinchina. On the pretext of preparing for a dogged resistance against possible French invasion of Tonkin they have formed a mobile militia commanded by retired mandarins in the provinces of Nam Dinh, Ninh Binh and elsewhere . . . The militia I refer to has never had government authorisation, although the mandarins have delivered mandates to the village chiefs to raise money. Some mandarins have told

[58]Ibid., p. 120.
[59]Taboulet, *La geste française*, p. 30.

me that an order has been sent from the capital to dissolve it,
but it has been ignored.[60]

And, as these militias undoubtedly took their rage out on people
whose Catholic faith was often thought to be at the root of the
country's problems, they created internal conflicts which equally
unauthorised French ventures were able to exploit.

When Francis Garnier's raid momentarily projected French imperial interests into Tonkin in 1873 without authorisation from Paris,
he took the citadel at Hanoi with a mere 212 men. The court's
inability to project its power into the region was also reflected when
Garnier enlisted such willing support among local Catholics that Phu
Ly, Ha Duong, Nam Dinh, and Ninh Binh provinces all offered
themselves up to his minuscule force with great rapidity. The court
thus had no alternative but to conclude the treaty of 15 March 1874
which recognised French sovereignty in Cochinchina in return for a
French withdrawal from the north, except for the retention of a
consulate and a small garrison in Hanoi.[61] However, the French
withdrawal only led to further violent upheavals in which the scholars
raised more unauthorised militias to exterminate Christians for their
support of Garnier, while a Le faction besieged Hai Duong.[62]

In 1874 the general helplessness of the court, which tried but failed
to restore order when it sent an ineffectual army north, was thus
reflected in various remarks by the emperor Tu Duc: 'in their hearts
the people are not determined', 'money and rice become scarcer
everyday', 'in the north we are pitted against the Khiet Dan barbarians so cannot send troops to the west. In the west we are pitted
against the Nguyen barbarians so do not dare send the army north'.[63]
This last comment of Tu Duc's is probably a classical allusion, for the
reference to the Khiet Dan barbarians and the Nguyen is obscure.
Yet, especially when such classicism only reinforced the scholarly
emperor's remoteness from reality, his allusion does give a fitting
sense of how the integrated regional power structure of the old
imperial army was breaking up under the extraordinary pressures of
French invasions.

As with the French occupation of the south, it is possible to argue

[60]Tuck, *French Catholic Missionaries*, pp. 77–78.
[61]Taboulet, *La geste française*, pp. 702–735 provides a range of French primary
sources on the Garnier mission. Tuck, *French Catholic Missionaries*, pp. 134–164 does
the same although in English translation. P.J. Honey, translator, *Voyage to Tonkin in
the Year At Hoi (1876)*, School of Oriental and African Studies, University of London,
1982, pp. 64–65 offers some details of the consulate.
[62]Tuck, *French Catholic Missionaries*, p. 158, p. 163.
[63]Dang Huy Van, 'Cuoc Dau Tranh', p. 30.

that the final French annexation of Tonkin and Annam was not inevitable. It was only by the narrowest of margins that the Ferry government survived an anti-colonial attack in 1881 in the National Assembly before it authorised the funds which initiated the last phase of the conquest. Yet once the Vietnamese court had appealed to the Chinese court for aid against the uprising of another Le pretender, and Chinese forces known as the Black Flags entered Vietnam in 1879,[64] the French reaction already made it very unlikely that either independent Vietnamese foreign policy initiatives or Chinese involvement in the region would be tolerated. In 1879 the Minister for the Navy in Paris immediately responded to the entry of Chinese forces into Tonkin by proposing the dispatch of twelve gun boats and 6,000 men. And while fear of becoming enmeshed in the political anarchy of Tonkin restrained the French government until Ferry was voted the funds in July 1881, Le Myre de Villers, the first civilian governor of Cochinchina, was urging involvement.[65]

At the same time as he recruited the first 1,700 strong Vietnamese regiment of *tirailleurs* (sharp-shooters) in 1879, Le Myre de Villers was telling Paris that he would not need any money for a northern expedition. He was also saying that 'in view of the impotence, not to mention the bad faith of the government at Hue, and given the bearing of the Black Flags, it seems essential to double the garrison at Hanoi'.[66] By April 1882 Commandant Rivière was thus sent to occupy the Hanoi garrison with 500 men and orders not to resort to force unless absolutely necessary. However, after some superficially cordial relations with the local mandarins, fighting broke out around the Hanoi citadel in the same month, and by the spring of 1883 the French government was envisaging a partial occupation of Tonkin in which Hanoi was to be securely held to ensure navigation of the Red River. As one historian has said of the Rivière mission, it was, 'the gearing'[67] which finally engaged the French in the final phase of the military conquest.

In the meantime, some of the mandarins at court who had long been opposed to modernisation and dealings with the French made renewed calls for guerrilla war. A lucid analysis of the reasons for such measures was included in a memorial to Tu Duc by the mandarin Nguyen Xuan On in the early 1880s, which stated that:

[64]G. Devéria, *Histoire des relations de la Chine avec l'Annam-Viet Nam du XVIème au XIXème siècle*, Paris, 1880, pp. 74–75. See also Lloyd E. Eastman, *Throne and Mandarins*, Harvard University Press, 1967; Henry McAleavy, *Black Flags in Vietnam*, London: Allen and Unwin, 1968.
[65]Franchini, *Les Guerres*, p. 99.
[66]Ibid.
[67]Ibid.

Our provincial capitals are built on exposed plains and near rivers
and the coast for ease of communications. But today the truth is
that for the enemy the provincial capitals are vital, while for us
attempts to hold them are very dangerous. Why is this? This is
because the enemy have very mobile ships and guns. Once they
have created a pretext for hostilities they bring their large ships
close (to our provincial towns) in order to fire their big guns.
Our army jealously guarding the town walls has no way of
avoiding the danger and so being frightened out of its wits melts
away. All the more reason for this is that our fortresses are no
higher than twenty or thirty feet and no more than two or three
feet thick, and the enemy uses ladders to climb the walls and
tunnels to attack them. This is why they could not help
winning.[68]

This is an excellent description of how French technology had con-
fined the Imperial Army to citadels, destroyed its power there, and
compounded the existing weakness of the court in the regions.
Furthermore, it was the basis on which Nguyen Xuan On advocated a
withdrawal from the coastal centers, and a general mobilisation of
the population for guerrilla war against an enemy which was unfam-
iliar with the country, the climate, or the feelings of the people:
'make fortresses out of mountains, make ponds out of crevices, place
guns so that they look down (on the enemy) from above'.[69]

While Tu Duc's response to this idea of abandoning the towns and
setting up bases in the mountains was negative — 'having people
migrate is not practical' —[70] it may have influenced the actions of the
high military mandarin, Ton That Thuyet, who began work on a
large fortified camp at Tan So in the mountains of north central
Vietnam in late 1883. The work was conducted by thousands of
people who toiled over the defences, dragged cannon into place, and
supplied the position with large quantities of rice.[71] In the north,
many provincial units from the imperial army also took to the
mountains as Général Bouet's Expeditionary Corps began to occupy
the Red River delta. But of course, all these efforts failed to have any
effect on the French. They were implemented too late and never
had the full support of the court,[72] which ordered the imperial army
to avoid contact with the French when it signed the Protectorate
treaty of August 1883. Clearly, the rulers in Hue had no confidence in

[68]Quoted in Dang Huy Van, 'Cuoc Dau Tranh', p. 36.
[69]Quoted in Ibid., p. 37, for other details see pp. 37–38.
[70]Quoted in Dang Huy Van, 'Cuoc Dau Tranh', p. 37.
[71]Marr, *Anticolonialism*, p. 49. Jean Chesneaux, *The Vietnamese Nation: Contribution to a History*, translated by Malcolm Salmon, Sydney, 1966, pp. 88–89.
[72]Marr, *Anticolonialism*, pp. 41–42.

their ability to go out into the countryside and lead resistance to the invaders as the Tran had done against the Mongols in the thirteenth century. Their authority had been too deeply undermined in the regions by their passive response to French power.

In 1883 and 1884 there some military engagements between French and Sino-Vietnamese forces. At the so-called Paper Bridge in May 1883, for instance, Commandant Rivière was killed and his column decimated by Vietnamese and Chinese troops firing the latest Winchester, Remington, and Martini rifles.[73] But, in general, 'passive resistance' was the hallmark of Vietnamese military operations until 1884. Some twenty four years after the French had noted the failure of the Vietnamese army to mass its forces for a counter-attack on the French position in the Saigon citadel in 1859, French dispatches were still making the same observations at the time of their occupation of Son Tay in December 1883:

> As before with Nguyen Tri Phuong at Ky Hoa, the Sino-Vietnamese did not try to profit from their numerical superiority. Instead of trying to throw their enemy into the sea by a determined offensive they locked themselves into an expectant attitude which left the French time to strengthen their position dangerously.[74]

The citadel at Son Tay fell quickly to the French after a Vietnamese officer provided unexpected assistance by opening the gates. Perfunctory royal resistance was then extinguished in March and April at Bac Ninh and Hung Hoa.

Tu Duc died in July 1883 before he had a chance to witness the Protectorate Treaty and the bitter end of this tragi-comic opera. In the following two years, as the French set about consolidating their new administration with many mandarins who defected to them and other new recruits, he was succeeded by no fewer than five sovereigns, three of whom committed suicide. As a French Résident Général was now to reside in the citadel at Hue, the Vietnamese guns on the ramparts were spiked in March 1885,[75] and, under a new convention of July Articles 4 and 5 sealed the fate of the old Imperial Army:

> Article 4. France puts at the disposal of the King of Annam a military mission, the cost of which will be supported by the royal treasury.

[73]Taboulet, *La geste française*, 792–796.

[74]Ibid., p. 817. The reference to the 'Sino-Vietnamese' army in the quotation reflects cooperation between the Black Flags and the Vietnamese.

[75]Nguyen The Anh, *The Withering Days of the Nguyen Dynasty*, Research Notes and Discussions No. 7, Institute of Southeast Asian Studies, Singapore, 1978, pp. 6–17.

The reorganised Annamese army will not exceed an effective force of 8,000 or 10,000 men and will be commanded by a French officer.
Article 5. The Tonkinese regiments at present at the service of France will remain distinct from the Annamese army.[76]

And with the sacking of the imperial palace by French officers and marines over a three month period from early July 1885, a jumble of broken walls and ruined temples bespoke the melancholy that settled over Hue's former glories.[77]

Yet the destruction of the court was not synonymous with the final conquest of the country. The French sacking of the imperial palace had been initiated by the actions of the regent, Ton That Thuyet, who ordered an attack on the forces of Général de Courcy on the night of 4 July 1885. While that attack failed, another massacre of Catholics began in the central provinces of Quang Tri and Binh Dinh,[78] and Thuyet did manage to take the boy king, Ham Nghi, out of the capital and declare the famous 'can vuong' movement to 'save the king'. This was done on the basis of such Confucian values as 'love of king', 'righteous duty', and on the need to restore 'the land to its frontiers'.[79] And when royal support was finally given to regional anti-French resistances it did tend to provide a political focus for an independence movement, even though it was far too late to save either the Nguyen dynasty or the ancient institution of the monarchy.

For the French, breaking the back of the resistance in hundreds of fortified villages was an expensive, bloody, and time consuming business. It was indeed the most difficult phase of the entire conquest and took 30,000 troops.[80] That the French were pitted against 'pirate bands' was the official rhetoric, but some perceptive French officials realised the hollowness of it. For example, with the recent example of Italian nationalist movements in mind, the Résident Neyret compared the resistance to the Carbonari when he explained in 1888 that

[76]Ibid., p. 20. This was the convention of 30 July.
[77]Ibid., pp. 18–19. Boissière, L'Indochine, pp. 259–267.
[78]Nicole Dominique Le, Les Missions-Etrangères et la pénétration française, Paris: Mouton, 1975, pp. 147–151. Tuck, French Catholic Missionaries, p. 206 says eight French missionaries and an estimated 25,000 Vietnamese Christians were killed.
[79]The 'save the king' movement was of course the Can Vuong movement which Marr, Anticolonialism, Chapter 3 has done much to elucidate. The other quotes come from the Can Vuong Proclamation which Marr presents on pp. 50–51. In note 21 on p. 51 there are details of the original source. Truong Buu Lam, Patterns, pp. 117–120 has another English translation.
[80]Boissierè, L'Indochine, p. 27.

for the last eight months I believed that the piracy was only an organization for pillage. But recently I have seen that I was wrong. If the piracy was only an association of brigands, it would have disappeared . . . The piracy is a kind of carbonarism.[81]

Of course, famous resistance leaders like Phan Dinh Phung and De Tham were still thinking in regional and monarchist terms. But as the resistance had outlived the real power of the monarchy for several years by 1888, what we see in the mind of at least one French officer is how the French invasion was beginning to place old political-military processes in Vietnam into new perspectives that linked them to modern world historical trends.[82]

The conquest literature is replete with examples where Vietnamese leaders, such as Phan Dinh Phung and De Tham, were able to draw taxes and corvée obligations from villages as they established formidable local defence systems that could obstruct French columns; these were for the most part dense thickets of sharpened bamboo stakes backed up with poisoned arrows from the crossbows of highland tribesmen, and Gras rifles that reached the resistance from diverse sources. One of the most piquant scandals of the period was in fact the discovery of an operation in which guns were being run to the resistance by a well known Swedish merchant in Hai Phong who was a close friend and confidant of the French Résident.[83]

Yet the French conquest was inexorable. A leader like De Tham, did manage to remain free until his head was cut off and paraded through the recalcitrant provinces in 1913. But the slow methodical campaigns of Général Gallieni between 1895 and 1897 finally extinguished

[81]Quoted in Charles Fourniau, 'Les traditions de la lutte nationale au vietnam: l'insurrection des lettrés (1885–1895), in Jean Chesneaux et al., *Tradition et révolution au Vietnam*, Paris: éditions anthropos, 1971, pp. 102–103.

[82]Like many of the other secret societies that proliferated in Spain, France, Germany, and Italy after the French revolution, the Carbonari had trans-European connections and an organisational structure and symbolism derived from eighteenth century freemasonary. To this extent it could not be described as modern. However, from the 1800s when successive popular uprisings marked the Napoleonic domination of Italy the political demands of the Carbonari and the other sects were very modern. As Stuart Woolf, *A History of Italy, 1700–1860: The Social constraints of Political Change*, London: Methuen & Co, 1979, p. 222 says, the 'egalitarian and democratic' nature of the sects 'tended to be displayed by patriotic demands for independence and a constitution.' In other words, they tended to display modern nationalist demands.

[83]Fourniau, 'Les traditions', p. 96 on the scandal, pp. 91–94 on defences. For an expansive colonialist accounts of the conquest see Charles Gosselin, *L'Empire d'Annam*, Paris: Perrin, 1904, and Thomazi, *La Conquête*. See also Paul Chack, *Hoang Tham Pirate*, Paris, 1933; Dao Trinh Nhat, *Phan Dinh Phung*, Saigon, 1957.

organised resistance. In his memoirs Gallieni attributed his success to 'a racial policy'[84] (*une politique de race*) in which he divided the regions up according to the 'sum of common or opposed interests' of the communities within them, and then applied the 'oil spot' technique:

> the country is cleared progressively by small military operations and, above all, by the population that has rallied to our army and been supported and supplied with munitions by us. For points of departure these operations have provisional posts which are successively extended as the purification progresses . . . This is the oil spot. One only moves into new territory after having completely organised that in the rear. They are the unsubdued indigenes of yesterday who aid us and who serve to prevail over the unsubdued of tomorrow.[85]

With the French able to divide the country up in this way and then rule it progressively with indigenous support there was no way resistance leaders like Phan Dinh Phung and De Tham could have held out indefinitely. And, as he died in 1897 suffering from dysentery and clawing at grass roots for food, Phan Dinh Phung spoke the truth for those who resisted the run of history: 'We live at a time when our families disintegrate, our country disappears, and our wives and sons are taken from us'.[86]

The resistance had saved neither the king nor the institution of the monarchy. The unprecedented power of the French had destroyed both and conquered the county. Without an independent monarch or the real prospect of ever having one again, the country was divided and ruled in the high colonial period between 1900 and 1939.

Conclusion: The Structures of French Colonial Rule, 1900–1939

Once the French had created the post of Gouverneur Général of Indochina and incorporated Vietnam into the 'Indochinese Union' along with Laos and Cambodia by 1887, ruling the country after the pacification campaigns was not difficult. All the French had to do was harden existing regional and ethnic divisions—Tonkin, Annam, Cochinchina, the Thai Country and so on—and rule through variegated administrative and legal systems that reflected practices both ancient and modern, regional differences, and the *ad hoc* development of

---

[84]Général Gallieni, *Gallieni au Tonkin (1892–1896)*, Paris: Editions Berger-Levrault, 1948, p. 87.
[85]Ibid., p. 156.
[86]Dao Trinh Nhat, *Phan Dinh Phung*, p. 7.

government agencies in the course of the piecemeal conquest of the country.[87]

In Tonkin, Annam, and Cochinchina the village councils of notables remained in place as the basic unit of administration, but were governed by different regulations in each region. At the higher levels of administration in Cochinchina, Provincial Administrators were the main agents of colonial power, and the region was administered directly as a colony of France through the Colonial Council set up in 1880. In Annam and Tonkin separate protectorates were set up, and a system of Résidents oversaw the activities of indigenous officials in the mandarinate; as a result, dual Vietnamese and French bureaucracies emerged in Annam, while the Services of the Gouvernement Général eventually incorporated all administrative functions in Tonkin.[88] In many cases, as Nola Cooke has noted, the functions of these administrative services were never clearly defined and often depended on the interpretations of incumbent individuals.[89] Meanwhile, an 'incredibly piebald judicial system', as Woodside has described it,[90] encompassed the Gia Long code of 1812–1815, French law, and special colonial decrees depending on the region and the race involved.

While these unrationalised systems of law and administration were riddled with contradictions, they were not necessarily a product of false consciousness on the part of the French. In so far as they reflected Vietnamese regionalism they were able and, in many cases as Woodside has argued, designed to accommodate traditional practices and customs to a significant extent.[91] By maintaining the old power structures such as the councils of notables, and the mandarinate no matter how they were re-modelled or how desiccated they would become by the 1930s, the French thus tended to stabilise their

[87]The administrative and legal status of the various parts of French Indochina has been discussed in many books. A good start point would be Paul Isoart, *Le phénomène national vietnamien*, Paris: Librarie Général de Droit et de Jurisprudence, 1961, Chapters 4 and 5.

[88]Nola Cooke's work is particularly valuable on Annam. See her 'Proteges and Protectors: Relations between the Protectorate Government and the Government of Annam, 1897–1925', M.A. Thesis, University of Sydney, 1980.

[89]Private communication, April 1988. Cooke, 'Proteges and Protectors', also offers a detailed analysis of the steps which the French took to re-model the mandarinate and set up its administration in Annam.

[90]Woodside, *Community and Revolution*, p. 24. On colonial law see Indochine Française, Section de l'Administration de la Justice, Exposition Coloniale Internationale, Paris, 1931, *La Justice en Indochine*, Hanoi, 1931. I am grateful to Nola Cooke for making this source available to me.

[91]Ibid., p. 24.

colonial rule. But by instituting new administrative systems such as the Services of the Gouvernement Général to extract taxes, oversee public works, and implement the alcohol, opium, and salt monopolies they were setting the economy up for long term exploitation and linking it to international markets. And, although the contradictions in this old-new system of colonial government generated serious regional revolts from time to time, it was a relatively simple matter for the Franco-Vietnamese colonial army to isolate and crush them.

In 1903 a second regular regiment of Vietnamese *tirailleurs* was raised for the colonial army to replace French and French African troops that were being withdrawn for service in other parts of the empire.[92] By 1930 of the colonial army's main strike force of thirty one battalions plus a regiment of artillery and other supporting units, twenty battalions were indigenous with a sprinkling of Vietnamese throughout the rest of the force. Twenty thousand of the thirty thousand regular troops in the country were indigenes.[93] In addition to these troops there was the colonial militia or 'Indigenous Guard' created in 1886 along the lines of the Bengal Police which the British had set up in India. Originally, it was recruited to take part in the conquest of Tonkin by canton chiefs who retained the same responsibility for recruiting under the French as they had in pre-colonial times. After the turn of the century it then carried out the role of a para-military force whose organisation like the regional forces of old was based on the provinces. In 1931 it numbered 15,220 plus 388 French officers and NCOs.[94]

Modern military technology and organisation had probably cut the size of the old Nguyen dynasty's regular army in about half, and substantially reduced the size of the para-military forces in the regions. With such a streamlined modern force the French could then override regional resistances to the colonial authority as it did most notably during the tax riots in Annam in 1908, the disturbances around Saigon in 1913, and the widespread uprisings in northern and central Vietnam in 1930 and 1931.

From around 1917 modern police methods also tended to reinforce the apparatus of the colonial state. In this year, the Special Police Branch of Indochina and the Directorate of Political Affairs both came under the Sûreté Général thus fusing the political and police

---

[92]Anonymous, 'La Défence de l'Indochine', *Revue des Deux Mondes*, XXXII, Mars/Avril, 1906, pp. 800–803.

[93]Exposition Coloniale Internationale de Paris, Commissariat Général, *Indochine Documents Officiels*, Paris, 1931, Vol. 2, pp. 28–34.

[94]E. Daufès, *La Garde Indigène d'Indochine de sa création à nos jours*, 2 Vols., Avignon, 1933–34, Vol. 1, Introduction.

functions of government at the highest level. After the uprisings in 1930 and 1931 a further expansion of secret police activities in Vietnam was also accompanied by the establishment of eleven new torture chambers in the Sûreté's main complex in Saigon. The increasing use of an international surveillance network which covered Singapore, Bangkok, Batavia, Tokyo, Hongkong, Shanghai and other southern Chinese cities, Paris and other major French cities, and a listening post at the French embassy in Moscow was also an aspect of modern police methods after about 1930.[95] Yet, while these police activities undoubtedly enhanced the oppressive power of the colonial regime in the short run, their effects should no be exaggerated.

What made French power unshakable before the Second World War was the way it broke up the unity of the old monarchical state, and reinforced the old and new institutions of the colonial period with modern military technology. Once the power and prestige of the monarchy had been destroyed there was no longer any political-military foundation for regional unity and independence. However, as the society was now caught between old and new systems, it was being pressed back into the past as much as it was being forced into the future. The birth of a new order was thus incipient in the death the old. And so the great problem which the French conquest set up for Vietnamese intellectuals in the twentieth century, was how the country's ancient political-military methods of constituting unity and independence could be given new force under the momentous changes that had overcome them in the modern world.

[95]Daniel Hémery, *Révolutionnaires vietnamiens et pouvoir colonial en Indochine*, Paris: François Maspero, 1975, Chapter 4, especially pp. 156–169.

2

Force of the New Nation: A Conceptual Construct, 1900–1939

Because of the power of the French colonial regime to divide and rule Vietnam, no anti-colonial party was to unite the regions and establish an independent government between 1900 and 1939. As already indicated, the uprisings that occurred in this period were effectively repressed. But if the strength of French rule in Vietnam was rooted in its power to intensify the regionalism of the old polity, its weakness was that it came from outside Vietnam and brought new political concepts with it that would ultimately undermine the foundations of colonial rule.

Western concepts of democracy, nationalism, and internationalism were integral to the technological imperatives that propelled Western expansion. Under the specific conditions of French rule in Vietnam we will see that there was no way the French presence in that country could suppress the idea of 'nation', even if French power could suppress its political manifestations for a time. Moreover, since the thrust of French colonial rule was to suppress the political manifestations of Vietnamese nationalism, colonial rulers also proved unable to repress Marxist-Leninist ideas of revolutionary 'internationalism' and 'world revolution'.

In themselves, there is no reason why these revolutionary ideas should have provided the only workable intellectual context for Vietnamese nationalism as they ultimately did. They did not provide the intellectual context in which nationalist movements developed in many other European colonies. However, we will see that the great importance of Marxist-Leninist internationalism in the Vietnamese revolution was that it provided the universalising creed which the Vietnamese needed to imagine an independent alternative to French colonialism in the 1930s, and, from 1938, it permitted this alternative

40

to take a national form within the old context of the Sino-Vietnamese relationship.

This chapter is therefore about the impact which colonial rule had on Vietnamese conceptions of an independent world order and on conceptions of how the armed forces of the modern nation would eventually be mobilised.

The Origins of a National Language of Opposition 1900–1930

Many historians have argued that it is legitimate to speak of a Vietnamese 'nation' before the French conquest.[1] Common language, culture, and ethnicity, together with a centralised administration and territorial contiguity can all be seen to have created a strong sense of group solidarity in pre-colonial Vietnam. Yet the 'loss of country' (*vong quoc*) to which turn of the century writings especially refer,[2] suggests very strong reasons why this old sense of group solidarity was not yet a 'nation'.

This 'loss of country' to the French was illuminated most powerfully in the writings of the Confucian scholar, Phan Boi Chau, who made the key observation in 1905 that 'Vietnam has disintegrated and the king disappeared'.[3] To understand this statement it is first necessary to realise that the term *trung quan* or 'loyalty to the monarch' encapsulated the idea of political obligation in pre-colonial Vietnam.[4] Since the monarch epitomised the country and the country

---

[1] For example Huynh Kim Khanh, *Vietnamese Communism 1925–1945*, Cornell University Press, 1982, p. 32 says that 'by the time of the French invasion Vietnam had developed the social and cultural attributes of a nation — a unified tradition, culture, and language, and an effective political and economic system.' Truong Buu Lam, *Patterns of Response*, p. 29 says anti-French resistance in the nineteenth century was nationalist. William J. Duiker, *The Rise of Nationalism in Vietnam, 1900–1941*, Cornell University Press, 1976, pp. 15–18 says that during the traditional period the Vietnamese already possessed a 'rudimentary sense of nationalism'. Pham Quynh, in an earlier undated work published in *Sud Est*, No. 13, Juin 1957, said 'Annam has always been a nation in full meaning of the word'.

[2] Phan Boi Chau, *Viet Nam Vong Quoc Su* [A History of the Loss of the Country of Vietnam], originally published in 1905 and translated from the original Chinese by Chu Thien and Chuong Thau, published by NXB Van Su Dia, Ha Noi, 1957, and reprinted with an introduction by Tran Van Giau in Paris in 1972, is the most famous statement on the 'loss of country'. For another *quoc ngu* translation and a copy of the original Chinese edition see *Dai Hoc Van Khoa* [Journal of the Faculty of Letters], 1959–1960 edition, Saigon, 1960, pp. 3–34. For a discussion of the work see Marr, *Anticolonialism*, pp. 114–119.

[3] Ibid., p. 51.

[4] Khanh, *Vietnamese Communism*, p. 29.

belonged to him, the concept of *quoc* or 'country' was inseparable from the concept of *quan* or 'monarch'. Loyalty to the monarch was thus inseparable from loyalty to the country, and these two loyalties were the foundation for Vietnamese political unity because they transcended regional loyalties and made the country, collectively, Vietnamese. In the seminal writings of Phan Boi Chau, therefore, when the unprecedented power of the French had destroyed the court and ruled out the possibility of the revival of an independent monarchy, the old foundation for a distinct sense of the Vietnamese collectivity had been destroyed, and gave birth to the spectre of 'the extermination of our race'.[5] But while Phan Boi Chau was so deeply uncertain about the future, French power had forced him to imagine the foundation for a new kind of collectivity.

At one point in his *History of the Loss of the Country* Phan Boi Chau wrote an unusual sentence: 'The country of Vietnam has people' (*Nuoc Viet Nam co dan*).[6] These words prefaced an explanation of why he had to describe to people the nineteen onerous French taxes that had replaced the two taxes imposed by the traditional court.[7] He was afraid that such a description would suffocate peoples' minds and leave them helpless and dizzy, but 'humane'[8] feelings dictated that he proceed for he did not know how people would be able to do anything about their plight if he did not. These 'humane' feelings were naturally those of a Confucian scholar, and it was the

---

[5]Phan Boi Chau, *Trung Quang Tam Su* [The Secret History of Trung Quang], originally written in episodes for a Chinese military journal between January 1921 and April 1925, translated by Nguyen Van Bach, and published by NXB Van Hoc, Ha Noi, 1971, p. 25 says 'they plan to exterminate our race'. Of course, in the context of this historical novel set at the time of the Ming occupation in the fifteenth century the 'they' were the Chinese rulers, but the novel was unquestionably rooted in contemporary concerns and any contemporary reader would also have undersdood that 'they' were the French rulers.

[6]Phan Boi Chau, *Viet Nam*, p. 55. Chinese scholars tell me this sentence is very odd in Chinese and could not have been written by a Chinese scholar. However, while line 7 of the 10th page of the Chinese text in *Dai Hoc Van Khoa*, 1959–1960 edition, shows that this is indeed what Phan wrote, I do not think Phan's construction can be explained simply in terms of his 'bad Chinese'. Phan could in fact write excellent Chinese as some of his poetry reveals, and I would argue that, as well as an attempt to popularise his message, Phan's construction reflects particular Vietnamese perceptions and conditions. It is also possible to argue that Phan's use of the Chinese character '*min*' for 'people' is part of an explicit heightening of the idea of 'the people' as citizens in a modern political sense.

[7]Ibid., pp. 55–76 may have been the first attempt by a Vietnamese scholar to systematically analyse the nature of French rule.

[8]Ibid., p. 55.

impact of the French occupation on these feelings that made Phan's assertion about Vietnam having people both significant and radical.

In olden times, the fundamental political question was whether or not the country had a good king. Despite cycles of drought, flood, epidemic, and war there was never any question that the country had people. If the country had a good king human affairs would be regulated because of his moral virtue and benevolence, and not because of any intrinsic virtue of 'the people'. With the French, such 'humane' rule in the Confucian sense became impossible, as Phan Boi Chau demonstrated in his famous *Letter Written in Blood*[9] while he was in exile in 1906.

In this statement he offered three reasons for the country's failure to meet the French challenge. First, 'the king did not know how to look after the welfare of the people'. Second, 'the mandarins did not care about the people'. Third, 'the people only care about themselves'.[10] Once we have therefore seen how the French conquest stripped away the political importance of the king and the mandarins, Phan presents us with a series of fascinating, radical formulations which isolate 'the people' (*dan*) as an independent political category. These formulation include the following: '(the people) establish the foundation for the wealth of our country', 'the people are of the country, and the country is of the people', and 'if we do not have people, then we do not have anything'.[11] In fact, as the good king and the country's capacity to find a new one had been eliminated, and as French power peeled away the protective layers of 'humane' rule and imposed nineteen taxes instead of two, we see how the existence of a Vietnamese 'people' was being placed in such a new light that they became the foundation for the entirely new political category of 'nation'.[12]

---

[9]I have used the edition of this long poem '*Hoai Ngoai Huyet Thu*' in Van Hoc, *Hop Tuyen Tho Van Yeu Nuoc va Cach Mang Dau The Ky XX (1900–1930)* [Collected Patriotic and Revolutionary Poetry at the Beginning of the Twentieth Century (1900–1930)], Hanoi: NXB Van Hoc, 1972, pp. 50–72.

[10]Ibid., p. 56. See Marr, *Anticolonialism*, pp. 129–131 for another translation and further commentary.

[11]Ibid., p. 56, p. 58. These ideas were also circulating in the *Dong Kinh Nghia Thuc* and throughout the entire country around the time Phan Boi Chau had written his letter. See p. 539, note, and p. 551 where the poem '*Ai Quoc*' (Love of Country), uses a line that Phan's uses in his *Letter Written in Blood*: '*dan la dan nuoc, nuoc la nuoc dan*' or 'the people are of the country, the country is of the people.'

[12]In other words, we are seeing a shift from the people as subjects to 'the people' as citizens. It is worth adding that the 'modernist tendencies' which Paul Mus, *Sociologie d'une guerre*, Paris: Editions du Seuil, 1952, p. 24 points to in the French administra-

From the 1900s 'nation' was rendered in Vietnamese as *quoc gia,
dan toc*, and *quoc dan*[13], but until at least the late 1920s we cannot
always be sure what the literati meant when they used these terms.
The term *quoc gia*, literally a 'country of families', was an ancient
term that can be found in Mencius.[14] It denoted the territorial
possessions of different feudal grandees, and well before the Tang
dynasty, it came to mean 'kingdom'. Thus, although the Japanese
had adapted the term to mean a nation-state with the three attributes
of territory, people, and sovereign legal powers in the nineteenth
century, we cannot be certain what classical scholars in Vietnam
meant for some time after they revived it in the 1900s.[15] There are,
however, at least two reasons why we can be sure that a modern
mutation in the ancient meaning of a term like *quoc gia* was occurring
at this time.

The first may be approached through the revival of the ancient
term *dong bao* to mean 'compatriots' under modern conditions. The
literal meaning of this term is 'of the same womb'. According to
Alexander Woodside[16] it had originally meant 'brothers' before
medieval neo-Confucian idealists had extended it to convey a sense
of the ideal spiritual nearness to each other of all people, not just
blood siblings. Then, suddenly, when the term is revived in the 1900s
such medieval universalism is modified to mean the prescriptive
nearness of all people to each other in a *quoc gia*, and this prescriptive nearness may be drawn out from some patriotic poems Phan Boi
Chau wrote in 1910.

It should be remembered that the old ideal of loyalty to the country
was synonymous with loyalty to the monarch. What Phan Boi Chau

tion after 1900 also reinforced this shift. For example, the creation of a regulated civil
state which increased controls over Administrators and Councils of Notables, and the
introduction of elections to constitute councils at various levels in the administration
tended to reinforce the notion of citizenship.

[13]Khanh, *Vietnamese Communism*, p. 29 and throughout stresses that 'patriotism'
(chu nghia ai quoc) was a motive force of Vietnamese group solidarity or nationalism
in the twentieth century and I would agree, but this still does not show how the old
political groupings took on a new political significance at the same time. In other
words, it does not define the fundamental building blocks of the modern Vietnamese
nation. Apart from the terms I have mentioned there were others like *nuoc, nuoc nha*,
and *nha nuoc* that came to mean nation or nation state. These were very old
Vietnamese as opposed to Chinese words for 'the country', and I have avoided them in
the present discussion, for any semantic change that comes over them in the twentieth
century must already be related to the changes that come over the other terms.

[14]Letter from Professor Alexander Woodside, September 25, 1986.

[15]Ibid.

[16]Ibid.

was therefore doing when he wrote poems like 'Love of Country' (*Ai Quoc*), 'Love of Community' (*Ai Quan*), and 'Love of Race' (*Ai Chung*) in 1910,[17] was helping to set up a new foundations for political obligation in a situation where the foundations for being loyal to the monarch had been deeply shaken. In other words, as all the elements of the old political order—the country, the people, the race—fell apart when the central element, the institution of the monarchy, was destroyed by French power, Phan Boi Chau was picking up the broken elements in his poems and relating each one to the other through 'love' (*ai*), thus setting up the idea of patriotism (*chu nghia ai quoc*) as the modern notion of political loyalty and obligation in a nation-state.[18]

But what is of particular interest is the way the categories of country, community, and race are all brought together without the monarch in a poem like 'Love of Community' and mutually prescribed in the term *dong bao*. For example, what we find in this poem, which begins with the couplet, 'The heavens gave birth to our unique race,/ the mountains and rivers constitute one special country of Vietnam', is the formulation '*dong chung, dong bao*' which conveys the sense that 'people of the same race (*dong chung*) are not only of the same race but also compatriots (*dong bao*)'.[19] Since patriotism fused love of people of the same race with love of country, and since compatriots were people with a prescribed nearness to each other in a *quoc gia*, we therefore see how the use of such terms permitted a conflation of the modern sense of national solidarity and ancient universal idealism, and gave terms like *dong bao* and *quoc gia* a special potency from around 1910.

Another reason why the term *quoc gia* incorporated a modern mutation in the ancient categories is that it was often used interchangeably with other new terms that came to mean 'nation' from the 1900s: *quoc dan*, literally 'a country of people', and *dan toc*, literally 'a people of clans'. In fact, these terms which placed an unprecedented accent on 'the people' (*dan*) could be used interchangeably themselves as late as the 1950s to mean 'people', 'citizen', 'nation', or

[17]Van Hoc. *Hop Tuyen Tho Van Yeu Nuoc*, pp. 76–81. These were not necessarily the first poems on these subjects. Other Confucian Scholars were also working on them around the same time as Phan Boi Chau. See the note on p. 539 for more information.

[18]This is even though Phan does not actually use the term 'patriotism' in the poems cited. It should also be remembered that as late as 1910 Phan was promoting Cuong De as a royal pretender, which indicates that ideas of 'loyalty to the monarch' still existed beside the new foundations for patriotism, even as he constructed them.

[19]Van Hoc *Hop Tuyen Tho Van Yeu Nuoc*, p. 79.

'nation-state'.[20] And so the very interchange of these ideas in the new terms, and the interchange of these new terms with old terms like *quoc gia* makes it clear that a modern mutation in Vietnamese perceptions of the political collectivity was indeed taking place in the first decades of the century. Furthermore, as we have seen, the sense of political obligation was being transferred from 'loyalty to the monarch' to 'patriotism'. The effect of French power was to topple the monarchy and bring 'the people' and 'the nation' into existence as political categories of fundamental importance in the twentieth century.

One other elaboration of the new terminology should be mentioned. In 1911 Phan Boi Chau's 'League for the Restoration of Vietnam' in Southern China called for a 'democratic republic' (*dan chu cong hoa*) and announced the formation of a 'revolutionary army' (*quan doi cach mang*).[21] Of course, plots surrounding these calls came to nothing because the French were far too strong. But as the new terms were inspired by Sun Yat Sen's republican revolution, what was at stake conceptually was a refinement of the role of 'the people' in modern times, for the Vietnamese phrase for democratic, *dan chu*, may be translated literally as 'the people as master'.[22] A revolution had certainly taken place in Vietnamese perceptions of political and social order.

The best demonstration of the connection between technological change and the evolution of a national political consciousness is the one between the modern printing press and the explosion of publishing it facilitated in the romanised Vietnamese script known as *quoc ngu* or the 'national language'.[23] For example, when the important colonial journal *Nam Phong* or *Southern Wind* was first published in

[20]For example, Diep Van Ky's use of the *dan toc* in *Su Cach Mang* [A History of Revolutions], Saigon, 1927, p. 34 clearly means 'nation' and 'nationalism' (*chu nghia dan toc*). Also see Khanh, *Vietnamese Communism*, p. 27, especially note 9. Also for an interesting example of the deliberate conflation of '*quoc dan*' (the people) and '*dong bao*' (compatriots) by Phan Boi Chau in 1913 see the quote heading p. 212 of Marr, *Anticolonialism*.

[21]Marr, *Vietnamese Colonialism*, p. 219.

[22]For another interesting example of the conscious placement of 'the people' as masters rather than subjects see Marr's 1913 quote from Phan Boi Chau heading p. 212 of Marr, *Anticolonialism*. Indeed, after asking the question 'Who are the masters?' (*Chu Nhan la ai?*) the quote answers 'Our people . . .' (*Quoc dan*).

[23]See David G. Marr, *Vietnamese Tradition on Trial*, University of California Press, 1981, pp. 161–167 for a discussion of 'The Quoc Ngu Explosion'. See also Nguyen Thanh, *Bao Chi Cach Mang Viet Nam 1925–1945* [Newspapers of the Vietnamese Revolution, 1925–1945], Hanoi: NXB Khoa Hoc Xa Hoi, 1984, Introduction and Chapter 1.

July 1917, one of its prime movers, Pham Quynh, presented readers with an entirely new idea. Because he felt that the pressure of change had made the personality of the Vietnamese people 'ambiguous and fleeting like a photograph out of focus', (a new metaphor in itself), Pham Quynh argued that 'the most important question of our time' was the question of developing a literature in the 'national language'.[24] Many other numbers of *Nam Phong* then took up the issue, and when Phan Ke Binh related his efforts at writing the heroic tales of Vietnamese history in the 'national language' to efforts of the writers of renaissance France who converted Latin tales of medieval heroes into colloquial French[25] the message was clear: French colonialism was bringing the concept of a distinct Vietnamese nation into focus.

It might also be added that when *Nam Phong* was first published in 1917 it had the words 'France Before the World—Its Role in the War of Nations' emblazoned in French across the title page. When some 100,000 Vietnamese went to the war with the promise of post-war reform from the colonial government, there was no possibility or even thought that the idea of 'nation' could be stifled in colonial Vietnam.

Of course the whole force of French colonialism suppressed any manifestations of the modern nation at the same time as it brought the concept of the nation into focus. By the turn of the century the futility of trying to fight the French army was clear to any thinking person, and with few exceptions among the elite the years through to 1925 or so were those of 'Great France' (*Dai Phap*). As small land owners and a petty bourgeois class emerged, learned French at school, sometimes went to France to study, and saw the new roads and railways being constructed and telegraph poles springing up like phallic symbols of modern progress, there was widespread if not unqualified belief that Franco-Vietnamese collaboration was the path to modernity. The vast majority of the elite, like Phan Chu Trinh, were calling for more education and reform within the compass of French rule. Many like Ho Chi Minh, who tried but failed to gain entrance to the colonial school at Marseilles in 1911, thought a French education would be of use to the country. Many others like Bui Quang Chieu who had studied agricultural engineering in Algeria were trying to apply their knowledge at home.[26] However, by the

---

[24]*Nam Phong*, July 1917. See article by Pham Quynh on the need for a 'National Literature'.

[25]I am again indebted to Professor Alexander Woodside for pointing this information out to me.

[26]John McAlister Jr., 'The Origins of the Vietnamese Revolution', Yale University PhD, 1966, pp. 29–53 on the French speaking elite; Isoart, *Le Phénomène*, p. 215 on

mid-1920s when the promises of reform that the French used to gain Vietnamese support during the First World War were not realised,[27] the Vietnamese intelligentsia became increasingly radicalised.

In January 1926, as the French and their collaborators tried to find a successor for the deceased puppet emperor Khai Dinh, the widening gap between those Vietnamese intellectuals whose self interest demanded a continuing and closer allegiance to the French[28] and the radicals was reflected in an article which linked the fate of the defunct monarchy to modern change. This article by the radical Nguyen Van Pho appeared in the journal *Viet Nam Hon* (Soul of Vietnam) under the title 'For the Suppression of the Monarchy of Annam. Proclamation to the People', and it said:

> The princes of the royal family are all ignorant beings; none of them has sufficient qualities to be king. To seek the will of God and examine the sentiments of the people, one could say that it is the end of royalty in Vietnam. In today's situation in our country, conserving royalty will only have disadvantages. Let our compatriots open their eyes and follow *the current which has led all the people on earth*. Let us try to overthrow this old statue. After its demolition, we shall reconstruct the social edifice to give a new life to our country, to demand our rights and our liberty.[29]

This current which led '*all the people on earth*' had begun to run through Vietnam when telegraph poles and steam ships had already linked it to the modern world, and new ideals like those of 'nation' first came to usurp those of 'the monarch's country' in the first decade of the century. And after the ideology of Franco-Vietnamese collaboration had dampened this current for many years, it began to

---

the hope of a favorable evolution of French policy especially after the First World War, and pp. 172–175 on roads and railways; Duiker, *The Rise*, see index on Phan Chu Trinh; Georges Boudarel et al., *La bureaucratie au Vietnam*, Paris: L'Harmattan, 1983, pp. 26–30 on Ho Chi Minh; Megan Cook, *The Constitutionalist Party in Cochinchina: The Years of Decline 1930–1942*, Monash Papers on Southeast Asia, Number Six, 1977, pp. 15–16 on Bui Quang Chieu.

[27]Isoart, *Le Phénomène*, p. 215.

[28]Gareth Porter, *Imperialism and Social Structure in Twentieth Century Vietnam*, Cornell University PhD, 1976, Chapter 1, shows how Vietnamese landowners and colonial economic interests prevented economically privileged Vietnamese from becoming radicalised. Page 31 says such people were in a position of 'conflict and dependence' on the French. Cook, *The Constitutionalist Party*, Chapter 2, is also a very worthy read on the subject.

[29]Quoted in Khanh, *Vietnamese Communism*, pp. 50–51, emphasis mine. *Viet Nam Hon* was printed in France not Indochina.

surge through literature of the late 1920s once the elite had become increasingly radicalised by the failure of reformist ideas.

In a work like the 1928 *History of Colonialism* by an underemployed official in the colonial education system named Dao Duy Anh,[30] the idea of a new Vietnamese nation in opposition to the old regime is very strong. Indeed, under the influence of modern revolutions in other countries such as Sun Yat Sen's in China, Dao Duy Anh was one of the first Vietnamese writers to link such concepts as 'people's power' or 'people's rights' (*dan quyen*) and 'people's livelihood' (*dan sinh*) with the concept of a 'people' or 'nation' (*dan toc*) in opposition to colonial rule.[31]

A work by the radical historian, Tran Huy Lieu, *Mirror for Restoring the Country*, published in Saigon in 1928[32] then puts this opposition into a wider context. The text is a translation from the Chinese; it concerns the Italian Risorgimento and plots the careers of Mazzini, Garibaldi, and Cavour. The book was designed to praise these nationalist leaders for their 'love of country' (*long ai quoc*)[33] and says in the translator's postscript that if the Vietnamese want to save their country they will have to follow their example:

> When we read the story of these nationalists how can we not think of the story of our own country; when we see these nationalist personalities how can we not think of the personalities of our own country.[34]

In other words, what numerous works like Tran Huy Lieu's did was to relate Vietnam to the modern world of burgeoning bourgeois nationalisms which had already toppled enfeebled monarchies all over Europe. When the refugees from these fallen thrones then retreated to the colonies to establish their absolutist regimes there, these would again be toppled in time by the force of modern nationalism.

Bourgeois nationalist opposition to the French colonial regime in Vietnam first took significant political form in 1927 with the foundation of the '*Quoc Dan*' or 'National' Party of Vietnam (*Viet Nam Quoc Dan Dang* or *VNQDD*) by the northern Vietnamese school teacher Nguyen Thai Hoc. After organising itself along old secret society lines and half along Leninist lines so that it pledged secrecy and loyalty to the Party's central committee, sub-committees, and

---

[30]Dao Duy Anh, *Thuc Dan Lich Su* [A History of Colonialism], Hue, 1928.
[31]Ibid, p. 86
[32]Tran Huy Lieu, translator, Lung Khai Sieu, *Guong Phuc Quoc* [Mirror for Restoring the Country], Saigon, 1928.
[33]Ibid., Introduction.
[34]Ibid., p. 81.

cells before ancestral alters, the Party began to plot an uprising. Regional and district committees planned uprisings in cities and towns, made bombs, and began to infiltrate Franco-Vietnamese colonial army units.

However, when the uprising broke out at the colonial army garrison at Yen Bai in February 1930 it was a fiasco.[35] The French soon had the situation under control and the uprising was suppressed with great thoroughness. But when the French captured the National Party's leader, Nguyen Thai Hoc, he addressed a letter to the French Deputies before his execution that outlined five changes the French would have to make if they wanted to stay in Vietnam without being troubled by revolutionary movements. At the same time, the letter summarised the aspirations of Vietnamese nationalists in 1930:

1) Abandon all brutal and inhumane methods; 2) Behave as friends to the Annamites and no longer as cruel masters; 3) Strive to relieve moral and material miseries by restoring to the Annamites elementary rights of the individual, freedom of travel, freedom of education, freedom of association, freedom of the press; 4) No longer favour the extortion of functionaries or their bad habits; 5) Give education to the people and develop indigenous commerce and industry.[36]

Refracted through these demands, therefore, was the vision of a democratic and industrialised nation state which modern ideas had formed in the minds of the radical Vietnamese elite by 1930, and which the French regime moved ruthlessly to repress.

Such ruthless repression of Vietnamese nationalism would then make resistance to the French more inevitable than ever as Nguyen Thai Hoc had implied. Yet, the success of French repression in 1930 was still indicative of the powerlessness of Vietnamese nationalism. What the word 'nation' defined in the late 1920s was still what it defined when turn of the century literati first constructed it: the loss of king and country and an awareness that 'the people' could be the only foundation for an independent Vietnam. In other words, all this definition did was to highlight the dislocation of the Vietnamese people in the world without suggesting how they might be relocated

---

[35]On the formation of the Vietnamese Nationalist Party see Hoang Van Dao, *Viet Nam Quoc Dan Dang: Lich Su Dau Tranh Can Dai, 1927–1954* [The Vietnamese Nationalist Party: A History of Modern Struggle, 1927–1954], Saigon, 1964. Also see A.B. Woodside, *Community and Revolution in Modern Vietnam*, Boston, 1976, pp. 59–67. For a detailed description of the uprising see Hoang Van Dao, *Viet Nam*, Chapter 6–7, and Cedric Allen Sampson, *Nationalism and Communism in Vietnam, 1925–1931*, University of California Los Angeles PhD. Chapter 7.

[36]Original text in French in Hoang Van Dao, *Viet Nam*, pp. 123–124.

under modern conditions. It offered no workable definition of the nature of French colonialism and what exactly would be necessary to overthrow it. What has to be done now, therefore, is to show how the ideology of Marxist-Leninist internationalism came to provide such a definition and place the idea of 'the people', if not immediately 'the nation', in an independent context.

Marxist-Leninist Internationalism and the Language of Revolutionary Universalism, 1925–1938

While nationalist terminology had gained a certain currency among the Vietnamese elite in the late 1920s this was also becoming true of the revolutionary terminology of Marxist-Leninist internationalism. Where the two terminologies were fundamentally related was in their perception of the importance of 'the people' or, in the case of the revolutionaries, 'the masses' (*quan chung*) as a modern political category. A major difference between the two, however, was that while the word 'nation' merely tended to reflect the particular impact of technology in Vietnam and on the position of the monarchy, the use of revolutionary terms including 'world revolution' (*the gioi cach mang*) and 'imperialism' (*de quoc chu nghia*), tended to universalise the Vietnamese experience of French colonialisation rather than to particularise it.

The idea that there was an imperialist world order and a potential for world revolution did not come to Vietnamese radicals in a moment. Asian intellectuals generally had not been able to make the connection between capitalism and colonial exploitation before Lenin's writings on imperialism, most notably *Imperialism: The Highest Stage of Capitalism*, had shown them how in 1919.[37] It was not then until the mid-1920s that Lenin's argument that the Western bourgeoisie had converted itself into a supra-national group which used its technology to enslave the technologically backward peoples of the world was incorporated into the thinking of at least one important Vietnamese revolutionary.

This was Ho Chi Minh. After his rebuff at the colonial school in Marseilles in 1911, he had drifted into socialist circles in France, taken a special interest in the Russian revolution, become a founding

---

[37]Jonathan D. Spence, *The Gate of Heavenly Peace: The Chinese and Their Revolution, 1895–1980*, Penguin, 1982, p. 151. The basic text is of course V.I. Lenin, *Imperialism: the Highest Stage of Capitalism*, in V.I. Lenin, *Selected Works*, 3 vols, Moscow, 1967, Vol. 1, pp. 673–777. See also Alfred G. Meyer, *Leninism*, Harvard, 1957, Chapter 11, and A. Reznikov, *Lenin and Revolution in the East*, Moscow, 1969.

member of the French Communist Party in 1920,[38] and embarked on a course of study in Moscow by 1924 when he made one of his earliest recorded statements on the subject of Western imperialism.

In this statement he noted the use of colonial troops in the First World War, and alleged that colonial soldiers stationed near the Pyrenees in France were used to put down a strike in 1917.[39] In a reference to Lenin's 1920 *Theses on the National and Colonial Questions* which called for 'the closest possible union' between the proletariat of Europe and the revolutionary movements of the East',[40] Ho was also saying in 1925 that 'Lenin established the basis for a new radical revolutionary era in the colonies'.[41] One of his longest and most detailed tracts on imperialist exploitation then came in the first eight or nine pages of his *Le procès de la colonisation française*[42] which was published in France in the same year. And before long, ideas such as those Ho was writing about in exile had begun to trickle into Vietnam via returned soldiers from the First World War, sailors working the international shipping lines, and émigrés in China.[43]

The publication of Dao Duy Anh's *History of Colonialism* in Hue in 1928 is a literary milestone in the Vietnamese revolution, if only because it provided the first generally available, full explanation of what imperialism might be to the Vietnamese:

[38]For an introductioyn to Ho see Jean Lacouture, *Ho Chi Minh*, Paris: Seuil, 1977, pp. 17–18; Charles Fenn, *Ho Chi Minh: A Biographical Introduction*, London, 1973.

[39]Ho Chi Minh, 'Tham Luan ve Van De Dan Toc va Van De Thuoc Dia tai Dai Hoi Quoc Te Lan Thu Nam cua Quoc Te Cong San', in *Ho Chi Minh Tuyen Tap* ['A Discussion of the National and Colonial Questions at the Fifth International Congress of the Communist International', in Ho Chi Minh Collected Works], Hanoi; NXB Su That, 1980, Vol. 1, p. 37.

[40]English translation of Lenin's *Theses* in R.F. Turner, *Vietnamese Communism: Its Origins and Development*, Stanford, 1975, pp. 305–309. For another translation and general background see Jane Degras, *The Communist International 1919–1943*, 3 Vols., Oxford University Press, 1956–1960, Vol. 1, pp. 38–47. On the Third International and its resolutions on the national and colonial questions see also V.G. Kiernam, *Marxism and Imperialism* , London, 1974, especially Chapter 1; Kermit McKenzie, *Comintern and World Revolution*, New York, 1964, Chapter 2.

[41]Ho Chi Minh, 'Le-Nin va Cac Dan Toc Thuoc Dia' [Lenin and Colonised Peoples], in *Tuyen Tap*, pp. 76–77.

[42]Ibid., pp. 81–89 under the title *Ban An Che Do Thuc Dan Phap*. The original was published in French by the Librarie du Travail, Paris, 1925.

[43]F. Trager, ed., *Marxism in Southeast Asia*, Stanford, 1959, pp. 107–111. Tran Huy Lieu, *Lich Su Tam Muoi, Nam Chong Phap* [A History of Eighty Years Resistance to the French], 2 Vols., Hanoi, 1961, Vol. 2, p. 9. As is well known Ho was at work addressing groups of Vietnamese troops in France waiting for repatriation in 1921 and 1922. See N. Khac Huyen, *Vision Accomplished? The Enigma of Ho Chi Minh*, New York and London: Collier-MacMillan, 1971, p. 18.

the countries of the world can be divided into two categories:
one category, rich and strong, occupying a very small (area),
and consisting of the great powers of Europe and America; the
other category, poor and vile, occupying a very large (area), and
consisting of colonies, protectorates, half colonies, and half
protectorates.[44]

And we have no doubt that the great powers were 'imperialist' for we
are told in terms that come straight from Lenin how

capitalism at its highest stage of development is called
"imperialism", that is to say, the stage when the capitalists use
political power to develop and support their capital in foreign
countries.[45]

The publication of Diep Van Ky's *History of Revolutions* in Saigon in
1927 should also be remembered in this context, for it had already
implied links between the ideas of imperialism and of world revolution:

from the outbreak of the October revolution, Russia . . .
initiated self determining nationalism, by giving people
everywhere one desire to resist imperialism and capitalism.[46]

Indeed, by 1927, intellectuals in Vietnam who used the new revolutionary terminology were conceptualising an imperial order that
exploited the Vietnamese people, and they were beginning to imagine links between what was happening in Vietnam and the whole
world.

As they began to imagine these links, however, the radical intellectuals had a theoretical problem that they have never solved. Marxist-
Leninist notions of 'world revolution' were clearly underpinned by
others of 'class struggle' (*giai cap dau tranh*), and, even if it were
possible to assume the existence of a foundation for 'class struggle' in
an overwhelming peasant society like Vietnam's,[47] no application of

---

[44]Dao Duy Anh, *Thuc Dan Lich Su*, p. 1.

[45]Ibid., p. 4.

[46]Diep Van Ky, *Su Cach Mang*, p. 34.

[47]It is difficult to argue that a foundation for proletarian class struggle existed in
Vietnam when the French actively stifled indigenous capitalism and the urban proletariat in the 1930s was minuscule, probably not more than 100,000. If one then departs
from classical Marxism and argues the existence of class struggle between various
agricultural classes — landlords, rich peasants, poor peasants, tenant farmers, agricultural laborers, and so on — the problem of applying these categories meaningfully in a
wide variety of regional and social contexts is a bewildering one. For some idea of what
Bernard Fall correctly called the 'comical' aspects of the first 'Population Classification
Decree' of March 1953 see his *The Two Vietnams: A Political and Military Analysis*,

this idea ever showed any sign of being able to overthrow the power of French colonialism. Indeed, while Ho Chi Minh had begun to use, but not explain, the idea of 'class struggle'[48] by 1927, and while the same may be said for radicals generally by the 1930s, we will see that it was a sufficiently unworkable idea for its main exponents in the Indochinese Communist Party (ICP) to abandon it as an element of public policy by 1939.

Yet the commitment of radicals to 'class struggle' because it was an inescapable tenet of 'world revolution' in the late 1920s and 1930s, still suggests the overriding need which they had to invoke universalism. In fact, when French power was so strong in the 1920s and 1930s that nothing was able to overthrow it, only some universal idea that related the conquest of the country to something beyond itself could make an independent alternative to colonial rule conceivable. And if we relate the new idea of 'world revolution' to the old Confucian idea of the 'great harmony' or 'great unity' (*dai dong*) which also appeared in the radical writings, it is possible to show how Marxist-Leninist internationalism fulfilled this overriding need.

In the ancient Confucian context the idea of the 'great unity' envisaged a world in which 'common spirit ruled all under the sky'. 'Robbers and filchers and rebellious traitors did not show themselves' such that the 'outer doors remained open and were not shut'.[49] It envisaged a utopian world in which all barriers between people were flattened. And as we are drawn back into the ancient language of the 'great unity', we are alerted to the importance which some Vietnamese radicals gave it in the modern world.

The modern word for 'world', *the gioi*, was in fact another revival of an old term in which *the*, 'time', and *gioi*, 'the directions' (north, south, east, west, up, down) had added up to the 'universe'.[50] When this word was used in modern times and linked up with the term 'revolution' we are thus alerted to the universalising effects of Marxism-Leninism on Vietnamese political thought. Ultimately, the

New York: Praeger, 1966, p. 155. An Article in *Nhan Dan* of 29 June 1956 raised further problems in a reference to the government's heavy handed land reforms of that time, when it said that 'a number of people not classified as landowners' resisted the government. Also, do tenant farmers struggle against poor peasants as well as rich peasants and landlords, and what happens if somebody fits into more than one class category? Finally, there is the well known fact that the majority of the leaders of revolutionary movements in Vietnam were from rich or gentry backgrounds.

[48]For example, Ho Chi Minh, *Tuyen Tap*, p. 234 uses the expression '*giai cap tranh dau*' in *Duong Cach Mang* [The Road to Revolution].

[49]Quoted in Martin Bernal, *Chinese Socialism to 1907*, Cornell University Press, 1977, p. 11. Chapter 1 is entitled '*Datong*', the Chinese equivalent of *Dai Dong*.

[50]Letter from Professor Alexander Woodside, 25 September 1986.

'great unity' of the ancient Confucian philosophers was not far from the equally spectacular view of the world that the Russian revolution and Lenin's notion of 'world revolution' had revealed to humankind. Lenin's utopian vision of 'world revolution' certainly raised class barriers to brace the revolutionary struggle, and for the Vietnamese this was new. But like the 'great unity', it finally flattened every known geographical, cultural, ethnic, barrier between peoples and included the whole world. And there is no doubt that a modern radical like Ho Chi Minh could see this connection.

The old word for 'world', which the revived word *the gioi* appeared beside in the first decades of the twentieth century, was *thien ha*, literally 'beneath heaven'. Therefore, when Ho Chi Minh wrote in 1927, '*thien ha dai dong—ay la the gioi cach menh*', 'the great unity under heaven'—that is the world revolution',[51] we see in the clearest possible terms how the universalism of the old concepts was being transferred to the new.

This transference may be depicted in the political-social realm. In pre-colonial Vietnam where 'the people' had not been recognised, society had been ordered hierarchically into four classes on the Confucian model: scholars, peasants, artisans, and merchants (*si, nong, cong, thuong*). Since the scholars had been displaced by the French and the merchants appropriated by them, this left the peasants and the artisans.[52] If, under the influence of Marxism-Leninism, a reversal in the order of the peasant and artisan categories and a modern mutation in meaning are then admitted – no one would deny the existence of some factory workers in colonial Vietnam – what comes into view are the modern categories of 'workers' and 'peasants' which together are synonymous with 'the people'. Since the modern Vietnamese words for worker and peasant, *cong* and *nong*, are the same as the old words for artisan and peasant,[53] the semantic shift for peasants is less visible than for workers. Nevertheless, in their alliance with 'the people' both the worker and peasant categories had taken on a new political significance and, at least conceptually, were a powerful force for change. It is therefore reasonable to say that the use of Marxist terminology with its accent on 'the people', 'the masses', and 'the workers' helped Vietnamese radical intellectuals clarify this revolutionary guardianship, and give 'the Vietnamese

[51]Ho Chi Minh, *Tuyen Tap*, p. 237 in an important tract called *Duong Cach Menh* [The Road to Revolution] which is discussed in detail below.

[52]The fact that the new category *tri tuc* of 'intellectuals' replaced the *si* for a time does not undermine my argument when they were powerless in affairs of state.

[53]The word *tho thuyen* is also commonly used for 'worker'. *Tho* can be translated as 'artisan' or 'workman'.

people' universal significance in the modern world through the doctrine of world revolution.

In the face of French power, Marxist terminology could therefore
maintain a conceptual focus on 'the people', and to support this
argument textually, we may refer to the seminal tract Ho Chi Minh
published in Canton in 1927 called *The Road to Revolution*.[54] This
tract was a primer for the intensive training courses the 'Revolutionary Youth League' was conducting from 1926 among Vietnamese
émigrés in China including Le Hong Phong, Ho Tung Mau, Le Hong
Son and Pham Van Dong.[55] And, as Huynh Kim Khanh has observed, it represented a 'new analysis' that went beyond 'nationalist'
terms when it stated that 'oppression gives birth to revolution' and
'workers and peasants are the masters of the revolution'.[56]

[54]I have used the edition published in Hanoi in 1980 in Ho Chi Minh, *Duong Cach
Menh* [The Road to Revolution] in *Tuyen Tap*, pp. 229–300. This full edition of *The
Road to Revolution* did not become available until 1980 and therefore poses problems
of interpretation. For one helpful critique see Vu Tho, 'Tu *Duong Cach Menh* den
Luan Cuong Chinh Tri cua Cong San Dong Duong [From the *Road to Revolution* to
the *Political Theses of the Indochinese Communist Party*], *NCLS*, No. 72, March 1965.
From this source we learn that on the basis of an early, if not a first edition of *The Road
to Revolution*, a Chinese communist argued in 1933 that while the work was 'light' on
the standpoint of the proletarian class, it 'reeks with nationalism' (*sac mui quoc gia*). In
1965, one Vietnamese Party historian, Vu Tho, answered this argument by saying that
even though *The Road to Revolution* did not attempt to present a comprehensive
Marxist interpretation of Vietnamese society or the Vietnamese revolution, it was
nevertheless 'impregnated' with a proletarian world view. Since Ho's tract rested on
such propositions as 'revolution is a task of the masses' and 'workers and peasants are
the root (*goc*) of the revolution', Vu Tho concluded that
   'if *The Road to Revolution* is a document that "reeks with nationalism", then that is
   not bourgeois nationalism, but the position of the proletariat as it first took shape in
   the national liberation movement in Vietnam'.
Despite their differences in emphasis, therefore, we find agreement between critics
who would undoubtedly have emphasised Ho's Marxist leanings as strongly as they
could have, that his tract was rooted in nationalism of some kind. While any changes
that have been made to the 1980 edition have very likely been ones to 'correct' Ho's
nationalist bias with infusions of Marxist-Leninist terminology, and while there is still
nothing in the 1980 edition that fundamentally contradicts a nationalist interpretation
of it, we then have a reasonable basis for saying that the 1980 edition has not basically
changed the emphasis of Ho's original work.
   [55]For a discussion of the Revolutionary Youth League see Khanh, *Vietnamese
Communism*, pp. 63–89; William J. Duiker, 'The Revolutionary Youth League:
Cradle of Communism in Vietnam', *China Quarterly*, July–September, 1972
   [56]Khanh, *Vietnamese Communism*, pp. 84–85. Ho's propositions can be found in
Tuyen Tap, p. 238. The term 'class' is also deployed on a number of occasions such as

Ho's statement begins by highlighting the difference between the old scholar, peasant, artisan, merchant social categories and the new revolutionary categories. This is done by making a Leninist distinction between 'people's revolution' (*dan toc cach menh*) and 'world revolution' (*the gioi cach menh*):

> The two kinds of revolution are different from each other because today's revolution does not yet make class distinctions, that is to say, the scholars, peasants, artisans, and merchants are equally united in their resistance to brute force. But in the world revolution the proletarian class stands at the head.[57]

As soon as this distinction is made between old Confucian and new Marxist categories is made, however, the passage continues:

> But the two kinds of revolution are still related to each other. For example, the Vietnamese people's revolution succeeds and weakens the French capitalists, and if the French capitalists are weakened it is easier for the French workers and peasants to carry out class revolution. And if the French worker-peasant revolution succeeds then the Vietnamese people will be able to have freedom.[58]

In Ho's thinking the people's and world revolutions are 'different' but 'related'. He is saying that there are no class distinctions in Vietnam *yet*, but relating the destiny of 'peasants' and 'artisans' who comprised 'the people' in Vietnam with the destiny of 'workers' and 'peasants' in France. In this relationship the switch from peasant-artisan to worker-peasant categories is thus implicit thereby universalising the Vietnamese experience. Indeed, collocated in the text with the passage that produces this switch is the important comment of Ho's that we have already discussed: 'the great unity under heaven—that is the world revolution'.

one on p. 257 where Ho confidently raises the Comintern slogan, 'the proletarian class of the whole world unite!'. Also see p. 234 where 'class struggle' is mentioned in passing. The scholarly writers including Khanh have of course been critical of Ho's failure to explain the application of Marxist theory to Vietnamese conditions. See William J. Duiker, *The Communist Road to Power in Vietnam*, Boulder, Colorado: Westview Press, 1981, p. 19; Alexander B. Woodside, *Community and Revolution in Modern Vietnam*, Boston: Houghton Mifflin Company, 1976, pp. 168–170. In my view, these writers, who were without access to a full edition when they wrote, overstate Ho's failure to explain Marxism because Marxism is not really the subject of Ho's tract. Although Marxism has a position of special prominence in it, its subject is the integration of old Vietnamese political categories with the changes that had overcome them in the modern world.
[57]Ho Chi Minh, *Tuyen Tap*, pp. 237–238.
[58]Ibid., p. 238.

A number of examples of world revolutions, which were meant to tap the collective historical consciousness of the Vietnamese, were then set out. The American revolution was an example of a people who rose to claim their liberty, freedom, and happiness.[59] 'Revolutionary courage' was what the Vietnamese could learn from the 'soldiers without uniforms', 'the people with torn clothes, emaciated faces, and empty stomachs' who rose in France in 1789 and 'defeated foreign soldiers'.[60] Then, the Russian revolution, which had completely overthrown the monarchy, the capitalists, the landlords,

> teaches us that if we want to have a successful revolution *the people* (*workers and peasants*) must be the root, we must have a strong party, we must have courage, a spirit of sacrifice, and we must have unity. In sum, we must follow Marxism-Leninism.[61]

Now, to understand this 'courage', 'spirit of sacrifice', and 'unity' Ho was using Marxism-Leninism to draw on for revolutionary purposes, it is necessary to realise that, in its own right, the concept of 'struggle' (*dau tranh*) is one with important associations in Vietnamese history. The struggles to establish prosperity and the unity and autonomy of a relatively small state on the border of the Chinese empire constitute major themes in Vietnamese history. Many Vietnamese writers have suggested as Luong Duc Thiep did in 1944, that history gave the Vietnamese people a 'potential for struggle'[62] that would help them survive the vicissitudes of modern times. What Ho was doing in his set of historical comparisons in 1927 was similar: he was appropriating the old sense of 'struggle', and using Marxism-Leninism to place it in a culminating world historical context with the Russian revolution where '*the people* (*workers-peasants*) must be the root'.

Ho had still not explained how the concept of 'class struggle' was supposed to work in Vietnamese society. When some attachment to the concept was nevertheless necessary to maintain an internationalist line, (and there is no doubt that many communists came to believe it), we therefore come up against one of the intellectual disjunctions that stems from the use of Marxism in Vietnam. Nevertheless, Ho had still tapped the collective consciousness of 'struggle'. Ideas of 'armed struggle' and 'mass struggle', if not 'class struggle', could then be used eventually with great force by Vietnamese Marxist-Leninists,

---

[59]Ho Chi Minh, *Tuyen Tap*, p. 242.
[60]Ibid., p. 244.
[61]Ibid., p. 255. Emphasis added.
[62]Luong Duc Thiep, *Xa Hoi Viet Nam* [Vietnamese Society], Hanoi, 1944, republished Saigon: Hoa Tien, 1971, see introduction.

because Ho had also clarified the worker-peasant categories of 'the people'. In sum, by relating the concept of world revolution to the 'great unity' and making a popular struggle its motive force, Ho had taken two very important conceptual steps. He had freed Vietnamese history from the course of French colonial rule, and, regardless of any problems the concept of class struggle might cause the ICP in the future, he had permitted radicals to imagine an independent alternative for 'the people' within a socialist world order.

Almost as soon as the ICP was formed under Ho's direction in Hongkong in February 1930,[63] there is a good example of how such an alternative was momentarily realised. At this time, just after the Party's program mentioned the need to establish a 'worker-peasant-soldier government' and a 'worker-peasant army',[64] it was swept up in the widespread uprisings which the nationalists touched off at Yen Bai in February. By May its cadres in the central provinces of Nghe An and Ha Tinh, and many other community leaders who could not be described as Party members, began to act on internationalist impulses if not the ICP's program itself. Indeed, although ICP cadres and other leaders were largely forced to react to the uprisings that were caused by rapacious taxation and extreme economic hardship at the time of the great depression,[65] they still managed to set up some rural 'soviets' and 'village self defence forces' (*doi tu ve*) which official histories in 1974 and 1981 refer to as the first units of the 'People's Army'.[66]

In a situation where the colonial regime lost control of the administration in significant areas of the countryside for months at a time, the new soviets represented the emergence of a new village

[63]There are numerous sources on the formation of the Communist Party. Ban Nghien Cuu Lich Su Dang Trung Uong [Central Board for the Study of Party History], *Lich Su Dang Cong San Viet Nam So Thao* [Draft History of the Communist Party of Vietnam, 1920–1954], Vol. 1, Hanoi, 1981, (Hereafter *LSDC*); and Khanh, *Vietnamese Communism*, Chapter 2 with notes for further reading in primary sources are good start points.

[64]*VKQS*, p. 10.

[65]There is a voluminous literature on the uprising in Nghe An and Ha Tinh. For some main Western sources see bibliography under Scott, James C.; Popkin, Samuel; Brocheux, P.; Duiker, William J.; Bernal, Martin; Osborne, Milton, 'Continuity and Motivation . . .'. Apart from the Vietnamese sources noted below also see Tran Huy Lieu, *Lich Su Tam*, and *Thai Lieu Tham Khao*.

[66]Ban Nghien Cuu Lich Su Quan Doi Thuoc Cuc Chinh Tri [Board for the Study of Army History in the Political Department], *Lich Su Quan Doi Nhan Dan Viet Nam* [History of the People's Army of Vietnam], Hanoi: NXB Quan Doi Nhan Dan, 1974, Vol. 1, (Hereafter *LSQD*), pp. 32–38. See also *LSDC*, Vol. 1, Chapter 2. For the origins of the term 'People's Army' see the next note.

administration. The village self defence units also represented what Engels had described as the 'self acting armed organisation of the population' at a time of great upheaval. They represented the first flickering of the independent Vietnamese 'nation in arms'.[67] But it is important to realise that the peasants themselves did not think in these terms as they rose up. They were far more likely to think in ancient terms. For example, one history based on local interviews says that at Ba Xa in Can Loc District, Ha Tinh, where the people formed a Self Defence Group that was eighty strong in August,[68] they decided to forge a 'new life':

> they worked together, ate together, there was equality with no division by rank, causing many people tears of happiness. Thinking back that until recently every day they had to bend their heads, bowing before and waiting upon the important figures and village bullies who were eating and drinking their fill at banquets, being beaten and cursed, they saw enough to understand the meaning of "liberation", "equality", and "freedom". No one spoke but everyone was happy, making concessions and sharing with each other.[69]

[67]In the writings of Marx and Engels, from which probably all modern theories of armed uprising spring, state power was thought to emerge from within the society to impose control over the exploited class, and the standing army and the police, essentially detached from the society were its chief instruments of force. In this conception the state was a form of institutionalised violence 'blocking up the pores of life', as Marx said in *The Civil War in France*. Lenin thus concluded in *The State and Revolution*, London reprint of the 1918 Moscow edition, p. 12, that 'the liberation of the oppressed classes is impossible without a violent revolution and without the destruction of the machinery of state power.' On the same page Lenin then refers to the standing army etc., as the 'special force' or 'special bodies of armed men'. He does this to make a distinction between the 'special force' of the state or the standing army, and what Engels in *The Origins of the Family, Private Property, and the State*, London, 1942, p. 195, p. 131, probably first called the 'people's army', as under conditions of early Athenian democracy, or the 'self acting armed organisation of the population'. This 'self acting' mechanism was thought of as a kind of popular armed organisation that would form automatically in a classless society as in the Paris Commune in 1871. With the French army defeated by the Prussians and with the National Guard in tact and ready for the defence of Paris, one of the first acts of the commune was to abolish conscription and the standing army and 'declare the sole force to be the National Guard in which all citizens capable of bearing arms were to be enrolled,' as Engels put it in his Introduction to Marx's, *Civil War in France*, in R.C. Tucker ed., *The Marx Engels Reader*, New York, 1972, p. 531. Lenin thus concluded in *The State and Revolution*, p. 43 and p. 143 that 'Paris armed was the revolution armed'. The standing army had been replaced by the 'nation in arms'.

[68]*LSQD*, p. 32. For the training of such units see Bernal, 'The Nghe-Tinh Soviet', p. 54, and Osborne, 'Continuity and Motivation', p. 43.

[69]Hoang Nhat Tan, *Xo Viet Nghe-Tinh* [The Nghe-Tinh Soviets], Hanoi, 1962, p. 105.

This account is certainly an emotional one. But the emotion is revealing, for as it welled up from the collective consciousness it displayed the utopian ideals of the 'great unity'. And as these ideals were associated with a soviet adminsistration and self defence forces, and tinged with modern notions of 'liberation', 'equality', and 'freedom', we see how the past was rushing up to help create alternatives to French colonial rule in Vietnam's modern revolution.

Of course, by late 1930 the Franco-Vietnamese colonial army had planted 122 military posts in the region and the soviets were crushed. The almost complete destruction of the ICP as soon as it was formed involved the execution or imprisonment of 90% of its leaders and the Party did not recover for years.[70] Yet what sets the rural soviet movement apart from the nationalist uprisings that preceded them is that radical intellectuals in Vietnam had begun to integrate the notion of popular uprising with an independent world view through the use of Marxist-Leninist terminology. Also, this terminology does a great deal to explain why the Communist Party eventually recovered from the French repression of 1930-31 while the Nationalist Party never really did.[71]

Because of institutional support from the Comintern, Marxist-Leninist internationalism was an ideology that some leading individuals could build into a vocation. After the destruction of 1930–31, some Vietnamese internationalists who went to find refuge and inspiration in the Soviet Union may well have felt like the Chinese intellectual Qu Qiubai when he made the journey in 1921:

The icy beams of the crystal moon struck in flashes through the windows of our compartment, and amidst these flashes and

[70]Tran Huy Lieu, *Lich Su Tam*, Vol. 2, especially pp. 72–78; *LSDC*, pp. 141–163; Duiker, *The Communist Road*, p. 41; Bernal. 'The Nghe-Tinh Soviet', p. 151; Osborne, 'Continuity and Motivation', p. 47.

[71]In this discussion I have avoided organisational factors as an explanation for the singular success of the Communist Party. This is partly because its Leninist style organisation has been discussed by many authors including Huynh Kim Khanh and Douglas Pike whose works can be found in the bibliography. More importantly, however, this is also because I do not think organisational factors deserve the attention they have received. I have seen no evidence which convinces me that the ICP's mode of organisation *per se* was any more effective than that of other anti-colonial parties like the Nationalists. Even though they never recovered as a political force after 1930–31 various nationalist parties like the VNQDD and the Dai Viet maintained some semblance of an organisational presence for years to come, and after all the organising that went on in ICP circles in the 1930s, we will see later that the French police still smashed the Party's organisations in Saigon in a few hours during the Nam Ky uprising in 1940.

dancing lights our train pushed on, drawing ever nearer to Moscow.[72]

Moreover, we know from a memoir by Ho Nam[73] of the kind of experience that was possible on arrival.

On the icy evening of 12 September 1931, a group of Vietnamese[74] in the club of the University of the Toilers of the East in Moscow were exhilarated by the solidarity which marked the first anniversary of the repression of the recent uprisings in Nghe An and Ha Tinh. An orchestra opened the meeting by leading a loud chorus of the *Internationale*. A succession of speeches by Comintern representatives, an art exhibition devoted to the theme of the oppression of Indochina, and a play performed by Vietnamese actors entitled 'The Success of the Indochinese Revolution' filled out the evening. Then, as the lights of the world revolution must have danced beneath a crystal moon when the members of the orchestra picked up their instruments to play a final chorus of the *Internationale*, we have some idea of how many Vietnamese came to believe that proletarian internationalism was, as one writer has recently put it, a 'moving spirit'[75] of the Vietnamese revolution.

As this spirit universalised the Vietnamese struggle it revealed visions of a new world order. Electrification leading to light, steel works, and power for the people was of course one of the catchcrys of the Russian revolution. And for all its deficiencies, the idea of an inevitable revolution that would electrify the world and give power to the people is a very important one for an understanding of why those Vietnamese who believed it have had such a major impact on their country's recent history.

Since the standing army had a monopoly on modern weapons, the repression of 1930–31 had shown there was no way popular forces would have the power to succeed in Vietnam without an international upheaval that substantially reduced the power of the French. Lenin's theory of imperialism and world revolution gave radicals such as Ho Chi Minh a view which permitted them to predict 'the Second World War'[76] and to believe that 'imperialism is almost at the end of the

---

[72]Quoted in Spence, *The Gate of Heavenly Peace*, p. 176.

[73]Ho Nam, *Ky Niem Nghe An Bao Dong* [Anniversary of the Nghe An Violence], no place, 1 August 1932. This memoir is a hand written document which comes from the Library of Congress in Washington.

[74]Ibid., p. 3.

[75]This phrase (*dong luc tinh than*) is in fact part of the title Tam Vu, 'Chu Nghia Quoc Te Vo San, Mot trong Nhung Dong Luc Tinh Than cua Cach Mang Viet Nam tu Sau Chien Tranh The Gioi Lan Thu Nhat den Thang 8–1945' NCLS, No. 82, 1979.

[76]*VKQS*, p. 12 records the prediction in 1930. The earliest prediction I have seen was in 1924 in Ho Chi Minh, *Tuyen Tap*, p. 54.

road'.[77] This belief in the imminence of a world crisis that would undermine the power of the French and create an opportunity to seize power, gave ICP cadres a sense of purpose that other anti-colonial parties did not necessarily enjoy in the 1930s. This sense of purpose, almost certainly helps to explain why a number of prominent radicals like Tran Huy Lieu and Le Tung Son defected from the Nationalist Party to the ICP in the early 1930s, at a time when the ICP was never farther from power.

To maintain the Comintern links that were necessary to imagine a new world, therefore, the ICP was never more firm about the need for 'class struggle', 'mass struggle', and 'world revolution'[78] as it rebuilt it cells in Vietnam from around 1933. For leading ICP cadres including Le Duan, Bui Cong Trung, Nguyen Van Cu, and Pham Van Dong who had been trained in Moscow,[79] the French repression in 1930–31 had confirmed that 'peaceful methods will have no effect whatsoever'.[80] Nevertheless, as it stressed 'armed violence','revolutionary violence', and the need to infiltrate the standing army in the 1930s,[81] the ICP was never any closer to achieving real power than any of the other anti-colonial parties in the country.

Duiker has pointed correctly to the inappropriateness of the ICP's emphasis on class struggle and the mobilisation of the urban proletariat when the vast majority of the population were peasants.[82] Then there were the bewildering policy changes that effectively placed the ICP on the same side as the colonial regime from around 1936 to 1938, after Stalin ordered world communist parties to adopt a popular front strategy against the rise of fascism.[83] Whether the ICP emphasised a Stalinist style class struggle and subversion of the standing army, or a Stalinist style Popular Front strategy against the rise of Fascism in the 1930s, therefore, it could not have been farther from mobilising the popular force of the modern Vietnamese nation.

Yet Khanh still alerts us to the reality that the only difference between the ICP and the thirty other parties that plotted the downfall of the French before 1939 but failed to develop after was 'internationalism'.[84] As already indicated, Marxist-Leninist inter-

[77]Ho Chi Minh, *Tuyen Tap*, p. 261 records this statement in 1927.

[78]*VKQS*, p. 41, pp. 86–87. Fulminations against 'reformism' and the 'pacifism of Ghandi' also rumble through this source. See p. 61, p. 64, p. 74.

[79]Tran Huy Lieu, *Lich Su Tam*, Vol. 2, pp. 116–119; Khanh, *Vietnamese Communism*, pp. 172–175 gives an interesting account of international support for the rebuilding.

[80]*VKQS*, p. 64, p. 86.

[81]This theme is emphasised throughout *VKQS*.

[82]Duiker, *The Communist Road*, Chapter 3.

[83]Ibid.

[84]Ibid., especially pp. 99–105 and pp. 172–176.

nationalism permitted the ICP to maintain from its inception that 'the Second World War will erupt' and eventually create conditions where 'the people' would be able 'to rise against the French'[85] and create a free place for themselves within a socialist world order. But to understand the real as opposed to the spiritual advantage which this expanded vision gave Vietnamese Marxists over their rivals in Vietnam, and also over Marxists with similar visions who never came to power in other European colonies such as Indonesia, India, and Malaya, it is necessary to remember Vietnam's relationship with China.

From 1937 when the international situation began to change dramatically with the Japanese invasion of China, the ICP was the only party in Vietnam with a sufficiently wide world view to place the fortunes of the revolution in a dynamic relationship with this change. Chinese Marxist-Leninist internationalists still had a long way to go to victory. But from 1937 they had begun to develop political-military methods that would be useful for mobilising 'the people' in Vietnam when the anticipated world crisis sufficiently undermined the power of the French colonial regime. Moreover, as Vietnamese internationalists revived ancient practices when they began to draw on appropriate Chinese models from 1938, we will see how they found that these were not ideologically bound by unpromising ideas of 'class struggle'.

As the Sino-Vietnamese relationship began to reassert itself in the late 1930s, so did Vietnamese nationalism. Indeed, nothing did more than the Japanese invasion of China to turn the ICP away from Comintern models based on class struggle, and to relate a growing Vietnamese interest in Mao's peasant based model of a war of 'national' liberation with the first serious external threat to the colonial regime. Vietnamese radicals, who had imagined an independent place for the people in a socialist world order, were now beginning to find themselves in a position to concretize this place in national terms. For these radicals, it was one of the great fortunes of the Vietnamese language that, as turn of the century literati had understood, talking about 'the people' could be the same as talking about 'the nation'.

The ICP and Mao's Model of a Revolutionary Guerrilla War of National Liberation, 1938–1939

The Japanese invasion of China in 1937 caused a great deal of interest in Vietnam for Vietnam was close to China, and it was widely believed that further Japanese expansion was inevitable. As one commentator put it in 1938, 'according to the Japanese master plan,

[85]*VKQS*, p. 12.

once they have ransacked China they will proceed with the ransacking of the Philippines, Indochina, Siam, Malaya, and the Dutch East Indies'.[86] Essays on Japanese expansion since the Russo-Japanese War, accounts of Japanese bombing of Chinese cities, stories of the work of well laid Japanese spy rings in China and Vietnam, and numerous books on the Sino-Japanese War itself began to inform an avid reading public.[87] Meanwhile, the colonial regime was incapable of formulating an effective defence policy.

The metropolitan government in Paris was unsympathetic to calls for more troops and military supplies at a time when war clouds were gathering in Europe. If anything, the Minister of Colonies, Georges Mandel, wanted a scaling down of colonial defences, for a considerable number of Vietnamese troops were in fact sent to France in 1939 and early 1940.[88] Moreover, any idea of arming the people and giving them the foundations for a defence industry would have undermined the colonial order. All the French in Indochina could thus do was to train a few thousand extra militiamen, comply with various Japanese demands over the closure of the rail link between Tonkin and China, and hope that the threat would go away.[89] But as the threat loomed

[86]Nguyen Duc Thuy, *Phuong Phap Khang Nhat cua Hong Quan Tau* [The Method of Anti-Japanese Resistance to the Chinese Red Army], Ha Noi, January, 1938, p. 1. For the ICP's official perception of the impending invasion see *VKQS*, pp. 121–124.

[87]For example, Nguyen Manh Bong va Mai Dang De, *Nhat Hoa Xung Dot Thuc Luc* [A Factual Record of the Sino-Vietnamese War], Ha Noi, 1938. Nguyen Hong, *Sam Vang Trung Nhat* [The Sino-Japanese Conflict], Ha Noi, 1938. Le Dong and Nguyen Huy, *Nhut Hoa Chien Tranh va Su Hoat Dong cua To Chuc ve Gian Diep Nhut* [The Sino-Japanese War and the Activities of the Japanese Spy Network], Saigon, 1937. Bao Hung, *Nhat-Nga Chien Tranh* [The Russo-Japanese War], Ha Noi, 1937. There were also a number of works devoted to the question of the defence of French Indochina. Nguyen Vy, *Cai Hoa Nhat Ban* [The Japanese Peril], Ha Noi, 1938, and *Ke Thu la Nhat Ban* [The Enemy is Japan], Ha Noi, 1939; Tri Binh, *Van De Thu Dong Duong* [The Problem of the Defence of Indochina], Saigon, 1939; Hoang Van Su, *Dong Duong Du Bi Chien Tranh* [Indochina Prepares for War], Hanoi, 1938.

[88]In the words of Général Catroux, *Deux actes du drame indochinois*, Paris, 1959, p. 7, pp. 22–23. Mandel took the view that 'the Empire was to form a reservoir of forces at the disposal of France at war'. David Marr told me about the troops who went to France.

[89]The French command in Indochina knew well that a major Japanese attack could not be repulsed along the Sino-Vietnamese border with the means at its disposal. A mobile defence of the region was precluded by the lack of roads. Yet a static defence from posts like that at Lang Son which one French general described as 'undefendable' was not viable either. These posts had been built at the turn of the century and could not stand up to an assault from modern weapons. See R. Bauchar, *Rafales sur l'Indochine*, Paris, 1946, p. 41; Philippe Devillers, *Histoire du Vietnam de 1940 à 1952*, Paris, 1952, p. 75; Général Sabattier, *Le destin de l'Indochine: Souvenirs et documents, 1941–1951*, Paris, 1952, p. 34.

larger, and Japanese diplomats discussed the possibility of stationing troops in Indochina in 1939, it was clear that the colonial government's fortunes were not the only ones at stake. While the colonial regime could do nothing to ensure the defence of the country, some in the ICP therefore began unofficially to consider alternatives to the Comintern line.

Tran Huy Lieu has made this categorisation of ICP opinion in the late 1930s: 'while there were comrades who decided to follow both the name and the form of the Popular Front in France', there were others 'who wanted to follow the example of the Popular Front for resistance to Japan in China'.[90] Tran Huy Lieu might have added that Vietnamese regionalism effected this break down of opinion. Those in Cochinchina were more likely to think in terms of the Popular Front in France than those in Tonkin who were closer to events in China and to the Sino-Vietnamese border across which any Japanese attack was likely to come. But, especially when the Popular Front government in France had fallen in 1937, some idea of the reason for this partial yet growing attraction for a Chinese style Popular Front can be found in two little known political-military tracts that were published in Vietnam in early 1938.

The Method of Anti-Japanese Resistance of the Chinese Red Army by Nguyen Duc Thuy, and *What Can the Chinese Do to Defeat the Japanese?* by Nguyen Van Tay[91] were nothing less than Vietnamese primers on the writings of Mao and other Chinese strategists who were concerned with guerrilla war and changes in CCP policy as a result of Japan's invasion of China. These books emphasised that the Maoist model of a popular front could provide a conceptual foundation for the mobilisation of the mass of the population who were peasants rather than workers. They also suggested how the ICP could take an independent course of action that was hostile rather than ambiguously supportive of the helpless colonial regime.

Such emphases were clear in Nguyen Duc Thuy's book, which consisted of a compilation of twenty one Vietnamese translations of

---

[90]Tran Huy Lieu, *Lich Su Tam Muoi*, Vol. 2, p. 124.

[91]Nguyen Duc Thuy, *Phuong Phap Khang Nhat cua Hong Quan Tau*, Ha Noi, January 1938, provides the fullest exposition of the military thinking of the Chinese strategists, and is based on attributed passages translated into Vietnamese from the Chinese strategists. Nguyen Van Tay, *Lam Sao Cho Tau Thang Nhat?*, My Tho, February 1938, consists of summaries rather than translations of unattributed Chinese writings which say more about the political foundations for military strategy than the strategy itself. Bui Cong Trung's introduction to Nguyen Van Tay's work says it is based on 'valuable' Chinese documents. Both these works were undoubtedly known in ICP circles. Bui Cong Trung was a well known ICP member.

tracts by Mao, Zhou Enlai, Zhu De, and other Chinese strategists. The translator says in his introduction that these were 'translated from Chinese documents'.[92] The tracts emphasised the CCP's policy of a 'United National Front', the abandonment of the 'Soviet' and 'Red Army' nomenclature, and the 'politics of democracy' and 'patriotism' to defeat 'imperialism'.[93] Thuy's compilation further offered an important passage from Mao which said:

> We temporarily stop the class struggle between workers and peasants and the bourgeois classes within the country because in a semi-colonial country like China the contradictions between China and external imperialism are greater than the internal contradiction between classes. Thus we must reduce the internal contradictions to resolve the external contradictions.[94]

Nguyen Van Tay's book, which consisted of a series of summaries rather than translations of the Chinese strategic writings, reinforced this theme in passages which elaborated on the need for the 'unity' of 'the entire masses'[95] in their resistance to Japanese imperialism in China.

In the political context in which Nguyen Duc Thuy and Nguyen Van Tay presented these arguments, they were clearly part of an attempt to formulate a new policy. With the fall of the Popular Front in France, and the failure of the old international line on class struggle which had proved to be as inappropriate in Vietnam as Mao had found it to be in China,[96] the new thrust which the Vietnamese observers of China were suggesting was nationalist.

Yet this was not an attack on internationalism. As Mao explained elsewhere,[97] since any revolution in the colonies and semi-colonies would be 'a great blow to imperialism', revolutionary colonies and semi-colonies would in any case have to be considered as 'allies in the front of the world socialist revolution'.[98] Marxist-Leninist internationalism was thus preserved even if the notion of 'class struggle' had to be temporarily abandoned to forge the United National Front. In short, class contradictions were still seen to exist, but the further

[92]Nguyen Duc Thuy, *Phuong Phap Khang Nhat*, p. 1.
[93]Ibid., p. 4.
[94]Ibid.
[95]Nguyen Van Tay, *Lam Sao cho Tau Thang Nhat*, pp. 22–24.
[96]Of course, Stalin was not stressing class struggle between 1935 and 1939. But especially when the French Popular Front Government fell in 1937 the idea of class struggle still was an important part of ICP thinking.
[97]Mao Tse Tung, *China's New Democracry*, Sydney, August 1945, reprinted from the January 15 issue of the magazine *Chinese Culture* under the title of 'The Politics and Culture of New Democracy'.

contradiction that they were not to be emphasised until the foreign imperialists had been defeated was overlooked.

The political opportunism of both Chinese and Vietnamese communists on this issue stands out. But as Nguyen Duc Thuy and Nguyen Van Tay brought Mao's model of a United National Front to the attention of radicals in Vietnam by 1938, the fact remains that a war of national liberation could now be fought using the same patriotic language of opposition to imperialism that nationalist radicals used in the late 1920s. The all important difference by the late 1930s, however, was that Mao had shown how this nationalist, democractic, and patriotic language of opposition to French rule could be used in socialist international context. In this context, the Molotov-Ribbentrop pact of September 1939 to April 1941 was obviously an acute embarrassment for the ICP. But as the outbreak of the Second World War led to the dissolution of the Comintern, and the ICP began to incorporate the use of Chinese models, it was the Sino-Vietnamese relationship that began mainly to constitute Vietnam's socialist internationalist context.

In this relatively restricted but increasingly practical sense, the Marxist-Leninist internationalism which Ho first outlined for Vietnamese in *The Road to Revolution*, was beginning to sit on concrete foundations. This was especially so when models of political and military struggle that were appropriate in a peasant society, came with Mao's United National Front. These were the models which Mao first systematized in his famous works *On Guerrilla War* in 1937 and *On Protracted War* in 1938.[99]

When Mao wrote *On Guerrilla War* he did not envisage for a moment that guerrillas could defeat a conventional army with tanks, artillery, and aircraft by themselves. He argued, however, that wherever guerrilla war was a protracted patriotic resistance war against foreign imperialists and their feudal lackeys it could be politically structured through a progressive mobilisation and organisation of the whole population. As communist cadres moved in among the population to 'arouse' and 'organise' it guerrilla units

[98]Ibid., pp. 10–11. Of course this lead was not entirely original. Lenin had raised it around 1920 in his polemic against Rosa Luxemburg on the National Question. See Meyer, *Leninism*, pp. 148–155.

[99]Mao Tse Tung and Che Guevara, *Guerrilla Warfare*, London, 1965 with an introduction by Captain B.H. Liddel Hart. This treatise written by Mao in 1937 should not be confused with 'Strategic Problems in the Anti-Japanese Guerrilla War', written in 1938 and published in English tanslation in Mao Tse Tung, *Selected Military Writings*, Peking, 1965. *On Protracted War* is also published in *Selected Military Writings*, pp. 187–267. For a general treatment of guerrilla war see Walter Laquer, *Guerrilla*, Boston, 1976.

would take shape.[100] Then, as political and social reforms and military training were conducted, people's committees and conventional forces would eventually rise within this structure.[101]

As this structure was being reflected in Vietnamese writings by 1938, Nguyen Van Tay emphasised China's need for the 'unified action' of the people and the army according to a 'sure military plan'.[102] He also highlighted the integration of political organisation with social reforms, literacy compaigns, and military training.[103] Meanwhile, Nguyen Duc Thuy's translations included a passage from Zhou Enlai which emphasised that *'our victory must depend on the participation of the masses in the resistance war'*,[104] and another from Zhu De which said 'the way of guerrilla war is also the highest form of resistance war of the masses'.[105]

Another feature of the passage from Zhu De is that it already identified the first stage of the Maoist style guerrilla war as the 'defence' (*phong ngu*) stage in which

the guerrilla army is able to establish many small bases in the enemy's rear, distinguish weak points in the enemy's forces and then use our main force (*chu luc*) to attack suddenly . . . [106]

In fact, while this could be the first use in Vietnam of the term 'defence' stage, it could also be the first use of the term 'main force' (*chu luc*) to describe the offensive elements of the guerrilla army which we will come across increasingly from the mid-1940s. And while I am not aware that Mao's second and third stages, or what came to be described in Vietnamese in the 1940s as the 'holding' (*cam cu*) and the 'general counter offensive' (*tong phan cong*) stages, had yet been identified in these terms in Vietnamese writings by 1938,[107]

---

[100]Mao Tse Tung and Che Guevara, *Guerrilla Warfare*, p. 32.

[101]As Lin Piao, 'Long Live The Victory of People's War', in the *Peking Review*, September 3, 1965 said of areas in which Chinese guerrillas were mobilised against the Japanese: 'In these base areas, we built the (Communist) Party, ran the organs of state power, built the people's armed forces, and set up mass organisations . . . Our (guerrilla) base areas were in fact a state in miniature.'

[102]Nguyen Van Tay, *Lam Sao cho Tau Thang Nhat*, p. 24.

[103]Ibid., pp. 24–25.

[104]Nguyen Duc Thuy, *Phuong Phap Khang Nhat*, p. 10. Italics in original.

[105]Ibid., p. 13.

[106]Ibid.

[107]It should be remembered that while Nguyen Duc Thuy's translations were published in Vietnam in January 1938, Mao's full elaboration of the three stages—defence, holding, and general counter offensive—did not come until his publication of *On Protracted War* in May 1938.

all three stages were implicit in a remarkable passage of Zhou Enlai's which Nguyen Duc Thuy presented in his compilation.

This passage, was entitled 'Guerrilla Strategy is the Main Strategy of a War of People's Liberation'.[108] It began:

> With respect to strategy we must use PROTRACTED WAR (*CHIEN TRANH LAU DAI*), with respect to (individual) campaigns we are in favour of RAPID STRIKES (*DANH DIET THUC MAU LE*), and with respect to tactics we must use MOBILE WAR (*VAN DONG CHIEN*). Why is this so? It is because China has not invaded any country but is only protecting itself and the method of fighting for self protection must be supple to ensure victory. China is inferior to Japan in the military armaments industry therefore it is not able to fight one rash life or death battle with the enemy as soon as the war breaks out.[109]

After emphasising the need 'to mobilise the masses and to organise the masses' to support the Chinese Army, the passage then describes the three classical stages of Maoist style guerrilla war even though it does not use of the terms 'defence', 'holding', and 'general counter offensive' stages to delineate them.

First, 'we must use small numbers to defeat large numbers of the enemy so that the method of following local circumstances will be most advantageous'. Second, once the strategy of using rapid strikes has yielded a sufficient quantity of weapons and begun to disperse and tire the enemy,

> the enemy will naturally not dare to scatter his forces anymore but will have to keep them concentrated . . . In this way we will be able to blockade the enemy and beseige him. This means we have encircled the enemy strategically and caused him to waste his strength and become helpless.

Third, once a 'democratic political foundation' has been established and the people have been mobilised and organised 'around us',

> We attack and destroy his reinforcements so that in his front there will be no way to advance and in his rear there will be no reinforcements. To advance will mean death and to withdraw will be equally dangerous. If the enemy cannot move then he will surely tire, his food will be bad, and his sleep troubled, and as this continues over a protracted period his situation will become increasingly perilous.

---

[108]Ibid., p. 10. The quotes below can be found on pp. 10–11. For an English translation of the full passage see the Appendix.

[109]Ibid. Capitals in original.

What was being set out in three stages was Vietnam's tradition of resistance to foreign invaders updated to take account of the power of modern military technology. The growing attraction of Mao's model to the ICP in the late 1930s was thus self evident.

This attraction did not necessarily mean that ICP strategists would slavishly apply Mao's model or even realise its full implications immediately. Although I know of no evidence to support an argument that ICP radicals came independently to the same conclusions as Mao by the late 1930s this is also not impossible. But when the ICP had been struggling hopelessly with Stalin's line for almost a decade, there is little doubt that Mao's model had a big impact on Party thinking at a time when the Japanese threat to the stability of French rule was looming.

When Vo Nguyen Giap published *The Proper Path: The Question of National Liberation in Indochina* in early 1939[110] both the book's title with its reference to 'national liberation' and its content indicate a clear awareness of Chinese developments as conveyed by Nguyen Duc Thuy and Nguyen Van Tay.[111] Giap argued that since the French were much more likely to come to an accommodation with the Japanese than arm the people, the ICP *itself* must now take the lead in the struggle for national liberation. This was to be done by expanding the Party's operations among the masses so that they could simultaneously prepare to defend themselves against attacks from the colonial government and continue the ongoing revolutionary struggle. Then, later in the year, with the end of the Popular Front in Vietnam, the outbreak of World War Two, and a new wave of colonial repression which saw many ICP members who were not able to escape to China back in jail,[112] it was to Mao's model that the ICP officially turned.

[110]Van Dinh (Vo Nguyen Giap), *Con Duong Chinh: Van De Dan Toc Giai Phong o Dong Duong* [The Proper Path: The Question of National Liberation in Indochina], Hanoi: Dan Chung, 1939. This book must have had considerable circulation for it has found its way into the Bibliothèque Nationale in Paris. I have largely followed Marr's succinct discussion of it in *Vietnamese Tradition*, pp. 328–329.

[111]It could be also argued that the well known publication in 1938 of a book entitled *The Peasant Question* by Vo Nguyen Giap and Truong Chinh further reflected the impact of Mao's model. The amount of detail in this book long puzzled me until I read the primers by Nguyen Duc Thuy and Nguyen Van Tay and was alerted to the impact of the ideas they contained on the ICP's line in 1939. See Christine P. White, translator, Truong Chinh and Vo Nguyen Giap, *The Peasant Question*, Data Paper No. 14, Southeast Asia Program, Cornell University, January 1974.

[112]Duiker, *The Communist Road*, p. 60 says that Governor Général Catroux announced in September 1939 his intention to undertake a 'total and rapid' attack on the ICP. Isoart, *Le phénomène*, p. 315 says 800 ICP members were imprisoned by September 1940.

At the Sixth Conference of the ICP's Central Committee held at Ba Diem in Gia Dinh between 6 and 8 November, senior cadres including Nguyen Van Cu, Le Duan, Phan Dang Luu, and Vo Van Tan met to announce a 'change in policy'.[113] Of course, the Party would never forget the workers and peasants. But it had become apparent that 'large numbers of middle and poor landowners and the local petty bourgeoisie also hate imperialism'.[114] It was now to be a 'United National Anti-Imperialist Front of Indochina' which took up the struggle and it included:

> All classes, factions, and anti-imperialist elements that want to liberate the nation in order to struggle against imperialist war, resist fascist invasion, overthrow the French, the monarchy, and all the servants of imperialism . . .[115]

Moreover, while the ICP was saying that it would 'always regard soviet power as the widest governmental form', it was also saying that it was now necessary to suppress the idea of a 'worker, peasant, soldier government' and replace it with a 'Federated Democratic Republic of Indochina'. In keeping with this change, the term 'National Revolutionary Army' also came to replace the more inflammatory 'Red Army', and self defence units were to be 'expanded widely' so that 'a thousand would unite as one' in the 'revolution for national salvation.'[116]

At the Sixth Conference of the ICP's Central Committee the class question was pushed ambiguously into the background. Nevertheless, the languages of nationalist and revolutionary opposition to French rule were first unified in ICP policy. The idea of the nation in arms, the 'People's Army' now had a foundation. In some regions, especially Cochinchina, it would be some years before these important developments would have a direct impact on the history of the Vietnamese revolution. Yet the foundations for a nationalist struggle against imperialism which the Sixth Conference put in place in 1939, could only be strengthened by events in 1940 and 1941 as the next chapter will show.

[113]*VKQS*, p. 127.
[114]Ibid., p. 130.
[115]Ibid., p. 129.
[116]Ibid., pp. 130–131, pp. 133–134. In November 1940 the name for the army was again changed to *Nhan Dan Cach Menh Quan* or People's Revolutionary Army, See p. 152 on this change.

Conclusion

In the first decade of the century the power of modern technology had forced Vietnamese intellectuals to use the word 'nation'. But the weakness of this idea, which radicals like Nguyen Thai Hoc realised at their executions in 1930, was that it incorporated no sense of the independent context necessary to bring the force of 'the people' and thus 'the nation' into focus under modern conditions. By the late 1920s a few radicals with experience of a wider world than that of the early nationalists were drawn to Marxist-Leninist internationalism because in the Vietnamese context it overcame this weakness. What Ho Chi Minh did in *The Road to Revolution* was to focus the concept of the force of 'the people' by integrating them into a modern international order that opposed colonialism. This was the socialist world order to which 'the Vietnamese people' were bound by 'worker-peasant' alliances and 'world revolution.'

Yet to maintain this universalism in the 1930s when the French were so strong, the ICP had no alternative but to maintain an emphasis on inappropriate Comintern models of class struggle which ignored the real force of the Vietnamese people who were peasants. Because of its internationalist perspective the ICP was the only party in the country prepared to relate international changes signalled by the Japanese invasion of China to the cause of Vietnamese independence. In other words, the ICP's internationalism finally enabled it to envisage a path to 'national' independence once knowledge of Mao's common sense connection between world revolution and national liberation began to circulate in Vietnam from 1938.

The publication of the Chinese translations is in fact an excellent example of how Marxist-Leninist internationalism had integrated the Vietnamese revolution with the country's tradition of resistance to foreign invaders. It will be recalled that in ancient times the acquisition of Chinese military books was a sign of a strong and independent Vietnamese state within the Confucian world order. In 1939 the modern Vietnamese nation-state was neither strong nor independent. It was nothing more than a concept. But, by 1938, knowledge in Vietnam of what would become the most influential Chinese military book ever, Mao's *On Guerrilla War*, was an indication that the concept of an independent nation-state within the socialist world order had an important tradition on its side.

3
Formation of the First Guerrilla Bases, 1940–1945

In 1961 Paul Isoart claimed convincingly that in 1939 'Vietnam was calm, the security perfect'.[1] There had been no significant disturbances in the colony since 1931 and French people could travel anywhere without danger. With the outbreak of World War Two, however, international events began to break this calm and cause a fundamental transformation in Vietnamese politics.

As the war made its impact on French Indochina, most notably through the Japanese occupation from September 1940, the colonial regime was permanently weakened. This did not mean that the French suffered an immediate loss of power over Vietnamese society, for the Japanese permitted the regime to remain in place so that they would not have to divert valuable resources from the Pacific. The French were thus able to repress two major uprisings that broke out in 1940, and maintained their power between 1941 and 1944 with regular waves of repression in a number of particularly troublesome regions. Yet the need for regular repression was itself a sign that something had changed in French Indochina. Furthermore, from around mid-1944 when the tide had turned against the forces of world fascism, the French became increasingly preoccupied with Japanese intentions in the event of an Axis collapse. With French attention thus diverted from the far northern border provinces where the ICP had begun building guerrilla bases in 1941, the stage was set for the emergence of the first units of the People's Army on a national scale in 1945.

The ICP initiative to build bases had been conditioned by earlier views that the outbreak of the Second World War would have a

[1]Isoart, *Le phénomène*, Paris, 1961, p. 301.

74

deeply disturbing effect on the colonial regime and stimulate Vietnamese nationalism. The Eighth Congress of the ICP's Central Committee at Pac Bo in May 1941 thus verified the trend in Party thinking from 1939 which suggested that, as in China, the idea of class struggle should be temporarily abandoned in the interests of a war of national liberation. In other words, because the ICP was a Party with an internationalist perspective it was able to anticipate the weakening effect the Second World War would have on the colonial regime. Because it was able to use Mao's model of a war of national liberation it was also the only Party in Vietnam able to integrate the Vietnamese struggle for independence with the events of the Second World War. Therefore, by using guerrilla strategies, and the important political-military technique of 'armed propaganda' which enabled the ICP to integrate political and military action in the cause of nation building, the ICP was able to break into the society at a point where French power was weakened by international events and begin to mobilise a national army by 1945. This is the main importance of the period of the Second World War in modern Vietnamese history.

Second World War and the Promise of Independence

In the fall of 1938, as war clouds were gathering in Europe, Ho Chi Minh, who had been predicting the Second World War since the early 1920s, travelled from Moscow to China as an agent of the Comintern. Here he spent some time with the Eighth Route Army in Yenan and worked concurrently as a radio operator and club manager at the Eighth Route Army's liaison office in Kwelin. He also sent articles back to Vietnam for publication in ICP journals under the name of P.C. Lin which almost certainly contained much about what the Chinese Communists were doing.[2]

In 1939, Ho moved closer to the Vietnamese border and by May 1940 or earlier, he had made contact with Vietnamese Party members in Kunming such as Vu Anh and Phung Chi Kien who had been in charge of ICP liaison with the Comintern. Ho also met cadres from within Vietnam, including Pham Van Dong and Vo Nguyen Giap who had fled Hanoi in May 1940 as the French drive against the ICP intensified. When he learned of the fall of France Ho anticipated the deeply disturbing effect this would have on the colonial regime and so made the decision to return to Vietnam and plot the course of the

---

[2]These articles are mentioned in King Chen, *Vietnam and China, 1938–1954*, Princeton University Press, 1969, p. 35. I have not been able to find copies of them but it is reasonable to assume that they contributed to the ICP's information on Mao's guerilla strategies in the late 1930s as discussed in the last chapter.

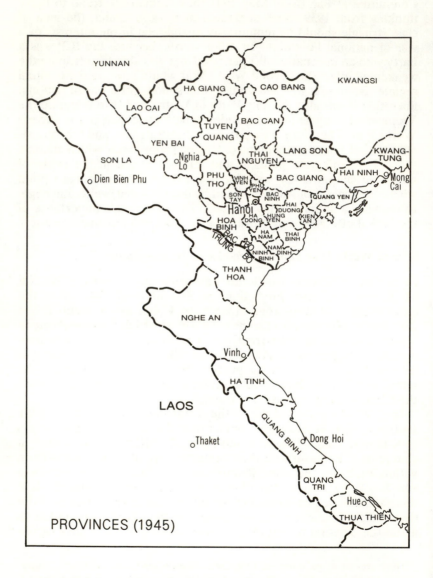

PROVINCES (1945)

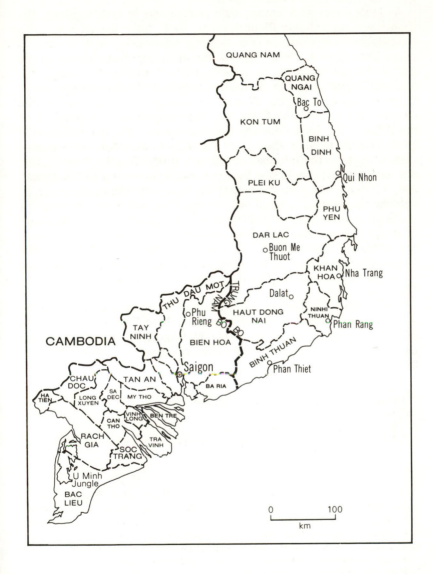

ICP's war time strategy.[3] The result of this decision was the Eighth
Plenum of the ICP's Central Committee at Pac Bo in Cao Bang
Province from 10 to 19 May 1941.

As Ho's return to Vietnam after thirty years in exile suggests, the
Eighth was no ordinary Plenum for the ICP, for it placed Vietnam's
struggle for independence in a dynamic relationship with the events
of the Second World War. Indeed, the most important feature of the
Eighth Plenum was that its policies related Vietnam's struggle for
national liberation to the international conflict. Some historians have
stressed that the Eighth Plenum represented a triumph for the
nationalist faction in the Party over the rampant internationalism of
the 1930s.[4] They have done this because it was at Pac Bo that the ICP
confirmed the trend of the earlier Plenums to abandon the notion of
class struggle in the interests of national unity. But the choice could
not have been a simple one between nationalism and internationalism. Vietnam was a small country whose revolution could never be
detached from international events especially when they were as far
reaching as the Second World War, and the Plenum was well aware
of this when it noted that 'the international situation will influence
the revolution in Indochina'.[5] Before discussing the resolutions of the
Eighth Plenum further, it is helpful to highlight the impact which the
outbreak of the Second World War had already had in Vietnam by
May 1941.

Well before the Plenum was convened Vietnam was disturbed by
international events. Even prior to the fall of France in June 1940
there had been a run on the banks in Saigon,[6] and in the Mekong
Delta the mystic leader of the Hoa Hao religious sect, Huynh Phu So,
told agitated audiences that

> Misfortunes of all kinds,
> Fires, floods, epidemics, misdeeds of war,
> The country will suffer,
> The catastrophe is almost upon us,
> The sun and moon will disappear from the sky,
> And smoke will envelop the earth,

---

[3]Ibid., pp. 33–48. For Ho's meeting with Giap see *Origins of the People's Army*, in
Russell Stetler ed., *The Military Art of People's War, Selected Writings of General Vo
Nguyen Giap*, New York and London, 1970, pp. 39–47. For Ho's return to Vietnam
also see Le Quang Ba, 'Reminiscences of Underground Revolutionary Work', and
Chu Van Tan, 'With Uncle Ho', *Vietnamese Studies*, No. 15, Hanoi, 1968.

[4]Khanh, *Vietnamese Communism*, Chapter 5 makes the main case for this.

[5]Extracts of resolutions of the Eighth Congress quoted in *LSQD*, p. 73.

[6]Khanh, *Vietnamese Communism*, p. 241.

There will be no houses, no trees, no grass,
Then there will be peace and perfect tranquility.[7]

At the same time the French did nothing to assuage local fears of the Japanese threat when they began to raise two 'Divisions de Marche'[8] for service in the Middle East. By December 1939 there were already a number of desertions from Colonial Army units around Tay Ninh, and at Cho Lon some 300 First World War veterans held a meeting and disappeared with their weapons. When the authorities then took disciplinary action against such acts of insubordination there were large protest meetings,[9] which finally merged with a number of minor disturbances and two major uprisings. Both of these, the Bac Son uprising near the Sino-Vietnamese border in September and the Nam Ky uprising in the Mekong Delta in November, may also be related to events surrounding Japan's need to occupy Indochina so that it could advance into the rest of Southeast Asia.

Franco-Japanese negotiations, in progress since 1939, appeared to be on the point of reaching peaceful agreement over the unrestricted entry of Japanese troops into Vietnam by September 1940. Either as a result of a local initiative or a high level move to embarrass the French and emphasise their own power in the region, however, the Japanese began their occupation of Vietnam with a surprise attack on the northern border post of Lang Son on the 22nd and 23rd,[10] and touched off the two uprisings.

After the fall of France and the alignment of the colonial army with Vichy, the soldiers who had originally been recruited to fight in the Middle East and Europe were purged. But then, in Nam Ky,[11] great

[7]Quoted in A. Savani, *Sectes et Groupements Armées du Sud Vietnam*, Centre de Hautes Etudes Administratives sur L'Afrique et L'Asie Modernes, (hereafter CHEAM), Paris, 1956, p. 5.

[8]René Bauchar, *Rafales sur l'Indochine*, Paris: Fournier, 1946, p. 30. However, Admiral Decoux, *A la barre de l'Indochine: Histoire de mon gouvernement général, 1949–1945*, Paris: Plon, 1949, p. 85 says that instructions came from Paris in 1938 to raise 10,000 *tirailleurs*. Then when general mobilisation was ordered the raising of three divisions for service in Libya and Syria was initially envisaged.

[9]*CMCD*, Vol. 10, pp. 17–19.

[10]Philippe Devillers, *Histoire du Viet Nam de 1940 à 1952*, Paris: Editions du Seuil, 1952, pp. 74–78, and J.T. McAlister, 'The Origins of the Vietnamese Revolution', Yale University PhD, 1966, pp. 89–100 provide discussions of events leading up to the Japanese attack. For a more recent discussion based on new sources see Vu Chieu Ngu, 'Political and Social Change in Viet-Nam Between 1940 and 1946', University of Wisconsin PhD, 1984, pp. 4–33.

[11]Nam Ky, Trung Ky, and Bac Ky, were the Vietnamese designations for southern, central, and northern Vietnam respectively.

discontent was caused by a renewed wave of recruiting for the colonial army[12] once the Siamese tried to take advantage of their Japanese ally's attack on Lang Son to wrest back territory in French Indochina they had originally seized from the Cambodians in 1794 but returned in 1907 under French pressure.[13] Large protest meetings encouraged by Japanese agents, ICP cadres, and Cao Dai leaders then broke out at recruiting centers in My Tho, Vinh Long, and Long Xuyen where some were calling for 'an uprising'.[14] There was no approval for this uprising from the ICP's Central Committee in the far north if only because it was so remote from southern events. It is also well known that when the colonial authorities heard of the plans of southern cadres on 22 November the ICP's urban cells were smashed in a few hours. But as the famous Vietnamese communist standard, the red flag with the yellow star, flew for the first time in the Mekong delta,[15] ICP members led crowds of peasants armed with machetes and bamboo spears in attacks on at least eight major and many minor locations. In fact, the uprising precipitated such a challenge to French authority that it was not until a large force of colonial infantry, artillery, marine, and air force units was concentrated in December that the uprising was crushed. Apart from the destruction of several villages, hundreds of captives, strung together with wire through their hands, were marched off to imprisonment or execution. As René Bauchar noted in his description of the repression, 'we were cruel'.[16]

Meanwhile, in the far north, the Japanese attack on Lang Son on 22–23 September precipitated the Bac Son uprising. The Japanese,

---

[12]*CMCD*, Vol. 10, pp. 19–20.

[13]On the Franco-Siamese War from November 1940 to January 1941 and the subsequent French cession of Battambang, parts of Siem Riep, and Kompong Thom, and southern Laos, (and the Japanese occupation of Cambodia) see Decoux, *A la barre*, pp. 123–147; Bauchar, *Rafales*, pp. 72–85; Général Sabattier, *Le destin de l'Indochine: Souvenir et documents, 1941–1951*, Paris: Plon, pp. 10–17.

[14]*CMCD*, Vol. 10, p. 17.

[15]Vien Su Hoc [Board for Historical Studies], *Tai Lieu Tham Khao Cach Mang Thang Tam (Tong Khoi Nghia o Hanoi va Cac Dia Phuong)* [Research documents on the August Revolution (in the General Uprising in Hanoi and Other Regions)], 2 Vols., Hanoi: NXB Su Hoc, 1960, (Hereafter *CMTT*), Vol. 2, p. 239. See also Nguyen Thi Thap, 'The Nam Ky Uprising 30 Years Ago', Vietnam Courier, 296, 23 November 1970, p. 2; and *LSQD*, pp. 57–69.

[16]Bauchar, *Rafales*, p. 71. Devillers, *Histoire*, p. 80 says that against thirty members of the French forces killed, 100 insurgents were killed in combat, 6,000 were arrested, and 'many others were maltreated'. There were several dozen executions of communists. Also see Vu Chieu Ngu, 'Political and Social Change. .', pp. 22–29 for an account of the uprising.

who had cultivated anti-communist elements in the remnants of Phan Boi Chau's Restoration League in the 1930s, defeated the French, decapitated the French commander, and sent a contingent of the League to start an uprising.[17] With the help of Vietnamese soldiers who had defected from the colonial army after its defeat the Restoration League began to attack the French administration. Before the League could create more than great excitement around Bac Son, however, the Japanese withdrew their support and permitted the French to chase the trouble makers back across the border.[18]

But, as the Bac Son uprising was suppressed and the French and Japanese worked out their *modus vivendi*, this would not be the end of the story. Against the backdrop of international upheaval projected into Vietnam it would only be the beginning, especially when the ICP's operative decisions at the Eighth Plenum revolved around the temporary abandonment of class struggle and the adoption of Mao's model of guerrilla war. In other words, when the Plenum noted that with the Nam Ky and Bac Son uprisings there had been a 'change' in 'brother bourgeois' and 'brother landlord',[19] it was not making its choice between nationalism and internationalism. In so far as it had a choice, the ICP was making it between the Russian model based on class struggle and the Chinese model which stressed national liberation as the best means of achieving independence in the modern world. And, when the Plenum decided on 'a new democratic Vietnam following the spirit of new democracy',[20] it is clear that there was a strong tendency for it to prefer the latter.

[17]John T. McAlister, 'The Origins of the Vietnamese Revolution', PhD, Yale University, 1966, p. 102 says that thanks to Japanese generosity the Phuc Quoc already had equipment estimated at 5,000 rifles, 20 automatic weapons, 25,000 rounds of ammunition, and 3,000 grenades. Also 'around 3,000' Vietnamese troops from the colonial army are thought to have gone over to the Phuc Quoc.

[18]McAlister, 'The Origins', p. 103. For a detailed Vietnamese account of the uprising see *CMCD*, Vol. 10, pp. 12–17. See also Tong Bo Viet Minh Xuat Ban [Published by Central Committee of the Viet Minh], *Bac Son Khoi Nghia* [The Bac Son Uprising], fourth edition, 1945. This source presents a critique for the uprising and is really a training manual based on the event. A more recent Vietnamese account with some emphasis on the role of ICP cadres leading up to the Eighth Plenum of the ICP's Central Committee is Hoang Quang Khanh, Le Hong, Hoang Ngoc La, *Can Cu Dia Viet Bac: Trong cuoc Cach Mang Thang 8–1945* [The Viet Bac Base Area: In the August Revolution], Viet Bac Publishing House, 1976, Chapters 1 and 2. As in the south, however, it should not be imagined that the ICP's Central Committee took a leading role or even approved of the initial Bac Son uprising.

[19]*VKQS*, p. 184, p. 188. Quotes from this source on the Eighth Party Plenum are taken from its published resolutions: 'Trung Uong Hoi Nghi Lan Thu VIII Dang Cong San Dong Duong', pp. 168–208.

[20]Ibid., p. 186.

Of course, the choice was neither simple nor clear cut. Through 1944 ICP documents continued to speak of the need to 'support the Soviet Union'. Internal Party critiques, not for general dissemination also continued to take the idea of class struggle seriously.[21] After all, the power of the Soviet Union to influence the outcome of the Second World War was so great that it could not be ignored. But when the Soviet Union was so remote, and its urban oriented strategies for revolution had come to nothing in Vietnam in the 1930s, what the Eighth Plenum did was to verify the late 1930s turn towards a more appropriate emphasis on Chinese models of guerrilla war within the context of new democracy in a peasant society. Therefore, the ICP did what the CCP had already done and abandoned the notion of class struggle, temporarily.[22] It was still absolutely essential for the ICP to maintain its socialist internationalist orientation, otherwise there would have had no workable context in which it was possible to imagine an independent Vietnamese nation. As the espousal of Russian revolutionary models was maintained to some extent and the idea of class struggle was abandoned temporarily, the new emphasis on Mao's revolutionary model permitted the ICP to define the united national front that would be necessary to exploit the crisis which the Second World War had created for French colonialism in Indochina.

What the temporary abandonment of class struggle meant in practical terms for the ICP from 1941 was the elimination of all political distinctions between 'workers, plowers, rich peasants, landlords, and local bourgeoisie who love the country'.[23] In organisational terms 'the unity of the entire people'[24] could then be achieved

---

[21]*VKQS*, p. 259 offers a call to 'Support the Soviet Union' in February 1943. Also, see *CMTT*, Vol. 2, p. 52, p. 232. My knowledge of how 'class struggle' continued to be taken seriously in internal party documents comes from discussions with David Marr.

[22]Ibid., p. 185, p. 191 rationalise this decision as follows:

> If at the moment we promote the slogan of overthrowing the landlords and redistribution the land to the plowers not only will we throw away an allied force, a supporting force in the revolution to overthrow the French and Japanese, but what is more, that force will go over to the side of the enemy and become its supporting force.

And:

> At present if we are not able to resolve the question of national liberation and do not demand independence and freedom for the entire nation then not only will all our peoples continue to live like cattle, we will not be able to demand what is in the class interest for ten thousand years.

Of course, all the other groups and classes in society were still to be led in their struggle against the French by the workers.

[23]Ibid., p. 185.

[24]Quoted in *LSDC*, p. 340.

under the 'Independence League of Vietnam' (*Viet Nam Doc Lap Dong Minh Hoi*)[25] which was usually referred to as the Viet Minh from its creation by the Eighth Plenum. Within the structure of the Viet Minh's national front, 'National Salvation Organisations' would unite functional groups of all conceivable descriptions—peasants, landlords, youth, women, Catholics, soldiers, intellectuals and so on. A 'Peasant National Salvation Organisation' (*Nong Dan Cuu Quoc Hoi*) would, for example, have the right to form a Viet Minh village and the most important group would have the largest number of representatives.[26] At canton, district, provincial, and national levels relevant National Salvation Organisations would likewise organise themselves and elect representatives to run the alternative adminis-tration. Because regional security was a fundamental aspect of ad-ministration, 'in each National Salvation Organisation we also select the most enthusiastic and loyal elements to organise National Self Defence and Guerrilla Squads' (*Tu Ve Cuu Quoc Hoi* and *Tieu To Du Kich*).[27]

Above all, however, it must be stressed that this conception of a national administration and defence system was integrated within the context of Marxist-Leninist internationalism. When turn of the cen-tury literati had begun to use new words to describe the 'nation' with its stress on 'the people' and 'people's rights', we saw in Chapter 2 that they could still not imagine an independent context for these modern political categories. But once the Viet Minh had made its modern categorisation of functional groups—workers, peasants, soldiers and so on—they could begin to talk meaningfully about 'national salvation' because they had an international context for it.

In the published resolutions of the Eighth Plenum the 'National Question' received much attention. However, it was still discussed in terms of the new 'nation's' relationship with the Soviet Union and China and the anti-fascist forces in the world. And while the Viet Minh's manifesto called many 'national salvation heroes' to mind—Trung Trac, Ngo Quyen, Tran Hung Dao etc.—it is still clear that the force of the tradition these heroes represented could not be consid-ered in isolation from the modern world where 'two hundred million people of the Soviet Union and four hundred and fifty million Chinese people are heroically fighting to kill the fascist invaders'.[28] Fundamentally, the only reason why myriad regional and functional

[25]On Regulations (*Dieu Le*) for the Viet Minh see *CMCD*, Vol. 10, pp. 53–55; *VKQS*, p. 194.
[26]*VKQS*, p. 195.
[27]Quoted in *LSQD*, p. 72.
[28]*VKQS*, p. 321. The 'National Question' is discussed on pp. 183–187. The manifesto of the Viet Minh can be found on pp. 317–322.

administrative units might transcend the parochialism which French colonialism thrived on and link up to build a nation was the promise of independence and a better life within a new international order. And the ICP began to set itself up to make this promise at the Pac Bo Plenum in 1941 because its perceptions of the importance of the Second World War for Vietnam were the context for the emergence of the imagined nation. As the ICP noticed with the outbreak of the Second World War and the uprisings in Nam Ky and Bac Son, 'time and space will work for us',[29] and

> when the Pacific War and the People's War in China have completely turned to our advantage the forces we will have ready will be able to lead a partial uprising in each region and will be able to achieve victories that will open the road to the general uprising.[30]

Even though it may not have predicted it for the right reasons,[31] the ICP now had its long-awaited crisis in world imperialism. Although the full effects of this crisis would not begin to work decisively in the Viet Minh's favour until late 1944 and early 1945, it was the context in which the first guerrilla units began to form in the face of residual French power.

Residual French Power and the First Guerrilla Units

The fall of France and the Japanese occupation in 1940 caused major unrest in Vietnam, but the decline of French power was not immediate. Both the Bac Son and Nam Ky uprisings were successfully repressed once the Japanese gave the French a free hand in the interests of their own trouble free occupation. It is also true that until 1945 the French presence was maintained in large tracts of the countryside with nothing more than a platoon of the Indigenous Guard to a province.[32] This was not the case in the Viet Bac region

---

[29]Ibid., p. 202.

[30]Resolutions of the Eighth Plenum quoted in *LSQD*, p. 73.

[31]For a discussion of the ICP's perceptions of the outbreak of the Second World War see Pham Xuan Nam, 'Ve Nhung Nguyen Nhan Phat Sinh Cuoc Chien Tranh The Gioi Thu Hai (Xet theo nhan dinh cua nhung nguoi cong san Viet Nam luc do)' [On the Causes of the Outbreak of the Second World War (As Understood by Vietnamese Communists at the Time)], *NCLS*, No. 5, September-October 1979, pp. 67–79. For another internationalist perspective see Nguyen Khanh Toan, 'Ve Nguyen Nhan Phat Sinh Cuoc Chien Tranh The Gioi Thu Hai' [On the Causes of the Outbreak of the Second World War], *NCLS*, November—December 1979, pp. 1–16.

[32]Isoart, *Le phénomène*, p. 318. For the waves of repression see the relevant chapters in *CMTT*, Vols. 1 and 2.

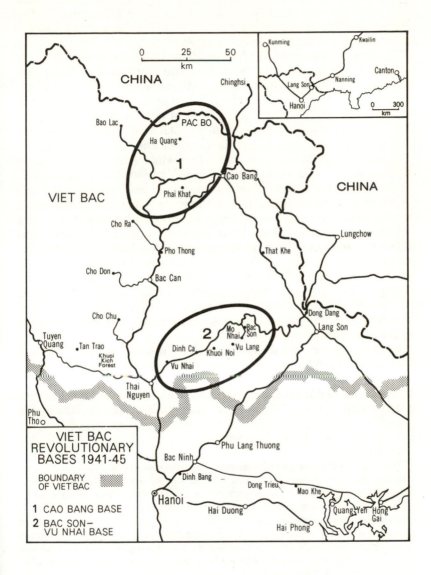

0 25 50
km

CHINA

Chinghsi

Bao Lac

PAC BO

Ha Quang

1

Cao Bang

CHINA

VIET BAC

Phai Khat

Cho Ra

Lungchow

Pho Thong

That Khe

Cho Don

Bac Can

Cho Chu

Dong Dang

Tuyen Quang

2

Mo Nhai

Bac Son

Lang Son

Tan Trao

Dinh Ca

Khuoi Noi

Vu Lang

Khuoi Kich Forest

Vu Nhai

Thai Nguyen

Phu Tho

VIET BAC
REVOLUTIONARY
BASES 1941-45

BOUNDARY
OF VIET BAC

1 CAO BANG BASE
2 BAC SON–
VU NHAI BASE

Phu Lang Thuong

Bac Ninh

Dinh Bang

Dong Trieu

Mao Khe

Hanoi

Hai Duong

Quang Yen

Hong Gai

Hai Phong

Kunming

Kwailin

Lang Son

Nanning

Canton

Hanoi

0 300
km

and one or two provinces like Quang Tri and Quang Nam where regular military operations were conducted by the French between 1941 and 1944 to repress revolutionary activities. But even in the Viet Bac, where the first units of the People's Army were formed in the wake of the Bac Son uprising and the Eighth Plenum, they initially had minimal success in mobilising popular support.

The first of these units, the Bac Son Guerrilla Unit, commanded by Nung minority leader, Chu Van Tan, and composed of thirty two 'party members and the most enthusiastic members of the revolutionary masses who had fought in the Bac Son uprising',[33] was formed in the Khuoi Noi forest near Vu Le on February 14. Once the Eighth Plenum had delineated the Bac Son-Vu Nhai area as the first guerrilla base area, the Bac Son Guerrilla Unit became the first platoon of 'The Army for National Salvation' (hereafter AFNS). After being shown a map of the world which Pham Van Dong had drawn with Vietnam and the Soviet Union coloured in red, members of the AFNS received some instruction in the ICP's policies and some basic training in military drills under the experienced supervision of Phung Chi Kien, a veteran of Mao's Long March.[34] A second platoon of the AFNS was then mobilised in September by the ICP's Central Committee Cadre, Hoang Quoc Viet, in the Khuon Manh forest near the burnt out village of Trang Xa.[35] However, as soon as the AFNS attempted to organise military and political training in the villages of Bac Son-Vu Nhai the main effect was to provoke another series of French patrols that fell heavily on the local population and routed the AFNS like ragged rebels.

From late June 1941 to March 1942 French forces swept through the Bac Son-Vu Nhai area and corralled people in camps at Na Pheo, Dinh Ca, Lang Giua, and Dong En while others fled into the jungle from villages like Dinh Ca and Trang Xa where 'columns of fire rose from burning houses'.[36] As its supporters were treated in this way the

---

[33]*LSQD*, p. 77.

[34]Ibid., pp. 76–79. Mai Elliot, translator, *Reminiscences on the Army for National Salvation: Memoirs of General Chu Van Tan*, Data Paper Number 97, Southeast Asia Program, Cornell University, September 1974, p. 76. On Phung Chi Kien see p. 49, p. 51. According to this source he was from Nghe An Province, spent about ten years in China, spoke good Chinese, studied in the Red Army University in the Soviet Regions, had been a company commander in the Red Army, and liked to tell stories about Mao's Long March. On his activities in the Viet Bac region see also Hoang Van Hoan, *Giot Nuoc trong Bien Ca: Hoi Ky* [A Drop of Water in the Ocean], Peking: NXB Tin Viet Nam, 1986, p. 128.

[35]*LSQD*, p. 81.

[36]Chu Van Tan, *Reminiscences*, p. 58; *LSQD*, p. 83.

AFNS itself was hunted at every turn, and its leader Chu Van Tan has described what life was like for the guerrillas at this time:

> Usually we built our huts near a stream. As soon as we finished cooking we poured water on the fire to wash away all traces. At first, we carefully made huts with roofs of palm leaves, but our life was so unsettled—we had to move and fight constantly—that we just cut banana leaves and used them to roof our huts. Sometimes we had to move before the banana leaves had time to dry.[37]

Class conscious Marxist historiography to the contrary, the AFNS did not survive because it 'clung' resolutely to the people.[38] Even though Chu Van Tan's memoirs often dwell nostalgically on the reliability of the masses, these are contradicted by many passages which show that precious food supplies usually depended on family or other close contacts, and even then villages were often watched for days before hunger overcame fear of French spies and the contacts were made. Usually without instructions from the Party, sick, substituting roots for rice, and so lightly armed that revolvers were known by name, sections of the AFNS had to hide in the jungle for months to avoid being betrayed by villagers and killed in ambushes like Phung Chi Kien in July 1941.[39] French patrols successfully divided the AFNS from the population who had good reason to believe that it was the source of its misery. All that saved the AFNS from destruction in March 1942 was its ability to move across an international border into China,[40] and remain there until the end of the year when it heard the French had left the area.

But even though the AFNS was able to take advantage of the departure of French forces from the region, and even though some sources suggest the 'continued'[41] development of bases in the Viet Bac from 1943, the troubles of the first guerrilla units were not over. Many sources stress that in 1943 and 1944 the French continued to perpetrate 'white terror'[42] or the 'systematic mop up of communist

[37]Chu Van Tan, *Reminiscences*, p. 117.

[38]*LSQD*, p. 87.

[39]Chu Van Tan, *Reminiscences*, p. 117.

[40]*LSQD*, p. 90 says that one section of the AFNS of forty two people left for China on 7 March while another number disbanded as a military unit to stay behind in the villages to maintain the infrastructure.

[41]*CMTT*, Vol. 1, p. 68.

[42]The Vietnamese borrowed this term from the Chinese, but as we will see in some detail in the next Chapter it had its roots in the French revolution. It was widely used in Vietnamese literature to refer to French repression. See for example, *CMCD*, Vol. 10, pp. 67–73.

activities'.[43] Philippe Devillers has said the French campaign in the northern provinces from late 1943 was designed to impose 'a policy of being present'.[44] By the end of the year a system of permanent patrols were thus organised by troops of the Indigenous Guard. During the first half of 1944 these patrols had forced the Viet Minh to take refuge 'in the roughest limestone regions, the most difficult to enter',[45] and French success against the rebels may be measured by Viet Minh sources:

At times the sun was down for days as they set fire to our jungle positions and killed suspects: Comrade Pham Van Dong's organisation was completely surrounded on a number of occasions and attacked by artillery fire. They paid much attention to Bac Kan (Province). On one occasion Comrade Vo Nguyen Giap and two units of reinforcements were surrounded for three days on a mountain top near The Ruc . . . Very many comrades were killed by the imperialists.[46]

Figures of 5,453 members of Viet Minh organisations and of 1,184 militia men in 1943 are also shown to have dropped somewhat in Vietnamese sources to 3,999 and 812 in 1944.[47]

Nevertheless, there is no doubt that the Viet Minh survived the various waves of 'white terror'. As we will see, part of the reason was the relative lack of attention the French patrols gave to Viet Minh activities in the most northerly provinces along the Sino-Vietnamese border, and part of it was the positive application of guerrilla strategies and propaganda techniques. In the meantime, however, there were important international events from around 1943 that would work gradually to reinforce the rise of the first guerrilla forces and undermine the residual power of the French.

In 1943 as portraits of Marshall Petain, 'the symbol of France', were hanging at 'post offices, administrative offices, barracks, villages, stations, and main cross-roads',[48] the German Army was crushed at Stalingrad and the Japanese Army began to suffer its first serious reversals in the Pacific. Gaullism gradually became more respectable in colonial society, and around the time of the Normandy landings in mid-1944 Governor Général Decoux, though as anti-Gaullist as ever, had to make a quick change of portraits.[49] But even

---

[43]Khanh, *Vietnamese Communism*, p. 276.
[44]Devillers, *Histoire*, pp. 107–108.
[45]Ibid.
[46]*CMCD*, Vol.10, p. 71.
[47]*CMTT*, Vol. 1 p. 93.
[48]Lucien Félixine, *L'Indochine livrée aux bourreaux*, Paris, 1959, p. 24.
[49]Khanh, *Vietnamese Communism*, p. 292.

with De Gaulle now installed in France, there was still the question of what the Japanese might do in the event of an Axis collapse to increasingly divert French attention from the actions of a few guerrilla bands in remote mountain regions.

As the Japanese position in the Pacific began to deteriorate, Japanese propaganda in Vietnam became more strident. Many authors have argued that the Japanese tried to intimidate the French and gain Vietnamese support for their war effort by sponsoring paramilitary organisations like the Advance Youth Guard and conducting a barrage of 'Asia for the Asians' and 'Greater East Asia' propaganda. Similarly, many have shown how the French attempted to counter the Japanese and win Vietnamese support by organising a sports and youth movement, following a 'policy of respect' to Vietnamese culture, and conducting their own 'Indochinese Nation' propaganda.[50] The assumption in most of these writings is that Vietnamese nationalism was stimulated by Japanese attempts to undermine the French, while French attempts to counter the Japanese only compounded their original problem. Both a Japanese sponsored organisation like the Advance Youth Guard, and a French sponsored organisation like the Sports and Youth Movement therefore had strong support in the south by 1945,[51] and both provided a large reservoir of recruits for the Viet Minh by the time they seized power in August 1945. Furthermore, although the Viet Minh was not widely known outside the Viet Bac before mid-1945, the arousal of nationalist sentiments in the community between 1941 and 1945 was not only a function of Franco-Japanese competition.

Once the Eighth Plenum of the ICP had concluded its deliberations the Party's leadership decided on a division of labour and broke up into two groups. One group under Ho Chi Minh, which included Pham Van Dong, Hoang Van Hoan, and Vo Nguyen Giap remained in the border region to supervise the building of guerrilla bases. The other group under Truong Chinh, which included Hoang Quoc Viet

[50]Ibid., pp. 238–249; Isoart, *Le phénomène*, Chapter 7; J. Lebas, 'Le mouvement de jeuness en Indochine', *L'Indochine*, 2, No. 37, 15 May 1951; Vu Chieu Ngu, 'Political and Social Change', pp. 106–108; and various others. For a dissenting opinion see Truong Buu Lam, 'Japan and the Disruption of the Vietnamese Nationalist Movement', in W. Vella, ed., *Aspects of Vietnamese History*, University of Hawaii, 1973, pp. 237–269. See also Decoux, *A la barre*, and Maurice Ducoroy, *Ma trahison en Indochine*, Paris: Editions Internationales, 1949 for primary French views. *CMCD*, Vols 8 and 9 provide primary Vietnamese views. Vol. 9 pp. 32–35 is particularly interesting on the youth movement's stimulation of Vietnamese nationalism.

[51]On the Advance Youth Guard see Jane Susan Werner, 'The Cao Dai: The Politics of a Vietnamese Syncretic Religious Movement', Cornell University PhD, 1976, p. 255. On the sports and youth movement see Devillers, *Histoire*, p. 85.

and Hoang Van Thu returned to the delta region to carry out clandestine Party work. In this division of labour at least one author has detected a 'factionalism' which he generally argues became the chief characteristic of the ICP's leadership.[52] Yet, whatever the merits of this argument, it is worth pointing out that at a time of general unease during the Second World War, the division did tend to facilitate the development of Vietnamese nationalist activities in some significant parts of Bac Ky and Trung Ky as well as the Viet Bac between 1941 and 1945.

In Hanoi itself nationalist activities were always difficult. Nevertheless, urban 'guerrilla cells',[53] formed by 1942 and smashed in 1943, were revived to some extent with the formation of various self defence groups in May 1944. As ICP cadres distributed leaflets and made contacts with intellectuals, youth groups involved themselves in public health programs, workers mounted a number of strikes and, 'to help people in Hanoi understand the Viet Minh better',[54] a 'Thai Nguyen Week' was organised in November 1944 to propagandize recent Viet Minh military actions in that region. In Bac Giang, where Truong Chinh was operating, there were some military training courses run from 1941, and by 1943 there were a number of 'Viet Minh groups'. Similar developments in Bac Ninh included the founding of a Central Committee publishing house in 1941, while the famous Party journal *The Flag of Liberation* (*Co Giai Phong*) continued to come off the presses that had been set up in Ha Dong in 1939.[55]

In a province of central Vietnam like Quang Tri, and in a couple of other provinces in southern central Vietnam the Viet Minh's program was known to some extent, as Party cells broke and reformed according to the rhythm of French repression.[56] However, while such activities would serve to strain the French and nurture nationalist sentiment, it would not be until well into 1945 that they would take the form of a guerrilla resistance which the course of the Second World War had helped to shape a good year before in the Viet Bac.

Attacks on village posts that resulted in the seizure of arms or the assassination of French sympathisers or village notables were frequently recorded by the administration in the far northern provinces

---

[52]Tai Quang Trung, *Collective Leadership and Factionalism: An Essay on Ho Chi Minh's Legacy*, Institute of southeast Asian Studies, Singapore, 1984. Pages 16–17 discuss the division of labour in 1941.

[53]*CMTT*, Vol. 1, p. 9.

[54]Ibid., pp. 9–17.

[55]Ibid., pp. 197–198, pp. 313–314, p. 330.

[56]Ibid., Vol. 2, pp. 46–47, pp. 92–94.

in 1943 and 1944. Some well informed officials like Major Reul, the Resident at Cao Bang, and Pierre Pontich, an Inspector of the Indigenous Guard, who tirelessly but unsuccessfully pursued guerrilla bands around the highlands in 1943 and 1944,[57] believed that these disturbances could be put down to 'communist agitation'.[58] Yet, by June 1944, the general preoccupation with the Japanese was such that, when one French Reconnaissance Unit sent to investigate some arms thefts and the burning of thirty Tho and Meo villagers alive in their houses near That Khe came under sporadic fire, it was at first puzzled. After further investigations revealed nothing, it assumed Japanese agents were responsible for the trouble.[59]

Meanwhile, even though the intelligence services continued to pay some attention to the Viet Minh, there was much to distract them from what was happening in the northern highlands. The Sûreté became increasingly interested in what support the Japanese might be giving Vietnamese nationalist parties in the towns and cities. The main military intelligence gathering body, the Office of Military Statistics, became exclusively occupied supplying the Allies with information on Japanese shipping and troop movements. Other branches of the pro-Gaullist resistance that operated their own spy networks with varying degrees of efficiency were also preoccupied with the Japanese.[60] Furthermore, it is clear that any good intelligence the French might have had on Viet Minh activities was not adequately assessed and disseminated.

The Commander of the Tonkin Division, Général Sabattier, for example, could only see a few 'incidents' around Dinh Ca in Cao Bang Province in late 1944. Admittedly, these merited attention because 'partisans had been taken, arms stolen, and notables assassinated'.[61] Yet, after two battalions made a sweep through the area the problem was soon forgotten and the winter of 1944–45 was only 'lightly troubled by local political difficulties',[62] at a time when we will see the Viet Minh was actually expanding its mass organisa-

---

[57]Général J.J. Fonde, 'Giap et le maquis de Cho Ra (Mars 1945–Mars 1946)' *Revue Historique Des Armées*, No. 2, 1976.

[58]Interview with Colonel Albert Reul, Paris, 28 May, 1981.

[59]Général Yves Gras, *Histoire de la guerre d'Indochine*, Paris: Plon, 1979, p. 27.

[60]For further information on French intelligence operations see Sabattier, *Le destin*, especially Chapter 5, and André Gaudel, *Indochine en face du Japon*, Paris: J. Susse, 1947. It is also significant that the northern provinces are hardly discussed in these sources. This is also a striking feature of Decoux's 500 page apologia, *A la barre*, where there is much however on 'Le Spectre du Coup de Force'.

[61]Sabattier, *Le destin*, p. 97. Meanwhile, the Viet Minh were referring to the Dinh Ca episode as an 'uprising'.

[62]Ibid.

tions and para-military units in the region. By the second half of 1944 French operations were not systematically aimed at the ICP at all, nor could they have been when Sabattier was not aware that guerrilla bases existed, and Général Gras has correctly observed:

> In these operations to maintain order he (Sabattier) saw above all a means to justify to the Japanese the placement of his forces in a position where he could counter aggression on their part.[63]

French military deployments were no longer dictated by the internal threat, but much darker forces and the death throes of world fascism towards the end of the Second World War. And as the darkness spread over French Indochina the Viet Minh would have greater opportunities to break into the villages unnoticed.

Armed Propaganda and the Origins of the People's Army

Although French patrols had dealt ruthlessly with the AFNS in Bac Son and Vu Nhai in 1941–1942 and continued to retain their effectiveness until mid-1944, these patrols had not been extended systematically into the northern most border provinces of Cao Bang, Bac Can, and Lang Son (hereafter Cao-Bac-Lang) where the mountainous terrain was particularly difficult. In Cao Bang, for example, Party cells were not seriously disrupted by colonial military operations in early 1941, and unlike the Bac Son-Vu Nhai area no enemy patrols are mentioned in authoritative sources for 1942.[64] It was not then until late 1943 and early 1944 that the region was caught up in another generalised wave of repression which nevertheless failed to arrest the development of Viet Minh activities. In this context it is also worth speculating that the Eighth Plenum at Pac Bo may have delineated the Bac Son-Vu Nhai area as the first guerrilla base area to cover its activities along the border. In any case, as the difficult terrain and isolated mountain valleys provided valuable camouflage, ICP cadres already had the opportunity to establish a foothold in this area in 1941 and 1942. And the way they went about this was to use armed propaganda.

Although the term 'armed propaganda' (*vu trang tuyen truyen*) was not specifically used until November 1944[65] after Ho had made a trip back to China and seen armed units using the technique there,[66] this

---

[63]Gras, *Histoire*, p. 28.

[64]*CMTT*, Vol. 1, pp. 81–93 gives the pattern of repression. *LSQD*, pp. 92–95.

[65]This was with the mobilisation of the 'Vietnam Propaganda and Liberation Unit' on December 22, 1944. This unit will be discussed later.

[66]Chen, *Vietnam and China*, p. 80.

was the technique essentially used from 1941. What it involved was the integration of political and military action in a bureaucratically underdeveloped peasant society by guerrilla units or even individual cadres. As such it was the mainspring of the modern Vietnamese army. But it is also important to realise that a similar integration of political and military action throughout Vietnamese history, had always been central to the creation of armies of resistance. This can be seen in the fifteenth century testament of Vietnamese resistance to Ming occupation under Le Loi, the *Binh Ngo Dai Cao*, which records that as he mobilised his army Le Loi 'raised the flag of righteousness'.[67] This meant Le Loi was demonstrating that his was a strong force in the land that demanded support because it was righteous and offered people the promise of more rice and a better life. When armed guerrilla units began to move into the villages of Cao-Bac-Lang in 1941 and 1942 under the 'red flag with the five pointed gold star'[68] which had first appeared in the Nam Ky uprising in late 1940, it was the same. They were demonstrating their power to demand support because they also offered the promise of a better life. The only difference was that their flag linked them to a modern world order with its heart in the ideals of the Russian Revolution. Instead of righteous rule in the Confucian sense, there would be cinemas for the people and highland villages festooned with electric light bulbs.[69]

In times both ancient and modern, armed propaganda clearly encompassed the use of force as the need to 'arm' the propaganda team implied. But still this was not a static concept that ultimately depended on terror for its success. In Vietnamese the modern word 'propaganda' (*tuyen truyen*) does not necessarily have the same limited meaning it does in English. It certainly conveys the idea of political indoctrination. But at least in the mid 1940s I would argue that it originally meant much more than this. *Tuyen* means to 'proclaim', 'to declare'. *Truyen* means 'to hand down', 'to communicate', 'to transmit' a tradition or inheritance, and it can be used in such compound words as *truyen dao* meaning 'to preach a religion'. The modern Vietnamese word for propaganda therefore literally conveys

---

[67] Tran Trong Kim, *Viet Nam Su Luoc*, Vol. 1, p. 238, p. 278.

[68] *LSQD*, p. 55 says in connection with one attack on the school at Vu Lang on 25 October:

> the revolutionary flag with the five pointed gold star on a red background was held high so that within only a few days the guerrilla forces grew to near 200 divided into sections of ten people.

It will be recalled that the flag was first flown in the Nam Ky uprising in November-December 1940.

[69] Isoart, *Le phénoméne*, p. 319.

the idea of political indoctrination within an appeal to traditional moral and ethical values which help legitimise the terrible acts that are a part of any war. 'Armed propaganda' was then the political-military technique used to integrate armed action with the political ideal which in Vietnam in the 1940s was national independence.

In its most rudimentary form in Cao-Bac-Lang in the early 1940s armed propaganda would have followed a description which the Inspector of the Indigenous Guard, Pierre Pontich, has left of Vo Nguyen Giap's activities:

> In certain remote valleys Van (i.e. Giap) opened the path, operating himself according to a standard technique. He would arrive alone in a hamlet, destitute like an outlaw offering to work in the fields. In return he received his food. The days passed. First tolerated, then accepted and listened to he assured himself of some solid support. At this moment he had won the game. The village provided intelligence and supplies for the commandos, and then furnished guerrillas. The opposition remained silent or was eliminated.[70]

A Viet Minh training manual, written close to August 1945, corroborates Pontich's account and fills it out:

> Propaganda teams must work hard. Sometimes they must help our people in their work or work their way into a crowd of people who are harvesting or transplanting in the fields and propagandise them.

The next step was

> to explain to them clearly that joining the revolutionary army is a responsibility of the people and a glorious honour. Clearly outline the long term gains if all the people are liberated and the short term gains if the revolutionary army becomes stronger every day and wins whereever it fights . . . (also) use pamphlets, cartoons, and slogans to carry out propaganda. But the most important means is verbal communication so that the propaganda teams organise meetings and lectures and use theatrical performances and songs (with accompaniment if possible).[71]

[70]Fonde, 'Giap et le Marquis', p. 114.

[71]Viet Nam Doc Lap Dong Minh, *Chinh Tri Vien Trong Quan Doi*, [Vietnam Independence League Political Cadres in the Army], Hanoi, 1945, pp. 13–14. Hoang Van Hoan, *Giot Nuoc*, pp. 210–211 also gives a description of propaganda activities incorporating the use of songs and participation in local weddings etc. . Page 214 also offers a definition of 'propaganda'.

These were the methods of the armed propaganda campaign after the Pac Bo Guerrilla Unit was formed in December 1941 under the command of the Tay ethnic minority leader and later divisional commander in the People's Army, Le Quang Ba.[72] However, these methods encompassed complexities which the above descriptions do not convey.

Because it was trying to enact a revolution of national liberation the armed propaganda campaign could not ignore the country's traditions. But because it could only conceive of national liberation within a modern socialist world order it could not ignore this force either. The whole point of the armed propaganda campaign was that like the political-military techniques that underpinned it, it reflected a meshing of continuity and change, a fusion of past and present. As units like the Pac Bo Guerrilla Unit went out to arouse the population, this fusion was exemplified in one of the many poems Ho Chi Minh wrote for the campaign.[73] *The History of Our Country*[74] used the six-eight rhyming scheme of classical Vietnamese poetry to play on ancient glories and harmonise their meaning with the modern world. It said:

> Our people were originally proud and brave,
> Many times we have struck in the north and cleared the east,
> Like our glorious ancestors the Dragon and the Fairy.

Therefore,

> Now the French have lost the country,
> They have neither the strength nor enough people to rule us,
> The Japanese bandits have just arrived,
> And their political foundations are not yet established,
> Also the Chinese, American, Dutch, and English,
> Are causing the Japanese trouble by fighting them everywhere,
> This is a good opportunity for us,
> To rise and restore the country of our ancestors.[75]

An image of the new nation that would arise from the rubble of world fascism was depicted in another poem of Ho's called *Geography:*

> Vietnam is in the shape of the letter S

---

[72]*LSQD*, p. 94.

[73]For a discussion of Ho's literary efforts at Pac Bo see Phan Ngoc Lien, 'Tim Hieu ve Cong Tac Van Dong Giao Duc Quan Chung cua Ho Chu Tich Trong Thoi Gian Nguoi o Pac Bo' [An Investigation of President Ho's Mass Mobilisation and Education Work in the Period He was at Pac Bo], *NCLS*, No. 14, 1973.

[74]*Lich Su Nuoc Ta* written in 1942 and published in Ho Chi Minh, *Tuyen Tap*, pp. 325–336.

A very beautiful peninsula,
On the Pacific coast,
In Southeast Asia.[76]

Lit up in poetry, as well as promises of electric light bulbs, was a place for Vietnam in the modern world even though its ancient traditions continued to be very forceful.

The meshing of ancient traditions and modern imperatives was also reflected at many levels as the first guerrilla units began to multiply. For example, it is certain that, like the Mac family who harassed the Le dynasty in the sixteenth century from the region around Cao-Bac-Lang,[77] the Viet Minh were largely dependent upon the ethnic minorities who populated the area for their early survival. We can say this because both the commander of the original Bac Son Guerrilla Unit, Chu Van Tan, and the commander of the Pac Bo Guerrilla Unit, Le Quang Ba, were from the ethnic minorities. Also, when the ICP's Eighth Plenum had stressed that 'with respect to ethnic minorities we must have specialist committees to mobilise them'[78] this was nothing new either. It had been common in earlier times for special military mandarins to be sent to take charge of frontier units whose special knowledge of the terrain and skill with cross-bows made them very useful against Chinese and other invaders.[79] Past and present were surely fused when cadres like Pham Van Dong and Vo Nguyen Giap were reputed to have been conversant with more than one highland language,[80] and when the figure of a highland specialist gone native in a loin cloth with blackened teeth and a cross-bow could appear in the literature of the 1950s.[81]

Congruence between ancient and modern military methods may also be found in the forms of military organisation. The most rudimentary form created by the armed propaganda teams was the

---

[75]Ibid., p. 333, p. 334.

[76]Quoted in Phan Ngoc Lien, 'Tim Hieu ve', p. 15.

[77]John T. McAlister Jr., 'Mountain Minorities and the Viet Minh: A Key to the Indochina War', in Peter Kunstadter, ed., *Southeast Asian Tribes, Minorities and Nations*, Vol. 2, Princeton University Press, 1967, p. 787.

[78]*VKQS*, p. 207; *CMCD*, Vol. 10, p. 89.

[79]For the use of ethnic minority troops during the Chinese invasion of 1077, for example, see *Our Military Traditions*, in *Vietnamese Studies*, No. 55, pp. 14–15.

[80]Pham Van Dong and Vo Nguyen Giap spoke Tay, Giap spoke Dao as well. See Le Quang Ba, '*Reminiscences*, pp. 49–50; *Reminiscences*, pp. 27–30.

[81]For example, see the story of Y Ngun 'a courageous young man who had completely transformed himself into a mountaineer, given up hair cutting, and filed his teeth to identify his life with the local population' in Selected Short Stories of the Resistance War, *The One Eyed Elephant and the Elephant Genie*, Foreign Languages Publishing House, Hanoi, 1959, pp. 61–81.

Village Self Defence Unit (*Doi Tu Ve*). At the next level were the National Salvation Guerrilla Cells (*Tieu To Du Kich Cuu Quoc*) recruited from the 'most enthusiastic' in the Self Defence Units, and as they developed they had a roving regional responsibility which took them beyond the village.[82] Finally, although one was not formed until December 1944, there were the Main Force Units (*Chu Luc*) which were the biggest, the best, and the most reliable units and could be called on for any task.[83] The official history explains it this way:

> Because our Resistance War was a war of the whole population, it was necessary to mobilise and arm the entire population, and so initially when we raised (local) forces to establish an army we had to maintain armed regional forces to coordinate their operations with each other. Moreover, main force units had the responsibility to lead the armed regional units, to help to train them, and to help to provide them with weapons where possible, so that these units would grow to full strength.[84]

Now, in all of this, there was no fundamental difference from the organisational differentiation and interaction of the ancient army. As we saw in Chapter 1, the army was divided into elite units which defended the court and regional units which had local responsibilities but coordinated their activities with elite units on big campaigns.

Another ancient-modern congruence has considerable political importance. As Viet Minh units at each level were organised on the modern Maoist 3 by 3 system—three to five men in a 'squad' (*tieu doi*), three squads in a 'platoon' (*trung doi*), and three platoons in a 'company' (*dai doi*) for tactical flexibility and ease of political control[85]—the system of having a 'political leader' (*chinh tri chi dao vien*)[86] paralleling the military commander with ultimate authority over him also had strong roots in ancient practice. In its twentieth

---

[82]*VKQS*, pp. 209–214 for organisational structure of units.

[83]Ibid., pp. 262–263 for instructions for the establishment of the Vietnam Propaganda and Liberation Unit. For structure, recruiting standards, and role of early armed units also see Van Tao, 'Mot Vai Nhan Dinh ve Qua Trinh Phat Trien cua Luc Luong Vu Trang Cach Mang Viet Nam, Vai Tro va Tinh Chat cua No trong Giai Doan Gianh Chinh Quyen Cach Mang' [Some Observations on the Development of the Vietnamese Revolutionary Armed Forces: Its Role and Character in the Period of Seizing Revolutionary Power], *NCLS*, No. 93, December 1966, pp. 17–18.

[84]*LSQD*, p. 192.

[85]In Vietnamese the 3 by 3 system of organisation was called the '*tam tam che*'. See *VKQS*, p. 118, p. 294.

[86]Ibid., pp. 210–211. As well as political officers there were 'Special Affairs Units' (*Dac Vu Doi*) to supervise political training and propaganda activities. In principle at least these contained specialist Inspectors, Weapons Instructors, and Medical Orderlies.

century formulation this idea of dual field command was first used by Trotsky at a time when the Soviet Red Army was largely dependent on officers of the old Tsarist regime.[87] But, especially in the nine-teenth century Vietnam, it will be recalled that the army was no stranger to either political control or dual command, even if these functions underwent some modification under modern conditions.

A distinction between nineteenth and twentieth century practices would be that, in the nineteenth century, political control was not a part of the dual command function at the lowest unit levels. Here, where command of fighting columns was often a dual function be-cause the units that constituted them could come from different regions, the function was shared by military mandarins. Yet at the higher levels of command, where there was an overlap in the func-tions of civil and military mandarins, where the court could send 'military secretaries' (*cai binh*) out to provinces and districts, and where civil mandarins tended to have precedence over military mandarins precisely because of the Confucian need for political control over the army,[88] the institutional parallels with the twentieth century certainly exist. Indeed, the idea of political control of the army, and the system of dual command necessary for exercising it, were already built into the structure of military organisation in the nineteenth century. The only difference was not then structural. It was the low level to which both the idea and the system were rationalised in modern times.

While the modern guerrilla and armed propaganda teams in Cao-Bac-Lang were a manifestation of twentieth century change and the Second World War, the development of their organisation, com-mand, and control systems did not therefore conflict with pre-colonial military methods. For this reason the success of the armed propaganda campaign in Cao-Bac-Lang by early 1943 was significant. On 1 January, for example, a 'students congress' (*hoc sinh dai hoi*) was organised in Ha Quang District in Cao Bang Province. Here, as part of the literacy campaign which cadres were expected to promote in the villages, tests were given in the national language to local people in cultural, political and military subjects as well as physical training.[89] In this same district alone in 1942–1943 the strength of the

[87]It should be remembered, however, that Trotsky's idea can be traced back to the French revolution where the first French Republic used a system of political inspectors to monitor the loyalties of the officer corps that had largely come from the army of the old regime. In England in the seventeenth century Cromwell's New Model Army also used a system of protestant chaplains for similar purposes. See Jonathan R. Adelman, *Revolution, Armies, and War*, Boulder, Colorado: Lynne Reiner, 1985.

[88]See Chapter 1.

[89]Phan Ngoc Lien, 'Tim Hieu ve', p. 14.

village para-military forces appears to have increased significantly; Vietnamese sources say they rose from 235 to 1,184 of whom 180 were organised into 'fighting squads' (*tieu doi chien dau*). Around this time, an alternate Viet Minh administration also began to emerge in the villages.[90] And, as the first signs of an embryonic state began to appear in the form of a public education system, expanding militia, and village administration in Cao-Bac-Lang by early 1943, they would gradually be extended into the original Bac Son-Vu Nhai base area as French power eventually receded there.

Once the refurbished AFNS was ready to return to the Bac Son-Vu Nhai base area from China by December 1942, liaison agents were first sent back to their home areas 'to set up infrastructure, make propaganda, consolidate the local organisation'.[91] Then, the units began to return. As this movement gathered momentum a 'Southern Advance Army' of 'nineteen self armed assault groups'[92] was also mobilised around Cao Bang to link up with the Bac Son-Vu Nhai area. Such groups moved from village to village organising self defence units and running short training courses. One Vietnamese historian also says that 'to nourish the spirit and will to struggle'[93] songs like 'The Song of the Self Defence Unit' and 'The Ten Viet Minh Policies'[94] were used. 'The Song of the Self Defence Unit' appears to have been a jaunty air,[95] but the blend of old Confucian strictness and new revolutionary zeal circumscribing the ten Viet Minh policies was serious:

1. Absolute obedience to orders from above.
2. Do not take as much as a needle and thread from the people.
3. Buying and selling must be carried out fairly.
4. It is absolutely forbidden to take public property for oneself.
5. Speak politely.

---

[90]Vien Su Hoc, *Cach Mang Thang Tam trong Khoi Nghia o Ha Noi va Cac Dia Phuong* [Board for Historical Studies, The August Revolution in the Uprising in Hanoi and Other Regions], (hereafter *CMTT*), Hanoi, 1960, Vol. 1, p. 93. *CMCD*, Vol. 10, p. 65 says 'throughout 1942 three of the new districts in Cao Bang were completely organised (*to chuc hoan toan*)'.

[91]Chu Van Tan, *Reminiscences*, p. 147.

[92]*LSQD*, p. 100. Hoang Van Hoan, *Giot Nuoc*, p. 213 also deals with the 'southern advance', while pp. 208–232 give an interesting general account of Viet Minh activities along the border.

[93]Phan Ngoc Lien, 'Tim Hieu ve', p. 17.

[94]Ibid.

[95]For the words of this song or at least another of the same name see Ho Chi Minh, *Ve Dau Tranh Vu Trang va Luc Luong Vu Trang Nhan Dan* [On Armed Struggle and People's Armed Forces], Hanoi:Quan Doi Nhan Dan, 1970, p. 413.

6. Wherever you stay the house and garden must be kept clean for the people.
7. Whatever is borrowed must be returned.
8. Whatever is broken must be replaced.
9. No bathing in front of women.
10. No alcohol, gambling, or opium.[96]

This code of behaviour, incidentally, was essentially the same as that of the People's Liberation Army in China.[97]

From a military point of view training covered basic drills and weapons handling, and these weapons must have been mostly wooden, for arms were scarce. Tran Huy Lieu says that

at the time (we) only had a number of blunderbusses, flintlock rifles, a hand full of grenades bought on the Chinese border and a number of rifles and short barrelled firearms manufactured by the tribesmen on the border.[98]

Nevertheless, a deficiency in weapons is perhaps the fundamental characteristic of any guerrilla army and in these terms it is not necessarily a handicap as long as tactical training is sound. While at Pac Bo in 1941 and 1942 Ho thus wrote a number of military pamphlets like *The Method of Guerrilla War*, and *The Experience of Chinese Guerrillas*[99] to help structure the training. Although it has been shown that the army suffered when the French made their last serious attempt to repress it from November 1943, guerrilla tactics of 'avoiding (the enemy) and entering the mountains and jungles'[100] were at least partly responsible for its survival. International events would then support this survival and help to generate substantial growth from about mid-1944.

Devillers says that by the autumn of 1944 the French administration believed it had 'reestablished the situation'[101] since it had eliminated the Viet Minh from entire districts, and therefore withdrew. But he adds that with the liberation of France from the Germans in August 1944 the authorities in Indochina chose to believe that France

[96]*LSQD*, p. 82.
[97]See Mao's 'Three Main Rules of Discipline' and 'Eight Points for Attention' in *Selected Military Writings of Mao Tse Tung*, Foreign Languages Press, Peking, 1966, p. 343.
[98]*CMCD*, Vol. 10, p. 65.
[99]Ho Chi Minh, *Ve Dau Tranh*, pp. 184–204.
[100]*LQSD*, p. 102. *CMCD*, Vol. 10, p. 72 also says that 'courageous elements were selected in each district . . . to form specialist armed units of from seven to twelve people with the responsibility of exterminating traitors'.
[101]Devillers, *Histoire*, p. 108.

'had recovered its prestige in the eyes of the population'.[102] In other words, in their haste to reassure themselves that the liberation of France would ensure continuity in French rule in Indochina, the French assumed that the Vietnamese would see events in the same light. By building on this illusion and ceasing operations in the northern provinces in August the French chose to overlook the fact that the dispersal of the Viet Minh did not necessarily mean victory. Dispersal of forces, indeed, is one of the characteristics of guerrilla tactics, and although the Colonial Army had enjoyed considerable success in dividing the Viet Minh from the population before mid-1944 there was still much they could not see. For example, the French could not see that on 25 February 1944 the Third Platoon of the AFNS was officially raised at a ceremony presided over by Hoang Quoc Viet at Khuoi Kich in Tuyen Quang.[103] Another thing the French failed to see with their attention on events in Europe was that, although armed units had been eliminated from many areas, secret ICP cells were still operating in a large number of villages.[104] Moreover, if the AFNS had had some experienced cadres killed or captured, there had been at least some opportunity to replace the departed on such occassions as the jail break at Cho Chu in early 1944 when seasoned cadres like Song Hao, Le Hien Mai, and Ta Xuan Thu escaped.[105] The official history is therefore correct to note that when the French ceased their operations in the northern provinces in August 1944 the revolutionary movement was 'still solid'.[106]

From this point the expansion of the Viet Minh was very much dependent upon changes in the international situation. However, at one point in late 1944 the ICP came very close to miscalculating the rate of change. Already on May 7 'Instructions for the Preparation of the General Uprising'[107] had been issued on the basis that 'all the forces of freedom and progress in the world are fighting with us . . . the glorious day of our people is not far off'.[108] By August the ICP's

[102]Ibid.

[103]*LSQD*, p. 104.

[104]Ibid., p. 102.

[105]*Ibid*, p. 105. For example, Song Hao immediately became Party Secretary for a sub-region. In 1961 he reached the rank of Lieutenant General.

[106]Ibid., p. 103. Hong Van Hoan, *Giot Nuoc*, also shows how the infrastructure remained intact around Cao Bang despite French action.

[107]These instructions are set out in *CMCD*, Vol. 10, pp 98–109. *LSQD*, pp. 106–107 discusses them. See also Hoang Van Hoan, *Giot Nuoc*, pp. 226–227, and Khanh, *Vietnamese Communism*, pp. 187–189, 'An Aborted Insurrection'.

[108]*Chi Thi* in *CMCD*, Vol. 10, pp. 108–109. But if all the forces of progress were on the side of the Viet Minh the instructions also stress that the Viet Minh had to 'contribute eagerly' to the victory of these world forces.

Central Committee began to issue letters of credit along with appeals to collect money to buy weapons,[109] and by November it was preparing to give the order for the uprising. But all that saved the ICP from another blood bath was Ho Chi Minh, who returned from China where he had been since August 1942[110] and wisely vetoed the plans on the grounds that although the northern highlands were ready the rest of the country was not.[111] Ho realised that the French and Japanese were still too powerful for a general uprising and that the international situation was still not sufficiently favorable to support such a major move. As they therefore waited for the end of the Second World War to produce a decisive collapse in the French and Japanese positions in Indochina the Viet Minh went on building their strength in the Viet Bac region.

On December 22, 1944, a date now remembered as the official birthday of the People's Army, the first main force unit was mobilised. This was the Vietnam Propaganda and Liberation Unit (*Doi Viet Nam Tuyen Truyen Giai Phong Quan*)[112] whose title encapsulated the methods and aims of the Vietnamese revolution, and whose composition reflected one strong strand of Vietnam's colonial history. Of the new unit's thirty four members 'not one person in the unit did not have a hatred for the imperialists, or have his house burnt, his property confiscated, his father, brothers, or sisters arrested or shot'.[113] Vo Nguyen Giap, an ICP member since 1933 and one of the Party's leading military figures since 1940 when he was forced to flee government repression in Hanoi, was placed in overall command. Operational command was given to Hoang Sam who had been born into a family of political refugees in Siam. He received a military education in China during a long stay there, reached high rank in the Kuomintang Army, fought against the Japanese, and changed sides to the Chinese communists before joining the Viet Minh. As such people began to concentrate their view of the world on minor enemy posts like those of Phai Khat and Na Ngan in Cao Bang Province on December 24 and 25, their successful armed attacks then made such effective propaganda that within a month the size of the unit had tripled.[114] And this propaganda was so effective because it was buttressed on all sides by the rapidly changing international situation towards the end of the Second World War.

[109]*LSQD*, p. 108.
[110]For Ho's stay in China see Chen, *Vietnam and China*, pp. 55–85. Hoang Van Hoan, *Giot Nuoc*, pp. 233–252 also offers an analysis of the reasons for Ho's trip.
[111]*LSQD*, p. 113.
[112]Ibid., pp. 114–126.
[113]*LSQD*, p. 118.
[114]*LSQD*, pp. 119–120.

Conclusion

With guerrilla tactics and armed propaganda to project the ideal of strength and a better life in the modern world the Viet Minh had begun to mobilise the force of the nation. This mobilisation had occurred in the remote northern provinces of Viet Bac once the international upheaval of 1939–1945 had opened a chink in the French armour there. In the rest of the country such mobilisation was not feasible because the French were still far too strong as their repression of the uprisings of 1940 had shown. But because the Viet Minh was a political and military organisation with an internationalist perspective it had still related the Vietnamese desire for independence with the events of the Second World War. Indeed, on the eve of the Japanese coup d'état of 9 March 1945 which would completely extinguish French power in the region, the Viet Minh was the only party in the country with an embryonic Army of National Liberation ready for rapid expansion.

4

Armed Propaganda, the Army, and the 'August Revolution', March 1945–August 1945

Western commentators on the rapid expansion of the Viet Minh's armed forces in 1945 frequently use the word 'terror'. This is especially so in accounts of the period after the Japanese extinguished French power in the 9 March coup d'état and gave the Viet Minh an unprecedented opportunity to expand its operations beyond the Viet Bac region. For example, one of the earliest accounts written by Bernard Fall in 1954 says that the anti-Japanese campaign which the Viet Minh conducted after 9 March was not characterised by action against the Japanese, but by a campaign of 'outright terror or intimidation of officials and prominent citizens in the nationalist zone.'[1] Fall is right to argue that the impact of Viet Minh actions on the Japanese was 'minute'.[2] But terror alone can hardly account for the rapid increase in the army's regular main force in the Viet Bac region from probably 500 in March to 5,000 in August. Nor can it account for the rapid proliferation of irregular armed propaganda units, national salvation units, self defence forces, and guerrilla units which probably included around 200,000 people in Bac Ky and Trung Ky by August.[3]

[1]Bernard B. Fall, *The Viet Minh Regime: Government and Administration in the Democratic Republic of Vietnam*, Data Paper Number 14, Southeast Asia Program, Cornell University, April 1954, p. 45, or *Le Viet Minh 1945–1960*, Paris, 1960, p. 162. also see note 32.

[2]Fall, *The Viet Minh*, p. 2, *Le Viet Minh*, p. 19.

[3]The March figure of 500 regular main force soldiers is notional. In May we know from *LSQD*, p. 138–139, there were thirteen main force companies. This would have been about 1,000 people, or more. The August figure of 5,000 was both claimed by Vietnamese sources and estimated by French sources. See John McAlister Jr., 'The Origins', p. 165; William S. Turley, Army, 'Party and Society in the Democratic

One obvious omission in Fall's analysis is the impact of the terrible famine in the northern half of the country in the winter of 1944–45. The famine helped focus support for the Viet Minh. Apart from the extinction of French power in the countryside, however, the most important consideration in the army's expansion was the nature of the Viet Minh's armed propaganda campaign which has been overlooked by Fall, as by every other writer on the subject. This campaign clearly involved an element of terror, but it was also a part of a much wider political-military process. As we have seen, the whole point of armed propaganda was to legitimise armed violence with the promise of rice and a better life; this was the foundation for the army's expansion, because the integration of political and military techniques merely reflected the army's wider integration with the society under modern conditions.

In this context it then becomes necessary to challenge established notions about the nature of the 'August Revolution'. Many theorists have cherished the idea that there was in fact a 'general insurrection' in August. However, this is impossible, for the armed propaganda campaign had already mobilised people in a series of revolutionary events that rolled through the countryside from 9 March and only culminated in the cities in late August after the Japanese surrender in the Second World War had created a power vacuum there. In sum, a balanced understanding of the progressive mobilisation of the population and expansion of the armed forces with armed propaganda between March and August 1945 tends to make the 'August Revolution' a misnomer.

The Japanese Interlude

As Japan's military position deteriorated in the Pacific in early 1945, and as it became clear to the Japanese Command in Vietnam that the Gaullists working in concert with the Allies would pose military problems for them, the fate of French Indochina was sealed in a coup d'état. On 9 March the French administration was toppled in the 'Bright Moon' Operation which led to the incarceration of the bulk of French civil and military officials within two days.[4] The Emperor Bao Dai was permitted to declare independence and national unity under Japanese tutelage and revoke the Protectorate treaty of 1884. He was

Republic of Vietnam: Civil-Military Relations in a Mass Mobilisation System', University of Washington, PhD, 1972, p. 8. For the militia forces around August, the figure of 200,000 is also notional and comes from a reading of *CMTT*.

[4] A detailed and helpful account of the 'Bright Moon' or 'Meigo' Operation is Vu Chieu Ngu, 'Political and Social Change', Chapter 7.

also permitted to ask the ailing and elderly Confucian scholar, Tran Trong Kim, whom the Japanese had maintained in Singapore and Thailand since 1943, to form a government.

Under these circumstances Radio Tokyo could announce with some accuracy that 'the colonial status of French Indochina has ended.'[5] But like the glow on a hilltop illuminated by the last rays of a setting sun, the Kim government was never more than the final reflection of Japanese power in the Pacific. Japanese diplomats promptly filled all the major residencies as fast as the French were removed from them; a Japanese Governor, Minoda, was placed in direct control of Nam Ky,[6] and polite instructions for Bao Dai from the commander of the Japanese Army sealed the new relationship:

> In this important period we wish to avoid changes and
> disturbances that would harm security and order. For this
> reason, we would like that, with regard to the political and
> military aspects, reforms be effected only within the most
> necessary limits of the strategic arrangements . . .[7]

Despite Japanese attempts to impose political and administrative stability on the country, however, the situation was so inherently unstable after 9 March that it is most unlikely a government as hastily formed and as politically restricted as Bao Dai's could ever have survived.

In the cities there was an explosion of political activity following the nationalist awakening during the Second World War. This activity signalled a widespread desire for political change and independence. By June political parties and associations of public servants, intellectuals, religious groups, and youth mushroomed all over the

[5]Quoted in Huynh Kim Khanh, *Vietnamese Communism*, p. 292. The simultaneous coup in Cambodia and Laos as well as Vietnam removed the French in these countries of Indochina too.

[6]For details of the Japanese Administration see Ralph B. Smith, 'The Japanese Period in Indochina and the Coup of 9 March 1945', *JSEAS*, 9, 2, September 1978. Official Vietnamese sources basically view the Japanese period as an extension of colonial rule. Tran Huy Lieu, et al, *Tai Lieu Tham Khao Lich Su Cach Mang Can Dai Viet Nam* [Reference Documents on Vietnam's Modern Revolution], (hereafter *CMCD*), 12 Vols., Hanoi, 1955, 1957–1958, Vol. 11, pp. 10–11, for example, states that on 9 March the 'Japanese enemy immediately took over complete power in Indochina and kept the old system of political administration intact in each region so that they could gradually put their supporters in power.' Khanh, *Vietnamese Communism*, pp. 292–294, however, emphasises that the Japanese were far more preoccupied with their own military problems than thoughts of long term colonisation.

[7]Tran Van Giau, *Giai Cap Cong Nhan Viet Nam* [The Vietnamese Working Class], Hanoi, 1963, 3, p. 196 quoted in Huynh Kim Khanh, 'The Vietnamese August Revolution Reinterpreted', *Journal of Asian Studies*, 30, 4, August 1971, p. 765.

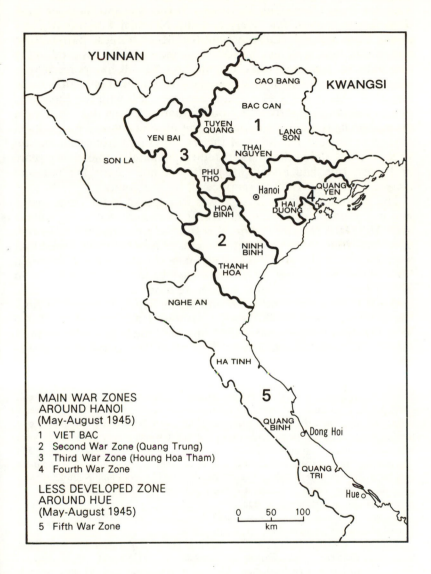

YUNNAN

KWANGSI

CAO BANG

BAC CAN

TUYEN QUANG

1

LANG SON

YEN BAI

THAI NGUYEN

SON LA

3

PHU THO

Hanoi

QUANG YEN

HOA BINH

HAI DUONG

4

2

NINH BINH

THANH HOA

NGHE AN

HA TINH

MAIN WAR ZONES
AROUND HANOI
(May-August 1945)

1   VIET BAC
2   Second War Zone (Quang Trung)
3   Third War Zone (Houng Hoa Tham)
4   Fourth War Zone

LESS DEVELOPED ZONE
AROUND HUE
(May-August 1945)

5   Fifth War Zone

5

QUANG BINH

Dong Hoi

QUANG TRI

Hue

0   50   100
km

country.[8] Apart from relatively well established political associations like the Cao Dai and the Hoa Hao religious sects and the Restoration League (*Phuc Quoc*), these included such groups as the New Vietnam Party (*Dang Tan Viet Nam*) in Bac Ky, and the Viet Nam Restoration Party (*Phuc Viet*) and the National Liberation Party (*Dang Quoc Gia Doc Lap*) in Nam Ky. Many of these parties were ephemeral. Insofar as they had an ideological basis as opposed to the raw patriotic sentiment that Huynh Kim Khanh has pointed out, many envisaged national independence within the framework of the monarchy. Many also had working arrangements with the Japanese, just as various ICP Advance Youth Guard factions did.[9] Yet such arrangements could not camouflage the universal desire for political change or prevent members of the Youth Guard from standing on street corners and in the markets telling people that 'the eighty years of French rule had ended', that they should 'learn the national language' and 'be ready to sacrifice all for the country.'[10]

The desire for political change was widespread in the cities, but it was in the countryside that the Kim government was most vulnerable. Here, the Japanese Army was still the government's mainstay, and, apart from some small detachments of twenty or thirty men that were located in the provinces, it was concentrated around the main lines of communication as it had always been. This meant that in March 1945, after considerable troop reinforcements from China in January to deal with the coup and an anticipated Allied landing, there were some 30,000 troops around Hanoi, possibly 5,000 around centers like Hue and Da Nang, and the bulk of the remaining 25,000 or so around Saigon.[11] In other words, no attempt was

---

[8]Khanh, 'The Vietnamese August Revolution', pp. 766–768.

[9]Foreign Languages Publishing House, *History of the August Revolution*, Hanoi, 1972, pp. 76–77 criticises the conservative parties for being 'pro-Japanese' and 'reactionary'. But p. 106–107 also notes that Viet Minh cadres 'who wanted to make use of the Japanese' had to be 'sternly criticised'. The desire which some cadres had to work with the Japanese is also indicated in the censure which was directed against them and reflected in various passages of *CMTT*, 2 such as p. 50, p. 254. Smith, 'The Japanese Period', p. 276 also says that the Advance Youth Guard Leader Pham Ngoc Thach was a 'friend' of the Japanese writer Komatsu Kiyoshi who was connected with the Japanese Cultural Institute in Saigon.

[10]Nguyen Van Mai, *Phong Trao Thanh Nien Tien Phong* [The Advance Youth Guard Movement], Saigon, 1947, p. 23, pp. 26–27.

[11]Philippe Devillers, *Histoire*, p. 279. Archives D'Outre Mer, Rue Oudinot, Paris, Indochine, Nouveau Fonds, Carton 123, Dossier 1112. (Hereafter, AOM, NF, C-, D-.), 'Effectif Japonais en Indochine'. McAlister, 'The Origins', p. 91 says Japanese troop strength in February 1945 was 61,775.

ever made by the Japanese to replace the French troops whose task it had formerly been to keep order in the countryside.

Such deployments left the Vietnamese troops of the old colonial army (*tirailleurs*) and the Indigenous Guard which became the Security Forces (*Bao An*) of the Tran Trong Kim government.[12] However, with the loss of their French officers, a change of name was not enough to turn these troops into an effective security force. Low morale was universal, many units had been infiltrated by the Viet Minh, and many others simply disintegrated as their members went home or joined the ranks of the revolutionaries. Also, where units did remain intact, their relationship with the society had often broken down to the extent that one commander of Vietnamese troops in the Hon Gay region said, 'the Vietnamese *tirailleurs* sought to exploit the population as much as they could'.[13]

This breakdown in provincial military affairs, however, did not necessarily mean that civil administration had ceased to function. The Kim government did attempt to reduced taxes and institute constitutional, judicial, and educational reforms. In central and southern Vietnam the government was able to stimulate the development of some political organisations and youth groups.[14] Although their residual power probably had little to do with the strength of the central government, provincial bureaucrats still tended to go about their business in these areas. Even in the north where the government's influence was slightest, officials in Thanh Hoa, for example, could still muster considerable armed force for some time after 9 March.[15]

Despite these qualifications, however, nothing does more to illustrate the overall weakness of central government, and set the stage for the emergence of the Viet Minh as the real power in the country-

[12]McAlister, 'The Origins', pp. 90–91 drawing on French sources says 'a total of 99,000 armed men were under French command during the occupation of whom little more than 74,000 were regulars including 19,371 Europeans in three services together with 54,649 indigenous troops. The remaining forces consisted of a local militia of 24,680 men with a cadre of 362 Europeans'. Vu Chieu Ngu, 'Political and Social Change', p. 360 says the Bao An was not created until August. However, Vietnamese histories like *CMTT* use the term extensively after March and so I have followed this usage unless it is clear from the sources that we are dealing with the Indigenous Guard.

[13]Jean Leroy, *Un homme dans la rizière*, Paris, 1955, p. 61.

[14]Vu Chieu Ngu, 'Political and Social Change', Chapter 8, offers the most detailed account of the Kim government's activities even if it does exaggerate their importance.

[15]*CMTT*, 1, p. 385 says of Thanh Hoa province that 'in many places the enemy was no longer able to collect taxes', there is a clear implication that taxes could be collected in other places. The same source also mentions the forces of the old regime often.

[16]*CMCD*, 8, pp. 69–78.

side, than reference to the terrible famine which struck northern and some areas of central Vietnam in the winter of 1944 and 1945.

The Vietnamese economy had originally undergone serious dislocation when it was cut off from metropolitan France in 1940. After the Japanese forced an economic treaty on the Decoux administration in May 1941, it was also exploited ruthlessly for the benefit of the Japanese war effort. Millions of tons of coal, precious minerals, rubber, and coffee were extracted from Vietnam by Japanese and Franco–Japanese companies and shipped to Japan at very low prices.[16] But the most damaging effect on Vietnamese society came from the shipping of rice to Japan by the Mitsui company in such large quantities and such low prices that it was barely disguised pillage. In 1943, for example, people in Bac Ky were paying 57 piasters for a picul of rice while the Japanese bought it for 13.41, and in 1945 while the people paid 800 piasters a picul the Japanese army paid 14.68.[17] The starvation which these figures imply was further exacerbated by the Japanese army's practice of making forced requisitions from villages. In some areas like Thanh Hoa peasants with no economic margin for error whatsoever were also forced to turn their rice fields over to the cultivation of other crops like jute for consumption in the war economy.[18]

But this was not all. Between May and September 1944 three typhoons struck the coastal region of Bac Ky. In normal times these would have already caused crop failures from flooding and placed the population in a perilous position. But with the cumulative effect of Japanese policies and French collaboration in them, general war time disruption which included the crippling of the transport system by Allied bombing in 1944 and 1945,[19] and astronomical inflation, the worst famine in living memory, struck northern and northern central Vietnam.

According to Tran Van Mai, who recorded his first hand experience of the famine in a novel called *Who Committed this Crime?*,

[16]*CMCD*, 8, pp. 69–78.

[17]Ibid., pp. 77–78.

[18]David Marr, 'World War II and the Vietnamese Revolution' in Alfred W. McCoy, editor, *Southeast Asia Under Japanese Occupation*, Monograph Series No. 22, Yale University, Southeast Asia Studies, 1980, pp. 133–134.

[19]The destruction by Allied bombing was considerable and comes out in many sources. For example, Nguyen Van Mai, *Phong Trao Thanh Nien*, describes how Advance Youth Guard members went to work to help victims of one heavy raid on Saigon and Cho Lon on 12 June 1945. Glimpses of the effect of bombing on the Hue to Saigon railroad can be found in Lucien Félixine, *L'Indochine livrée aux bourreaux*, Paris, 1959, for example. p. 50.

The starvation began in early October (1944). Earlier than any other year the weather was cuttingly cold. The north wind howled and it pierce through the rags of the hungry and poor . . . It was so cold that people would lie in haystacks, covering themselves up with banana leaves. They were so hungry that they had to eat marsh pennywort, potato leaves, bran, banana roots, and the bark of trees . . . Regardless of the time of the day or night, the hungry people over and over again would hug each other and would moan tragically . . . On the streets (in provincial towns) there were only the municipal ox carts rolling along in the process of collecting corpses. On one cart we saw that there were from five to seven corpses piled in a disorderly way on top of each other . . . The scenes of people dying were beyond description . . . [20]

Meanwhile, in the centre of Hanoi, the corpses were not even collected. Françoise Martin has described how, as public health services broke down completely, 'bodies black and bloated' lined the streets while footpaths were turned into 'latrines' and 'enormous rats multiplied in total security'.[21] Up to two million people thus died in northern Vietnam in the Winter of 1944–1945 as the Emperor Bao Dai went hunting in the central highlands, and the feeble Prime Minister, Tran Trong Kim, tried but failed to carry out effective relief.[22]

The appalling state of affairs in the north did not extend into southern Vietnam. In 1944 and 1945 the southern harvests were good, fish were plentiful, fish sauce was easily obtained, and the fleet of junks that operated the southern coastal trade did brisk business.[23] One French prisoner of the Japanese who was moved the 1010 kilometers from Hue to Saigon by train between 7 and 13 August has also described how there was no overt hostility to the French along

[20]Tran Van Mai, *Ai Gay Nen Toi?* [Who Committed this Crime?], Saigon, 1956. I quote from Ngo Vinh Long's translation in *Before the Revolution: The Vietnamese Peasant Under the French*, MIT Press, 1973, pp. 221–276.

[21]Françoise Martin, *Heures tragiques au Tonkin*, Paris, 1948, pp. 98–105.

[22]Bao Dai, *Le Dragon d'Annam*, Paris, Plon, 1980, p. 99 shows his surprise at hearing about the Japanese coup when he reached Hue on the night of 10 March 'après deux journées passées dans ma résidence de chasse près de Quang Tri'. Smith, 'The Japanese Period', pp. 289–290 gives an account of what the Kim government was doing during the famine. Vu Chieu Ngu, 'Political and Social Change', pp. 363–365 discusses the efforts which Tran Trong Kim made to sponsor Famine Relief Associations in the south so that rice could be sent from the south to the centre and the north. However, as one contemporary source, Nguyen Van Mai, *Phong Trao Thanh Nien*, p. 22 particularly notes, even though the Youth Guard collected food in Saigon for famine relief in the north, 'there was no way to transport it'. On the figure of two million deaths see Khanh, *Vietnamese Communism*, p. 301, note 1.

the route until he reached Saigon, and how the biggest obstacle to obtaining fruit, eggs, and other food items from Vietnamese vendors at the stations was the Japanese guards.[24] Such evidence supports David Marr's argument that, as opposed to families in the north, most families in southern and southern central Vietnam 'were able to cope'[25] in 1945. As we will see, these important regional differences would be reflected in the different paths the Viet Minh took to power later on. But there is no doubt that a combination of raging famine in the north, very weak central government in Hue, and general discontent in all major centres first gave the Viet Minh its opportunity to expand beyond the Viet Bac area and become the dominant force in all the land by late August.

Armed Propaganda and the Eruption of the Vietnamese Revolution

With almost certain prior knowledge of the coup on 9 March, the ICP's Central Committee met in Dinh Bang village in Bac Ninh that night. It decided that because of the 'political crisis', the 'frightful famine', and the anticipated 'Allied landing in Indochina to attack the Japanese', the 'pre-insurrectional period' (*tien khoi nghia*) had begun.[26] Above all, it stipulated that 'armed people must be led in attacks on imperialist paddy stores to put an end to the catastrophic starvation' while guerrilla units were mobilised to 'open a wide guerrilla war . . . to take the initiative in the task of driving the rapacious Japanese Army out of the country'.[27] With the French army imprisoned, except for two columns under generals Sabattier and Alessandri that had escaped the Japanese dragnet on 9 March and were now marching to China,[28] the Viet Minh declared its anti-Japanese Resistance Movement.

From the strictly military point of view Fall was correct to describe the anti-Japanese movement as 'minute'.[29] There were very few clashes with the Japanese, and such claims as those which the official sources make when they say that revolutionary forces killed 'fifty'

---

[23]Commandant Jean Simon, *Experiences d'action politico-militaire au Centre-Vietnam*, CHEAM, Paris, 1957, p. 82.

[24]Felixine, *L'Indochine livrée aux bourreaux*, pp. 46–64.

[25]Marr, 'World War II and the Vietnamese Revolution', p. 135.

[26]*LSQD*, p. 129 quoting 'Instructions of the Standing Committee of the Central Committee on the ICP', 12 March 1945.

[27]Ibid., p. 130.

[28]Général Sabattier, *Le destin de l'Indochine: Souvernir et documents*, Paris: Plon, 1952, Chapters 8 and 9. A. Patti, *Why Vietnam? Prelude to America's Albatross*, University of California Press, 1980, pp. 88–89.

[29]Bernard Fall, *The Viet Minh*, p. 2; *Le Viet Minh*, p. 19.

Japanese at Deo Khe in March and another 'sixty' at Deo Chan in May are difficult to believe.[30] However, to imply with Fall and others like Duiker who emphasises the 'minuscule'[31] size of the Viet Minh's armed forces, that the anti-Japanese campaign was of little importance in the history of the Vietnamese revolution is to overlook the nature of the Viet Minh's armed propaganda efforts. This oversight then leaves the undue emphasis which many writers place on Viet Minh 'terror'[32] unchecked, because they have no other explanation for the Viet Minh's rise to power.

'Hundreds'[33] of village notables and mandarins were intimidated, dispossessed, beaten, and killed in the course of the revolution. Although we will see in the next chapter that most of this violence occurred after August, it was Viet Minh policy after March to 'confiscate the property of traitors and enemy agents',[34] and by at least May 'Military Tribunals' (*Toa An Quan Su*) were established in some areas like Bac Giang[35] where spies and traitors were executed. However, the unconscious fear of those Western writers who terrorise themselves in their accounts of the Viet Minh stems largely from unwarranted cultural assumptions.

Many Western writers including Fall and Duiker use the idea of 'terror' to explain the development of the Viet Minh 'regime' in 1945 and 1946. While Fall tells us of the 'outright terror and intimidation' of the Viet Minh 'regime', Duiker refers to 'a policy of brutality and terrorism' and to how 'terror squads' were 'established'.[36] The assumptions in such references may then be described as historically specific, because they clearly rest on notions of 'government by intimidation' and of a 'system of terror' which go back to 'the reign of

[30]*CMTT*, 1, p. 135; *LSQD*, p. 145.

[31]Duiker, *The Communist Road*, p. 103.

[32]Terror is emphasised by many writers apart from Fall and Duiker, *The Communist Road*, p. 111, p. 117. p. 122. For example, Devillers, *Histoire*, p. 181; Isoart, *Le phénomène*, p. 343. The idea that Viet Minh rule was based on terror was also a major premise in the outpouring of literature on psychological warfare in the 1950s and 1960s. For example, see Yvonne Pagniez, *Le Viet Minh et la guerre psychologique*, Paris, 1955. Of course, it would be a foolish person who denied the Viet Minh used force, but the fundamental issue is surely the universal one in which political power has to be given by people who then have it turned back on them.

[33]Devillers, *Histoire*, p. 180.

[34]AOM, NF, C. 123, D. 1112, Vietnamese Newspaper Reports.

[35]*CMTT*, 1, p. 207.

[36]Fall, *The Viet Minh Regime*, p. 45; Duiker, *The Communist Road*, p. 117, p. 122. There would also seem to be a problem with Duiker's full sentence on p. 122 that 'Terror squads were established to punish traitors'. Are 'traitors' a category of people normally associated with repression by terror? See also note 32 above.

terror' in the French revolution between March 1793 and July 1794.[37]
This period of French history, in which 'the terror' had a beginning
and an end, has also given us the term 'red terror' to mean the
remorseless shedding of blood by the revolutionary regime. The
'white terror' then applied to the counter-revolution that followed
the 'red terror'. What is therefore remarkable about any emphasis on
the Viet Minh's 'outright' 'policy' of terrorism, is that while it
assumes a specific regime of terror by 'reds', the Vietnamese term for
'terror', *khung bo*, and various phrases based on it, do not convey
this Western assumption.

Khung bo is a pejorative term without any assumption of the
specificity of a 'reign of terror'.[38] By the 1940s it had been built into
phrases like *khung bo do*, 'red terror', and *khung bo trang*, 'white
terror', which the Vietnamese borrowed from the Chinese, the
Russian, and, ultimately, the French revolutions. But even if we
accept that these Vietnamese phrases bring us closer to Western
assumptions, the frequent occurrence of the term 'white terror' to
refer to French police operations between 1941 and 1944 in the
revolutionary literature, and the arguably not so frequent occurrence
of the phrase 'red terror' to refer to the actions of the Viet Minh
regime after mid-1945 in conservative writings,[39] reflect political
realities that reverse the Western assumptions.

In Vietnam, the so-called 'white terror' largely *preceded* the so-
called 'red terror'. With the relatively minor qualifications of the
Soviet movement in 1930–31, the shortlived uprisings in 1940, and
parts of Viet Bac by late 1944, the 'reds' only established a 'regime'
once power of the 'whites' was progressively extinguished in 1945.
Therefore, as an application of Western assumptions to Vietnamese
conditions would lead to the striking conclusion that the counter-
revolution largely began before the revolution, Western writers who
imply the specific use of 'terror' as a method of government in the
Vietnamese revolution can not be describing what they think they
are.

This is especially so when they overlook the fact that the Viet Minh
can not be held responsible for all the acts of violence that occurred

[37]The quotes and information on 'terror' are drawn from *The Oxford University
Dictionary*, 1932 edition, Vol. 11, p. 216. For a majestic, conservative discussion of the
nature of 'the terror' in a Western context see Hannah Arendt, *On Revolution*, New
York: The Viking Press, 1963.

[38]David Marr alerted me to this point.

[39]For examples of 'white terror' between 1941 and 1944 see Chapter 3, and *CMCD*,
Vol. 10, pp. 67–73. Examples of the use of the term 'red terror' in the period of the
Viet Minh's rise to power can be found in the *VNQDD* press. See Duiker, *The
Communist Road*, p. 111.

when social order had broken down in large areas of the countryside and when banditry and anarchy were widespread. The cause of this situation was the terrible famine which Franco-Japanese policies and practices exacerbated rather than relieved. What is therefore most remarkable about the Viet Minh between March and August are its attempts to recreate social order with armed propaganda.

The idea of *recreating* social order is important, for the endemic use of the verb 'to control'[40] in Western literature is another barrier to understanding the Viet Minh's rise to power in 1945. The assumption that armies must be able 'to control' populations to expand and mount revolutions is in fact another reason for the emphasis on 'terror' in the Western literature, because it suggests the primacy of domination. But, while Viet Minh leaders naturally wanted whatever control they could get, they had no infrastructure of any kind in place in most parts of the country *before* March. What we find in the Vietnamese literature is that terms for 'control' such as *'kiem soat'* and *'kiem tra'* are used infrequently. They also tend to be used in a specific way as in a 'control commission' (*uy ban kiem tra*), rather than in a general way as in English expressions such as 'social control' or 'political control'.

In the Vietnamese literature the key word is unquestionably *'doan ket'* ('unity').As Ho Chi Minh put it, the secret of revolutionary success in Vietnam was *'doan ket, doan ket, dai doan ket'*,[41] and since *'doan ket'* is usually translated as 'unity' we may translate 'unity, unity, greater unity'. But in the present context a more operative translation suggests itself. The literal meaning of *doan* is 'group', 'band', 'party', and of *ket* is 'to join', 'to connect'. When Ho Chi Minh thus appealed to the population to *'doan ket* around'[42] the National Liberation Committee in August 1945 what he was calling for was groups of people—villages, hamlets, communes, guerrilla units—to connect or link up around the Viet Minh infrastructure which he thought was the foundation for what I will call this 'linkage' (*su doan ket*).[43]

The significance of the Viet Minh's political-military infrastructure lay less in its power to control and terrorise people than in the links it made between people and regions through mobilisation and organisation. These links alone could integrate the force of the modern Vietnamese nation. Woodside recognised this in his comment that

---

[40]For example, Khanh, *Vietnamese Communism*, p. 323 has a map entitled 'Areas under Viet Minh control as of 17 August 1945'.

[41]Ho Chi Minh, *Ve Dau Tranh Vu Trang*, p. 84.

[42]Ho Chi Minh, *Tuyen Tap* [Collected Works], Vol. 1, Hanoi: Su That, 1980, p. 248.

[43]Ibid., says *'Viet Minh la co so cho su doan ket'*.

Viet Minh 'planning'—he does not use the word 'control'—was
'remarkably decentralised.'[44] In fact, Woodside recognised that the
chain of functional and regional groupings in the society had no
centre, and that what the Viet Minh needed at this stage was political
and military linkage that touched off revolutionary social responses
as it generated its own momentum and progressively unified the
modern nation.

Le Thanh Nghi captures this point in his observation that once
armed propaganda units set up Viet Minh infrastructure in one area,
the news spread to neighboring areas 'in a flash',[45] preparing the path
for the next advance of the armed propaganda unit. Tran Huy Lieu,
drawing on the 1946 publication of Vo Nguyen Giap's book, *The
Liberated Zone*, also indicates that the operations of the Propaganda
and Liberation Army Units between March and August were characterised by

> Armed propaganda, that is to say, the opening of attacks and
> ambushes on the enemy to achieve victories that create
> confidence among the people, at the same time as the people are
> propagandised and organised.

Once the remnants of French Administration had then been replaced
in an area by the revolutionary regime the process of building the
army developed in the following way:

> Cadres of the propaganda units were deployed with regional
> armed units to organise new Liberation Army platoons and
> prepare to continue the fight against the Japanese.[46]

In other words, while it may be that Tran Huy Lieu tends to
exaggerate the amount of armed conflict with Japanese forces, the
Japanese presence was essentially used as a propaganda weapon by
the Viet Minh to create their infrastructure in the villages. Hence, by
employing such slogans as:

> Not a grain of paddy to the Japanese!
> Not a cent in taxes to the Japanese!
> Not a soldier for the Japanese Army!
> Not a coolie for the Japanese!,[47]

by already implementing rudimentary land redistribution in some

---

[44]Alexander Woodside, *Community and Revolution in Modern Vietnam*, Boston,
1976, p. 216.
[45]Le Thanh Nghi, *Con Duong Cach Mang*, pp. 22–37 and especially p. 25.
[46]*CMCD*, 11, p. 33.
[47]AOM, NF, C. 123, D. 1112. See compilation of Vietnamese Newspaper Reports
from 1945.

areas like Bac Giang, [48] and by attacking provincial grains stores where considerable quantities of rice—sometimes as much as 100 or even 1,000 tons[49]—had been accumulated for collection by the Japanese Army, the Viet Minh were attacking the symbols of foreign domination and linking people together in the struggle for national independence. Some idea of the scale of these actions after the Japanese coup is given by one authoritative source which lists around ninety attacks in seventeen northern provinces.[50]

What happened in Thai Nguyen was typical of the Viet Bac region. After a rice store was opened at Dinh Ca on 15 March, and a national salvation platoon captured thirty six rifles and took over the Vo Nhai district offices on the 21st, similar events occurred all over the province. At Dinh Hoa soon afterwards two National Salvation Platoons rapidly took the local military post without resistance, captured 100 weapons, released prisoners from the Cho Chu jail, and opened four large rice stores; at Dai Tu on the 27th district officials were forced to flee, tax records burnt, and a store house opened; at Phu Luong on the 24th the district offices were occupied, although this district was not completely liberated for some time because a Japanese post at Phan Me continued to guard a coal mine there. Apart from the fleeing officials at Dai Tu, some twenty eight soldiers from the Indigenous Guard were killed and forty three wounded in an ambush after they tried to break out of the military post at Dinh Ca.[51] This was the revolution in Thai Nguyen and, despite some other slight clashes with Japanese forces in the other provinces of the Viet Bac[52], it had the same profile there as the region was largely liberated by May.

In northern provinces outside of the Viet Bac like Bac Giang, Bac Ninh and Dong Trieu where there were no regular Liberation Army

[48]*CMTT*, 1, p. 207. See also Le Thanh Nhgi, *Con Duong Cach Mang: Tap Hoi Ky Cach Mang ve Dong Chi Hoang Van Thu, Le Thanh Nhgi, Nguyen Duy Trinh, Tran Do*. [The Revolutionary Road: Revolutionary Memoirs of Comrades Hoang Van Thu, Le Thanh Nghi, Nguyen Duy Trinh, Tran Do], Hanoi: Thanh Nien Publishing House, 1970, p. 33.

[49]*CMTT*, 1, p. 301 gives a case in Hung Yen where over 100 tons were captured, p. 367 gives a case in Ninh Binh where 100 tons were distributed to the poor, and p. 73 says that at Cho Chu in Thai Nguyen there were 4 rice stores and that 'each rice store had over 1,000 tons'.

[50]*CMCD*, 11, pp. 103–130. The provinces were Bac Ninh, Bac Giang, Hung Yen, Thuan Thanh, Ninh Binh, Phuc Yen, Vinh Yen, Vinh Phuc, Son Tay, Ha Dong, Kien An, Ha Nam, Thanh Hoa, Nghia Lo, Hoa Binh, Thai Nguyen, Tuyen Quang.

[51]*CMTT*, 1, pp. 72–73.

[52]For example, Ibid., pp. 134–135 gives details of the battle at Deo Khe in Tuyen Quang where 50 Japanese were allegedly killed. This figure is almost certainly inflated.

Units, local 'Assault Propaganda Units' and 'National Salvation Units'[53] had nevertheless sprung up. These units were calling for attacks on rice stores at large public meetings, and distributing anti-Japanese leaflets within days of the coup. They were also supported by local Viet Minh cadres, and the mass organisations and self defence forces that began to take shape with the attacks on the rice stores. As one French report of 1945 noted that 'nothing could have been better to raise the combative spirit of the peasants than this excellent method of struggle',[54] it then went on to cite a number of Viet Minh newspaper reports which described attacks on rice stores and military posts soon after 9 March. For example, the attack on the post at Tra Cu in Bac Giang Province on 13 March was described as follows:

> Two hundred inhabitants also attacked the stores at Tra Cu post, but the post was defended by many soldiers and the attackers were forced to withdraw with four dead. The following day the peasants returned to attack the post with more than 2,000 and succeeded in confiscating all the paddy, arms, ammunition, and medical supplies they could find there.[55]

The effect of such victories on the development of people's armed forces in Bac Giang may then be measured by an account from one of the earliest histories of the revolution:

> if the establishment of armed forces was previously only a number of small and secret organisations, after 9 March, self defence units and fighting self defence units sprang up openly everywhere. Many military training classes were opened. Very many weapons of different kinds, (captured from the French, Japanese, and Indigenous Guard, and donated by the people) were used to form many armed units . . . The Party was then able to raise both concentrated provincial companies, and concentrated district platoons.[56]

Apart from possibly Bac Ninh and Dong Trieu where at least two people who worked for the Japanese were executed,[57] military development in the other northern provinces was not as rapid as it was in Bac Giang. In places like Hai Duong and Thanh Hoa, for instance,

---

[53]*CMTT*, 1, p. 203, p. 204, p. 213.

[54]AOM, NF, C. 123, D. 1112, Vietnamese newspaper reports from 1945. Some attacks are recounted in Le Thanh Nghi, *Con Duong Cach Mang*, 22–23. Also see note 35 below.

[55]AOM, NF, C. 123, D. 1112. Newspaper reports.

[56]*CMTT*, 1, pp. 203–204.

[57]Ibid., p. 225.

the armed propaganda campaign did not really get under way until April or May. Also, in central Vietnam, with the exception of Quang Tri and Quang Ngai where self defence forces began to come into existence in March, there was little armed propaganda until around mid-year, and in the south there was virtually none until August when Viet Minh cadres began to influence the actions of various youth movements. Nevertheless, as attacks of rice stores continued in the northern regions and spread into the central regions by April and May, the Viet Minh were clearly able to organise large numbers of people for further action.

In this context it should also be realised that defections from Tran Trong Kim's security forces played a role in many of the Viet Minh's successes. The exact number of soldiers from colonial army units and the Indigenous Guard who went over to the Viet Minh between March and August will never be known. However, there is little doubt that the ICP's longstanding policy of infiltrating the colonial army was having a significant effect.[58] One source estimated that by August 4,000 *tirailleurs* had joined the Viet Minh, [59] and others make numerous references to support which Viet Minh military actions received from old colonial soldiers. For instance, at Bac Giang on 4 April, a member of the post at Hiep Hoa facilitated a Viet Minh attack by opening the gates after prior consultations,[60] and one account of a successful Viet Minh attack on the Tam Dao post which resulted in the death of some ten Japanese soldiers began: 'On 6 April the political prisoners destroyed the prison. Our troops reinforced by soldiers of the Indigenous guard attacked the Japanese barracks.'[61]

With little or no power in place to repress it in large areas of the northern countryside, the Vietnamese revolution had erupted. By April 1945 National Liberation Committees (*Uy Ban Dan Toc Giai*

[58]Fall, *The Viet Minh*, p. 2, says the Viet Minh 'won many recruits particularly among the Vietnamese soldiers of disbanded French colonial forces who became the hard core of the Viet Minh's nascent army and who arc today (1954) the elite of the military cadres of the DRVN'.

[59]Tran Van Giau, *Giai Cap Cong Nhan*, 3, p. 235. It should also be noted that the Viet Minh had 'specialist committees' whose task it was to infiltrate colonial army units and encourage their defection. See Nguyen Hoai, 'Ve Cong Tac Binh Van trong Thoi Khang Chien Chong Phap, 1945–1954', ['About the Work of Mobilising Soldiers in the Period of the Anti-French Resistance War'), *NCLS*, No. 97, April 1967, p. 13. Also see note 11 above.

[60]*CMTT*, 1, p. 205. For other examples, see pp. 205–206, p. 218, p. 221.

[61]AOM, NF, C. 123, D. 1112, Vietnamese newspaper reports. This report says there were twenty Japanese in the post, but *CMTT*, 1, p. 190 is almost certainly closer to the mark when it says ten.

Phong)[62] were beginning to appear in the villages of many Provinces in Bac Ky, and parts of Trung Ky as a result of the Viet Minh's armed propaganda campaign. By early May the Viet Minh's main force units in the Viet Bac, that is to say, the best armed units with the highest level of training, discipline, and ICP participation whose responsibility it was to set up the village militia, 'were no longer a few platoons and companies, but had developed into many companies'.[63] In one or two other regions like Bac Giang we have also seen that 'concentrated' units, or quasi-regular units, had come into existence. However, even the many main force companies were having great difficulty integrating the scores of irregular semi-armed and unarmed bands that the revolution had spawned once masses of starving people began to break the constraints of eighty years of systematic colonial repression. This was the case in the wide arc of provinces around Hanoi and in Quang Tri to the south of Hue. These exigencies brought about the ICP's first Bac Ky Revolutionary Military Conference at Hiep Hoa in Bac Giang Province from 15 to 20 April, and force us to consider the expanding army's intitutional links with the society.

The Army in Society

The April Conference was presided over by the ICP's General Secretary, Truong Chinh. It was attended by cadres from all over Viet Bac, Hoa Binh, Ninh Binh, and Thanh Hoa, and its assumption was that 'sooner or later the Allies will enter Indochina'.[64] But in the Conference's view this was all the more reason for 'a truly large development of guerrilla army units' so that the Viet Minh would be in a position to 'occupy the essential points and keep the initiative'[65] once the Allies had served their purpose and eliminated the Japanese in the cities. In fact, the ICP was attempting to relate the mobilisation of the army to international events as well as to domestic developments, and so a new structuring of the forces began by May.

Ho Chi Minh first moved his headquarters from the border area to the more central location of Tan Trao in Tuyen Quang Province and proclaimed the Viet Bac region 'the Liberated Zone'.[66] He also

---

[62]For a discussion of the administrative forms taken by the revolution see *CMCD*, 11, p. 50, pp. 55–60.

[63]*LSQD*, p. 133.

[64]Ibid., p. 135.

[65]Ibid.

[66]Ibid., pp. 137–138. Five War Zones, were delineated for Bac Ky and Trung Ky. *CMCD*, 11, p. 46 actually delineates seven War Zones for the entire country, but as we

delineated five new War Zones and placed them under the political and military command of various newly elected members of the Bac Ky Revolutionary Committee. These members were Vo Nguyen Giap, Chu Van Tan, Van Tien Dung, Le Thanh Nghi, and Tran Dang Ninh who were ordered 'to command the War Zones in northern Indochina on the political and military fronts at the same time as they had responsibility for assisting the whole country on the military front.'[67] And if the formation of the new political-military administrative boundaries could lead Truong Chinh to remark that 'a new Vietnam came into being'[68], we may add that a new army came simultaneously into being.

On May 15 the Army for National Salvation and the Propaganda and Liberation Army were formally disbanded in Thai Nguyen Province. Virtually all members of these forces now became cadres in the new Liberation Army of Viet Nam (*Viet Nam Giai Phong Quan*), and the ranks were expanded with new recruits who 'had already carried out work among the masses in their regions and had become propaganda cadres'.[69] The Liberation Army now consisted of thirteen companies or possibly 1,000 to 1,300 men under direct military command, as well as numerous regional platoons and companies that had sprung from the People's Revolutionary Committees in the villages of Viet Bac. Weapons were in relative abundance as several thousand rifles of various descriptions and at least a few machine guns and sixty millimetre mortars had fallen into the hands of the armed forces. Hundreds of tons of assorted ammunition were also available, and 'Liberation Army Paddy Stores' (*kho thoc Giai Phong Quan*) were set up in the villages to feed soldiers.[70] However, to achieve more than the most superficial understanding of all these developments an important question must be asked about the army's relationship with its social base. How was the society at large going to support, that is, feed, cloth, and equip a rapidly expanding army in a country so recently ravaged by famine?

One political training manual in circulation in the Viet Bac area by at least June 1945, and now at rest in the recesses of the Bibliothèque Nationale in Paris, suggests a reasonable approach to this question.

---

will see only 4 in Bac Ky and a fifth in Trung Ky came into existence before August by which time the old delineation was largely superceded.

[67] Resolutions of the Bac Ky Revolutionary Military Conference, 15–20 April, 1945, quoted in *LSQD*, p. 137.

[68] Truong Chinh, *Cach Mang Thang Tam*, (The August Revolution), Hanoi, Fifth Edition, 1955, p. 13.

[69] *LSQD*, p. 140.

[70] Ibid., pp. 140–141.

The manual, *Japanese Resistance Work in Rear Areas: Questions and Answers*,[71] poses and answers a series of thirty five questions. These begin by establishing that 'rear area work is very important' because 'the rear area is our base, the origin of our vanguard'. A series of questions and answers then deal with the election of 'people's committees' which were necessary to organise the mass organisations. Finally, the manual deals with concrete kinds of community support that the mass organisations would have to channel to the army:

Q. What is the People's Government's position with respect to the people who work for it?
A. At the beginning when the Government does not yet have finances it can only help officials and army men to a limited extent and order the people to help their families. For example, a family with a person in the ranks of the revolutionary army will receive help in plowing, transplanting, collecting firewood, and carrying water from the other people in the village. When a soldier's parents are sick then the village committee looks after them etc. When the property of Vietnamese traitors is divided up then those families receive the first portions.
Q. What do we mean by mobilising the people to participate in the resistance war?
A. (For the people) resistance war . . . means helping by organising the elimination of traitors, the setting up of self-defence guards, organising armed units, carrying out scorched earth tactics (*lam vuon khong nha trong*), destroying roads and bridges, and mobilising people to join the army . . .
Q. What can the people in rear areas do to help the Liberation Army?
A. a) Establish Liberation Army supply stores that are stocked with the help of the people or the confiscated paddy of Vietnamese traitors that support the Japanese.
b) Help with clothing, medicinal herbs, food, shoes, etc . . .
c) Help by guiding the army along the road. When the Liberation Army is launched into battle then the self defence

[71]Ban Bien Tap Bo Chinh Tri Khu Giai Phong Xuat Ban [Published by the Editorial Committee of the Political Department of the Liberated Zone], *Cong Tac Khang Nhat Hau Phuong: Van Dap* [Japanese Resistance Work in Rear Areas: Questions and Answers], Viet Bac, May? 1945. This does not appear to be a translation from Chinese as some other manuals in use at the time were. See the bibliography, section 3, under Viet Nam Giai Phong Quan for manuals that have, or very likely have been translated from Chinese. The first manual listed under this heading states explicitly that is a translation from Chinese, and the kindred subject matter of the other two manuals listed suggests that the same is true of them. Perhaps *Cong Tac Khang Nhat* was an original Vietnamese manual because it dealt with specifically Vietnamese problems.

forces help by carrying their equipment, preparing the battle field, and rescuing the wounded.
d) Mobilising ever greater numbers of youth, men, and women to join the ranks of the Liberation Army.[72]

In fact, what we have here is a clear explanation of those well worn words, 'People's War, People's Army'.[73] At every level of military enterprise the entire population in liberated areas was to be linked to the army in a corporate effort to expand it. To use a military metaphor, armed force units were merely spear heads. The shafts which propelled them were the mass political, social, and economic organisations which mobilised the support of the entire population. Or, in more binding terms, Vo Nguyen Giap serves us well with a metaphor from the science of chemistry: the military, he says, was 'organically'[74] related to the body politic. Therefore, it is of fundamental importance to the history of the People's Army to understand that armed units were bound to the society in a complex web of political-military relationships, and it is by no means coincidental that this organic relationship was reinforced in the army's training.

Like its predecessors, the Bac Son Guerrilla Unit, The Army for National Salvation, and the Propaganda and Liberation Units, the Liberation Army was trained in its social and political as well as its military roles. In addition to instruction in drill, weapons, and guerrilla tactics according to the principle of 'old soldiers lead new soldiers, skilled people help unskilled people',[75] soldiers studied the ten point Viet Minh aims and the ten point disciplinary code which forbade such things as rough talk, bathing in front of women, and 'taking as much as a needle and thread from the people.'[76] Moreover, after the April military conference gave orders 'to unify political and military training',[77] and Hoang Van Thai opened the Official Japanese Resistance Military School for Liberation Army cadres near Tan Trao in July, surviving training manuals show that the aim of the School's courses was

To create a number of command cadres and political cadres with the ability to command a platoon and become the soul and

---

[72]Ibid., pp. 10–11.

[73]This is of course the title of the famous collection of articles on Liberation War by Vo Nguyen Giap first published in 1961 and followed by several editions.

[74]See Vo Nguyen Giap's introductory essay in Ho Chi Minh, *Ve Dau Tranh*, p. 79. Here Giap actually uses the word 'huu co' or 'organic' to describe the relationship between the military and the political as Ho saw it. However, I believe my extrapolation is justified because this was clearly Giap's and the ICP's perception too.

[75]*LSQD*, pp. 139–140.

[76]See Chapter 3, note 96.

[77]*LSQD*, pp. 135–136. *CMCD*, 11, p. 67.

strength of the National Salvation Army. Therefore, this training program consists of two parts; one part military, and one part political work in the army. The military part is based on the knowledge necessary for a person to command a company.[78]

On the military side, the manuals reveal a sophisticated grasp of training techniques such that trainee platoon commanders in any modern army would have found familiar. From basic drill and parade ground manoeuvres training progressed through a series of graded lessons in squad, platoon, and company operations, and all the elements of guerrilla tactics were practiced: scouting, patrolling, night patrolling, night firing, attacking, withdrawing, dispersing, and use of terrain.[79] As groups of 100 students[80] were rotated through the courses that probably lasted no longer than two weeks in the beginning, the training must have been very compressed and its quality at this stage should not be over-rated. Nevertheless, this was not a military training program for a band of raffish rebels. It was a well conceived and properly constructed course of instruction for a modern army that was confident in its legitimate relationship with the rest of society.

This relationship becomes concrete when the political part of the course is considered. According to the manuals of the Japanese Resistance Military School, political training was carried out in informal lectures and guided group discussions (*thao luan*) on a range of subjects which set the army's internal politics and discipline within the broadest political framework. For example, the six subjects laid down for theoretical consideration were:

1. The spirit of responsibility and discipline of cadres.
2. The world situation.
3. The situation in Indochina.
4. The revolution of (national) liberation.
5. The manner of carrying out tasks and leadership.
6. Political work for leaders.[81]

Internal military discipline and political work was thus integrated into a vertical hierarchy of revolutionary political relationships on a world scale. Then, in the syllabus for practical political training for cadres,

[78]Ban Bien Tap Bo Chinh Tri Khu Giai Phong Xuat Ban [Published by the Editorial Committee of the Political Department of the Liberated Zone], *Muc Dich va Phuong Phap Huan Luyen* [The Aims and Methods of Training], May? 1945, p. 1.

[79]Ibid., pp. 2–14. see also Viet Nam Giai Phong Quan [Vietnam Liberation Army], *Phan Tich Dong Tac Quan Su* [an Analysis of Military Work], Hanoi, 1945, pp. 1–11.

[80]*LSQD*, p. 141.

[81]*Muc Dich va Phuong Phap Huan Luyen*, pp. 14–15.

the dynamics of the army's integration with the local society can be seen in the balance that was set up between work 'inside the unit' (*doi noi*) and work 'outside the unit' (*doi ngoai*).

Practical political work 'inside the unit' consisted of students preparing political documents for the army, writing political slogans, and organising theatrical performances that would 'forge' keen and discipline fighters. Complementary political work 'outside the unit' was then practiced:

> Groups go to make propaganda, organise the people, (arrange) banners, and write mass training slogans. They organise meetings to unite the army and people, carry out practical efforts to help the miserable masses, and organise welcoming parties for people who support the school or local community.[82]

The training of cadres at the Japanese Resistance Military School therefore shows that by mid-1945 the army was taught to think of itself as a fighting force whose internal constitution grew out of a reciprocal relationship with the society that directly sustained it. Army units certainly had their own group solidarity and institutional identity. They were after all the community's fighting arm. (In 1945 and 1946 it was also still possible for units to follow the 'feudal' practice of identifying with individual commanders.) However, the army's internal stability and particular identity could only be maintained if the army was politically relevant in the society, and this meant the army had to be seen to champion mass social and political objectives. Put another way, the military simply could not function let alone expand unless it was capable of exerting a significant political influence in the society.

It must be remembered, however, that neither the regular Liberation Army nor its training had much direct influence beyond the Viet Bac before August 1945. When the need 'to reorganise self defence units and guerrilla cells into units of the Liberation Army outside the Liberated Zone'[83] was stressed at Tan Trao in May we are again reminded of how myriad irregular self defence forces and guerrilla units had already sprung up outside ambit of Liberation Army, ICP, or even Viet Minh control. Conversely, it is clear that the level of political action and organisation by ICP and Viet Minh cadres determined the level of development in the armed forces. If mass organisations were not strong and linked up in a region, the resources necessary to 'emancipate' (*thoat ly*) people from work in the fields for the creation of regular units could not be mobilised. And when a

---

[82]Ibid., p. 15.
[83]*LSQD*, p. 159; *VKQS*, p. 310. Emphasis added.

region was thus limited to irregular units their level of training would be low, so that any idea of coordinated action according to the plans of higher commands could be forgotten for some time to come.

Yet once the Vietnamese revolution had erupted and the April Military Conference began to restructure its anti-Japanese resistance campaign, the Viet Minh had begun to push the level of political organisation along in large areas of the northern countryside. Around this time the sources begin to register the names of important cadres like Nguyen Binh, To Huu, Nguyen Chi Thanh, and Vuong Thua Vu who often had to break out of jail before they organised regional propaganda drives about the Liberation Army and the Liberated Zone.[84] Needless to say, they went on to develop the Viet Minh's political infrastructure, set up self defence forces and guerrilla units, and open many political and military training courses. Although it would be at least another year before there would be anything like an integrated main force and regional force structure, the tendency was already for independent regional developments to be linked together and reinforced by armed propaganda.

The Armed Propaganda Campaign

Between May and August armed propaganda was used to establish five war zones (*chien khu*) out of those which had been delineated at the April conference. The first of these was naturally the Viet Bac Zone which had been liberated by April. The Second War Zone (Quang Trung) covered the provinces of Hoa Binh, Ninh Binh, and Thanh Hoa by May; the Third War Zone (Hoang Hoa Tam) covered Phu Tho and Yen Bai Provinces by June; the Fourth War Zone was established in the northeastern provinces of Quang Yen and Hai Duong by July; and the Fifth War Zone in Trung Ky (Phan Dinh Phung) delineated a northern area of operations around Vinh Thuy and a southern area around Nui Lon in Quang Ngai Province south of Hue by May.[85] Since there is no need to say more about the way army was expanding in the Viet Bac, we may therefore go straight out into the other War Zones where the official history generally stresses the effectiveness of the 'armed propaganda'[86] campaign, but does not

---

[84]Many jail breaks are mentioned in the sources. For example, *LSQD*, p. 128; *CMTT*, 1, p. 73; *CMTT*, 2, p. 8, p. 34, p. 49, pp. 50–51; and Vuong Thua Vu, *Truong Thanh trong Chien Dau* [Coming of Age in War], Hanoi: NXB Quan Doi Nhan Dan, 1979, pp. 28–43 has a long account of a break out at Nghia Lo.

[85]Foreign Languages Publishing House, *History of the August Revolution*, pp. 100–105; *LSQD*, pp. 147–154; *CMCD*, 9, p. 85.

[86]*LSQD*, p. 147–148.

necessarily give a good sense of the resistances it had to overcome.

A particular problem in the Second War Zone was the relatively strong resistance of the old regime. As sizeable contingents from Tran Trong Kim's security forces continued to move around the province trying to collect taxes, a number of Self Defence Force soldiers were killed in some skirmishing with them. One attack on a plantation at Da Nam in Thanh Hoa by Self Defence Forces from nearby villages also failed on 12 May when four of the attackers were killed.[87] But while such difficulties were compounded by the 'struggle'[88] which assault propaganda teams had to suppress Dai Viet elements in May, and Japanese patrols in May and June that committed atrocities in Thanh Hoa, destroyed a Buddhist Temple, and commandeered a quantity of rice earmarked for famine relief,[89] they were not insurmountable. On the contrary, as they provided the Viet Minh with good propaganda, at least those problems posed by the Security Forces and the Japanese tended to stimulate rather than restrain political-military expansion.

Quynh Luu and Lu Phong in Ninh Binh therefore became increasingly important base areas for the Second War Zone by early May, and an armed forces training centre had opened. By the end of the month Vuong Thua Vu had also begun another school for cadres at Phu Long village which had two intakes of forty five cadres from surrounding provinces per month. Furthermore, two new units of the National Liberation Army were formed locally. The first of these, formed on 20 May with forty one people and twenty one rifles, was the Vietnam Propaganda Liberation Army Unit. The second, which was formed by forty people not long after a half day battle with Japanese troops on 4 July, was the Second Liberation Army Platoon of Quynh Luu. The creation of 'many other self defence units, especially a platoon of emancipated women under comrade Que'[90] also accompanied the formation of these two main force units.

In the Third War Zone significant resistance to the armed propaganda campaign came again from conservative groups which revolutionary histories describe as 'Vietnamese traitors'[91] because of their alliances with the Japanese. These included Dai Viet and VNQDD elements. Nevertheless, many Viet Minh propaganda meetings and attacks on grain stores had led to the creation of numerous armed

---

[87]*CMTT*, Vol. 1, pp. 383–388.
[88]Ibid., p. 384.
[89]Ibid., p. 384, p. 387.
[90]Ibid., pp. 368–370.
[91]For example, this term is used extensively in the account of Phu Tho Province in Ibid., pp. 143–162.

units by mid year and the generally high prestige of the Viet Minh. In Phu Tho one particular victory over the Security Forces in March gave a further fillip to military expansion, as guerrilla units up to sixty and seventy people strong now appeared in the province.[92] In Yen Bai there were similar developments as clashes with Japanese forces and Bao An in early July made such good propaganda that there were 'over 500 people' in armed units and military courses were in operation in that province.[93]

In the Fourth War Zone, where the future commander of the Nam Bo resistance, Nguyen Binh (Nguyen Phuong Thao), first became prominent, the extreme weakness of the old regime was itself a problem because of the depredations it encouraged by bandit groups along Colonial Route 18 between Bac Ninh and Mong Cai.[94] But as at least the worst of these depredations were stopped by a combination of negotiations and repression in June, the weakness of the old regime in the Fourth War Zone had other advantages for the Viet Minh as it led to a series of defections by Tran Trong Kim's Security Forces.

In the Fourth War Zone the sources stress the shortage of weapons which the Viet Minh initially experienced in March as youth groups ran around looking for Viet Minh cadres to direct them.[95] But by May, after some intensive propaganda operations, many defections from the Security Forces and such windfalls as a Hotchkiss machine gun taken from a Japanese ship at Hai Phong, the scarcity of arms was eased. Many posts and grain stores were then taken 'easily' by local 'guerrilla units'. Half-hearted Japanese attempts to repress the revolutionary movement from around 10 June had no effect at all unless that was to stimulate political-military development. By June political training courses for groups of fifty cadres were also under way at Bac Ma Temple.[96] Therefore, by June-July the area was effectively liberated, Viet Minh and National Salvation Organisations had 'sprung up like mushrooms' and

> from a position (in March) where regional revolutionaries did not have a single weapon to defend themselves, (they had reached) a position where they had 970 weapons of various kinds; formed concentrated guerrilla units with a strength of almost 5,000 (not counting regional units); taken ten military posts and two Quoc Dan Dang and Dai Viet training

[92]Ibid., p. 146.
[93]Ibid., pp. 170–171.
[94]Ibid., p. 215.
[95]Ibid., p. 217.
[96]Ibid., pp. 218–235; *LSQD*, p. 150.

camps; . . . exterminated and scattered many bandit groups; and established security for the people.[97]

Furthermore, by August units in the region could boast that they

already know how to destroy bridges, to destroy roads . . . to paralyse enemy movement; in deploying the army we always know how to move from this place to another place to conceal our movements from the enemy . . .[98]

And here we have a good example of how the capacity for planned and coordinated action tended to increase with the level of organisation and training in a region. Political development then tended to be commensurate with strategic flexibility, for at Dong Trieu, Chi Linh, Mao Khe, and Trach Bang Revolutionary People's Committees were soon in place.

Finally, in the Fifth War Zone were Nguyen Chi Thanh and To Huu were at work, developments were not as spectacular as they were in the others. From March moves to establish Viet Minh infrastructure and Self Defence Forces in Quang Tri were made, but it was not until July that various factions working in the province were unified, anti-Japanese propaganda was widely disseminated, and a National Liberation Committee established.[99] By early August there were probably several thousand people in the local self defence forces. However, when one history says that 'news of the continuous victories of the army of the Soviet Union'[100] spurred movement on in Quang Tri after July we are reminded that developments in even the least developed War Zone in Vietnam cannot be separated from international events. For these events constituted the wider international context in which the armed forces of the new Vietnamese nation were growing.

From the Japanese point of view, the rapid deterioration of their position in the Pacific forced their Army in Vietnam to protect its rear. This had been the motivation for the March coup and, although the official history overstates the 'many patrols'[101] the Japanese made across the Lo River and into the Second and Fourth War Zones from May, it was also the motivation for what another Vietnamese source has accurately described as the 'scattered'[102] Japanese actions in

[97]Ibid., p. 233–234.
[98]Ibid., p. 234.
[99]Ibid., Vol. 2, p. 51.
[100]Ibid., pp. 51–52.
[101]*LSQD*, p. 143.
[102]*CMCD*, 11, p. 75 describes the Japanese as '*le te*' (scattered or sparse), and p. 76 says the Japanese were essentially restricted to the towns. Major Thomas, 'Report on

these areas. But as we have seen these confused Japanese military actions tended to stimulate the internal development of the Viet Minh's armed forces, they also had the effect of reinforcing the internal development because of the external support they attracted for the Viet Minh.

By late 1944 Americans in the China theatre were aware that the Viet Minh had given assistance to an American pilot named Shaw who had been shot down over Tonkin. We also know that Ho Chi Minh made a special visit to Kunming in late 1944 to talk to the American Air Force Commander, General Chennault, about the possibility of support for the Viet Minh's anti-Japanese resistance.[103] By early July 1945 the Americans were then saying that 'there were about 3,000 armed guerrillas in Tonkin'[104] who were hostile to the Japanese. Consequently, the decision was taken to parachute a small party—the Deer Mission—into Tuyen Quang under a Major Thomas to link up with the Viet Minh and 'set up a base near the Hanoi-Lang Son road and railroad, and to destroy, blow up, and render useless as much of the road and railroad as possible'. 'Secondary to this was the gathering of intelligence'[105] on Japanese movements.

After Major Thomas and two other members of his party landed unceremoniously in the trees of Tuyen Quang on 16 July they were 'greeted by 200 armed guards of the Viet Minh party . . . a very impressive reception committee'. Speeches were exchanged and 'we were introduced to Mr Hoo, party leader, who welcomed us and presented us with a fatted calf and some Hanoi beer for our supper.'[106] But what also impressed Major Thomas was that on the same day the Deer Mission landed in Tuyen Quang a strong Liberation Army force of 500 had significantly assaulted the nearby post of Tam Dao, garrisoned by twenty to forty Japanese troops and seventy members of the old Indigenous Guard. Indeed, Major Thomas thought it worth mentioning in his report that when the Liberation Army overran the garrison and killed at least eight of the Japanese they 'suffered casualties in so doing'.[107] Together with the impressive reception committee and the beer and fatted calf, the attack on Tam Dao was clearly part of a propaganda campaign to gain American

---

the Deer Mission', in *Hearings before the Committee on Foreign Relations United States Senate, Ninety Second Congress, Second Session on Causes, Origins, and Reasons of the Vietnam War*, Washington, May 9, 10, and 11, 1972, p. 260 notes that the Japanese did not even patrol the main road from Phuc Linh to Thai Nguyen.

[103]Chen, *Vietnam and China*, p. 93; Hoang Van Hoan, *Giot Nuoc*, pp. 245–246.

[104]Thomas, 'Report on the Deer Mission', p. 256.

[105]Ibid., p. 251.

[106]Ibid., pp. 256–257.

[107]Ibid., p. 258. *LSQD*, p. 150.

support. And it worked, for, on the strength of their good impression of the Viet Minh's potential as a fighting force, the Americans began to airdrop some 5,000 weapons to the Liberation Army and trained about 100 soldiers in their use—'the boys picked it up fast'.[108]

Meanwhile, the political impact of this American support was at least as important as the military. Jean Sainteny, who arrived in Hanoi in late August, gives us some idea of this impact in his memoirs when he describes the propaganda value of American aid to the Viet Minh. According to him there was a widely held opinion among the people that U.S. aircraft regularly flying over Hanoi by this time

> were those of the young Viet Minh Air Force based at secret aerodromes in the mountain region. The proof of this was after all marked on the wings of these aircraft where the population could distinguish the star which figured on the new red flag of Vietnam.[109]

Clearly, the significance of international support for the Viet Minh cannot be computed in ordinary terms. American aircraft certainly dropped 5,000 modern weapons to the Viet Minh by early August, and this has allowed historians to establish a perfect symmetry between the weapons and the strength of the Liberation Army which they say was also 5,000 by this time.[110] But what this figure camouflages is that the 5,000 soldiers and weapons merely represented the tip of the political-military pyramid, and that beneath it the impact of international support was already reinforcing the internal constitution of the armed forces of the new Vietnamese nation, such that 150,000 to 200,000 people were probably in the irregular armed units

[108]Ibid., p. 259–260. As if to highlight Allied confusion about what was happening in Vietnam some of the 5,000 weapons were dropped by the British (using US aircraft) to French commandos holding out in the Sino-Vietnamese border area. Obviously the Viet Minh got to them first. See McAlister, 'The Origins', pp. 164–167 for a discussion of the 5,000 weapons.

[109]Jean Sainteny, *Histoire d'un paix manquée*, Paris, 1967, p. 124. Hoang Van Hoan, *Giot Nuoc*, p. 245 tells us there was in fact some talk amongst the Viet Minh about building a small airstrip in the Viet Bac for the purpose of receiving American aid, and this idea may have been circulated in the propaganda campaign. Another example of the influence of early Viet Minh forays into 'foreign affairs' came in late August in Saigon. In fact, one major reason for the Viet Minh's ascendancy over numerous other parties manoeuvering for power was the ability of the southern Viet Minh leader, Tran Van Giau, to build up the argument that his was the only party 'strongly supported by the Allies with arms, equipment, and training'. Quoted in Patti, *Why Viet Nam?*, p. 186.

[110]See note 3 above.

by August, and countless thousands more were involved in mass organisations that had linked up to support them.

These figures do not mean that political-military developments were even, and in many areas knowledge of the Viet Minh was still quite vague in early August. Vietnamese sources are correct to be quiet about the Catholic Bishoprics of Phat Diem and Bui Chu in Bac Ky, most of the area from Nghe An to Thua Thien in Trung Ky, and all of Nam Ky. But by early August at the latest, the Viet Minh had a continuous system of political-military linkages, that is, a system of interrelated People's Committees and regional armed units, from the Liberated Zone in the Viet Bac region to the northeast coast through the Fourth War Zone, and to Thanh Hoa in northern Trung Ky through the Second and Third War Zones. The Fifth War Zone in Quang Tri and Quang Ngai to the south of Hue also had at least tenuous communication links with the Liberated Zone.

At the administrative head of this superstructure stood the Provisional Leadership Committee. It had a Political Department, a General Staff, a Department of Finances and Economy, a Department of Communications, a Department of Culture and Social Welfare. At the military head of this superstructure were the regular units of the Liberation Army. But once again the political, administrative, and military elements of the quasi-Viet Minh Government must be linked up. The Leadership Committee's General Staff clearly had a military function, and so too did all the other departments in one way or another. For instance, the Political Department was responsible for mobilisation.[111]

The importance of this extensive armed propaganda success for an understanding of the development of the People's Army and the Vietnamese Revolution is thus twofold. First, established notions about the size and nature of Viet Minh military expansion between March and August must be discarded as too simplistic: Fall's idea that the Japanese Resistance War was 'minute', and Duiker's that the Viet Minh's armed forces were 'minuscule'. Secondly, our expanded understanding of how the army developed in an organic relationship with the society necessitates a reevaluation of the events of August which brought the Viet Minh to power in all the major centers in Vietnam. Indeed, the expansion of the armed propaganda campaign from north to south and from the countryside into the urban centers must now be seen as an indispensible condition for the revolutionary events of August.

---

[111]Khanh, *Vietnamese Communism*, p. 312.

Armed Propaganda and the Seizure of Power in August

Once the Americans had dropped their atomic bombs on Japan in early August the fate of the Japanese regime in Indochina was sealed like the French regime before it. With foreknowledge of the Japanese surrender on 14 August Ho Chi Minh convened a National Party Congress at Tan Trao on the 13th and issued 'Military Order Number 1': 'The hour of the general insurrection (*tong khoi nghia*) has arrived. This is the opportunity for the People's Army of Vietnam (*Quan Dan Viet Nam*) to seize power and national independence'.[112] Here it should be stressed that the term 'Liberation Army' was not used, for it could provide little more than a model for political-military development outside the Viet Bac. What 'Military Order Number 1' envisaged was the seizure of power by people all over the country whose political and military organisation had hardly begun. The organisation of the People's Army would grow out of the uprisings themselves. But while the opportunity for the People's Army to expand on a national scale was certainly at hand, the order's use of the term 'general insurrection' is open to serious question.

The term *tong khoi nghia* is translated into English as 'general insurrection' or 'general uprising'. The meaning of '*tong*' is 'general', and, while there are no linguistic difficulties here, important conceptual problems are exposed when it is remembered that from at least the Eighth Plenum of the ICP's Central Committee in 1941 the concept of a series of 'partial' (*tung phan*)[113] insurrections was stressed. How, then, could there have been a 'general' insurrection in the second half of August when revolutionary power had already been established in some parts of the country after the 9 March coup, and the Viet Minh's propaganda units had already worked their way into many other areas?

By 1963 an awareness of this problem prompted some Party writers in Vietnam to argue that 'the insurrection began in the countryside and concluded in the cities'.[114] Then by 1970, Le Thanh Nghi, who

---

[112]Quoted in *LSQD*, p. 159. For full text see *CMCD*, XII, pp. 21–22.

[113]Resolutions of the Eighth Congress of the ICP's Central Committee quoted in *LSQD*, p. 73.

[114]'Tim Hieu Tinh Chat va Dac Diem cua Cach Mang Thang Tam' ['An Investigation of the Character and Special Points of the August Revolution'], *Su That*, Hanoi, 1963, p. 61. Also see Ho Hai, 'Mot Vai Y Kien ve Moi Quan He giua Nong Thon va Thanh Thi Nuoc Ta trong Thoi Ky 1939–1945' [A Few Ideas on the Relationship between the Countryside and the Cities in the Period 1939–1945], *NCLS*, pp. 12–19, especially p. 18 which argues that the nature of the August revolution was not 'simple' and tends to give more weight to the revolutionary impetus from countryside than that in the cities.

commanded the Second War Zone between April and August 1945, correctly pointed out that

> When speaking of the August Revolution, it must be remembered that regional insurrection movements had already broken out in many parts of the country from 9 March to August 1945.[115]

Clearly, there had been no 'general' insurrection in August 1945 and thus no 'August Revolution' in the literal sense of the term. There had rather been a series of revolutionary insurrections that began on March 9 and culminated in the cities *in August* once Japanese power there was eliminated by the Americans. But this is only the beginning of the problem. The complex question of why the ICP used the term 'general insurrection' in 1945 if it did not accurately describe events still remains, and to gain a purchase on this question it is necessary to examine the ICP's use of the term *khoi nghia*.

As previously mentioned the term *khoi nghia* was an ancient one used to describe a morally sanctioned 'righteous uprising' against corrupt and foreign imposed central authority. As it then came into the twentieth century through the writings of literati like Phan Boi Chau the term retained its old meaning to the extent that it pervaded popular perceptions during all the major uprisings against the French colonial authority with the possible exception of ICP inspired soviet movement in Nghe-Tinh in 1930–31. Moreover, in Phan Boi Chau's novel, *The Secret History of Trung Quang*,[116] the 'righteous uprising' gained its momentum in the countryside as the 'righteous army' (*nghia quan*) established the same kind of political-military links the Viet Minh had established in the society by August 1945, before it finally spilt over into the administrative centers once the main enemy garrisons there had tired of the struggle. The difficulty with this conception for radical intellectuals in 1945, however, was that so much of their anti-colonial thinking in the 1930s had been permeated by their commitment to the doctrines of proletarian internationalism.

We saw in chapter 2 that a range of Marxist-Leninist terms dominated the radical literature of the 1930s. While an old term like '*khoi nghia*' thus went into eclipse, Ho Chi Minh's revolutionary vanguard in *The Road To Revolution* was 'to make revolution' (*lam cach mang*). Other typical term in ICP documents were 'armed violence' (*vu trang bao dong*) and 'armed struggle' (*vu trang dau tranh*). But,

---

[115]Le Thanh Nghi, *Con Duong Cach Mang*, p. 22.

[116]Phan Boi Chau, *Trung Quang Tam Su* [The Secret History of Trung Quang], written in Canton and first published there in a military magazine between 1921 and 1925, Hanoi, 1971.

while French power had precluded any possibility of a revolutionary insurrection in the 1930s and ICP documents could say what they liked because they would never be tested, this would not be the case after the outbreak of the Second World War. Now, when revolution was really in the air, the radical literati were forced to make a conscious effort to relate the revolution to Vietnam's cultural traditions and so the old word *'khoi nghia'*[117] reappeared with a vengeance. Yet when it did reappear around the time of the ICP's Eighth Plenum in May 1941, the old meaning of the word was if not confused, then complicated by the new use which radicals gave it.

On the one hand, the Viet Minh had clearly found it necessary to employ the word *khoi nghia* for the power of its old meaning to communicate a meaningful political message to the people. In 1945 the Viet Minh also used the word to describe revolutionary events in both rural and urban centers so that the old conception of the uprising spreading from the countryside and finally engulfing the administrative centers was maintained. Yet there is still no doubt that when Marxists use the word to describe the events of August they mean to convey a sense of what they perceived to be a Russian style urban insurrection. For example, in the 1955 Vietnamese language edition of Truong Chinh's 1946 publication, *The August Revolution*, under heading *'Khoi Nghia Thang Tam'* the words *'Ngay 19, ca thu do dung day'*[118] are written. When the 1977 Hanoi English language edition is consulted we find the heading is translated as 'The August Insurrection' and the words as 'On 19 August, the entire capital rose up'.[119] From internal evidence in the Vietnamese edition, and a comparison of the two editions, what Truong Chinh means by *khoi nghia* is clear: an 'insurrection' in which the urban masses 'rose up'. Hence, the use of the word *khoi nghia*, and, by extension, the use of the term *tong khoi nghia* in the literature poses a fundamental dilemma which stems from the introduction of revolutionary theories based on Marx's critique of capitalism into an agrarian society.

The revolutionary literature is rooted in a conceptual disjunction which reflects the need of a small technologically backward nation to find appropriate international support for its desire for independence in the modern world. Because Hanoi theoreticians have not generally acknowledged this dilemma, they have therefore tended to explain the events of August in unconvincing terms. The 'August Revolution', they were fond of saying in the 1960s, was characterised by its

---

[117]For example, the Nam Ky uprising in 1940 is referred to as a 'khoi nghia' in resolutions of the Eighth Plenum in *VKQS*, p. 183.

[118]Truong Chinh, *Cach Mang Thang Tam*, Hanoi, 1955, pp. 14–15.

[119]Truong Chinh, *The August Revolution*, in *Selected Works*, Hanoi, 1977, p. 18, p. 20.

'rural-urban balance' and the ICP's masterly 'combination' or 'coordination' of political and military action.[120] Other theoreticians like William Turley have also claimed more recently that the military played a 'supportive' role in 'the August Revolution'.[121] However, the primitive state of Viet Minh communications and lack of centralised control rules out the view from Hanoi—the 13 August order for the 'general insurrection' at Tan Trao was not received by the Hanoi City Committee until the 16th—and our expanded understanding of the army's organic relationship with its social base makes Turley's view seem very narrow. What must be done about the events of August, therefore, is to discard existing theories and describe the culmination of a good old fashioned *khoi nghia* updated to take account of modern conditions in its application of armed propaganda.[122]

[120]For an introduction to theories on the 'August Revolution' see Duiker, *The Communist Road*, pp. 100–105, and Woodside, *Community and Revolution*, pp. 225–234. These works contain references to relevant Vietnamese readings. In addition to these readings there are a number of others which deal specifically with the relative roles of political and military action in the Vietnamese Revolution. See Le Quoc Su, 'Kheo Ket Hop Cac Hinh Thuc Dau Tranh Chinh Tri va Vu Trang trong Cach Mang Thang Tam' [The Skillful Combination of Political and Military Forms of Struggle in the August Revolution'], *NCLS*, No. 50, May 1963; and To Minh Trung's answer to Le Quoc Su in an article of the same title in *NCLS*, No. 53, August 1963. The following should also be consulted: Nguyen Cong Binh, 'Khoi Dau va Ket Thuc cua Cach Mang Thang Tam' ['The Beginning and End of the August Revolution'], *NCLS*, No. 51, June 1963; and Truong Chinh, 'Mot So Van De ve Cach Mang Thang Tam' ['A Number of Questions About the August Revolution'], *Hoc Tap*, No. 92, September 1963.

[121]William turley, 'The Vietnamese Army', in Jonathan R. Adelman ed., *Communist Armies in Politics*, Boulder, Colorado: Westview Press, 1982, p. 66.

[122]There is of course the doctrine of the spontaneous uprising which is a mystical one because it means that uprisings can occur for no external reason. Duiker, *The Communist Road*, p. 321, is one who emphasises the role of 'spontaneity' in revolutions. He distinguishes this 'spontaneity' from political 'manipulation' by the communists, but this is a false distinction. French imperialism, the application of electrical currents to people's genitals in French torture chambers, the famine, the Japanese coup, and the destruction of Japanese power at Hiroshima and Nagasaki could hardly be seen to constitute political manipulation by the Viet Minh. However, I would be surprised if Duiker did not acknowledge that such phenomena were external causes of the Vietnamese revolution. In other words, just because there was no ICP leadership, control, or political manipulation in many places this does not mean there were no external causes of the revolution, that it was spontaneous. By deflecting attention from the external causes of revolutions the mystical idea of 'spontaneity' can then protect the limited idea of 'manipulation' when the two ideas are deployed as complements. Because 'spontaneity' can be used to 'fill in' where 'manipulation' breaks down, 'manipulation' tends to be left unchallenged and so retains an influence that is out of proportion to what it can really explain.

The largely unopposed seizure of power in the cities was characterised by an urban extension of armed propaganda, which Truong
Chinh identified as the 'armed demonstration'.[123] This generally
meant that self defence forces, armed propaganda units, and youth
groups from the countryside took over public facilities in the capitals
and delivered speeches as semi-armed crowds of peasants also came
to town. However, these demonstrations did not occur according to
some master plan by the ICP. What is most remarkable about
'Military Order Number 1' and its call for the 'general insurrection'
on the 13th is that not many people received it. As Truong Chinh
noted in his 1955 edition of *The August Revolution*, 'many places' had
not yet received the order for 'the general insurrection' when people
began to 'rise up in front of the confused Japanese'.[124] In fact, people
without instructions from the ICP or the Viet Minh had been rising
up in many places since March. When news of the Japanese surrender began to circulate in August, armed demonstrations would have
brought the rural revolution into the cities with or without 'Military
Order Number 1' for the 'general insurrection'.

The Viet Bac is one place where it might be argued that the seizure
of power was not unopposed, for armed demonstrations there involved Liberation Army attacks on Japanese garrisons at Thai
Nguyen and Tuyen Quang. At Thai Nguyen, for example, where '30
to 40' Japanese were garrisoned, there was intermittent firing between the 21st and the 25th.[125] But when the Viet Bac had been 'the
Liberated Zone' since May, and the only casualty at Thai Nguyen
appears to have been a Japanese woman civilian shot through the
arm, this demonstration of military might was hardly essential to the
seizure of power. The 'battle' for Thai Nguyen was thus an armed
propaganda operation which the Liberation Army mounted to enhance its own heroic image, and to reinforce the effect of less
militarised demonstrations in the rest of the country.

In Bac Giang, after months of mobilisation in the countryside and
some land reform, around 1,000 self defence and guerrilla soldiers
were ready to seize power. The Province Chief and the Indigenous
Guard then handed the capital over to a ten man Self Defence Unit
when it entered the public buildings on the 18th, and crowds
gathered.[126] In Ha Tinh after a large meeting on the 15th to tell

[123]Truong Chinh, *Cach Mang Thang Tam*, p. 23.

[124]Ibid., p. 15. This reference which shows that the ICP and the Viet Minh did not
have communications with 'many places' has been deleted from the 1977 English
language edition of the work. See Truong Chinh, *The August Revolution*, Hanoi, 1977,
p. 20.

[125]Thomas, 'Report on the Deer Mission', p. 261.

people about the situation inside the country and outside the country, and to 'introduce the Cao-Bac-Lang War Zone' seven truck loads of self defence fighters motored into the capital from the countryside and marched into the bank and the administrative offices on the 17th. On the 18th an armed demonstration marked the final seizure of power in Ha Tinh,[127] as it also did in Hai Duong where one history says the situation in the countryside had been 'ripe' for some time.[128]

On the 19th power was then seized in Hanoi. In 1944 and the first half of 1945 where had been numerous strikes and meetings in the city as clandestine ICP cells organised some workers, and students. From around mid-1945 armed propaganda groups had also been entering the city from the countryside to stimulate urban military development. On one occasion in July, for instance, contemporary accounts tell how 'Armed Propaganda Brigades' brazenly entered the Ecole Professionnelle in the city and 'after posting sentries on the entrances the orators . . . called on the students to take up the struggle against the Japanese fascists. The Japanese soldiers entered when all was over.'[129] Nevertheless, the development of armed propaganda units and self defence forces in the city was not impressive by mid August, for the biggest problem local Party leaders had once the Japanese had surrendered and the countryside was rising around the city, was how they might arrange a sufficiently large demonstration of support for the Viet Minh.

This problem was solved by the Tran Trong Kim government. On the 17th it organised a mass meeting of functionaries in front of Hanoi's Opera House to try and bolster support for Bao Dai's regime, and the Viet Minh took it over. With armed propaganda activists located strategically in the crowd, red flags with gold stars rose above it. A short scuffle took place on the platform, impassioned speeches called on people to rally to the cause of national independence, and three shots were fired (into the air). Groups of Tran Trong Kim's security forces in the area then slung their rifles and joined the crowd as it marched off gaily in a downpour of rain to show its solidarity with the Viet Minh outside the Governor General's Palace.[130]

But as the rain continued, the local Party Committee was concerned that it might wash the urban revolution out unless extra action was taken. When the bad weather began there were perhaps 800 to

[126]*CMTT*, Vol. 1, pp. 207–210; *LSQD* p. 163.
[127]Ibid., Vol., 2, p. 27; *LSQD*, p. 163.
[128]Ibid., Vol., 1, p. 257.
[129]AOM, NF, C. 123, D. 1112. Vietnamese newspaper reports.
[130]*CMTT*, Vol. 1, pp. 36–41; *LSQD*, pp. 168–170; Patti, *Why Vietnam?*, p. 164–165.

900 workers, students, and 'peasant youths' with seventy weapons in the city's self defence forces. But one Hanoi history tells us that the rain 'dissolved' some of these forces which the Committee though were 'not very strong' and could not 'guarantee' the revolution in any case.[131] And so as 'peasant youths' already made up a proportion of the city's self defence forces, thousands of peasants armed with agricultural implements had to be mobilised 'outside the city' in Ha Dong and Bac Ninh to 'enter the city' under the supervision of Viet Minh armed propaganda teams on the 19th.[132] When the Viet Minh's Provisional Direction Committee to power in Hanoi, therefore, we see how the most effective part of its power base was still in the countryside, and how misleading it is to argue that 'the entire capital rose up'.

Nevertheless, the seizure of power in Hanoi had a great influence on political developments in the rest of the country. By the 22nd power had been seized in almost every northern province—Hoa Binh and Hai Phong had to wait until the following day—and in some provinces like Ninh Binh, where the urban seizures were notably 'easy', some of the demonstrations were more 'automatic' than armed. According to one source, however, there was a Liberation Army detachment under a Comrade Luong Nhan in Ninh Binh by the 19th, which on the 20th may have been involved in leading a large crowd of peasants into the capital with the Viet Minh flags flying and banners reading, 'Support the Viet Minh', 'Exterminate Vietnamese Traitors', and 'Overthrow the French and Japanese'.[133]

In central Vietnam the pattern of the rural revolution culminating in the cities was the same as news from the north flashed around the countryside. In fact, events in the central provinces offer a particularly good sense of the flash effect of armed propaganda. Many of these provinces had been spared by the famine and by July the general level of political and military development could not be compared with the north. Yet from early August working political-military links were established rapidly between the provinces as cadres moved around the countryside,[134] passing on what information and orders they had to help local committees to make operative decisions about their seizures of power. By at least mid-month self defence forces, assault propaganda and guerrilla units such as the famous Ba To Guerrilla Unit in Quang Ngai, and at least one main force Company were thus carrying out propaganda and mobilising

[131]Ibid., p. 41.
[132]Ibid., pp. 40–41, pp. 45–46.
[133]Ibid., p. 371.
[134]Ibid., Vol. 2, p. 160, p. 167.

people in the countryside for their march on the cities.[135] After news
of the seizure of power in Hanoi on the 19th, the seizure of most
central cities with armed demonstratons took place 'easily'[136] on the
22nd and 23rd. 'People's Tribunals' were then set up in a number of
areas, and at least four people were executed in Quang Tri and
another four in Khanh Hoa before the end of the month.[137]

In the meantime, the most important central city to be caught in
the flash was Hue. As the Ba To Guerrillas and other armed units
mobilised tens of thousands of peasants in the countryside for a
march on the Imperial Capital on the 22nd,[138] the Emperor Bao Dai
received a visit from the Imperial Post Master. A telegram had
arrived from 'A Committee of Patriots Representing All Sections and
All Strata of the Population'[139] in Hanoi, respectfully requesting that
his majesty abdicate. On the morning of the 23rd he then found
himself in splendid isolation as 'neither Tran Trong Kim nor any of
his ministers appeared at the palace. Only a few guards whose duty
was the opening and closing of doors lounged in the deserted
courts.'[140] In fact, thousands of peasants from outlying districts under
Viet Minh leadership had entered the city and power had already
passed into the hands of the Viet Minh. The stage was set for the
most central event in modern Vietnamese history: the abdication of
Bao Dai and the legitimisation of the country's first republican
government on a national scale.

Before Bao Dai actually abdicated on the 30th, however, the news
from Hanoi and Hue was the factor of overwhelming importance in
the seizure of power in Saigon on the 25th, and all other southern
provinces by the 28th. There had been no famine in the south, and
after the repression of the Nam Ky uprising in 1940 there was almost
no Viet Minh infrastructure in place to mobilise and organise revolutionary forces before at least July.[141] The most important armed

[135]*LSQD*, p. 162. *CMTT*, Vol. 2, p. 57 notes plans to set up 'Liberation Army' Unit,
along with self defence and security forces.
[136]This word is used to describe the seizure of power in many central provinces. For
example, see *CMTT*, Vol. 2, p. 15 for Nghe An, p. 100 for Quang Nam, p. 120 for
Quang Ngai, p. 153 for Phu Yen, p. 161 for Khanh Hoa.
[137]Ibid., p. 58, p. 163.
[138]*CMTT*, Vol. 2, pp. 84–86. Woodside, *Community and Revolution*, p. 230 drawing
on Vietnamese sources says that 150,000 people are claimed to have entered Hue
whose normal population was not more than 50,000.
[139]Bao Dai, *Le Dragon d'Annam*, p. 118.
[140]Ibid.
[141]By late 1944 there had been some signs of a revival. For an assessment of the Viet
Minh strength in the south see Jane Werner, 'The Cao Dai: The Politics of a
Vietnamese Syncretic Religious Movement', Cornell University PhD, 1976, pp.
256–261.

groups in the south therefore owed little if any of their development
to the Viet Minh. The Cao Dai Army was first formed by Cao Dai
dignitaries, the Advance Youth Guard was first formed by the French
in the Sports and Youth campaign, and both of these forces had been
taken over and trained by the Japanese by early 1945. Viet Minh
cadres and sympathisers had certainly infiltrated the ranks of the
Youth guard by this time. However, rather than declare an anti-
Japanese Resistance War, the Advance Youth Guard lined the
streets and organised big ceremonies in Saigon to welcome the
Japanese Governor, Minoda, when he arrived to take charge of Nam
Ky on 15 March.[142]

When the Japanese then handed their control of the south over to
the Bao Dai Government on 14 August, a United National Front,
composed largely of elements with long Japanese associations, took
control of the Saigon administration on the 16th and held it for a
week. On the 19th, the same day the Viet Minh came to power in
Hanoi, Bao Dai's Viceroy, Nguyen Van Sam, also arrived in Saigon
to take charge of a large quantity of arms which the Japanese handed
over for the creation of a militia.[143] Therefore, it was only after the
Viet Minh's culminating armed propaganda victories in Hanoi and
Hue caused word to circulate in Saigon on the 22nd that the Emperor
Boa Dai was going to ask the Viet Minh to form a government and
abdicate, that the United National Front was undermined.

With the help of the argument that the Viet Minh was the only
group with Allied support, and also the backing of the Advanced
Youth Guard by this time,[144] the southern communist leader, Tran
Van Giau, was able to form a coalition front of the old parties that
had worked in alliance with the Japanese and the Viet Minh under his
chairmanship. This front which came into being on the 23rd was the
Executive Committee of Nam Bo, and in the face of a large meeting
which the old regime organised in support of Nguyen Van Sam on the
24th, the Committee ordered an even larger counter-demonstration
on the 25th when it first 'came before the eyes'[145] of the people.
These people, who included Advance Youth Guards, workers,
peasants, women, Cao Dai, and Binh Xuyen bandits, made up a truly
vast concourse that could have been a million strong, and many were
armed with spears and swords. Moreover, these people 'poured'[146]

---

[142]Nguyen Van Mai, *Phong Trao Thanh Nien*, p. 7.

[143]Patti, *Why Viet Nam?*, pp. 183–187.

[144]*CMTT*, Vol. 2, p. 227 shows how the Advance Youth Guard began to prepare for
an uprising in Saigon from the 21st.

[145]Ibid., p. 228. P. 227 also indicates that the Viet Minh did not in fact 'go public' in
Saigon and Cho Lon until a meeting on the 20th.

[146]*LSQD*, p. 171.

into the southern capital from surrounding provinces like Gia Dinh,
Cho Lon, My Tho, Bien Hoa, Thu Dau Mot in cars, on trains, and on
foot to support the Viet Minh's call for national independence.[147]

After receiving a Viet Minh delegation from Hanoi under Tran
Huy Lieu on the morning of the 30th, Bao Dai handed over his gilt
seal and sword and read his abdication speech before a hastily
assembled crowd on the Ngo Mon Terrace at the Imperial Palace in
Hue that afternoon:

> We cannot help but feel a certain melancholy at the thought of
> Our glorious ancestors who had struggled for 400 years to make
> Our country great . . . We cannot help but have feelings of
> regret at the thought of the 20 years of Our reign, during which
> We have not been able to render any appreciable services to
> Our country . . .[148]

This event of great symbolic importance was then followed by two
others. One of these on 19th August was the arrival in Hanoi of 1,000
troops of the Liberation Army fresh from the 'battle' of Thai Nguyen
to the cheers of enthusiastic flag waving crowds.[149] The other was Ho
Chi Minh's proclamation of the national independence of the Democratic Republic of Vietnam before a vast and euphoric audience in Ba
Dinh square in Hanoi on 2 September.[150]

For some sixty years the Nguyen Dynasty had been held in place by
French imperial power. But the imperialist world order to which the
Nguyen Dynasty had aligned itself had failed the people because it
had ignored the force of twentieth century change and suppressed
Vietnamese independence. It was thus inevitable that a Party like the
Viet Minh whose alignment to a modern world order that promised
freedom and a better life would sweep the Nguyen Dynasty aside
once the imperialist power of France and Japan had failed it. Between March and August 1945 the society's regional and functional
groupings had linked up beneath the Viet Minh and raised it to
national prominence because it provided the only focus for a unified,
independent, and modern Vietnamese nation. And, as the armed
forces grew at the core of the new nation, it was not coincidental that

---

[147]*CMTT*, Vol. 2, pp. 227–228. *LSQD*, pp. 171–172. Patti, *Why Viet Nam?*, 183–187.

[148]Quoted in Bernard B. Fall, *The Two Viet-Nams: A Political and Military Analysis*,
New York, Washington, London: Praeger, 1964, p. 203. I have made a slight change to
Fall's translation on the basis of Bao Dai *Le Dragon d'Annam*, p. 120. For Bao Dai's
general view see pp. 119–121. For Tran Huy Lieu's view see his article, 'Tuoc An Kiem
cua Hoang De Bao Dai' ['Dispossessing the Emperor Bao Dai of the Seal and Sword'],
NCLS, No. 18, September 1960, pp. 46–51.

[149]*LSQD*, p. 173.

[150]*CMTT*, Vol. 1, p. 60 says '50 van' or 500,000 people were in Ba Dinh Square.

the Liberation Army had its name changed officially to the People's Army of Vietnam[151] with the declaration of the independence of the Democratic Republic on 2 September.

This declaration represented nothing less than the integration of the Vietnamese identity in the modern world, and it had been largely achieved by an accumulation of forces in the countryside whose armed and unarmed components were organically related. As soon as the armed propaganda campaign mobilised peasants to seize power in any place some had spears, a few might have had bird guns. Further definition of the armed forces then depended on the availability of weapons and on the development of unarmed mass organisations which the peasant mobilisation had created the need for in the first place. As armed self defence forces and guerrilla units formed first, and then regular units emancipated from work in the fields were formed in greatly increasing numbers by late August and early September, their survival depended on increasingly well developed institutional links with the society. This was the structure of the People's Army which began to crystallise as support for the Viet Minh surged into the cities between 18 and 28 August. And this was the army that would resist French forces as they tried to reverse the trend of modern history and reoccupy Vietnam almost immediately after the declaration of independence.

[151]*LSQD*, p. 174.

5
State Apparatus and the Army, September 1945–December 1946

The national independence which Ho Chi Minh declared on 2 September 1945 was based on the unity of Bac Ky, Trung Ky, and Nam Ky because the Viet Minh had come to power in all three regions and linked them together. But almost as soon as it had been created this national unity was threatened by a range of mutually supporting external and internal pressures that tended to accentuate regional differences.

As a result of decisions made by the great powers at Potsdam in July 1945 Vietnam was divided into two zones of occupation for the purpose of disarming the Japanese. South of the sixteenth parallel a British Indian Division under General Gracey was eventually to carry out this task, and north of the sixteenth parallel a Chinese occupation force under General Lu Han was to do the same.[1] Underlying differences in north-south political and military development were then intensified as the British almost immediately facilitated the French reoccupation of the south, and a combination of insufficient forces and the Chinese occupation temporarily blocked the French advance into the north. As war immediately broke out in the south the central government in Hanoi placed great hope in left wing political forces in France and embarked on negotiations to try to resolve Franco-Vietnamese differences. In the north the army thus

---

[1] In view of British imperial interests in Southeast Asia it is significant that Stein Tonneson, *1946: le déclenchement de la guerre d'Indochine*, Paris: L'Harmattan, 1987, pp. 12–13, has shown that the British were keen to have all of Indochina in their theatre of operations and to supervise the disarming of the Japanese in the entire country. The decision to divide the country was insisted upon by Roosevelt who did not want to offend Chiang Kai Shek unnecessarily.

enjoyed fifteen months of relative peace which enabled it to build on its already high level of political and military development there. Yet there is still a most important sense in which the unity of the Vietnamese nation was maintained despite the great regional differences that emerged.

One of the earliest studies of the Democratic Republic of Vietnam prepared for the French Expeditionary Force in 1945 stated clearly that 'the proclamation of the independence of Vietnam has unquestionably created universal enthusiasm among the Annamite people'.[2] Moreover, although the differences in regional development were great it will be shown that they were still shaped by the same underlying political structures in all regions. Initially in both the north and the south these underlying political structures would manifest the same weakness in the Vietnamese polity as the foreign armies of occupation entered the country. This weakness was the tendency which the polity had to fragment under pressure as it had done during the French conquest in the nineteenth century. In the south, armed units formed in late August and September 1945 therefore disintegrated with the first touch of French pressure because of internal faction fighting. And, in the north, the Viet Minh did battle with various conservative factions like the VNQDD that returned to Vietnam from exile in China under the protection of Lu Han's army. By December 1946 when full scale hostilities broke out in the north as well as the south, however, Ho Chi Minh's central government in Hanoi had still maintained the unity of the Vietnamese nation because its armed propaganda campaign had established links between all the regions as they embarked on their anti-French resistance war together.

The Paradox of the Central Government

It is proper to speak of a central national government in Vietnam in this period because Ho Chi Minh's government in Hanoi was the only political force in the country to symbolise national unity and exercise power in all three regions of Bac Bo, Trung Bo, and Nam Bo[3] to any extent.

This is not a popular view. Most Western historians have emphasised the government's weakness. For example, Duiker says that

---

[2]Service Historique de l'Armée de Terre, Château de Vincennes, Etat Major Interarmées Forces Terrestres, Carton 68, (Hereafter SHAT, C.-), *La République Démocratique du Vietnam*, Saigon, December 1945, p. 40.

[3]These administrative categories are the same as Bac Ky, Trung Ky, and Nam Ky or northern, central, and southern Vietnam.

Ho's government was 'shaky at best',[4] and others like Chen imply that because of men like Major Thomas and his Deer Team before August it was artificially 'made' in America.[5] One difficulty with this emphasis, however, is that it is contradicted by the government's survival and the expansion of the army from 5,000 in August 1945 to some 80,000 in late 1946,[6] at a time when the government came under extreme international pressures which accentuated the internal pressures it already had to deal with. Certainly, Ho's government was faced by great disorder, and Duiker is correct to note that the Communists now confronted a political situation of 'almost unprecedented complexity'.[7] But when the survival and consolidation of the government is remembered it may be argued with equal certainty that there is much more to the story than writers like Duiker and Chen suggest. In particular, an understanding of the nature of Ho's government in 1945 demands some discussion of what might be described as a fundamental paradox of Vietnamese government: the contradiction between the autocratic centralism of the state in a constitutional sense and the almost complete decentralisation of the state apparatus in a territorial one.[8]

At its most extreme between 1500 and 1800, this paradox was reflected in both the maintenance of the symbolic authority of the central court under the Le dynasts and the complete administrative division of the country under the Nguyen and Trinh dynasties. In the nineteenth century the tendency was then for a greater concentration of power at the centre with the establishment of a single court under the Nguyen dynasty at the geographically central location of Hue. But the ease with which the French were able to break up the polity and divide and rule it still revealed the force of Vietnamese regionalism. Without autocratic-centralism there would be no higher political focus for the unity of the regions within a greater world order, and without territorial decentralisation of administration re-

[4]William J. Duiker, *The Communist Road to Power in Vietnam*, Boulder Colorado: Westview Press, 1961, p. 107.

[5]King C. Chen, *Vietnam and China, 1938–1945*, Princeton, 1969, p. 114. What Chen is reflecting here of course is the French perception of American aid to the Viet Minh.

[6]See note 123 below.

[7]Duiker, *The Communist Road*, pp. 107–108.

[8]An awareness of this paradox is at least incipient in many of the early French writings on Vietnam like M. De La Bissachère, *Etat Actuel du Tonkin, de la Conchinchine, et des royaumes de Cambodge, Laos et Lac-Tho*, 2 Vols., Paris, 1812, Vol. 1, Part 2, Chapter 1, and it comes out strongly in a more recent work like Vu Quoc Thong, *La décentralisation administrative au Viet Nam*, Presses Universites du Viet Nam, 1952, p. 31.

flecting regionalism there would be no foundation for a central government in the society. In 1945 and 1946, therefore, both autocratic-centralism and territorial decentralisation were in operation.

From 2 September 1945 Ho's government in Hanoi ruled through thirteen ministries (*bo*) whose prestige was reinforced by the ex-Emperor Bao Dai in the office of Supreme Political Advisor.[9] These ministries stood at the apex of an embryonic and, in many parts of the country like the south, still non-existent state apparatus whose projected constitution was characterised by its extremely centralised nature. As Ginsburgs has written:

> Systematic review and control over all the activities of every public institution by a complex succession of superior supervisory agencies, culminating in the personal office of the President of the Republic became the new rule.[10]

In many respects this high degree of centralisation was only a continuation of colonial and pre-colonial practice where all legislative, executive, and judicial powers were concentrated in the monarch and the Gouverneur Général. But the Viet Minh were also reacting against the great division of colonial Vietnam, and if anything the tendency was for greater centralisation than ever before.

Certain decentralised public institutions created by the French like Chambers of Commerce and Agriculture immediately disappeared.[11] In a spate of revolutionary decrees between September and December 1945 the Mandarinate and the Village Council of Notables were abolished and replaced by a parallel system of 'People's Committees' (*Uy Ban Nhan Dan*) and 'Resistance Committees' (*Uy Ban Khang Chien*) with an ascending succession of supervisory agencies from village to national level. This centralised government structure was reinforced with revolutionary attempts to suppress ceremonial rituals, banqueting, and superstitious visits to fortune tellers who might tell lies about 'Uncle' Ho. By attacking these customs which tended to reinforce regional power structures, the effect would be to centralise the power of the Viet Minh government as it broke into the society to implant new unified national political structures there. Furthermore, the centralising impact of modern technology

---

[9]Chen, *Vietnam and China*, p. 111–112 lists the ministries. For Bao Dai's description of the use Ho Chi Minh made of him see *Le Dragon d'Annam*, pp. 135–153.

[10]George Ginsburgs, 'Local Government and Administration in North Vietnam, 1945–1954', *The China Quarterly*, No. 10, April–June 1962, p. 166. Ginsburgs uses Russian sources.

[11]Vu Quoc Thong, *La décentralisation*, p. 294.

can not be forgotten. As soon as it came to power Ho Chi Minh's government took control of the main radio transmitter at Bach Mai and requisitioned all the printing apparatus and stationery supplies it could. This tendency to monopolise the means of communication then enabled the army of anti-imperialist writers in Tran Huy Lieu's propaganda ministry to propagate the unified line of the central government: national independence and the program of the communist party.[12] Vu Quoc Thong who has studied Viet Minh decrees in 1945 and 1946 therefore says that they did not show 'any measure'[13] of decentralisation.

Paradoxically, however, any idea of central government would have been meaningless in Vietnam in 1945 and 1946 unless the state apparatus was able to reflect wide variations in regional political development. These variations will be highlighted later, but what must be recognised here is the important sense in which Ginsburgs' 'complex succession of superior supervisory agencies' culminating in the person of the President was as much an aspect of Vietnamese regionalism as it was of autocratic centralism. This centralising supervisory mechanism was in fact the unified state's only way of both transcending and linking the plethora of village, district, provincial, and regional committees because of their great regional differences and multiplicity. In other words, rigid autocratic-centralism was an automatic and inevitable reflex of regional diversity within unity, or what is more formally referred to as 'democratic centralism'.[14] And the implications of this 'democratic centralism' for a cohesive understanding of Viet Minh government in 1945 and 1946 are important.

At a time when the country was being invaded by British, French, and Chinese armies it may well have been that the new government was a little 'shaky' at the centre. But paradoxically this is not the heart of the matter. The heart of the matter is that the central government was being *pumped up* by the interaction of armed

---

[12]Bernard B. Fall, *Le Viet Minh 1945–1960*, Paris, 1960, pp. 76–78. Devillers, *Histoire*, pp. 178–180. Paul Isoart, *Le phénomène*, p. 343.

[13]Vu Quoc Thong, *La décentralisation*, p. 294.

[14]In institutional terms this democratic centralism emerged in the Constitutional Decree No. 63 of 22 November 1945 as 'two categories of organs of authority', namely people's councils and administrative committees. On the institution of these organs of authority Ginburgs, 'Local Government', p. 177 then notes that:

> The former, elected by the population at large through direct and universal suffrage, were described as 'representative organs of the people', while the latter, indirectly chosen by the plenary councils and functioning as executive bodies, were designated as 'administrative organs representing simultaneously the people and the government.'

Ginsburg quotes here from the Constitutional Decree.

propaganda and the almost universal desire for independence in the regions. Put another way, the central government's real power was paradoxically in the regions because this is where its armed propaganda operations were simultaneously demonstrating the strength of the Viet Minh and building the state apparatus in 1945 and 1946.

Of course, as the regions broke up and absorbed the impact of the extraordinary combination of British, French, and Chinese invasions, the central government had to play an increasingly prominent leadership role to keep its armed propaganda pump in operation. This was so in all regions, but especially in the south. The Chinese created various complexities for the government in the north that will be discussed later, but it was the arrival of the British Indian Division under General Gracey in Saigon on September 12 that created the greatest immediate difficulties. Gracey's mission was to disarm the Japanese. But by the 22nd he had also released the 11th French Colonial Infantry Regiment from its Japanese prison, rearmed it, and permitted it to clear the Saigon docks and occupy public buildings in the city.[15]

The Vietnamese immediately responded by declaring a guerrilla war to resist the French re-occupation of the southern half of the country. However, as the French rapidly built up their forces in the south it soon became clear that universal hostility would not be enough to stop the spread of French power. Unless armed propaganda units actually went into the villages to compete with the French, encourage confidence in the central government, and build the state apparatus and the army, the failure of the central government to maintain national unity would inevitably emerge and accentuate regional differences. This was especially true in the south where the Viet Minh's institutional development was virtually non-existent, and where the first touch of French pressure caused bitter internal conflicts in resistance politics.

Initial Disorder in Nam Bo

Once General Gracey had declared martial law in Saigon on 22 September and permitted the 11th French Colonial Infrantry regi-

[15]Daniel Bart Valentine, 'The British Facilitation of the French Re-Entry into Vietnam', PhD, UCLA, 1971 is a symphatetic discussion fo the British involvement in Vietnamese affairs and the pressures which led to Gracey's decision. So too is Peter Dennis, *Troubled days of peace: Mountbatten and South East Asia command, 1945–46*, Manchester University Press, 1987. For a less symphathetic discussion see George Rosie, *The British in Vietnam: How the Twenty Five Year War Began*, London: Panther, 1970.

ment to begin its 'Opération de Force'[16] in the city the Vietnamese responded. At Cay Moi on the morning of the 23rd a meeting of local ICP delegates and the Nam Bo Committee under the northern cadre, Hoang Quoc Viet, ordered a general strike, and declared guerrilla war that began with an attack on the city's electricity and water supplies.[17] However, although hostility to the French clearing operations was virtually universal, internal divisions within the southern resistance soon became a major problem for the central government in Hanoi.

From late August the People's Committee in Nam Bo under Tran Van Giau had already begun the difficult task of trying to rationalise the military potential of the south. Three hundred 'workers assault units'[18] with a strength of 15,000 were formed to take the role of Saigon's self defence forces. The Republican Guard (*Cong Hoa Ve Binh*) comprising four divisions of at least 17,000 men was also formed to weld the disparate armies of the southern provinces into a cohesive military force.[19] The First Division (*De Nhat Su Doan*) essentially consisted of three old French colonial units from the Civil Guard who had supported the Viet Minh around Saigon in August— the Mobile Brigades from Chi Hoa and Gia Dinh and the Auxiliary Brigade. Newly formed Youth Guard and workers units were added to the division which then had a total strength of some 10,000. The Second Division (*De Nhi Su Doan*) was organised from Dai Viet elements, miscellaneous soldiers from the colonial army, and various new youth groups. Its strength was reportedly around 1,000. The Third Division (*De Tam Su Doan*) was formed by some 5,000 members of the Japanese formed Advance Youth Guard. And the Fourth Division (*De Tu Su Doan*) was formed from disparate groups such as supporters of the Trotskyites and what the official history describes as 'reactionary religious cast-offs'.[20] By this the official history presumably means the Catholics around Ben Tre, and followers of the Cao Dai and Hoa Hao Religious Sects. However, by claiming that the strength of the Fourth Division only amounted to 'about 1,000',[21] the official history seems to be underestimating its

---

[16]André Teuiliers, *La guerre du Vietnam*, Paris: Lavauzelle, 1979, p. 32.

[17]Ban Nghien Cuu Lich Su Dang Trung Uong [Board of Historical Research of the Central Committee of the Party], *Lich Su Dang Cong San Viet Nam, So Thao, 1920–1954* [Draft History of the Vietnamese communist Party, 1920–1954], (hereafter *LSDC*), Hanoi: Su That, 1981, p. 464.

[18]*LSQD*, p. 168.

[19]Ibid., pp. 187–188.

[20]Ibid., p. 188.

[21]Ibid.

strength because other sources indicate that the Cao Dai alone in late 1945 had an army of 7,000 to 8,000.[22] At any rate, the constitution of the Republican Guard certainly reflected the enormously complex pattern of political life in Nam Bo, and as such it is not surprising that its history is one of great internal conflict.

Even before the arrival of the British on September 12, and the French attacks of September 22, serious conflicts had broken out, most notably between the Viet Minh and the Hoa Hao whose leader Huynh Phu So, had long harboured visions of being 'King'[23] of an independent realm centered on the 'western capital',[24] Can Tho. Here, fighting broke out on 8 September, as Hoa Hao Generals Tran Van Soai and Lam Thanh Nguyen led 10,000 of the faithful armed with batons and sabers in a bid to take the town. Many were killed as the Viet Minh repulsed the attack. Brothers of both Huynh Phu So and Tran Van Soai were caught and executed. General Lam Thanh Nguyen was also caught, put in a sack, and thrown into a river, but he escaped 'with the help of a genie'.[25] After this battle the Viet Minh tried to placate the Hoa Hao by offering Huynh Phu So a position on the People's Committee of Nam Bo. This had little effect, for once the Viet Minh were thrown on the defensive by French attacks into the Mekong Delta in October the Hoa Hao quickly took advantage of the situation to conduct what Savani has described as a 'terrible'[26] retaliatory massacre. Although Viet Minh-Cao Dai and Viet Minh-Catholic relations did not immediately degenerate to the same extent as Viet Minh-Hoa Hao relations, there were still serious tensions which could not be camouflaged under the strain of French attacks from 23 September. By the end of the month the Fourth Division of the Republican Guard simply disbanded itself as some Cao Dai units sought refuge at Tay Ninh while others broke up and either joined elements of the old Japanese sponsored Advance Youth Guard or went home.[27]

To deep sectarian conflict, the sheer confusion arising from complicated and often clandestine political manoeuvering must be added as a cause of division in the southern resistance. As soon as the French

---

[22]Général Yves Gras, *Histoire de la guerre d'Indochine*, Paris: Plon, 1981, p. 56.

[23]Hoc Tu, *Nhung Ngay Dau cua Mat Tran Nam Bo* [The First Days of the Battle on the Southern Front] Hanoi, 12 November 1945, p. 21.

[24]A. Savani, *Sectes et Groupements Armées du Sud-Vietnam*, Centre de Hautes Etudes Administratives sur l'Afrique et l'Asie Modernes, (hereafter CHEAM) Paris, 1956, p. 7.

[25]Quoted in Ibid.

[26]Ibid., p. 8.

[27]Hoc Tu, *Nhung Ngay Dau*, p. 19.

attacked Saigon on 22 September fighting broke out between Advance Youth Guard Groups earlier formed by the Japanese (the Third Division of the Republican Guard), and new Viet Minh Youth Units (elements of the First and Second Divisions), as well as all these groups and the French. One contemporary account described the situation:

> At this time, the eruption of a Viet Minh Youth movement to repress the Advance Youth Guard was a mistake that resulted from the quite large number of party factions. It was a mistake because the Viet Minh Youth incorrectly thought that the Advance Youth Guard did not support the Viet Minh because it had been formed during the period when the Japanese still had power. But the truth was that the person who formed the Advance Youth Guard was Tran Van Giau, Head of the Executive Committee, (precursor to the Nam Bo People's Committee), who stood in the background while Dr Pham Ngoc Thach carried out the work of training the youth. In reality the Viet Minh Youth was the same as the Advance Youth Guard. The only difference was that one group was set up in the period while the Japanese were still in power, and the other group was set up in the open after the coup d'état.[28]

These were some of the difficulties facing the Nam Bo People's Committee as it withdrew in disarray to the Mekong Delta in late September, and the French began to capitalise on what one official history has called 'our weak spot'.[29]

As the French built up the strength of their army in the south to 30,000 by January 1946, they occupied all the major towns in Nam Bo, Southern Trung Bo, Cambodia, and Southern Laos by February,[30] and revived the policy of 'divide and rule'. By mid-1946 the new French High Commissioner of the French Administration, Admiral Thierry d'Argenlieu, had 'recognised' a 'Republic of Cochinchina' and proclaimed the ethnic minority areas of the central highlands an 'autonomous region'. As d'Argenlieu also began to talk of the administratively non-existant region of 'Southern Annam' in similar terms, and attempts were later made to establish other autonomous zones among ethnic minorities in the northern regions of Hoa Binh and the Thai Country, it is also remarkable that until at least 1948 French officials assumed that the status of Tonkin, Annam, and

[28]Ibid., p. 20. See also Tran Tan Quoc, *Saigon Septembre 45*, Saigon: Viet Thanh, 1947, p. 39. Although the title is in French the text is in Vietnamese.
[29]*LSQD*, p. 466.
[30]Gras, *Histoire*, p. 62. Teuliers, *La guerre*, pp. 33–38.

Cochinchina was still defined by nineteenth century agreements with the Court of Annam.[31]

In late 1945 and 1946, however, there were two important factors which tended to ensure the survival of the southern resistance. The first factor, based on the widespread hostility to the French, was the diffuse nature of the southern resistance which gave the French no centre to strike at. The second factor was the central government's ability to structure the regional resistance forces using armed propaganda. Indeed, the survival of the southern resistance rested on the paradox of Vietnamese government, for while the central authority and the decentralised regional resistance were eventually integrated the French still had no centre of resistance to capture.

Integration of the Southern Resistance

In Saigon, even though the French had demolished the Republican Guard by the end of September 1945, it still took two full months for them to establish firm control of the city.[32] Even then assassinations of collaborators, and small scale attacks such as that of the youth Le Van Tan, who turned himself into a 'living torch'[33] as he blew up a petrol dump on the night of 17 October, were never entirely eliminated. In other urban centers like Bien Hoa, Xuan Loc, Qui Nhon, Phan Thiet, Phan Rang, and Nha Trang the French reoccupation often had to be facilitated by British and Japanese forces already in situ because of the tenacity of the local resistance.[34] At Xuan Loc on 30 November, for example, it was only after French forces with British and Japanese units attacked the town with tanks and artillery

---

[31]The quotes are quoted in Joseph Buttinger, *Vietnam: A Political History*, New York: Praeger, 1968, pp. 250–252. On the 'autonomous zone' around Hoa Binh see Ngo Tien Chat, 'Ve Nhung Cuoc Dau Tranh Vu Trang cua Nhan Dan Cac Dan Toc Tinh Hoa-Binh trong Cuoc Khang Chien chong Phap' [On the Armed Struggle of the Peoples of Hoa Binh Province in the Anti-French Resistance War (1945–1956)], *NCLS*, pp. 44–54, especially p. 46. On the Thai Country and on assumptions of the old treaties see Franchini, *Les Guerres*, Vol. 1, p. 394, p. 397. In fact Franchini also reminds us that one of the biggest difficulties the French had in trying to persuade Bao Dai that he should form a government in 1948 was that he, like the revolutionaries, opposed the division of the country.

[32]Teuliers, *Le guerre*, p. 32.

[33]*LSQD*, p. 193.

[34]For a contemporary Vietnamese account of the resistance in these locations and others see Hoai Tan, *Chien Cong Oanh Liet cua Dong Bao Nam Bo* [The Glorious Resistance of Our Compatriots in Nam Bo], Hanoi, November 1945; Hoai Tan, *Trung Bo Khang Chien*, [The Resistance War in Trung Bo], Hanoi, 1946.

that the local resistance forces withdrew. According to one Vietnamese eye witness, after 'the sound of gunfire shook the sky from 11 am
to nightfall'[35] the defenders withdrew to the Ba Ria-Phan Thiet road
junction, laid mines in the road and dropped trees across it to impede
the movement of armoured cars.

The occupation of the towns, then, was only the beginning of
French problems. Traversing the countryside and moving between
the towns often posed bigger military problems for the French than
entering them even though offensive military opposition was seldom
encountered. During the advance of one French armoured column
on My Tho sixty kilometers to the south of Saigon on October 15
progress was 'very slow':

> On the route which traversed the embankments of water logged
> paddy fields for three quarters of the distance, all the bridges
> had been destroyed and the peasants had dug numerous ditches
> in the road. Each time it was necessary to fill up the holes,
> repair the road, and rebuild the bridges. With bulldozers in the
> lead the column of armoured cars made slow progress without
> either firing or receiving a single shot. It traversed the deserted
> countryside and abandoned villages. That night it had not passed
> Tan An half way along the route to My Tho.[36]

One other example which brings all the main elements of the military
situation into focus during the reoccupation of the south is that of the
coastal town of Nha Trang. Here, a battalion of the 6th Colonial
Infantry Regiment was disembarked from the warship *Richelieu* on
20 November, but only after Japanese troops in the town had already
been ordered to occupy key points.[37] By the end of November one
contemporary Vietnamese source says 'there was not one shadow of
a Vietnamese'[38] in the city, and all the routes out of it were blocked.
Despite some subsequent patrolling supported by naval gunfire on
prepared Vietnamese defence works to the north and west of the
town, local resistance forces kept the Franco-Japanese garrison from
breaking out of it until two armoured columns arrived on 29 January
1946.

The experience of these relief columns is instructive. Not only did
the one coming from Ban Me Thuot in the central highlands under
Colonel Massu have its progress retarded by the usual obstacles, but
for the first time a French column had to fight its way through a
strong blocking force in the Ma D'Rac Hills. The second relief

[35]Hoai Tan, *Chien Cong Oanh Liet*, p.16.
[36]Gras, *Histoire*, p. 58.
[37]Ibid., p. 60. Hoai Tan, *Chien Cong Oanh Liet*, p. 14.
[38]Hoai Tan, *Trung Bo Khang Chien*, p. 35.

column moving from the south along the coastal route only had to deal with the usual obstacles.[39]

From the French point of view, there was already a paradox between the deceptively easy reoccupation of southern centers by February 1946 and the widespread resistance in the countryside. This paradox is reflected by Général Gras who, writing in 1979, described the French reoccupation of the south as 'a vast military promenade across the countryside',[40] but added on the next page that, in one two month period of operations alone, certain units of the 9th Colonial Infantry Division lost a third of their strength through men killed, wounded, and sick. This paradox was also reflected by the French minister Léon Pignon who, in mid-1946, complained of the 'extreme naivete'[41] of the French military which claimed control of all the towns and 80% of the villages but had been forced to withdraw most of its small posts in the countryside because they could not be defended at night. In fact, even as the French Commander, Général Leclerc, announced triumphantly on 6 February 1946 that 'the pacification of Cochinchina and southern Annam has been achieved',[42] the relative speed with which the French army had occupied the towns already contained the seeds of its destruction.

French commanders had insufficient troops to control territory outside the main centers, and so resistance forces remained invulnerable no matter how disorganised and divided they might have been. Since there was no fighting as yet in the north, the central government had every opportunity to project its power into the south and impose some structure on the resistance there through armed propaganda. This was the second reason why the southern resistance not only survived but was gradually integrated as an arm of national defence in 1946.

As early as April 1945, the Bac Ky Revolutionary Military Conference was aware that the expansion of the new state apparatus would pose special difficulties in the south even if the French had not re-invaded. In fact, the Conference already anticipated the need for 'Southern Advance Units' (*Nam Tien Bo Doi*) to establish 'liaison' or 'contact' (*danh thong lien lac*) with southern cadres 'under direct

---

[39]Gras, *Histoire*, p. 63.

[40]Ibid., p. 63.

[41]Quoted in Tonnesson, *1946*, p. 52.

[42]Quoted in Teuliers, *La guerre*, p. 35. It should also be remembered, however, that in January 1947 Leclerc observed in a report to the French government which was soon ignored that this victory would be useless unless the French acknowledged the force of Vietnamese nationalism, that 'anti-Communism will be a useless tool as long as the problem of nationalism remains unsolved.' These words of Philippe Devillers are quoted in Dunn, 'American Policy and Vietnamese Nationalism', p. 83.

command of the Revolutionary Committee'.[43] For several months after the April Conference there is no further mention of the Southern Advance Army in the official documents. No doubt the tumultuous events taking in the country deferred the development of such a force. As soon as the Viet Minh came to power, however, all possible direction and assistance for southern cadres was forthcoming from the central government.

Although it does not use the term 'Southern Advance Army' one French source of 1953 noted that by early September 1945, before the French reoccupation began, 'a detachment of the Liberation Army . . . about 200 strong arrived at Bien Hoa (near Saigon) to reinforce the provincial forces and were stationed in the forest at Vinh Cuu'.[44] The source, goes on to say that the detachment 'that came from the north' immediately opened a military school at Vinh Cuu and many other places to train cadres and guerrilla fighters, and this claim is supported by a recent Vietnamese source.[45] Three days after Franco-Vietnamese hostilities began in Saigon on the 25th of September Ho Chi Minh made an impassioned appeal to 'Southern Compatriots' over the radio station at Bach Mai. In this appeal Ho said 'we would rather die free than live as slaves'. He predicted ultimate victory because the struggle for the Vietnamese people was 'just', and he assured Nam Bo that:

> The government and the entire nation will do all they can to help the soldiers and people who are currently making sacrifices to build strong foundations for the independence of the country.[46]

According to Vietnamese accounts several thousand cadres and soldiers arrived in the south by the end of 1945.[47] No doubt because of its relatively high level of political-military development, Bac Giang is one northern region which is singled out in the sources for its prompt response to calls for soldiers for the southern front, while two presumably prominent southern advance cadres, Hoang Dinh Rong

---

[43]VKQS, p. 284.

[44]SHAT, C. 94, *Essai sur l'historique des unites Viet Minh dans le secteur de Bien Hoa (Sud-Vietnam)*, Secteur de Bien Hoa, Avril 1953, p. 40.

[45]Ibid. The recent Vietnamese history is Ban Chap Hanh Dang Bo Dang Cong San Viet Nam Tinh Dong Nai [Executive Board of the Party Branch of the Vietnamese Communist Party in Dong Nai Province], *Dong Nai: 30 Nam Chien Tranh Giai Phong (1945–1974) So Thao* [Dong Nai: A Draft History of Thirty Years of Liberation War (1945–1975)], Dong Nai Publishing House, 1986, pp. 31–38.

[46]Ho Chi Minh, *Ve Dau Tranh*, pp. 163–164.

[47]LSDC, p. 468 says 'hang van' or 'a column of ten thousand'. LSQD, p. 211 says there were 'more than ten Southern Advance Brigades and Companies' in late 1945.

and Dam Minh Vien, have been mentioned by Hoang Van Hoan. It is also clear that as soon as the Viet Minh had seized power in central Vietnamese provinces like Quang Tri and Binh Thuan in late August military preparations to thwart the return of the French intensified immediately and that these included the mobilisation of 'southern advance' forces.[48]

Such forces were involved in the fighting around Saigon, the southern highlands, and the coastal towns of southern Trung Bo. The difficulty that Colonel Massu's column had encountered in the Ma D'Rac Hills in January 1946 may also have had something to do with the deployment of elements of the Ba To guerrillas into that region because of what the official history describes as their 'considerable experience in previous guerrilla operations to overthrow the French and Japanese'.[49] Furthermore, the general tone of contemporary sources does confirm more recent official accounts of the enthusiasm with which northern youth 'took the road to war amidst excitement.'[50] Yet, when northern reinforcements did little to impede the French re-occupation of at least the major centers, it must be emphasised that their main impact in the south was not directly military.

Writing after the country was united in 1975, Vo Nguyen Giap left a heroic image of the sons of the revolution marching south in 1945 and 1946 'with the best weapons we had at the time, with new outfits, shining stars on new caps, padded jackets, and leather boots'.[51] Such an image might be treated with skepticism from a material point of view when the north was being picked clean by the Chinese army of occupation before it had time to recover from the famine, new uniforms could only have been in very short supply, and other sources describe southern advance units dressed 'in rags'.[52] But from a political point of view Giap's image should not be taken lightly. What it projected was both the desire to build a strong new nation with a modern army and the central government's intention to develop the organs of state power in the south for this purpose. As

---

[48]*CMTT*, Vol. 1, pp. 212–213 for Bac Giang; Vol. 2, p. 60 for Quang Tri and p. 185 for Bing Thuan. Hoang Van Hoan, *Giot Nuoc*, p. 264 for the leaders.

[49]*LSQD*, p. 194.

[50]*LSDC*, p. 468. The contemporary sources I am referring to are Hoc Tu, *Nhung Ngay Dau*, and Hoai Tan's writings *Trung Bo Khang Chien* and *Chien Cong Oanh Liet*.

[51]Vo Nguyen Giap, *Unforgettable Days*, Hanoi: Foreign Languages Publishing House, 1978, p. 56.

[52]Ngo Van Chieu, *Journal d'un combattant Viet-Minh*, translated by Jacques Despuech, Paris: Editions du Seuil, 1955, p. 56.

the decisions of the April Bac Ky Military Conference and evidence of the arrival of northern cadres in the south before the French attack show, the French invasion only heightened the need for such development. The forces sent from the north in 1945 and 1946 were designated as the 'Southern Advance' forces because their primary purpose was to advance into southern society to develop the organs of state power that could provide the only foundation for national integration and the final defeat of the French. This was armed propaganda writ large.

Such a method of imposing order on the southern resistance was then reinforced by changes in the leadership. Tran Van Giau, the original President of the Nam Bo People's Committee was demoted as a result of the failure to contain the situation in late September. At the 23 September Cay Moi meeting at which war was declared the prominent role of the northern cadre Hoang Quoc Viet[53] suggests that Tran Van Giau was already in eclipse. As the 'biggest Party Conference' yet held in Nam Bo at Thien Ho in My Tho Province on 25 October noted that the organisation of the Republican Guard was 'not correct', that it was too 'complicated' and ignored 'principles',[54] Tran Van Giau's name is not mentioned at all. On this occasion Hoang Quoc Viet represented the Standing Committee of the Central Committee and some new figures appeared: the northerner Ton Duc Thang, the southerner Pham Van Bach, and possibly the southerner Le Duan.[55]

By November other important command appointments also indicate the major reorganisation that was under way in Nam Bo. In this month Pham Van Bach had become President of the Nam Bo People's Committee. Ton Duc Thang took over the Nam Bo Resist-

[53]*LSDC*, p. 464.

[54]*LSQD*, 195.

[55]Ibid.; Devillers, *Histoire*, p. 156. Unlike the other two Pham Van Bach was almost surely not a member of the ICP, but rather a well known lawyer and teacher from Chau Doc who cultivated leftist connections and thus made the transition from member of the Japanese sponsored United National Front to Chairman of the Provisional Executive committee of the Nam Bo. This information was given to me by David Marr. With respect to Le Duan, Ban Chap Hanh Dang Bo, *Dong Nai*, p. 68 contradicts the French sources when it suggests he arrived at Xuan Loc in the south in May 1947. However, it may be that Le Duan had travelled back and forth between the south and north by this time, and given the adminstrative shake up in late 1945 it is possible that the French sources are more accurate in this case. It may also be added that after his association with Tran Van Giau and the September failures, Hoang Quoc Viet does not then seem to have retained high office after the Thien Ho Conference, although Ban Chap Hanh Dang Bo, *Dong Nai*, p. 39 says he represented the Central Committee at another conference at Duc Hoa in December 1945.

ance Committee, and Nguyen Binh, who we have met as the successful commander of the Fourth War Zone north of Hanoi before the
seizure of power in August, arrived in mid-November to take command of southern military affairs. Finally, in early 1946, no less a
figure than the Commander in Chief, Vo Nguyen Giap, made a tour
of inspection which took him as far south as Nha Trang.[56]

With such central government attention to the southern leadership
the departments of Nam Bo's People's Committee were also straight-
ened out. From early 1946 there existed departments for Economics,
Interior, Culture, Public Health, Agriculture, Finance, Information
and Propaganda, and Military Affairs. The delegate for Military
Affairs on the People's Committee became the government's direct
link to the Resistance Committee which was directly responsible to
the People's Committee for its conduct of military operations.[57] Later
in the war, however, the functions of the two committees were to
merge as the whole country came under military administration.

To bolster this evolution of the organs of state power the central
government further projected its authority into the south in a number
of ways. At the time of the general election on 6 January 1946, for
example, Ho Chi Minh stressed its propaganda importance for the
south. 'Tomorrow', Ho said on 5 January,

> our people will show the soldiers in the southern region that: on
> the military front, soldiers use guns and bullets to fight the
> enemy, on the political front, the people use voting leaflets to
> fight the enemy. Each voting leaflet has the force of a bullet.[58]

There was no doubt about who would win the election, which was
clearly part of the overall propaganda campaign to convince the
southern population and resistance that it had the support of the
central government and the rest of the country. The death of some
forty cadres during the election campaign in the south then suggests
the efforts being made by the government to consolidate its position
there. Some of these deaths reflected incidents such as those at Tan

---

[56]Ibid. SHAT, C. 116, *Documentation de Cochinchine 1940 à 1948, D. Plaine des
Joncs*, Annex IV notes that Le Duan was in charge of regional forces. This source also
suggests that Le Duan became prominent in the organisation of regional forces in late
1946. However, see note 55 above. Ban Chap Hanh Dang Bo, *Dong Nai*, p. 36 tells us
about Nguyen Binh. Duiker, *The Communist Road*, p. 117 tells us about Giap.

[57]These statements were made on the basis of a comparison of SHAT, C. 66, *La
République Démocratique*, Annex A, 'Committee de Resistance Cochinchine', (i.e.
under Tran Van Giau), and Shat, C. 166, *Documentation de Cochinchine 1940 a 1948,
D. Plaine des Joncs*, Annex IV, 'Committee du Nam Bo', (i.e. under Pham Van
Bach).

[58]*LSDC*, p. 454.

An where the French bombed a polling booth, but in some regions such as Ba Ria, there is also evidence of conflict between the Viet Minh armed propaganda units and local Partisan Units (*Than Binh*) which the French set up in some villages.[59]

One other method of demonstrating both central government concern and capacity to influence southern affairs takes us into the field of logistics. Indeed, French and Vietnamese sources show that the central government 'made a great effort'[60] to organise the supply of weapons and equipment to the south. By late 1945 special economic cadres were already at work exploiting the black market in Saigon and extracting 'loans' from Chinese merchants. The capture of French weapons was also so successful that successive French Commanders in the south had to issue special directives to the Expeditionary Corps on this 'serious problem'.[61] Yet such sources of supply were not adequate to make the south self sufficient, and the government moved in many directions to help make up the short-fall.

Some idea of how the logistics of the southern resistance were integrated with the north can be gleaned from a reading of Nguyen Thi Dinh's memoirs.[62] In a tale of high adventure she has described how, after going to Hanoi in March 1946 with requests for arms and money, she returned to Ben Tre in the Mekong Delta with a sampan load of twelve tons of weapons. These arms were actually collected in Quang Ngai in Central Vietnam where dumps were being built up from sources in Canton and Hong Kong.[63] From Quang Ngai the weapons were transported by the still functioning train to Tuy Hoa (Phu Yen) where they were loaded onto sampans and covered with fishing nets and jars of fish sauce for the final leg south. French sources also show that similar shipments 'arrived regularly'[64] in the south with the help of numerous assistance committees along the central coast such as the one at Phan Thiet where the local merchants lent out their fleet of junks to run guns.[65] From such coastal centers jungle trails and elephants were also in common use as supplies filtered in to the resistance around Saigon. Moreover, some mention

[59]Ibid., p. 455. Ban Chap Hanh Dang Bo, *Dong Nai*, pp. 51–56.

[60]SHAT, C. 102, D. *Trafic d' Armes*, 'Ravitaillement en Armes des Forces de Guerrilla au Sud 16ème Parallele', Saigon, Décembre 1946, p. 1. For Vietnamese confirmation see note 62, for example.

[61]Pierre Boyer de Latour, *De l'Indochine à l'Algérie. Le martyre de L'Armée Française*, Paris: Les Presses du Mail, 1962, p. 48.

[62]Tran Huong Nam (ghi), *Khong Con Duong Nao Khac: Hoi Ky cua Ba Nguyen Thi Dinh*, [No Other Way: The Memoirs of Nguyen Thi Dinh], Hanoi, 1966, pp. 30–43.

[63]SHAT, C. 102, D. *Trafic d'Armes*, 'Ravitaillement en Armes', p. 2.

[64]Ibid., p. 3.

[65]Ibid.

should be made of other Southeast Asian sources of supply to the southern resistance which were centered on the commissariat the Viet Minh ran in Bangkok.[66]

This commissariat was run by Tran Van Giau after his demotion as Chairman of the Nam Bo Committee.[67] It included a small mortar bomb factory, and did business with a range of shady arms dealers of no known nationality (and undoubtedly Thai officials) who were eager to capitalise on the large quantity of American and Japanese armament that lay around Southeast Asia after the Second World War.[68] In addition to the Bangkok operation a network of overseas government-agents, that according to Lucien Bodard was known as 'the overseas regiment',[69] obtained weapons from Singapore, and went shopping as far afield as Burma and Indonesia where chemicals for bombs, batteries, and medical supplies were especially sought.[70]

Therefore, big efforts in the field of logistics, complete reorganis-ation of leaders and departments, and a major armed propaganda campaign in the south all support the official history when it says that by the first half of 1946 the southern resistance was 'firmly main-tained'.[71] From around this time independent French sources also note the tell-tale development of the literacy campaign by armed units around Saigon,[72] and a recent Vietnamese source says that 'with the method of small, dispersed, and sure attacks, the armed propaganda units were now rather more active (than before)'.[73] An at least tempor-ary and partial accommodation was reached with the religious sects with the inclusion of a 'Cao Dai Councillor', Cao Trieu Phat, on the Nam Bo People's Committee.[74] And, as small but regular guerrilla units were building their bases in many areas around Saigon and the Mekong

[66]Ibid., p. 5.

[67]McAlister, 'The Origins', p. 295.

[68]SHAT, C. 102, D. *Trafic d'Armes*, 'L'Approvisionnement en armes et munitions des forces vietnamiennes', Saigon, Janvier 1947. See also Claude Guiques, 'Panoplie Viet Minh', *Indochine Sub-Est Asiatique*, No. 7, Juin, 1952.

[69]Lucien Bodard, *La guerre d'Indochine*, 5 Vols, Paris: Gallimard, Vol. 1, 1963, p. 74.

[70]SHAT, C. 102, D. *Trafic d'Armes*, 'Ravitaillement en Armes', Saigon, Décembre 1946, p. 3.

[71]*LSQD*, p. 200.

[72]Bodard, *La guerre*, Vol. 1 p. 275 writes about armed units near Hoc Mon carrying out a literacy drive, although one need not agree with his conclusion that the anti-illiteracy campaign was 'a form of evil' because he had heard that anyone who could not read within six months would be beheaded.

[73]Ban Chap Hanh Dang Bo, *Dong Nai*, p. 55.

[74]SHAT, C. 116, D. *Documentation de Cochinchine 1940 à 1948, D. Plaine des Joncs*, Annex IV.

Delta,[75] Resistance Committees were beginning to develop strategic coordination and establish 'plans for action'[76] at provincial level. Two further steps were then required before southern units were finally integrated into the system of national defence.

The first was signalled in May 1946 when the government in Hanoi issued Order Number 71 and began a major reorganisation of military administration. The Army of National Defence now became the 'National Army' (*Quan Doi Quoc Gia*),[77] and the entire country was divided into twelve 'War Zones' (*Chien Khu*).[78] Nam Bo was divided into War Zones 7, 8, and 9 and southern Trung Bo was divided into War Zones 5 and 6. Around this time the official history notes a training drive all over the country,[79] and the organisation of southern forces was consolidated into *Chi Doi* by the end of the year.[80] The term *Chi Doi*, which is sometimes translated into English as 'brigade', referred to a sizeable body of troops formed from disparate elements that often operated independently as sub-units. Although their strength varied greatly, some *Chi Doi* of 1,000 people

---

[75]*LSQD*, p. 199. Bases were being built in Go Vap, Thu Dau Mot, Hoc Mon, Rung Sat, Ben Cat, Trang Bang, and Dong Thap Muoi. For a lengthy discussion of military developments in the area southeast of Saigon see Ban Chap Hanh Dang Bo, *Dong Nai*, pp. 36–63.

[76]Ibid., p. 61.

[77]Ibid., p. 234.

[78]*LSQD*, p. 234, note 1 lists the following twelve War Zones at the end of 1946:

War Zone 1: Cao Bang, Bac Can, Thai Nguyen, Phuc Yen.

War Zone 2: Son Tay, Ha Dong, Ha Nam, Nam Dinh, Ninh Binh, Hoa Binh, Son La, Lai Chau.

War Zone 3: Hai Phong, Kien An, Thai Binh, Hung Yen, Hai Duong (except Dong Trieu, Chi Linh).

War Zone 4: Thanh Hoa, Nghe An, Ha Tinh, Quang Binh, Quang Tri, Thua Thien.

War Zone 5: Quang Nam, Quang Ngai, Binh Dinh, Cong Tum, Gia Lai.

War Zone 6: Phu Yen, Khanh Hoa, Ninh Thuan, Binh Thuan, Dac Lac, Lam Vien, Dong Nai Thuong.

War Zone 7: Ba Ria, Bien Hoa, Thu Dau Mot, Tay Ninh, Gia Dinh, Cho Lon, Sai Gon.

War Zone 8: Tan An, Go Cong, My Tho, Sa Dec, Vinh Long, Tra Vinh, Ben Tre.

War Zone 9: Chau Doc, Long Xuyen, Ha Tien, Can Tho, Soc Trang, Bac Rach Gia.

War Zone 10: Lao Cai, Ha Giang, Yen Bai, Phu Tho, Tuyen Quang, Vinh Yen.

War Zone 11: Ha Noi.

War Zone 12: Lang Son, Bac Giang, Bac Ninh, Hai Ninh, Hon Gai, Quang Yen (including Dong Trieu and Chi Linh).

[79]*LSQD*, pp. 234–235.

[80]For an example of how 4 Chi Doi were created in one region see Ban Chap Hanh Dang Bo, *Dong Nai*, p. 46, p. 57.

divided into three *Dai Doi*, or what is usually translated into English as 'Company', were in existence by late 1946.[81] Since the official history says there were some twenty five *Chi Doi* in the south by this time[82] the total strength of the National Army's main force in this region may be computed at around 15,000 to 20,000.

The second step which helped to integrate the south into the national military administration was the making of an important link that strengthened the chain of political-military command from the central government to the smallest provincial *Chi Doi* in the south. In late 1946 as the northern half of the country braced itself for war, a regular northern regiment was moved into Quang Ngai Province in Southern Trung Bo's War Zone 5, and a special command post was set up under the Central Committee member Pham Van Dong to oversee southern affairs for the Central Government.[83]

By this time the key southern strategic area to the west of Saigon known to the Vietnamese as Dong Thap Muoi and to the French as the Plaine des Joncs (Plain of Reeds) had already become a major military base. This semi-aquatic, highly inaccessible, and sparsely populated area of some 10,400 square kilometers contained the most important southern command posts (those of Nguyen Binh and Tran Van Tra the commander of War Zone 8), and a developing network of mobile military schools, rudimentary hospitals, workshops, rice stores, and radio posts. Strategically, the Plain joined War Zones 7 and 8 and had direct access to War Zone 9 as well as to Cambodia through which many important southern supply lines ran from Thailand. The Plain also commanded the major Saigon-Phnom Phen and Saigon-My Tho-Vinh Long axes. Because of the southern command's institutional and radio links with the central government in the north, the some 6,000 regular and 10,000 irregular troops in and around the Plain by late 1946 could then have their operations integrated with the national defence strategy.[84] Thus, as early as the Franco-Chinese Treaty of February 1946 the Hanoi government could order an intensification of guerrilla action in the south, and from this time French sources note that guerrilla offensives from the Plain of Reeds

[81]SHAT, C. 94, *Essai sur l'historique*, pp. 40–42.

[82]*LSQD*, p. 234. By way of comparison with the north, at the same time as the loosely structured *Chi Doi* were being consolidated in the south they were being replaced in the north by the more tightly structured *Trung Doi* or Regiment. In other words, unit designation in the two regions further reflected the political differences between them.

[83]Ibid., p. 269.

[84]SHAT, C. 116. *Documentation de Cochinchine 1940 a 1948, D. Plaine des Joncs*, pp. 1–6. In 1940 the population had been estimated at '20,000 Cambodians, 80,000 Annamites, 10,000 Chinese'. As well as being Military Commander of Nam Bo Nguyen Binh also commanded War Zone 7.

were coordinated with various phases of Franco-Viet Minh negotiations throughout 1946.[85]

By at least mid-year the resistance in Nam Bo had been effectively
linked up with the central government through armed propaganda.
Yet it can never be forgotten that the nature of the link itself reflected
Vietnamese regionalism. The Plain of Reeds with one significant
logistics line that ran into Southeast Asia lay in an ecological zone
very different from any other area of major military importance. This
Plain and the area immediately surrounding it could be the cradle of a
guerrilla force, but Nam Bo unlike Trung Bo and Bac Bo did not
have mountains that could hide whole armies, and later it would have
no access to secure rear areas in China. On a political level also, the
bitter divisions that the French re-occupation initially revealed in the
resistance might have been smoothed over in 1946, but they never
entirely disappeared during the war. By 1947 we will see that the Viet
Minh had once more fallen out with the religious sects. Later,
Nguyen Binh would come into conflict with the central government
because of his independent approach to the war which was basically a
reflection of southern conditions. Yet these southern differences can
still be integrated into the unity of the nation, because they were
reflected in the political-military institutions that constituted the
power of the central government. The problems which the central
government had to deal with in the north in late 1945 and 1946 were
at once very similar to and very different from those in the south.

Dealing with Disorder in the North

The Chinese occupation of the north created a distinct set of conditions there that served to accentuate underlying north-south differences in 1945–1946. As distinct from the south, a combination of the
Chinese presence and a shortage of French troops blocked the French
advance into the north and led to Franco-Vietnamese negotiations
which, whatever else they were intended to achieve,[86] gave the

---

[85]Vo Nguyen Giap, *Unforgettable Days*, p. 114. Gras, *Histoire*, pp. 136–139. Duiker,
The Communist Road, p. 122 says 'In June Nguyen Binh lauched an offensive
northwest of Saigon, near the towns of Bien Hoa, Ben Cat, and Thu Dau Mot.' On
other offensives see Tonnesson, *1946*, pp. 53–54.

[86]As we will see, the idea that the French would inevitably attempt to invade the
north and that the negotiations were the 'shield' behind which the government
developed the army was widely believed at the time. However, we will also see there
are many clear indications that Ho Chi Minh's government tried to come to a peaceful
accomodation with the French in its negotiations. There is much on the negotiations in
Vo Nguyen Giap, *Unforgettable Days*, although it could hardly be said to offer a

government fifteen months to develop its forces before the outbreak of full-scale hostilities. When this major difference was superimposed on other underlying north-south differences like the nature of the terrain and the economic situation, we will see that the northern army was at a very different level of development from its southern counterpart when full scale hostilities began in the north in December 1946. Nevertheless, these differences cannot be kept in perspective unless fundamental similarities in the society's reaction to foreign occupation in both north and south are recognised. It must be shown first that, just as British and French intervention in the south caused serious internal conflict in the southern resistance, the Chinese occupation of the north, and the negotiated phasing in of French troops after April 1946, had a similar effect there even though it ran along different lines.

When the Chinese army of General Lu Han began its occupation of the country in late 1945 it sponsored the return of violently anti-communist remnants of the *Quoc Dan Dang* (VNQDD) and the *Dong Minh Hoi* (DMH) to Vietnam from exile in China. With Chinese protection these groups began to recruit their own armies around Phu Tho, Viet Tri, and Vinh Yen.[87] One French report gives some impression of the level of anti-government military development in its description of the DMH's army in early 1946:

> The Dong Minh Hoi's Army has been formed in China. The cadres have been trained by the Chinese at the Whampoa Military College. The units have been equipped by the Chinese on the same scale as the units of the central government (i.e. Chinese). This army therefore represents a solid force (of around 5,000) . . . the main force of the Dong Minh Hoi is still in the Tonkin Delta . . . preparing for a coup d'état.[88]

To understand fully the problems these armies created for the government, however, it is necessary to place their activities in the context of the Franco-Vietnamese negotiations which had begun in late 1945.

---

critical account. From the French point of view see Gras, *Histoire*, pp. 111–122. Devillers, *Histoire*, provides a more scholarly account in his Chapters on the Franco-Viet Minh Conferences at Dalat and Fontainebleau. Tonnesson, *1946*, is a valuable account of the period from September to December. Bao Dai, *Le Dragon d'Annam*, pp. 127–172 could also be read.

[87]Devillers, *Histoire*, Chapter XI has a good description of the problems which the VNQDD and Dong Minh Hoi caused the government. See also *LSQD*, p. 204, pp. 214–215, p. 241.

[88]SHAT, C. 88, *La République Démocratique*, p. 61.

A standard explanation for the negotiations throughout 1946 and since has been that the government was buying time to build up its forces for the French invasion of the north that everyone expected. As *Truth* said on 21 March 1946 the negotiations were the 'shield'[89] behind which the country readied its defences, and in 1979 Vo Nguyen Giap supported this argument when he stated that

(the negotiations were an aspect) of the fight for time that would enable us to strengthen the political power of the people, strengthen the forces of the revolution, and prepare to resist the new invasion plans of the enemy.[90]

Yet, while the belief that the French would attack the north was widespread, it is unlikely that Ho Chi Minh's motives for negotiating were as simple as the standard argument suggests.

A notable feature of official Vietnamese statements surrounding the negotiations is their assumption of the possibility of peaceful settlement with the left wing forces in 'new France'.[91] For example, if we take the Central Committee's instructions to cadres at the time of the Franco-Vietnamese accord of March 1946,[92] the idea that war was probable certainly lurked behind directions to 'preserve our real strength and gain a breathing space to strengthen our new position, reorganise the ranks of the revolution'. Yet not once do the instructions speak of the inevitability of war. The preliminary convention signed on March 6 might not have recognised Vietnamese independence, but it had recognised that Vietnam was a self governing free state, and this was a 'first step'. Hence, shooting at French colonial-

[89]Nha Xuat Ban Su That [Truth Publishing House], *Cuoc Khang Chien Than Thanh cua Nhan Dan Viet Nam* [The Sacred War of Resistance of the Vietnamese People], (hereafter *CKCT*), 4 Vols, Hanoi, 1958–1960, Vol. 1, p. 71. The same idea also came out strongly in an interview with Mr. Hoang Xuan Han, Paris, 29 May 1961. Mr Hoang Xuan Han was involved in the negotiations in 1946.

[90]Vo Nguyen Giap, *Dien Bien Phu*, Hanoi: Quan Doi Nhan Dan, 1979, pp. 19–20. It is also worth noting that from the French point of view Tonnesson, *1946*, could be read as an extended discussion of French determination to re-occupy the north, while Gras, *Histoire*, p.65 described the French occupation of Cochinchina, Cambodia, and Southern Laos as a 'preliminary' operation.

[91]This term was used in Party documents and in the press. See note 90 and *CKCT*, Vol. 1, pp. 70–71 for examples of its use.

[92]Ban Chap Hanh Trung Uong Dang Cong San Viet Nam [Executive Board of the Central committee of the Communist Party of Vietnam], *Van Kien Dang ve Khang Chien chong Thuc Dan Phap, Tap 1 (1945–1950)* [Party Documents on the Resistance War against the French Colonialists, Vol. 1 (1945–1950)], (hereafter *VKD*), Hanoi: NXB Su That, 1986, pp. 47–56. The quotes in the following paragraph come from p. 48, p. 49, p. 51, p. 50. For 'new France' see p. 48.

.ists and not believing in the correctness of an accord with France were popular tendencies that

> come out of a proper spirit of loving the country, but are light headed and could very easily push our people into unprincipled and ungovernable actions and easily provoke the reactionaries.

As careful distinctions were made between reactionary and progressive French elements in many contemporary statements, and as old slogans like 'fight the French colonial invaders' yielded to more conciliatory ones in which 'the French and Vietnamese peoples are united against the French reactionaries', the explanation that the negotiations were a 'shield' for defence preparations does not tell the whole story. In part, this explanation was itself a shield for the government's complex motives.[93]

The great difficulty which the government had as it treated with the invader, was that the main concession it made was very unpopular. When the government signed the March 6 Accords it agreed to the location of 15,000 French troops in the north to safeguard French interests pending a final Franco-Vietnamese settlement. Ho Chi Minh offered his people the reasonable argument that this concession would ensure a Chinese withdrawal from the north. But as French troops were phased into the north between April and July, the French Captain Le Flahec, whose task it was to negotiate the detailed deployment of French troops with Vietnamese and Chinese authorities, has described the 'profound bitterness'[94] with which his mission was received.

As his party travelled along the road three or four kilometers from Nam Dinh in April he described its reception as follows:

> our small group whose itinerary had been announced several days before already had the surprise of being stopped by an impressive martial display: batteries of sub-machine guns concentrated on the route . . . men lying almost everywhere in the rice fields . . . soldiers armed to the teeth with grenades,

---

[93]Tonnesson, *1946*, has presented other evidence that the Vietnamese government was serious about arriving at a negotiated settlement. In fact, his entire discussion revolves around the argument that neither the Vietnamese nor the French governments wanted war between September and December 1946. More evidence that the Vietnamese were serious is also bound to come out, for when I made the mistake of accepting the popular Party line in an earlier draft David Marr was able to draw on some reading he has been doing to make me think again.

[94]Capitaine Le Flahec, *Quelques missions en pays Viet Minh (Souvenirs)*, CHEAM, No date, p. 6.

knives, pistols, sub-machine guns and with an air as menacing as possible.[95]

What is of course remarkable about this scene and others Le Flahec encountered is that the soldiers did not shoot. By April the government must have established good discipline in the armed forces at Nam Dinh and many other areas for widespread hostilities not to have broken out immediately against the French. Yet, as nationalist sentiment boiled over into anti-French boycotts, strikes, and attacks in other places, inadequate training of units and frequent lapses in the cumbersome command system could lead to serious indiscipline and undermine the government's delicate negotiations with the French.

On April 28, for example, a minor battle developed after a Vietnamese post at Hai Phong fired on French civilians.[96] In early August a sizeable battle which involved French armoured cars, artillery, and aircraft also took place around Bac Ninh when Vietnamese troops fired on a French convoy headed for Lang Son. As the size of this battle and the deep anger of official Vietnamese accounts of how the French provoked it suggest,[97] the decision to fire on the convoy could very well have come from local committee level and, if not, local committees must have supported the decision once it had been made. Therefore, as we return to conservative groups like the VNQDD and DMH, it was in an atmosphere of great and complex tensions, of unacknowledged warfare in some places and restraint in most others, that they may be seen to have exacerbated the difficulties which the government already had.

As early as December 1945 VNQDD propaganda had vilified the government as follows:

> The truth is that the government tells the population to collaborate with the French.
> The truth is that the government is powerless.
> The truth is that the propaganda bureau specialises in lies.
> The truth is that the government uses terror and that it has become a specialist in making money from collections and subscriptions.

[95]Ibid. This source also gives examples from other parts of the country.

[96]Franchini, *Les guerres*, Vol. 1, p. 304

[97]The Vietnamese account of the affair is *CKCT*, Vol. 1, pp. 122–123, *Su That*, No. 48, 9 August 1946, which claims convincingly because of the detail it provides that French provocations were 'meticulously' prepared. On the other hand, Gras, *Histoire*, p. 128 is less convincing in his brief account which described the 'veritable ambush' of the convoy.

The truth is that Tran Van Giau and the members of the Youth Committee of Cochinchina are all deserters.[98]

To counter the effects of this propaganda inside Vietnam (and also to project a moderate image to the French) the government took various steps. For instance, once the ICP had cleverly dissolved itself in November 1945 to dampen criticism about the government being a group of radical communist terrorists, elections were held on 6 January 1946 and fifty of the three hundred seats in the National Assembly were allotted to the conservative parties.[99] But just as the Nam Bo Committee failed to pacify the Hoa Hao by offering Huynh Phu So a place in 1945, the elections and an offer of seats in the National Assembly failed to placate the conservative parties in the north and quell the conflict.

At this time Devillers says that Hanoi was 'a city without law'.[100] The VNQDD kidnapped, tortured and murdered members of the Viet Minh and the Viet Minh did the same to the VNQDD. Two Viet Minh prison registers captured by the French in December 1946 give some impression of the scale of the internal conflict between September 1945 and January 1946 even though they only give the barest hint of what was happening around Hanoi. One of these registers lists details of 225 arrests around Hanoi between December and January of which all were made for political reasons, and the second register accounts for sixty-four political prisoners deported to Bac Kan between September and February 1946.[101] And, in this context of

[98]The VNQDD Journal 'Truth', 12 December 1945, quoted in SHAT, C 88, *La République Démocratique*, pp. 24–25.

[99]Tonnesson, *1946*, p. 45 tells us that the conservative parties were given the opportunity to present candidates at the elections but did not take it. Following pressure from the Chinese these parties were then given the right to the non-elected seats in the assembly. However, Tonnesson's claim that 70 of the 300 seats were for non-elected representatives seems high. I have therefore followed Chen, *Vietnam and China*, p. 130 who says 50. On the elections also Devillers, *Histoire*, pp. 200–201, *LSDC*, pp. 454–455. There are a number of contemporary Vietnamese political pamphlets on the elections in the Bibliothèque Nationale in Paris which I imagine could provide the raw material for an interesting essay on Vietnamese perceptions of democracy and constitutionalism. See for example, Hoi Van Hoa Cuu Quoc Viet Nam [Vietnam National Salvation Cultural Organisation] *Quyen va Bon Phan Lam Dan* [The Rights and Duties of Citizens], Hanoi, 1945; the same author, *Hien Phap la Gi?* [What is a Constitution?], Hanoi,1945; Viet Nam Dan Chu Cong Hoa Nam Thu Hai [Democratic Republic of Vietnam Second Year] *Tong Tuyen Cu Ngay 6–1–1946* [The General Elections 6–1–46], Hanoi, no date.

[100]Devillers, *Histoire*, p. 197.

[101]SHAT, C. 88, *Le Viet Minh et Le Parti Communiste Indochinois*, Hanoi, 1949,

attacks on the government's authority and counter attacks by the government, it is necessary to raise the question of 'terror' once more.

As we saw in the last Chapter, the Viet Minh's rise to power from March to August was accompanied by a some violence even though the Viet Minh was by no means always responsible for it. Then, after August there is evidence of a degree of state sanctioned brutality. French sources note the killing and abuse of mandarins and notables in a number of regions by 'armed groups often unknown to the population.'[102] In all likelihood, some of these groups were the 'Assault Squads' of the Public Security Service (*Cong An Xung Phong*) created in early 1946.[103] Moreover, the government clearly sanctioned the purge of old regime figures like Pham Quynh, Ngo Dinh Khoi, and Bui Quang Chieu, and many lesser figures like the French spy, Bao Tao, who was dragged before one of the many People's Tribunals (*Toa An Dan Chung*) in Trung Bo and executed. As the journalist Hoai Tan recorded Bao Tao's execution: 'at five o'clock on the morning of 30 September in the execution grounds at Vinh near the Office of Justice a single shot brought his vile life to an end'.[104] This was real satisfaction.

Yet after eighty years of systematic colonial repression it is hard to see how the spilling of some blood could have been avoided. This is especially so in a highly charged revolutionary situation when the country was being occupied by three foreign armies, and when the violence of conservative groups like the VNQDD left the government with no alternative but to take repressive action. As the official journal *Truth* explained on 19 July, the VNQDD

> creates many difficulties for our diplomacy and does not take the higher interests of our people into account. The government is forced to take action. The Office of Public Security has been put to work!'[105]

In fact, the anti-government and anti-French violence of the conservative parties was so irrational that it finally prompted the French to approve of the government's liquidation of them.[106] And, when

---

Annex 5. The registers were captured in December 1946. Also see Fall, *The Viet Minh*, p. 51.

[102]Isoart, *Le phénomène national*, p. 51.

[103]*LSQD*, p. 221, p. 231.

[104]Hoai Tan, *Trung Bo Khang Chien*, p. 18.

[105]*CKCT*, Vol. 1, p. 112.

[106]At least some French concurrence was needed for the government's move against the VNQDD and Dong Minh Hoi because some French troops were already located in the north and no misunderstandings that might lead to premature hostilities with the French could be permitted. See Devillers, *Histoire*, p. 278.

the government did move against VNQDD and DMH bases around Phu Tho, Yen Bai, Viet Tri, and Vinh Yen in July and August 1946,[107] the National Army's rapid success there further highlights the inadequacy of those theories which try to explain the government's survival in terms of 'terror' and 'a policy of brutality and terrorism'.[108]

The VNQDD and DMH bases collapsed once their Chinese protectors had withdrawn from the north because the government's foundations in the society were deeper and wider. Moreover, the government's success against the conservative parties was a perfect example of its integration of internal political development with international diplomacy. By negotiating with the French and agreeing to the location of some French troops in the north the government had eliminated its problems one by one: French troops in the north guaranteed the withdrawal of the Chinese, this withdrawal guaranteed the defeat of the conservative parties (especially when the French supported the government in this respect), and the defeat of the conservatives reinforced the internal unity that the central government's armed propaganda campaign had been creating in the northern provinces just as it had been in the south.

In late 1945 and 1946 the official history states that the Army for National Defence

> executed propaganda and education work, mobilised people, proselytised the enemy, and organised . . . following the (earlier) experience of the Party and the Liberation Army in mobilising the masses.[109]

To promote this campaign the armed propaganda teams could organise theatrical performances in the villages, occasionally punish traitors and redistribute their property, offer crash courses in military drills, and involve themselves in promoting literacy.[110] And it is a reflection of the popularity of this campaign that village dogs were often the biggest obstacle to armed propaganda teams in large tracts of the countryside. These animals had to be repressed by government decree because they barked at cadres and sometimes bit them.[111]

[107] LSQD, p. 215.

[108] For example, Duiker, The Communist Road, p. 111, p. 117, p. 122.

[109] LSQD, p. 212.

[110] For a general discussion of the literacy campaign see Nguyen Trong Con, 'Vai Net ve Phong Trao Diet Giac o Viet Nam trong 5 Nam Khang Chien chong Phap (1945–1950)' [A Few Lines on the Movement to Wipe Out Illiteracy in Vietnam in the First 5 years of the Resistance War against the French (1945–1950)], NCLS, No. 3, May-June 1979, pp. 38–46.

[111] Uyen Loewald, Child of Vietnam, Melbourne: Hyland House, 1987, p. 50. Loewald's reference to dogs also finds support in Nam Cao's popular short story, Doi Mat [The Eyes], which can be found in various editions of his collected works.

Some indication of the width of the government's foundation in the society by mid to late 1946 is thus contained in official claims that there were 'almost a million'[112] people in the village Self Defence Forces (*Tu Ve*). If the real figure was not this high it must have been close because Giap tells how self defence units based on the National Salvation Youth League in the north 'were organised in almost every hamlet, village, street, and factory',[113] and French sources agree:

> Each street and village had its self defence groups comprising all the eligible young people to carry arms, as well as selected old soldiers. In the minds of the government the self defence groups placed under the authority of the People's Committees would become guerrillas in the case of a French invasion.[114]

There is also no doubt that the army viewed these developments as central to the process of consolidating the government's power, for Giap, who was a member of the government as well as the commander in chief of the army, has described how

> In areas not yet at war, (the self defence forces) proved an efficient instrument of dictatorship for the revolutionary power, ensuring security for the Party, the State, and Front Offices, and economic and national defence establishments maintaining peace and order, and suppressing reactionaries.[115]

The term 'efficient instrument' should be qualified here, for Giap does not tell us about the lack of training and indiscipline in the self defence forces as well as the National Army that we have already noted. But, given the extremely complex regional development of these forces, what is at least as remarkable as their indiscipline is the general level of restraint they demonstrated and the way the power of the central government was being consolidated in the provinces through armed propaganda.

By operating in the same political structures as the Southern Advance Units, the National Army had again created a high degree of political and military unity in the northern provinces. This unity had progressively reinforced the strength of the central authority so that the government not only had a political foundation on which to further reinforce regional unity, but it also had an extremely flexible foundation on which to deal with the complex external pressures that bore down on it. In other words, such regional unity *around the centre*

---

[112]Ibid., p. 230.

[113]Vo Nguyen Giap, *Unforgettable Days*, p. 86.

[114]Devillers, *Histoire*, p. 184.

[115]Vo Nguyen Giap, *Unforgettable Days*, p. 86.

guaranteed the survival of the national government under modern conditions because such a government was the only one that could focus the general desire for independence. The central government's general ability to restrain the population in the north, and to coordinate its diplomacy with guerrilla offensives in the south[116] shows that this was so.

At the same time, however, it must not be forgotten that since the central government's power was in the regions its existence also depended on the regional differences which gave the anti-French (and later anti-American) resistance its resilience. Indeed, there were many reasons why the army's development in the north had a very different character to its development in the south, even if the underlying political structures in all regions were similar.

Expansion of the Army in the Northern Regions

The geographical proximity of the earliest guerrilla bases in the Viet Bac to the densely populated northern plains was one reason for relatively rapid military expansion in northern society after August 1945. In the wake of the Viet Minh's cumulative armed propaganda victories between March and August village self defence units sprang up almost everywhere in Bac Bo and much of northern Trung Bo. As already noted there were about a million people in such organisations by late 1946. When this very rapid expansion then occurred during fifteen months of relative peace, the Viet Minh had the opportunity to develop a regular force with a level of military training, organisation, and logistics infrastructure that was not possible in the south where the resistance was involved in a guerrilla war. Also, even though the Viet Minh was not involved in full scale hostilities in the north as it was in the south, it had a particular set of problems in the north which had a further bearing on the distinctive nature of military development there.

In the north the Viet Minh were operating at a general level of poverty that was not easily imaginable in the south. Quite apart from the lingering effects of the famine of the winter of 1944–1945 most sources agree that the Chinese occupation created additional economic hardship.[117] To disarm about 30,000 defeated Japanese soldiers General Lu Han had led an 180,000[118] strong army of

[116]See note 84 above.

[117]Patti, *Why Vietnam*, chapter 30 provides the most detailed and interesting account of Chinese plunder.

[118]Ibid., p. 562, note 18 says 180,000 was the approximate total that was rotated through Vietnam during the period of occupation. There were never more than 50,000 troops in garrison at any one time.

occupation into northern Vietnam, and it descended on the country like a plague of locusts. (Chinese plunder of Vietnamese towns and cities went as far as water taps and roofing tiles.) Thus, although the Chinese occupation gave the Viet Minh time to organise their forces in the north, it also accentuated the problem of how the government was going to marshall the resources to train, lead, equip, and, above all, feed the regular soldiers that would have to be recruited from the village self defence forces and incorporated into regular forces capable of fighting the French.

In 1946 units of the National Army were basically no different from the self defence forces who supported themselves in the villages around which they operated. The problem of feeding the army was thus a problem of increasing production in the community at large. As soon as Ho Chi Minh's government came to power it announced that its first priority was 'the opening of an immediate campaign to increase production so as to overcome the famine'.[119] A little later Ho indicated the military implications of the production drive in an appeal to peasants:

> Soldiers go forth to preserve the country. Peasants go forth to help the soldiers. The two sides of the task are different but they are really related . . . At the present time we have two most important tasks: alleviating the famine in the north and the resistance in the south.[120]

Since the task was two sided the official history says that as the army units went out to repair dikes and cultivate the fields:

> Soldiers of the National Army who had vegetables ate vegetables, those who had rice gruel ate rice gruel, they wore good clothes and rags . . . (At the same time) the soldiers went forth with the people to increase production realising Ho Chi Minh's slogan "an inch of earth is an inch of gold".[121]

And on this slim basis the army grew.

Instead of the relatively few and more loosely structured *Chi Doi* which characterised southern military organisation in 1946, the more numerous quasi-regular main force units that characterised northern organisation were more tightly structured battalions (*Tieu Doan*) and regiments (*Trung Doan*). The size of these units varied a great deal,

---

[119]*LSDC*, p. 436. This was the first of six priorities. In order the others were: the anti-illiteracy campaign, the organisation of an election, the organisation of a program of education against colonialism, the reduction of taxes, the promulgation of freedom of religion to promote unity between Catholics and non-Catholics.

[120]Ho Chi Minh, *Tuyen Tap* [Collected Works], Hanoi: Su That, 1980, Vol. 1, p. 378.

[121]*LSQD*, p. 209, on sending soldiers to repair dikes see *LSDC*, p.445.

but in 1946 battalions of 500 men and regiments of 1,500 men would not have been unusual. Such large units were usually raised from the local self defence and guerrilla units in a particular area by existing National Army armed propaganda teams and designed to operate as units within a tighter command structure than their southern counterparts. This structuring was at least begun by January 1946 when the army's political leadership was centralised in Hanoi under the 'Central Committee's Army Member (*Trung Uong Quan Uy*) to help the Executive Committee of the Party lead the army'.[122] But far more than the centralisation of the army's political leadership was necessary to staff the some thirty quasi-regular regiments with perhaps 60,000 troops in existence by late 1946.[123]

The first military school to open after the declaration of independence was probably the Military Administrative School in Hanoi which received 300 cadets on 14 October, 1945. Within a year numerous cadre schools such as the Tran Quoc Tuan Military Academy in Thai Nguyen and the Ho Chi Minh Self Defence School in Hanoi had opened 'to create cadres urgently for the armed forces'.[124] Many regional committees also opened military schools in Bac Bo and Trung Bo in conjunction with existing local units, and the old Japanese Resistance School had its name changed to the Viet Nam Cadre School and greatly expanded its training program.[125] It should be added, however, that conditions in these schools could leave much to be desired as short rations, long hours, and strident political cadres were sometimes known to exhaust trainees and even cause them to run away.

Meanwhile, one group of people whose skills must have been in great demand was a group the official history only mentions in passing as 'former soldiers who loved the country'.[126] On the eve of the Japanese coup d'état in March 1945 there were around 50,000 Vietnamese soldiers in the Franco-Vietnamese Colonial Army. There were also around 22,000 in the Indigenous Guard,[127] and by late 1946 perhaps 2,000 to 4,000 old colonial troops had deserted

---

[122]*LSQD*, p. 211.

[123]*Ibid.*, p. 234. This source also gives the total strength of the regular army north and south as 80,000. French sources say that by mid 1946 the army in the north was around 30,000. See Devillers, *Histoire*, p. 283, and Gras, *Histoire*, p. 88. This figure obviously does not include the some 20,000 regulars in the south and it also does not allow for another six months development.

[124]*LSQD*, p. 210. For the Military Administrative School see Vu Chieu Ngu, 'Political and social Change', p. 435.

[125]*LSQD*, p. 210.

[126]Ibid.

from their units in France and returned to Vietnam. Some were possibly permitted to return to their villages by the French, but many others had to return via Viet Minh reception centers in Bangkok, Udon, and Laotian trails.[128] In the quasi-regular army that numbered about 60,000 in the north and 20,000 in the south by late 1946, therefore, the recruitment of even 10,000 trained ex-colonial officers and troops would have represented a significant infusion of military skills.

Some idea of this infusion comes from a number of sources. Ngo Van Chieu says in his memoirs that when he was put in charge of thirty men in October 1945 'for the most part these were old *tirailleurs* of the French'.[129] Chieu's battalion commander, a former adjutant of *tirailleurs*, is also reported to have boasted 'without us who would have officered the army?'.[130] Furthermore, while the official history says that 'military documents of the French and Japanese Armies were searched for and studied',[131] the continuing influence of French military practice may be detected in a comparison of various military manuals. If M. Reinert's, *Manoeuvre (1915): Translation en Quoc Ngu*, that was in wide use in the Colonial Army is compared with the Viet Minh's 1945 manual, *An Analysis of Military Work*, it is clear that sections on basic drills in the second manual have been copied more or less word for word from the first.[132] For such reasons Bernhard Fall's long standing comment that disbanded colonial forces 'became the hard core of the Viet Minh's nascent army'[133] must be taken seriously, even though Fall's analysis ignores the fundamental force of the nation that brought old colonial soldiers into the army in the first place.

Another contribution to northern military development that must be taken seriously, but not exaggerated, is the Japanese contribution. The Viet Minh were ready to utilise any resource that would help build the army, and, even though official Vietnamese sources barely mention Japanese aid, there was considerable time in the north for

[127]Amiral Decoux, *A la barre*, p. 85.
[128]Lieutenant Hanns, *Les forces armées du Viet Minh dans le Viet Nam du Nord*, CHEAM, 1950, p. 3. For details of Vietnamese mutinies in French units in France in late 1945 see AOM, NF, C. 102, D. 978.
[129]Ngo Van Chieu, *Journal d'un combattant*, 47–48.
[130]Ibid., p. 54.
[131]*LSQD*, p. 210.
[132]Compare M. Reinert, *Manoeuvre, Traduit en Quoc Ngu (Extrait du décret du 25 Août 1915)*, Hanoi, 1916?, p. 19, p. 30 and Viet Nam Giai Phong Quan [Vietnam Liberation Army] *Phan Tich Dong Tac Quan Su* [An Analysis of Military Work], Hanoi: Le Van Tan, 1945, p. 1, p. 8. See also Truong Chinh, *The Resistance Will Win*, in *Selected Writings*, Hanoi:Foreign Languages Publishing House, 1977, p. 169.
[133]Fall, *The Viet Minh*, p. 12.

the Viet Minh to make use of Japanese deserters—there were some 2,000 to 4,000 in the country—[134] who cooperated with the Viet Minh between August 1945 and December 1946. On the other hand, McAlister's unqualified emphasis on the 'important assistance of deserters from the Japanese Army'[135] must be treated with caution when it is based French sources which had an obvious interest in depicting the Viet Minh as Japanese puppets.[136]

According to French records of Japanese testimony in late 1946, one group of Japanese, who were motivated by the desire to 'create the necessary bases for aiding the resurrection of Japan' after the Second World War, was organised around the 'Japanese Organism for Collaboration and Aid for the Independence of Vietnam'.[137] The Organism's headquarters were in Thai Nguyen under a Lieutenant Colonel Mukaiyama formerly of the Staff of the 38th Army, and it had branches throughout Bac Bo and Trung Bo: Hanoi, Hai Phong, Nam Dinh, Son Tay, Dong Trieu, Lao Kay, Bac Quang, Vinh, Hue, Quang Ngai. Around the headquarters in Thai Nguyen there were some 1,500 Japanese and a further 2,500 around the other locations.[138] But, while this organisation appears impressive, its significance for the Viet Minh must have been limited by the confusion and frustration that surely characterised its operations in the face of defeat at home and revolutionary upheavals in Vietnam.

Yet it is still clear that one area in which the Japanese renegades made some contribution to the Viet Minh was in military training. Ngo Van Chieu explains in his memoirs how in December 1945 'because we had everything to learn'[139] his unit accepted training from a Japanese officer who spoke Vietnamese and others under his leadership, Vietnamese militia who had served with the Japanese during the War. It is also well known that Japanese officers were sprinkled through the military schools.[140] With Lieutenant Colonel

[134]See note 138.

[135]McAlister, 'The Origins', p. 299.

[136]On this point scc Vu Chieu Ngu, 'Political and Social Change', pp. 440–442. Thierry d'Argenlieu, *Chronique d'Indochine, 1945–1947*, Paris: Albin Michele, 1985, p. 81, gives some idea of the contemporary French attitude to Japanese aid to the Viet Minh.

[137]Commandement Français en Extrême Orient, Etat Major, 'Les Viet Minh Utilisent des Japonais', Saigon, 1947, Pièce 9, 5 December 1946, Hanoi, p. 1. The information in this document was based on Japanese testimony by a Lieutenant Colonel Saito and a number of other Japanese officers to the French Staff.

[138]Ibid., pp. 1–3. This source thus agrees with Patti's figure of 4,000 in *Why Viet Nam?*, p. 341. On Japanese attitudes see Chieu Ngu, 'Political and Social Change', pp. 439–442.

[139]Ngo Van Chieu, *Journal d'un combattant*, p. 60.

[140]Devillers, *Histoire*, p. 282.

Mukaiyama at the Viet Minh training centre in Thai Nguyen, for example, was the chief artillery instructor Lieutenant Nishizawa from the 51st Regiment of Mountain Artillery, while a Chief Sergeant Horiuchi from the Kempeitai was attached to the Viet Minh Cadre School in Son Tay.[141]

In the field of logistics even greater numbers were involved. Of the 1,500 Japanese around Thai Nguyen some 900 were combatants and some 600 were service personnel, the majority of whom 'worked in the arms factories'.[142] Once the government set up an Ordnance Office in the Ministry of Defence on 15 September and further organised numerous Army Supply and Manufacturing Agencies by mid-1946,[143] a number of Japanese could also have been involved with many times more Vietnamese personnel in converting old French industrial establishments into weapons workshops (and possibly the clothing and shoe factories which the Vietnamese sources also note)[144] in various parts of the country. Around Thai Nguyen, for example, the evidence shows one complex of fifteen weapons workshops run by a man named Inuge, a former member of the Showa Tosho Company in Hai Phong. This complex produced ten pistols a day, and fifty rifles and three or four machine guns a month.[145] (The quality of the pistols was good, the rifles average, and the machine guns poor—the working parts often jammed after firing only five or six rounds). Also, even though the Chinese Army had come to Vietnam to disarm the Japanese, at least some of the mountain artillery of the still heavily armed 900 combatants already mentioned around Thai Nguyen may well have found its way into the hands of the National Army which formed its first official artillery unit in June.[146]

One factor which such Japanese military assistance helps bring into perspective, therefore, is the extent to which northern conditions were leading to the creation of a regular army rather than a guerrilla resistance as had evolved in the south. Of course, in late 1946 the army was still very far from reaching a level of development in any region that could pose a significant threat to a sizeable French force. But, in the north, where the army was biggest and most regular an

---

[141]Commandement Français, *Les Viet Minh Utilisent*, Pièce 1.

[142]Ibid., Pièce 9, pp. 2–3. *LSQD*, p. 208 mentions 'Japanese' sources of supply in passing. See also Edgar O'Ballance, *The Indochina War*, London, 1964, p. 55.

[143]*LSQD*, p. 207, p. 235.

[144]Ibid. This source also stresses the rapid development of the primitive arms industry in the villages.

[145]Commandement Français, *Les Viet Minh Utilisent*, Pièce 9, pp. 2–3.

[146]Ibid. *LSQD*, p. 234.

important trend emerged as the Chinese occupation and the Franco-Vietnamese negotiations gave the Viet Minh time to make use of Japanese aid. Indeed, the relatively high potential for military development in the north and the corresponding high demand for foreign aid went with the fact that the north had its back to China. The full significance of this simple geographical fact would not become apparent until 1949–1950 when Mao Zedong's victories in China would open the ordnance depots of that country to the Viet Minh. But by 1946 the gap between the levels of military development in the north and south had already begun to grow. And here it must be added that, even in 1946, the north already enjoyed direct logistics connections with China.

McAlister's conclusion that Chinese sources of supply were responsible 'for most of the high quality weapons which the Viet Minh received' is difficult to fault.[147] By 17 September 1945 Ho Chi Minh declared a 'gold week' that was designed to raise funds for weapons purchases. The official history indicates that negotiations were soon under way with the 'Chinese' as well as the 'Japanese' Armies[148] to obtain weapons of all descriptions, ammunition, and uniforms. French archives provide such examples as that of one Poon Kong Mou, a native of Hai Nan who arrived in Hanoi with the Chinese Army in late 1945 and made several transactions with the Vietnamese government. One of these in 1946 is said to have concerned a large quantity of weapons—3,000 rifles with fifty rounds of ammunition each, twenty five heavy machine guns, thirty light machine guns, ten heavy mortars, and ten light artillery pieces—which the Ordnance Office sent junks to collect from Hai Nan.[149] Throughout 1946 and in early 1947 many other missions to buy arms, uniforms, printing presses, and paper were also sent to Hong Kong and Canton by people like Nguyen Duc Thuy the Chief of Chinese Affairs in the Foreign Ministry and Special Envoy to the Ministry of Defence.[150] As we have seen, some of these supplies found their way into the south to support the government's armed propaganda campaign. But as the level of military development in the south began to diminish in relation to the level in the north, the vast bulk of supplies from China were used where they were most needed in the north.

There is no doubt that the northern half of the country was at a much higher level of military development than the south when the Franco-Viet Minh negotiations broke down and full scale hostilities

[147]McAlister, 'The Origins', pp. 303–304.
[148]*LSQD*, p. 208.
[149]SHAT, C. 102, D. *Trafic d'Armes*, 'L'Approvisionnement en armes'.
[150]Ibid.

broke out on 19 December. Around this time, Party documents made the point themselves when they contrasted the situation in the northern and southern regions:

> In Nam Bo, where the terrain is difficult and preparations were less, the resistance has already been underway for over a year. (In the north) we have advantageous terrain, more supplies, and will be able to fight a resistance war for many years, until victory.[151]

However, while French intelligence reported that Giap had 35,000 troops with artillery and mortars around Hanoi in early December,[152] it must be kept in mind that this relatively high level of development generated its own problems.

Around mid-October, as the Vietnamese Government began to protest French moves to reestablish their customs control over the port of Hai Phong, the Central Committee had met at Ha Dong behind the ornately carved ironwood doors of the former Province Chief's mansion.[153] The recently published resolutions of this meeting reveal that military administration was still knotted with many problems reflecting rapid development, inexperience, and regionalism. The system of political officers still had to be integrated more effectively into the national defence infrastructure. The military command system had to become less cumbersome. The performance of cadres had to be lifted and military training standardised in schools in different regions. Factories and workshops had to have a unified system of production. The distribution of weapons had to be rationalised. Quinine had to reach soldiers in places where they could catch malaria. In view of the general shortage of supplies, weapons, and medical services the numbers flocking into the national army had to be stemmed at the same time as regional units and village self defence forces still had to be consolidated.[154] Despite all these problems, however, the army was preparing to fight.

After much deliberation the Party Secretary, Truong Chinh, affirmed around 19 October that 'we must be determined to fight the French'.[155] Soldiers were to be reminded that the Franco-Viet Minh accords were only temporary, and the senior training cadre at the

---

[151]*VKD*, p. 85. The Statement was made on 5 November 1946.

[152]Tonnesson, *1946*, p. 169.

[153]For a description of the meeting see Vuong Thua Vu, *Truong Thanh trong Chien Dau* [Coming of Age in War], Hanoi, 1979, pp. 73–75. This meeting coincided with the failure of the negotiations at Fontainebleau and the return of the Viet Minh delegation headed by Pham Van Dong.

[154]*VKD*, pp. 75–82.

[155]Quoted in *LSQD*, p. 243.

Tran Quoc Tuan Military Academy, Vuong Thua Vu, was given responsibility to organise the defence of Hanoi.[156] By late November he therefore tells us there were five regular battalions in the capital with 1,500 weapons, twelve suicide squads, thirty special guerrilla units, and many irregular self defence groups including a platoon of Buddhist monks under one Abbot Minh. Many government offices had already moved to Ha Dong from where they would eventually withdraw to the Viet Bac base area,[157] although some were trapped in Hanoi when the war broke out. Apparently, right up to the last moment, not everyone believed that war was imminent or that the Franco-Vietnamese accords were temporary.

But the war was imminent and, even if some quirk of fate had protracted the negotiations for a time, it was inevitable by late November. After the intractable customs dispute culminated in the notorious French naval bombardment of the civilian centers of Hai Phong on the 23rd and the simultaneous French occupation of Lang Son, the French noticed that the evacuation of Hanoi was being stepped up and defence works were being dug—mainly individual fox holes all over the city and trenches around government buildings. The French commander, Valluy, anticipated a Vietnamese attack, and Giap anticipated a French one. After the southern commander, Nguyen Binh, had sent a telegram north urging attacks on the Hanoi water works, electricity plant, and other facilities, Giap sent the following message south on the 30th: 'Total agreement with your intentions. We are preparing. As soon as news of the French attack on Hanoi is confirmed, all the fronts in Nam Bo will attack at the same time.'[158] Then, by the 19th when war broke out, events had become so confused in Hanoi that the only conclusion the most meticulous analysis we have of them has reached is that 'the information at our disposal does not permit us to reach a conclusion on the origin of the (Vietnamese) attack of 19 December'.[159]

---

[156]Ibid., pp. 243–244; Vuong Thua Vu, *Truong Thanh trong*, p. 76. For evidence of other plans and for the defence of Hanoi based on French intelligence sources see Tonnesson, *1946*, pp. 160–161.

[157]Vuong Thua Vu, *Truong Thanh trong*, pp. 77–106 on preparations for the battle. See also *LSQD*, pp. 261–263. Gras, *Histoire*, pp. 135–136 discussed the Viet Minh's 'combat government'.

[158]On Hai Phong and Lang Son see Chesneaux, *Tradition et révolution*, pp. 272–288, Gras, *Histoire*, pp. 142–148, Tonnesson, *1946*, pp. 100–120. On Vietnamese defence preparations in Hanoi see Devillers, *Histoire*, p. 345. The quote comes from Tonnesson, *1946*, p. 23.

[159]Tonnesson, *1946*, p. 232 for quote, chapters 5 and 6 for general discussion. Vuong Thua Vu, 'La vérité sur le 19 décembre 1946 à Hanoi', in L. Figuères, *Je reviens du Viet-nam libre*, Paris, 1950, pp. 181–194. *LSQD*, pp. 261–269. Devillers, *Histoire*, pp. 349–353; Gras, *Histoire*, pp. 149–155.

There is, however, a conclusion of overriding importance that the evidence does permit us to reach. This is that despite the great variations in regional military development, the whole nation was unified in its anti-French resistance war once the Viet Minh attacked the Hanoi water works, electricity plant, and other facilities at 8 pm. that night.

6
Shaping the People's Army in the People's War, 1947–1949

From almost the moment the lights went out in Hanoi on 19 December 1946 and full scale nation wide hostilities began with the French, the institutional foundations of the People's Army came under great pressure. By the end of March 1947 the quasi-regular forces of the north had been dispersed and the French had reoccupied the major centers in the northern half of the country. By mid-year the embryonic administration which had come to life in late 1945 and 1946 had largely ceased to function, and without it the development of the army was in great danger of being stifled. Yet, because the French would not agree to give Vietnam its independence, the resistance never ceased.

The point of this chapter, therefore, must be to show how the Vietnamese were able to adapt creatively to the pressure of total war by the time that the communist victory in China in 1949 opened a new era in the army's development. In particular, the decimation of the large quasi-regular units that were thrown recklessly into battle against the French in 1947 and the associated collapse of public administration led to a fundamental reappraisal of military strategy and administration. By 1948 attention was given to breaking large main force units of the army down into small guerrilla detachments to stimulate the development of regional militia and local administrative units, because these were the indispensible foundation for ongoing mobilisation of people and resources. So, as in other periods of the army's growth and consolidation, what developed between 1946 and 1949 was a revival of the armed propaganda campaign designed to integrate the political and military development of the society at war.

As a result of this campaign, and an associated development of economic organisations that will be discussed because they were the

nexus between the army and the society, the Viet Minh were beginning to rebuild large main force units on the shoulders of the regional
militia by 1949. Indeed, by this time the French were being held and
gradually weakened by the integrated development of regional militia forces and consolidated main force formations, which is to say the
ancient force structure of Vietnamese armies was reemerging under
modern conditions.

Failure of the People's Army in 1947

According to recent Vietnamese sources the battle for Hanoi was
'glorious victory'.[1] By holding the French Army for sixty days until
the last elements of the Capital Regiment were withdrawn from the
city in mid-February the battle is said to have defeated the enemy's
plans for a lightning victory, and, along with the resistance in other
cities like Hue and Da Nang, created a shield behind which the
resistance was further organised in the interior. In the words of the
official history the battle for Hanoi helped 'create the conditions for
all the country to change over to resistance war'.[2] However, contemporary Viet Minh sources, which hardly mention battles like those
fought in Hanoi except to criticise them, tell a different story.

The 1958 volume of articles compiled from the official Party
journals *Truth* and *Inner Life* for 1947, *The Sacred Resistance War of
the Vietnamese People*,[3] is one such source. Even though it was
selectively compiled there are any number of articles from 1947 in the

---

[1]*LSQD*, p. 280.

[2]Ibid. This theme runs through other Vietnamese accounts of the battle that were
penned well after the event. See, for example, Vuong Thua Vu, *Truong Thanh*, pp.
73–147; Nguyen Huy Tuong's 1958 novel *Song Mai voi Thu Do* [which may be roughly
translated as The Capital Lives Forever], in Nguyen Huy Tuong, *Tuyen Tap* [Collected
Works], Hanoi, 1978. However, it does not run through Tonnesson, *1946*, Chapter 6
which offers a good analysis of the available sources on the battle.

[3]*CKCT*. Volume 1 covering the period 23 September 1945 to December 1947 was
published in 1956. Along with Volume 1, Volume 2 which covers the period January
1946 to December 1950 and was published in 1960 has also been extensively used in
this Chapter, especially for the Party critique of the military situation in early 1947.
This critique begins about mid-1947 and goes on into 1948. Volumes 3 and 4 also
published in 1960 and covering the period January 1951 to July 1954 are used
extensively in the next Chapter. The main Party journals represented in the compilation are *Su That* [Truth]; *Sinh Hoat Noi Bo* [Inner Life]; and *Nhan Dan* [The People].
VKD, pp. 123–125 gives interesting details of editorial policy for *Truth* in April 1947,
but its thirty five page record of the resolutions of the April 6 meeting of Central
Committee cadres, pp. 95–130, which is the first major Party document for 1947 says
nothing directly about the battle for Hanoi.

volume which consistently support an interpretation of events that is far removed from more recent ones, and the authority of the articles may be judged from a comment in one history that *Truth* and *Inner Life* were 'always used to educate cadres, Party members, and soldiers'.[4] Indeed, from around March 1947 when the French had occupied almost all the main northern centers and were soon demonstrating that coordinated airborne and riverborne operations could penetrate any area held by the Viet Minh, the journals reflect the seriousness of the situation in some of the most direct and incisive criticism of political-military administration to be found in the available literature.

As Ho Chi Minh's government was forced to move from Ha Dong – ten kilometers to the west of Hanoi – to the jungles of Thai Nguyen to avoid capture in January 1947,[5] one critic reviewing the next five months for *Truth* showed how the intricate administration the government had sought to erect since 1945 became unworkable. This critic noted how a 'plan was slow in coming out', how 'orders and instructions were not concrete', and how:

The organisation of our units was still slapdash. It can be said that from the form of organisation to the system of administration nothing was clear. Units were not quite regular units and not quite guerrilla units. Each zone simply followed its own developments concerning tactics and organisation. At the same time the way our cadres worked was also poor so that each time an order to set something in motion needed coordination it seemed to be too difficult.[6]

By early 1947 it is clear that Bac Bo had learned nothing from the earlier failure of the Republican Guard in Nam Bo, for the confusion was complete.

As we will see in more detail later, some of this confusion arose from the inept application of Maoist style guerrilla strategies. Initially, however, the greatest difficulties arose as incompetent cadres and local committees tried to apply regular positional strategies and the tactics of the old colonial army.[7] As these cadres threw all available manpower into battle in many places and got their regular and regional units mixed up, not only were the units being exhausted and often decimated by the French as at Ha Dong, Cau Dam, Cho

---

[4]*LSDC*, p. 545.
[5]Gras, *Histoire,* pp. 159–160.
[6]*CKCT*, Vol. 2, pp. 40–41.
[7]Truong Chinh specifically criticised the use of old colonial tactics in *The Resistance Will Win,* in *Selected Works,* p. 168.

Ben, and Kien An in the first half of 1947,[8] but the whole foundation
of the people's army was being undermined. In another review of the
situation looking back over the opening of hostilities in the north
from April 1948 *Truth* observed that

> when the resistance war broke out in all the country, because
> the (local committees) in many areas wanted to confront the
> enemy's fierce attack they concentrated excessive numbers of
> people in the militia. Gradually, the funds of the resistance
> committees were not able to support the cost and the
> committees quickly dissolved or went running around from one
> province to another trying to do something. So what this did was
> detract from the idea of a resistance war of the people's militia
> and also mistake the significance of the organisation of the
> people's militia.[9]

In other words, as the local militia went off to fight unwinnable
battles and funds dried up and local committees disintegrated, there
was no longer any foundation for the mobilisation of people and
resources necessary to replace the originally mismanaged losses in
the militia. As one Viet Minh strategist, Tam Nguyen, further explained in July 1947:

> Looking back over the six months of war in all the country we
> clearly see that the mobilisation of the people has not been keen
> enough and that there are even places where it is still neglected.
> From the time the self defence war broke out in all the country
> because they were too eager to fight the enemy cadres as well as
> mobilisation committees in various areas directed themselves to
> work on the battle front. Committees with responsibility for
> youth, women, workers, peasants, etc., in some places ceased
> their activities or broke up so that cadres could go and do other
> work.[10]

In Tam Nguyen's view such basic failures in political and organisational work had led to a 'loss of spirit' in both the army and the
society at such times as the French attack on Hue when 'our army was
thrown into confusion, the battle front around Hue collapsed, and
the enemy overflowed into the districts and villages of Thua Thien.'[11]

Of course, given French military superiority their advance into
Thua Thien could not have ultimately been stopped. But what Tam
Nguyen was stressing was that if all the effort was thrown willy-nilly

[8]*CKCT.*, Vol. 1, p. 204.
[9]Ibid., Vol. 2, p. 26.
[10]Ibid., Vol. 1, p. 191.
[11]Ibid., p. 192.

onto the battle front, when it inevitably collapsed there would be no Viet Minh organisations left in the villages and no guerilla units to support them, even though the French did not have the manpower to occupy even a fraction of the villages. From the institutional point of view, the regular units, whose source of supply and manpower were the villages and their militia units, would then be cut off from their social base and eventually disintegrate like the regional militia before them. From the interrelated strategic point of view, if there were no regional units to defend the villages, harass the French, liquidate pro-French organisations as they sprang up, and leave the regular army free to concentrate and carry out offensive operations at opportune times, then the people's army would completely lose the initiative. In sum, *Truth* was saying that if the deficiencies resulting from an inability to mobilise the population were not overcome 'the protracted resistance war will become increasingly difficult. Not only will we be unable to prolong the war we will still face further defeats.'[12]

Contemporary Viet Minh accounts therefore make it clear that in 1947 the Vietnamese revolution was in great jeopardy. In Bac Bo the army had disintegrated into numerous scattered bands. The embryonic state apparatus of 1945 and 1946 had ceased to function under the strain of French attacks and the chaos that accompanied the departure of tens of thousands of refugees into the countryside. And with the war leadership in disarray in Bac Bo, the war effort in the other regions was carried on with varying degrees of failure. In Trung Bo there was hardly any mobilisation and where there was in Thu Thien, for example, it soon collapsed. In Nam Bo, although Nguyen Binh's distinctive policy of 'a general offensive to mix up, blockade, destroy, and strike the enemy on all fronts everywhere'[13] did succeed in tying down some 38,000 men or 40% of the French Expeditionary Force in the first half of 1947,[14] it still failed to prevent the French from building up the military superiority in the north that at least temporarily eliminated the government's power to direct a national war effort. If the French had not remained intransigent on the fundamental question of Vietnamese independence there is every possibility that an alternative solution to that proposed by the Viet Minh could have evolved.

[12]Ibid., p. 190.

[13]Quoted in *LSQD*, pp. 294–295.

[14]Gras, *Histoire*, p. 177. The French Commander in the south at the time, General Pierre Boyer de Latour, gives an account of the situation in the south in his memoirs, *Le Martyre de l'Armée Française*, pp. 110–112.

However, the French did remain intransigent as any number of historians have shown,[15] and to this extent a Viet Minh victory was inevitable. Once the French refused to acknowledge the Vietnamese desire for independence, the disintegration of the Viet Minh's administration exacerbated French problems in some important ways, because it became increasingly difficult to locate and destroy the opposition. Under such circumstances French military operations were then doomed to lose their momentum, while the Viet Minh had the opportunity to rebuild a war administration and define a suitable military strategy.

An Operational Military Strategy for Vietnam

As we have just seen, the loss of power and strategic initiative which the Viet Minh suffered in the north the first half of 1947 is reasonably explained in the Party critiques as a result of the disintegration of the regional militia. This loss of power highlights the central importance of reconstituting the regional militia if the army was to develop. However, it should be remembered that the Party critiques used in the above analysis do not date from the period of initial failure, but from mid–1947 to mid–1948.

The significance of this dating is that as much as Party strategists began to criticise the performance of the local committees and regional militia from mid–1947, no attempt had previously been made by the Party to define a comprehensive strategy into which a regional militia might fit. Ho Chi Minh's vague statement about 'Protracted Resistance War' of 5 November 1946, and the Central Committee's equally vague instructions of 22 December[16] could not be described as comprehensive. Indeed, as the impulse to prepare for regular war in Bac Bo and Trung Bo in 1946 led to a repetition of the initial failure in Nam Bo, it was not until mid–1947 that the attention given to the regional militia in the Party journals reflected a wider formulation of strategy.[17]

This formulation clearly had to take account of the failure of

---

[15]For example, R.E.M. Irving, *The First Indochina War*, London, 1975; Devillers, *Histoire*. For the official Vietnamese response to French intransigence see *VKD*, pp. 130–136.

[16]*VKD*, pp. 84–85, pp. 88–94.

[17]Of course, the major reforms in administration and strategy in the south in 1946 meant that by 1947 the regional militia was being consolidated in many provinces, and in some like Bien Hoa and Ba Ria the consolidated main force units, the Chi Dois, were even coordinating their operations with the regional militia. See for example, Ban Chap Hanh Dang Bo, *Dong Nai*, Chapter 2. For main force-milita coordination see p. 77.

regular positional strategies against the French, and so the need for protracted guerrilla strategies was apparent. As already indicated, however, the formulation also had to take account of the failure of Maoist style guerilla strategies that were subsumed in the general rout of early 1947. From the outset, and increasingly as the regular formations crumbled, we know that some commanders used guerrilla tactics ineptly, for by mid-year they were being criticised for offering no resistance to the enemy. As Truong Chinh noted in a reference to one case around Thai Binh in April 1947, confusion in the local command 'caused sorrow and shame to the troops who were indignant at not being allowed to fight'.[18] Thus, at the same time as they clarified the need for protracted guerrilla war, it is important to emphasise that the Viet Minh strategists also clarified the need to distinguish its conduct in Vietnam from its conduct in China.[19]

[18]Truong Chinh, *The Resistance Will Win*, in *Selected Works*, p. 175.

[19]I have seen one short reference to the difference between Vietnamese and Chinese conditions made in a Party document of April 1947 in *VKD*, p. 103. There is nothing in *CKCT* until about July when the subject becomes more prominent.

In the voluminous western literature on the subject of guerrilla war in the 1960s and 1970s I am aware of no attempt to differentiate Chinese and Vietnamese tactics. This is not surprising for those who believed that the Vietnam War was caused by advances in the Asiatic dominion of Chinese communism. However, even in a work like Georges Boudarel's 1971 'Essai sur la pensée militaire vietnamienne', in Chesneaux et al., *Tradition et révolution*, pp. 460–495 which gives a good sense of the subtlety and variety of Vietnamese strategy, nothing is said about the differences. One reason for this could have been that the Vietnamese themselves did not want to highlight the differences when they were receiving much aid from China during the Vietnam War. However, the official history of the army mentioned the differences between Vietnam and China and also Vietnam and Russia when it was written in 1974. See *LSQD*, p. 300. More recent sources like *LSDC*, pp. 540–541 also offer a brief discussion. Although it suffers from a paucity of primary Vietnamese source material and is misleading in places, Eugene K. Lawson, *The Sino-Vietnamese Conflict*, New York: Praeger Special Studies, 1984, points us in the right direction.

One contemporary work which is generally considered to be a basic text on Vietnamese strategy, Truong Chinh, *Khang Chien Nhat Dinh Thang Loi* (The Resistance Will Win), first published in September 1947, is critical of Viet Minh commanders who mechanically applied Maoist tactics although it does not seem to have been very explicit on this point. I say *seem* because I have not been able to read an early edition of Truong Chinh's work. In so far as I have used *The Resistance Will Win* I have used the 1977 edition in Truong Chinh, *Selected Writings*, Hanoi: Foreign Languages Publishing House. But in the following discussion I have relied far more on the contemporary Party journals which unless otherwise cited come from *CKCT*. The advantage of using this source is that, as *LSDC*, p. 525, note 3 says, *The Resistance Will Win* was originally compiled from a series of edited articles from *Truth* published between May and August 1947.

In China, the Viet Minh strategists now began to note, there were vast spaces which the Japanese (the Sino-Japanese War was still the model in Vietnam) could not even strike at let alone occupy, and even a protracted guerilla war had well defined fronts and wide ranging battles of movement. On the other hand, in Vietnam with its relatively small area and French mobility 'the war does not follow a determined front. It can spread very rapidly at several points'.[20] By neglecting the difference between Chinese and Vietnamese realities and waiting for fronts to form and battles of movement to develop, the People's Army in Vietnam was without a meaningful strategy.

One prominent writer on military questions for *Truth*, Hong Nam, thus observed in late 1947 that 'the French always attack our towns and cities to defend their position, and our army always waits for them to attack'.[21] Hong Nam went on to explain that

> From the time the war broke out in all the country until now our army—including regular, guerrilla, and people's militia units—has got mixed up . . . Speaking generally we have lost the initiative on more occasions than we have gained it. Experience shows each of us that the enemy rarely meets resistance on the road as he advances which means he has no difficulty in advancing. Our position is never-guaranteed. The enemy's tactics are to take a position and then reinforce it. Once they reinforce it they sweep the surrounding area. When the sweep is over they advance again and continue as before . . . Here is a great deficiency on our part.[22]

Even before he had published this explanation Hong Nam had already decided in an earlier edition of *Truth* that:

> We must clearly understand the differences between the character of the Sino-Japanese . . . and Vietnamese-French Wars. China fought Japan for eight years to win a victory that depended on guerrilla tactics and a protracted war strategy. But compared to our neighbor, if we have a strong wall of solidarity we only have a limited area of land. The secure rear areas in China were Trung Khanh, Van Nam, and Tu Xuyen. However, our secure rear area is non-existent or only exists between the people (who are all) close to the main front. This fluid rear area forces us to have a completely different concept of guerrilla war.[23]

[20]Dang Tri Dung, 'Les Mouvements Strategiques', in *Traduction de deux articles extraits de la publication Viet Minh intitulé: Quan Chinh Tap San*, Etat-Major des F.T.N.V., Hanoi, 1950, p. 18.

[21]*CKCT*, Vol. 1, p. 209.

[22]Ibid., pp. 273–274.

[23]Ibid., p. 272.

In particular, in a small country like Vietnam where freedom of manoeuvre was so restricted that strategic rear areas could only be conceived of in mystical terms of solidarity between people, what evolved was a kind of strategic involution. Here the idea of involution is not meant to convey entanglement or stifling intricacy. It is meant to convey a sense of internal dynamism that came when strategy was based on irreducible social units: people and houses. The irreducible relationship between strategy and society was then conveyed in the slogans of the time: 'each person is a soldier', 'each house is a fortress', 'each village is a battle front', and in areas where there was no jungle or mountain cover, 'jungles and mountains are made out of people'.[24] In this unusually concrete definition of *people's war* it was by detaching their strategy from the territorial restrictions which favoured the French and making *people* in each region, each village, and each house the basis of strategy that the Viet Minh could counter French mobility.

In tactical terms, when each house was literally a fortress and the war could spread without warning, guerrilla operations would have to encompass a whole range of overlapping possibilities. As in China tactics would have to be defensive as far as they preserved the main force from destruction. But this was about as far as the resemblance between Vietnamese and Chinese guerilla tactics went. In Vietnam unless guerilla forces also engaged the enemy in relatively intense offensive operations that at least retarded his advance, or held towns and bases until a superior concentration of enemy force and survival demanded that 'positional war' merge with 'mobile guerrilla war', there would be no way of inflicting casualties on the enemy, keeping him divided, and beginning to wrest back the initiative.[25]

Even though the Viet Minh were not conforming to an established strategy in the early stages of the war, one glaring difference between Mao's model and Vietnamese practice was the Viet Minh's repeated attempts to hold towns—Saigon, Hanoi, Hue, and many others.[26] In fact, Mao would have styled this strategy as feudal. But from a strategic point of view in Vietnam, one had to exact a maximum toll from the French consistent with the principle of preserving the main

[24]Ibid., Vol. 2, p. 29. *LSDC*, p. 576.

[25]On the relationship between positional war and mobile war and on the subject of gaining the initiative see Hong Nam's article in *Truth* of July 1947, *CKCT*, Vol. 1, pp. 207–210 which contrasts battles fought in Vietnam in 1947 with fighting around Shanghai in 1931. See also *LSDC*, p. 523, especially note 1; and note 27 below.

[26]Later in the war the Viet Minh even occupied towns as at Dong Khe during the border campaign of late 1950. In fact, here the battle for the town went through three phases: Viet Minh occupation in May 1950, French reoccupation in the same month, and finally Viet Minh reoccupation in October.

force.[27] Because space was so restricted positional war was a necessary facet of Vietnamese strategy and the only question of importance was the extent to which it was used.

One way of tuning positional tactics to the need for dispersal was
the extensive use of tunnel systems in lowland areas. By the late
1940s extensive tunnel systems were in use in villages to the north of
Hanoi, for as one user has stated, tunnels 'gave (us) and immense
advantage, permitting movement without being seen and attacks on
the adversary in unsuspected places.'[28] But the relationship between
positional war and mobile war was also very much a matter of local
circumstances and the tactical skill of local commanders.

Given the relatively unorganised and untrained nature of popular
armies, the problems of coordinating positional and mobile strategies
should not be underestimated. Orders could be blocked and confusion transmitted as at the battle at Thai Binh in April 1947. Local
guerrillas might destroy roads and bridges at the wrong time, and we
will see that supplies of ammunition ran out in some important
positions. Yet regardless of the level of organisation, discipline, and
military training in a region, problems of tactical coordination in a
battle were usually problems of coordination between village militia
and regional units, and these could be solved locally through
common experience, better organisation, and training as the war
progressed.

Village militia and at least regional units would soon get to
know each other when they sprang from the same villages. Apart
from the myriad military schools that had opened by 1947, offensive
operations were usually planned minutely and rehearsed by 1948.
Any change in enemy tactics—say in the use of armoured cars or
surveillance towers as in Cochinchina—was studied by special groups
who then ran courses on their findings. News of new methods also
travelled quickly, for it is known that knowledge of the success which
some were having with the use of underground hides and tunnels in

[27]Truong Chinh outlined the method of doing this in September 1947:
At first we apply positional war in the streets, holding on to every house, every
street, every quarter, (battles in Hanoi, Nam Dinh, Hue). Then we withdraw from
the towns, using positional warfare tactics to bottle the enemy up in the towns for a
certain time (battle in Hanoi etc.). Simultaneously, small units of our forces
penetrate the streets and use guerrilla warfare to harass the enemy. Guerrilla
warfare complements and helps positional warfare.
See Truong Chinh, *The Resistance Will Win*, in *Selected Works*, p. 143. See also note
25 above.
[28]Quoted in James Pinckney Harrison, *The Endless War: Fifty Years of Struggle in
Vietnam*, London: Free Press, 1982, pp. 195–200, pp. 260–262 gives accounts of tunnel
tactics. However, these accounts focus mostly on the period after 1965.

the north had led to excavations beneath some southern villages by 1948. In any case, the level of coordination necessary for village guerrillas to place bamboo stakes in the fields to impale French paratroopers, while regional units set up ambushes and then broke contact if they were losing was not overwhelming.[29] And provided such rudimentary coordination was possible in many regions *any* action against the enemy in one region would tend to weaken him in another.

A summation of the national strategy which therefore encompassed the need to 'mobilise the whole nation against the invader',[30] and tactics which demanded that Viet Minh forces everywhere develop the capacity to 'coordinate defensive tactics with offensive tactics'[31] was then offered by Truong Chinh writing for *Inner Life* in October 1947:

> The enemy attacks us on top, we attack him underneath. The enemy attacks us in the north, we attack him in central and southern Vietnam and Cambodia and Laos. The enemy violates one of our territorial bases, we immediately strike hard at the enemy's belly and back. The enemy comes and goes, we cut off his legs, destroy his roads. Regular units and people's guerilla units coordinate their action with each other according to conditions, and rise up and annihilate the enemy.[32]

The assumption here is one of a country strategically divided into various political entities, weak in isolation but strong when they combine and coordinate their efforts in support of the whole. Indeed, this was the strategic assumption reflecting the political ideals of 'solidarity' and 'unity' which pervades Viet Minh literature.[33] The institutional foundations for such a strategy were then interlocked with the strategy itself.

An Operative Resistance Administration

At the highest reaches of strategy Truong Chinh assumes a degree of regional autonomy when he writes of the people's guerrilla units,

[29]Ban Chap Hanh Dang Bo, *Dong Nai*, Chapter 2 offers many insights into how one region worked on coordinating its war effort between 1947 and 1949. Page 91 mentions the influence of northern experience on the first underground excavations of hides etc. beneath villages in 1949.
[30]Dang Tri Dung, 'Les Mouvements Strategiques', p. 18. This is perhaps the basic theme of Vietnamese strategic writing in the anti-French phase of the war to 1954.
[31]*CKCT*, Vol. 1, p. 208.
[32]Ibid, p. 239.
[33]For example, Ho Chi Minh, 'Ky Niem 6 Thang Khang Chien' [On the Occasion of Six Months of Resistance War], *Tuyen Tap*, Vol. 1, p. 419 stressed in June 1947 that the 'only' aim of the war was 'unity and independence for the Fatherland'.

'acting according to conditions'. But he also assumes that the villagers were aware of a power beyond the region that gave them strength if they complied with it. This was the power of the state, and in Truong Chinh's terms it was realised when regular units detached from regional responsibilities, 'coordinate' their actions with the regional units. The regional and regular units represented the need for regional autonomy within state unity, but they were also mutually supporting as were the state and its regions. To build up our idea of the institutional foundations for an independent strategy, therefore, it is necessary to show how the administrative reorganisation that began in late 1947 was locked into it from its inception.

From October 1947 Fall and Ginsburgs[34] tell us that the plethora of elected popular assemblies the government had legislated for in 1945 and 1946 (but which had long ceased to operate) were formally suspended. After this suspension the former Resistance Committees at each territorial level were fused into more streamlined commmittees known as 'Resistance and Administration Committees' (*Uy Ban Khang Chien Hanh Chinh*).[35] When the French October-November campaign in the Viet Bac then dispersed the organs of central government new administrative units were decreed to 'strengthen the war leadership',[36] as the official history puts it. Groups of villages, districts, and provinces were now placed under a single administration that was usually integrated with the military command, especially in battle areas and areas close to other areas under French control. These groupings were known as 'Inter-Villages' (*Lien Xa*), 'Inter-Provinces' (*Lien Tinh*), and 'Inter-Zones' (*Lien Khu*). By March 1948 the country was divided into six *Inter-Zones*, plus a special zone for Saigon.[37]

In theory the principle of democratic centralism still pertained, but with the suppression of elections for the popular councils at each level and the National Assembly the principle only applied to the Resistance and Administration Committees. At village and provincial level where Resistance and Administration Committees com-

---

[34]For the constitutional outline of the administration I have relied heavily on Fall, *Le Viet Minh*, pp. 75–79, and Ginsburgs, 'Local Government'. Bernard Fall's essay 'Local Administration under the Viet Minh', *Pacific Affairs*, 1954, Number 1, and Vu Quoc Thong, *La décentralisation*, Part 3, Chapter 1 should also be consulted.

[35]Fall, *Le Viet Minh*, p. 79. Ginsburgs, 'Local Government', p. 188.

[36]*LSQD*, p. 333.

[37]Ibid., pp. 333–4. It is interesting that while they involve themselves in general policy overviews the Party documents published in *VKD* for 1948 are not forthcoming on these important administrative changes. This would suggest that the Viet Minh Front and the Army had a high degree of autonomy in both policy formulation and implementation.

prised five to seven members, three of the five were still elected by popular assembly but their appointment had to be confirmed by the next highest authority. Two members could also be appointed from above. On each committee the member responsible for military affairs was invariably an appointee. At the Inter-Zone level the committee again consisted of five to seven members who were all appointed by the President of the Republic on the advice of the Supreme Council of National Defence, and it was into the hands of these Inter-Zone Committees that most of the real power to execute the war devolved. For example, these Committees were vested with extraordinary police and judicial powers. They could initiate prosecution before military tribunals, grant pardons or reduce sentences, they had control over censorship and confiscation of property, and they could delegate power to lower levels. Moreover, these Committees were responsible for devising programs for the recruitment of the regional militia and supervising their conduct.[38]

Now, insofar as I have followed the standard Western sources on Viet Minh administration to this point I have no disagreement with them. However, when these sources move form their outline of the contents of the constituional decrees to the actual operation of the administration there are internal inconsistencies that reflect on the whole system of administration in theory and practice. For instance, Fall and Ginsburgs both acknowledge that the new administration was not established in a moment, and Ginsburgs even says that 'to a large extent' the decrees ordering the implantation of the administration were 'never fully realised because of the constant and dire pressure of adverse external forces'.[39] Both writers also correctly emphasise that the new administration was highly militarised. Fall called it a 'combat administration.'[40] Yet, despite the high degree of militarisation, if the constitutional decrees outlining the administration 'were never fully realised', and if the pressure of war led to the evolution of a light weight 'combat administration' it is difficult to reconcile this institutional development with the totalitarian image of administration that both writers try to project. Ginsburgs writes of the 'uninterrupted routine subordination and accountability of local organs' that was 'in effect', and Fall stresses the 'excellent pretext' which the war gave the Viet Minh to consolidate its control over the resistance committees.[41]

But from mid–1947 the Viet Minh's basic problem was that to a

[38]Ginsburgs, 'Local Government'.
[39]Ibid., p. 194.
[40]Fall, The Viet Minh, p. 16.
[41]Fall, Le Viet Minh, p. 75; Ginsburgs, 'Local Government', p. 203.

large extent there was no functioning administration over which they might extend their control. From mid–1947 the Viet Minh were confronted with the problem of building a new state apparatus which would enable the centre to direct and coordinate regional affairs. Moreover, when the country was at war the survival of the central authority itself depended first on a capacity to establish a *regional* militia in support of a *regional* administration and this clearly precluded the development of totalitarian rule. At the same time, however, the imposition of an adminstration from above which the Western sources notice was a reality. But in Vietnam this imposition must be understood in terms of the inherent regionalism of the polity that demanded suitable demonstrations of central government to override it or the regions would have no reason to support the central government. As the paradox of Vietnamese government discussed in Chapter 5 evolved in the late 1940s, a situation developed where Party control of regional affairs came to be maximised through the Inter-Zone Committees appointed by the ministry of National Defense; however, administration remained highly decentralised as the armed propaganda teams of the People's Army went out into the society to carry out mass mobilisation.

From the related strategic point of view this capacity for administrative decentralisation within a centralised state offered the Viet Minh great flexibility. By decentralising the administration at the highest levels and grouping villages, districts, and provinces together at the lowest levels the government was creating groups of relatively autonomous yet mutually supporting political-military administrative units which its task was to lead and coordinate. If the French occupied a village or a province, the occupied area would be surrounded by other villages or provinces in the administrative system. The occupied area could then be re-integrated into the resistance administration once French commitments elsewhere forced them to weaken their grip on the area. Strategy and administration were thus interlocked at an institutional level, and, of course, at a practical operational level they were interlocked by the integrated political-military technique of armed propaganda. In an institutionally underdeveloped agricultural society this was the only way the Communist Party had of mobilising people to support the state apparatus and the army at the same time.

Revival of the Armed Propaganda Campaign

The Party's role in reviving and guiding the armed propaganda campaign was crucial, even though Vietnamese sources do not tell us much about the practical aspects of it. After its official dissolution in 1945, the Party's clandestine political work over the next five years merely shades the contemporary literature. Moreover, although they do offer full accounts of the Party's policies in the period, the draft history of the Party published in Hanoi in 1981 and other recent sources still do not tell us much about its operations.[42] As already suggested, however, the appointment of Party members to key defence posts on the Inter-Zone Committees is virtually certain. Although it is almost as certain that recent official histories of the Army and the Party inflate their figures, these and other sources also indicate that, while very many regional units would not have had Party Cells in 1947, the number of Party members in the army increased to several thousand by 1949.[43] Furthermore, when the Party's, or more accurately, the leadership of the Party's monopoly on the main resistance publications was coupled with the presence of political officers in almost all the sizeable regular units and training centers, the Party did have the means to guide and check the armed propaganda campaign.

Even before the French had finally withdrawn from the Viet Bac in the autumn offensive, Truong Chinh was therefore using *Inner Life* to propagate the party line on what had to be done after the battle:

We must pay special attention to making propaganda out of the Viet Bac victories inside and outside the country. Even though they might be small (we must) use (these) victories to the limit for propaganda. That is a pressing task. To carry out propaganda we need to mobilise newspapers, organise poetry readings in praise of the Viet Bac resistance, organise exhibitions of war booty, organise military parades, and give medals to soldiers with credit in the Army of National Defence as well as in guerrilla units and the people's militia.[44]

---

[42]The draft history is *LSDC*. Other recent sources include *VKD* and *LSQD*.

[43]For example, Ban Chap Hanh Dang Bo, *Dong Nai*, p. 74 says that no units of platoon or company strength in that region had Party members in mid-1947, although by the end of the year Party Cells were being established. *LSQD*, p. 381 says there were 40,000 Party members in the army by late 1949. This seems questionable when *LSDC*, p. 545 offers the equally questionable statement that by late 1947 there were 'over 70,000' people in the Party. Even if both these figures were accepted, and even if we allowed for the recruiting of Party members in 1948 and 1949 the proportion of Party members which *LSQD* says were in the army in 1949 still seems high. A figure of 40,000 Party members in 1949 represents about 40% of the army's main force strength which was in the vicinity of 80,000 to 100,000 troops. Nevertheless, these shaky figures do suggest that the number of Party members in the late 1940s was substantial.

[44]*CKCT*, Vol. 1, p. 134.

At the same time, to rationalise the popular political goal of national independence, the new emphasis on propaganda was harmonised with themes of Marxist-Leninist internationalism.

Ever since the end of the Second World War internal Party analyses and the official media had begun to reveal a world in ferment. Because it became general editorial policy in April 1947 for mass journals like *Truth* to concentrate on internal matters while the government information and broadcasting services concentrated on 'international propaganda',[45] the coverage of international events in different outlets could be uneven. Nevertheless, news of the independence movements in Burma, Malaya, and Indonesia, the emergence of socialist regimes throughout Central Europe, and the Communist Party's leadership of the growing anti-war movement in France, were all widely disseminated in the mid to late 1940s.[46] Since 1946 the great strides of the People's Army in China had also come in for attention in the journals. *Truth* noted in February that 'the situation in China will have an influence on Indochina that will not be small'.[47] Later it said that the impact of the Chinese people's victory in the world and in Indochina would be 'resounding', although by January 1948 internal Party analyses were also anticipating that the French and Americans would try to block 'unified action between the Vietnamese National Army and the Chinese Liberation Army'.[48]

Such, therefore, was the political context in which 'the special development of armed propaganda' was emphasised at the April 1948 meeting of the Central Committee, and cadres like Bui Quang Tao and Song Hao were given responsibility for 'building armed propaganda units like those in the days before the August Revolution'.[49] In setting out this example the Central Committee again seems to have overlooked the experience in Nam Bo, for it will be remembered from the last chapter that the major reorganisation of 1946 had already meant the revival of armed propaganda and small unit action by 1947. But because the central imperative in 1948 in Bac Bo and Trung Bo was the reconstruction of the regional forces, what occurred was the breakdown of existing regular units into 'Independent Companies' (*Dai Doi Doc Lap*) whose primary task was 'to help

[45]*VKD*, pp. 123–125.

[46]These themes run through *CKCT* from 1946 and continue to run to 1949 and beyond. They are also a feature of internal Party analyses. For example see *VKD*, pp. 25–27, pp. 95–97 for two particularly clear Party statements on the world situation in November 1945 and April 1947 respectively.

[47]*CKCT*, Vol. 2, p. 11.

[48]Ibid., p. 119; *VKD*, p. 168.

[49]*LSQD*, p. 315. However, the idea was incipient in internal Party deliberations from at least October 1947. See *VKD*, p. 155.

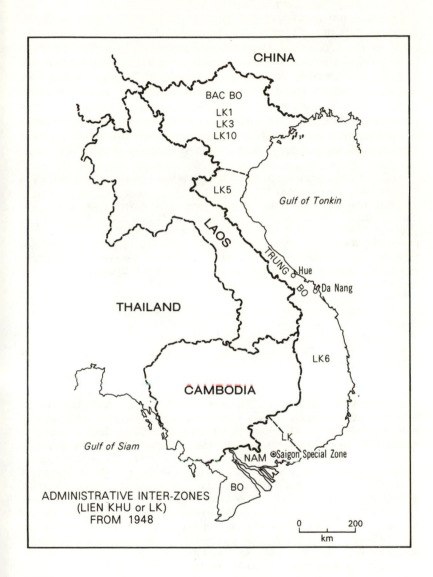

CHINA

BAC BO

LK1
LK3
LK10

LK5

LAOS

Gulf of Tonkin

TRUNG BO

Hue

Da Nang

THAILAND

LK6

CAMBODIA

LK

Gulf of Siam

NAM

⊙Saigon Special Zone

BO

ADMINISTRATIVE INTER-ZONES
(LIEN KHU or LK)
FROM 1948

0   200
km

(village) guerrillas become regional units'.[50] A new phase in the war had begun to emerge.

Up to the French offensive in the Viet Bac which had been designed to put a political seal on the rapid reoccupation of all the major centers in the country by the end of 1947, Viet Minh sources refer to the 'defence'[51] (*phong ngu*) phase of the war, although 'uncontrolled defence' would probably be a more accurate description. From December 1947 when the French withdrew from the Viet Bac and French sources begin to talk of 'stagnation'[52] in their military operations, both contemporary and more recent Vietnamese sources refer to the 'holding' (*cam cu*) phase of the war.[53] From 1949 there would then be much discussion of the point where the 'holding' phase merged with the 'general counter offensive' (*tong phan cong*).[54] But

[50]*LSQD*, p. 349. For a list of Main Force Units in the Army of National Defence in Autumn 1947 see p. 309, Note 1.

[51]Apart from the Maoist texts that were translated into Vietnamese in 1938 and which are discussed in Chapter 2, the earliest statement I have seen on the Maoist style phases of the war is a very brief outline of them in an internal Party document of 22 December 1946. A less brief description was given to cadres at the Central Committee Conference of April 1947. See *VKD*, p. 90, p. 103. The first media statement I have seen of the phases was in an article in *Truth* of 18 March 1947 which explains that 'we are in the defence phase'. See *CKCT*, Vol. 1, pp. 164–165.

[52]Gras, *Histoire*, p. 213.

[53]*CKCT*, Vol. 2, pp. 36–44 contains a May 1948 articles from *Inner Life* entitled 'Push the War Strongly into the New Phase'. This was the "Holding phase" (*cam cu*) or what is sometimes translated as "the stage of equilibrium".

[54]*CKCT*, Vol. 2, pp. 119–127 contains an article by Truong Chinh from *Inner Life* of 14 February 1949 which says on p. 119 that the war was still in the holding phase but with the advances being made by the Chinese revolution 'we must make every effort to prepare for the counter offensive and advance to the third phase'. Of course, Truong Chinh devotes Chapter 10 of *The Resistance Will Win* to the three phases of the protracted war which we saw in Chapter 2 were originally conceived of by Mao Zedong in *On Guerrilla War* in 1937. However, a reading of *CKCT* articles from March to August 1947, from which we have seen *The Resistance Will Win* was originally composed, does not suggest that the Party had yet offered a full discussion of the phases in 1947 as a reading of the 1977 edition of *The Resistance Will Win* suggests. Of course we have also seen that *CKCT* does not offer a complete set of articles from the journals, but there is no reason to doubt that those published give a very good idea of the main currents of strategic thinking. For an interesting discussion of the phases of the war in retrospect see Bui Dinh Thanh 'Mot Vai Y Kien Gop vao Viec Nghien Cuu Cac Giai Doan cua Cuoc Khang Chien' (A Few Ideas on the Study of the Phases of the Resistance War), *NCLS*, Number 45, December 1962, pp. 12–18, p. 32. Recent French works on the war generally agree with the Vietnamese periodisation of the war. For example, Tuelieres, *La Guerre*, structures its account of the war around Chapters entitled 'Le Viet Minh Se Défend', 'Le Viet Minh Se Rénforce', and 'Le Viet Minh Attàque'.

in the 'holding' phase in early 1948 the remnants of the Army of National Defence did not 'dig in' and build fortifications as a more conventional army may have been expected to do. It began to fortify itself by 'digging in' to the society through armed propaganda. And this remarkable development tends to refute Paul Mus's poetic assertion that in popular opinion the army's development was placed in the realm of the 'secondary considerations' of military and financial means that 'will of their own accord put themselves into the hands of the party that has received the mandate of heaven'.[55]

There could be no better evidence of the primary institutional importance of the army in the society in 1948 than the Party's need to break the regular units down into armed propaganda detachments to mobilise people and reorganise political-military affairs in the provinces. With the suppression of elections, and the widespread disintegration of the elected local committees during the period of French reoccupation from September 1945 to March 1947, there was simply no means of mobilising people in many regions. In Vietnam where the political and military institutions cannot finally be separated, and where the army was the only developed organ of Party power it was natural for the army to play a central role in the mobilisation process through armed propaganda.

A second reason for the primary importance of the army was that despite the eviction of the Councils of Notables in the villages and the revolutionary rhetoric since August 1945 the revolution had remained very superficial. There had been no fundamental redistribution of wealth and virtually no land reform. As almost all social categories remained strongly attached to particular interests, there was no new social or economic foundation to change the age old need for demonstrations of central government authority if the particular interests were to be linked and the country united. Truong Chinh clearly pointed to the particular interests and still relatively undiminished wealth of the rich peasants in *The Resistance Will Win* when he asked 'how much money is just lying around in strong boxes at the bottom of family chests and is not used in production beneficial to the country.'[56] Many writers in the Party journals also acknowledged that

> precisely because the work of reducing land rents and interest
> rates has not yet been perfected there are a number of comrades
> in the fields who are not really concerned about the new
> democratic system and are indifferent to political mobilisation.[57]

[55]Mus, *Viet-Nam: Sociologie d'une guerre*, p. 31.
[56]Truong Chinh, *Selected Works*, p. 204.
[57]*CKCT*, Vol. 1, p. 194.

Clearly, when similar tracts calling for the urgent need to 'reduce rents, reduce interests'[58] (*giam to, giam tuc*) were to pass through the press for several years to come, such political indifference could not ultimately be overcome without demonstrations of armed strength.

Another reason why Paul Mus's interpretation of the army's role in the society is misleading is that the country was at war: at war with the French Expeditionary Corps, and, it must be said, at war with itself. One effect of the tensions in the Vietnamese polity between the centre and the regions was that there always tended to be a potential for resistance to any centralising authority. In normal times such resistance was muted by the power of the state. But at a time when sustained French military action heightened the potential for regional resistance, it was inevitable that the army would play a major role in creating and often enforcing the unity in the society that the government perceived to be in its interests.

In some cases where resistance to the Viet Minh was well supported, organised, and geographically concentrated the Viet Minh found themselves engaged in an open civil war. This was so with the religious sects in the south who rallied to the French in 1947 and groups of Catholics in various parts of the country—Ben Tre in the south and the Bishoprics of Phat Diem and Bui Chu in the north.[59] In many other cases there were problems with ethnic minorities who did not always 'unyieldingly'[60] follow Ho Chi Minh and the Party banner as recent Vietnamese histories say. In fact, in a minority area like the southern highlands the English journalist Norman Lewis described in 1951 how both French and Viet Minh 'tommy gunners'[61] sought to gain the allegiance of the Rhade minority. Lewis also said of the southern highland centre of Ban Me Thuot that 'before 1946 there had been a native town, but it had been burnt down in trouble with the Viet Minh'.[62]

To the many major pockets of hostile or passive resistance to the Viet Minh there were also many individuals, small groups, and villages scattered throughout the countryside which the Viet Minh did not trust even in areas under firm control. Whether or not this

[58]For example, Ibid, Vol. 2, pp. 31–35 for May 1948, pp. 83–85 for October 1948. In 1949 and 1950 there were also numerous calls to improve the life of the workers and peasants.

[59]There are numerous works documenting the position of the sects. See for example the works listed in the bibliography for A. Savani and Jane Werner. On the Catholics see Bernard Fall, *The Viet Minh*, pp. 69–70, and Lucien Bodard, *La guerre*, Vol. 2, pp. 402–420, for a general introduction.

[60]*LSQD*, p. 203.

[61]Norman Lewis, *A Dragon Apparent*, London: Jonathan Cape, 1951, p. 142.

[62]Ibid., p. 88.

lack of trust was justified, it manifested itself in the general run of spy scares and in various other ways. For example, in many parts of central and northern Vietnam Catholic villages were only allowed to arm themselves with spears and lances,[63] and when French attacks were anticipated on Thanh Hoa, Nghe An, and Ha Tinh provinces in early 1949 orders emanated from the Resistance and Administration Committee of Inter-Zone 4 to 'establish lists of reactionaries in all localities—intellectuals, Buddhists, Catholics—to facilitate their imprisonment . . . on news of an attack'.[64] Armed propaganda units in the region then played a prominent role in preparing the local defences (although the French did not attack as anticipated). Indeed, refugees from the region told the French that 'armed guerrillas' were sent into the countryside to organise 'meetings and demonstrations',[65] to prepare various lines of defence that fell back from the coast to the hinterland, and to place pressure on those who might be reluctant to carry out a scorched earth policy.[66] In applying such pressure on this and other occasions, it may have been that armed propaganda units sometimes acted with unnecessary force and without proper authorization or justification. Yet the potential for resistance to the Viet Minh was certainly there, along with the heightened wartime need the army had to repress it in its own interests and those of the state.

Verification of the need for the army to overcome resistance in the society may also be found in French controlled areas which offer a mirror image of areas controlled by the Viet Minh. Like the Viet Minh the French understood the importance of carrying out armed propaganda, and frequent accounts of this French action in Viet Minh journals indicate their sensitivity to it. *Truth* thus noted in March 1947 how

> the enemy's attack to the west of Hanoi clearly shows the enemy deceive and propagandise our people as they fight. They distribute pamphlets, make announcements and cajole the people into staying home and working.[67]

[63]*SHAT*, C.97, 'Note Pour Monsieur Le Conseiller Politique', Saigon, 25 November 1949.
[64]*SHAT*, C.97, French translation of a Viet Minh instruction, Instruction Number 129, VP/KC, from the Resistance and Administration Committee of L.K. 4 to all District Committees dated 3 March 1949 entitled 'Mesures à prendre en cas d'offensive française dans le L.K.4.'.
[65]Ibid.
[66]*SHAT*, C. 97, document entitled 'Situation dans la region de Vinh', Janvier 1949, Hanoi, containing refugee reports of 7 February and 23 February 1949. Some idea of who the people were that were forced to leave their homes is suggested by refugee reports of the burning of the Chinese and Catholic quarters in Vinh in Thanh Hoa.
[67]*CKCT*, Vol. 1, p. 164.

Perhaps the most spectacular French armed propaganda success was the well known mobilisation of an effective army of 12,000 Catholics around Ben Tre in the Mekong delta by Colonel Leroy.[68] But there were many others especially in the main rice growing deltas where village self defence units (*groupes d'auto-defence*) and pro-French organisations had sprung up by 1948–1949.[69] This development occurred as the French strategy turned from the idea of a rapid victory to that of consolidating their hold on the main rice growing areas to try and starve out the Viet Minh.

At the same time, however, just as there was resistance in the Viet Minh areas that had to be overcome, there was also resistance in even the most consolidated French areas that the Viet Minh could seek to exploit. A good idea of the way these forces of resistance structured the Viet Minh's approach to the war is contained in the following summary of the situation in French occupied regions in mid-1948:

> In the beginning when temporary enemy influence is still strong, people's militia forces are able to disperse as the masses fear the enemy and do not dare to preserve and protect the guerrillas. But the truth is that not all people are equally afraid, that not all villages are equally under enemy control. We are very able to take advantage of these conditions even if they are only fragile and uncertain to gradually take unit members and cells and multiply them for wide action later. It is also true that in many enemy occupied areas regional guerrilla cells are still surviving . . . (however) experience has made us see that if you do not prepare and deploy secret guerrilla cells and do not immediately pacify pro-French organisations when they first spring up, if excessive fear of the enemy leads to a withdrawal of guerrilla forces from enemy controlled areas too soon, if people's militia units are not raised on the earliest possible day, the earliest possible hour, the enemy will quickly create his bases and be relatively secure in many places.[70]

The Viet Minh's operational assumption was not based on an expectation of infallible support from the masses. It was based on the reality that pro-French organisations would 'spring up' where the French were strong, but that there would always be points of resistance to the French which could be exploited by the flexible armed propaganda action of Guerrilla Cells, Special Action Units, and Independent Companies. In such a conflict victory would then go to

---

[68]Leroy, *Un homme*, pp. 140–167. Harrison, *The Endless War*, pp. 170–172.

[69]Anonymous article, 'Jeunes Armées', *Sub-Est*, Number 2, July 1949, p. 31; Boyer de Latour, *Le Martyre*, pp. 123–124. Teulieres, *La Guerre*, pp. 57–66.

[70]*Truth*, 8 April 1948 in *CKCT*, Vol. 2, pp. 27–28.

the side with the best propaganda, and the greatest capacity to defend its supporters. In sum, victory would go to the side with the best armed propaganda.

As local committees and units were established in the armed propaganda campaign, therefore, it was imperative that the new political-military regime did not degenerate into warlordism. As we will see, various campaigns to raise the cultural level of the troops, to involve them in agricultural work, and to stop high-handed dealings with the population were initiated by the Party. This was because it was vital for the resistance regime to reflect popular aspirations, and to establish supportive institutions that would ensure recruits and supplies for the army. Indeed, victory could never go to the side whose distribution of the burdens of war was fundamentally inequitable. As the armed propaganda campaign mobilised an ever increasing number of people in the anti-French resistance war, it is necessary to explain the developing economic nexus between the army and the society in 1948 and 1949.

Supporting the Expanding Popular Forces

Especially when the government complained that it only had a limited budget which had to be set aside for the maintenance of the regular main force units, it was essential that some way be found to make the regional militia self-sufficient, or the corner-stone of the Viet Minh's political-military strategy could not be set in place. One Viet Minh strategist, Le Liem, who was later praised by Party historians for the 'clarity' of his thinking on the problem of feeding the regional militia, explained in April 1948 how self-sufficiency was to be achieved:

> concentrated people's militia units have the function of
> preparing for war so each day they must eat, drill, and wait to
> fight the enemy. So why do we not give them the function of
> producing as they fight? A wide campaign to mobilise the masses
> can help the militia concentrate on an agreed piece of land. This
> will give them a number of fields for themselves, or enable them
> to work in conjunction with families near by. Then, by
> stipulating the method of concentrating quickly when the need
> arises, they will be able to fight the enemy on the land they have
> the function of defending.[71]

However, it is not difficult to imagine the problems of implementing such a system in the villages where land was such a jealously guarded commodity.

[71]Ibid., p. 26, pp. 28–29.

A year after Le Liem presented the Party line in *Truth* the 1949 training manual *Self Sufficiency* said the problem was that people still did not understand the slogan 'regional forces must be self sufficient'.[72] According to the manual, this slogan and Le Liem's idea of 'producing as you fight' 'does not mean that combatants must produce at the same time as they fight the enemy'.[73] No. What self sufficiency meant was that the armed units and the population in each region worked in a reciprocal relationship to produce necessities. The region's armed units had to contribute what they could to production but when they were fighting they obviously had to depend on the population for support. The population was also a part of the people's army and it was a collective responsibility for all 'to know how to assure the defence of their region and their means of production at the same time'.[74]

The primary response to this problem after the Resistance and Administration Committees had been placed on a firm footing in each region was to set up 'Self Sufficiency Committees'.[75] These consisted of economic cadres whose task it was to explain the government's policy, plan production, allot fields to the regional forces through negotiations with people in the village, and generally implement what came to be known as the system of 'small scale'[76] economic activity.

This system of production did not mean that output was to be small. On the contrary, one expert on economic affairs outlined the purpose of the system in 1949:

> the execution of small scale, dispersed (economic activity) will not only benefit us in our defence against the enemy destruction and bombing, it will also help us a great deal to (increase) the quantity produced.[77]

The government thus launched numerous movements in the late 1940s to encourage people to emulate high productivity in some area of the country throughout the rest of it.[78] Many songs and poems which associated patriotism and productivity, such as 'The Song of

[72]Quan Doi Quoc Gia Viet Nam [National Army of Vietnam], *Cung Cap Tu Cap* [Self Sufficiency], Viet Bac Inter-Zone, 1949, p. 4.
[73]Ibid.
[74]Ibid.
[75]*CKCT*, Vol. 2, p. 40.
[76]Ibid., p. 141.
[77]*CKCT*, Vol. 2, p. 141.
[78]*LSDC*, p. 531, pp. 570–571. *LSQD*, pp. 299–313. On the emulation movement in general also see *CKCT*, Vol. 2, pp. 22–25. For the seminal Party instructions of 27 March 1948 see *VKD*, pp. 197–208.

the Peasant Soldier',[79] were also used in the emulation and armed propaganda campaigns to encourage hard work, as every group in the society—family, village, zone, national salvation organisation, armed unit—was expected to maximise output from the scarce resources immediately available. About all the government then had to do was outline policy, send out economic cadres to the provinces, and occasionally crack the whip.[80]

By the end of the decade the success of the 'small scale' system of production was beginning to show. Of course, there was still no widespread success in the area of land reform, reduction of rents and taxes, but the progress in self sufficiency was encouraging in many regions. One journal article thus noted in 1949 how

> although they are still not numerous, cattle raising farms have been established in some places; (some) pigs and chickens have died of disease but thanks to attempts to increase production their numbers have still increased greatly.[81]

In some provinces like Phuc Yen moves to plan rice production had been extended to all villages where conferences of women, youth, worker, and peasant associations were frequently held to reach accord and establish norms. In other provinces like Nghe An, and especially Thanh Hoa, which it is not generally realised became one of the main rice suppliers for the Viet Minh's armies in the early 1950s, the first 'cooperatives' began to operate.[82]

To some extent the picture which the journals paint of economic development is tinged with utopianism. For example, journal reports of the large-scale irrigation projects in Quang Tri, the introduction of fertilizer to some central provinces from the north, the campaigns to improve farm implements, and the worthy cases in Inter-Zone 5 where members of village organisations were each given fifty cotton plants to tend around their houses[83] should be treated with healthy skepticism. The Party journals were after all setting up models for emulation, and the Viet Minh were never able to achieve fully their goal of scaling off their zones and cutting commerce with people in the occupied zones.[84] Nevertheless, the evidence of progress in the

---

[79]*CKCT*, Vol. 2, p. 253.

[80]For example, in a clear contradiction of the Marxist view of history *CKCT*, Vol. 2, p. 180 shows that *Inner Life* criticised the working class in April 1949 for 'relying on the government and not knowing about self organisation and taking up the task of improving (their own self sufficiency)'.

[81]*CKCT*, Vol. 2, pp. 141.

[82]Ibid., pp. 190–196.

[83]Ibid., pp. 251–258.

[84]In fact, in the south, the reverse tended to occur where the French successfully

journals cannot be ignored when the army continued to expand and the thrust of their accounts is supported by French sources.

Some of these sources show that the policy of self sufficiency was extended with some success to a range of important commodities like paper, medicines, pig fat soap, pig bristle tooth brushes, and a range of chemicals—antimony, sulphur, and acids.[85] Other French Army sources also show that in some areas it was becoming increasingly difficult for French garrisons to break the Viet Minh's economic blockade. In Thua Thien in 1949, for example, one French report noted that while French forces had difficulty in resupplying themselves from local resources, 'most of the time, the enemy is able to resupply his posts by third parties who go secretly to buy necessary merchandise in the villages'.[86]

With respect to weapons and ammunition the idea of self sufficiency largely meant that regional forces had to make the best use they could of captured weapons. However, these could be augmented by the local arms workshops.[87] When the government moved from Hanoi in December 1946 the original idea had been to evacuate machinery from the towns and set up 'self sufficient factories'.[88] Yet, despite recent claims that

> From the outbreak of the war in all the country to the summer of 1947 the working class moved 38,000 tons of machinery and material and already produced over two million guns, mines, grenades . . . to supply the armed forces . . .[89]

the Chief of Ordnance in the Ministry of National Defence, General Tran Dai Nghia, wrote in 1950 that in 1947 the policy of setting up 'self sufficient factories' 'was a complete failure; the quantity produced was negligible and the quality virtually nil'.[90] Thus, it was not

blockaded Viet Minh zones to cut them off from external sources of supply by 1949. There is a large body of literature on the economic war. From the Viet Minh point of view the articles by Truong Chinh and Xuan Truong in *Truth* in May 1948, *CKCT*, Vol. 2, pp. 35–38, pp. 44–46, provide a good introduction. One could start in the French literature with J. Despuech, *Le trafic des piastres*, Paris, 1953 and André Clermont, 'L'Economie Viet Minh', Indochine Sub-Est Asiatique, Number 19, June-July 1953.

[85]For a description of chemical works and paper making see Leo Figures, *Je reviens du Viet Nam libre*, Paris, 1950, pp. 61–62. Also see note 82.

[86]SHAT, C. 108, D. 'Contributions et Impots', Report of 13 August 1949.

[87]Figuères, *Je reviens*, p. 64 describes a mortar bomb workshop.

[88]Tran Dai Nghia, 'Les Méthodes de la Production D'Armement', in *Traduction de deux articles extraits de la publication Viet Minh intitutlé: Quan Chinh Tap San*, Etat Major des F.T.N.V., Hanoi, 1950, p. 5.

[89]*LSDC*, pp. 537–538

[90]Tran Dai Nghia, 'Les Méthodes', p. 5.

until around 1949 when the government had established various
'Supply Transport Offices' (*Cuc Tiep Te Van Tai*)[91] and numerous
staging posts were set up by the army to facilitate the circulation of
war supplies and material in the war zones that local arms production
enjoyed some limited success. Now arms workshops could be set up
'in series'[92] so that machines and artisans could be allocated to
particular jobs. Components and materials for, say, mortar bombs
and barrels of various calibers could then move more efficiently
through the production cycle. However, while the arms industry in
the villages could make a small contribution, it was not the kind of
industry that could ever have given the Viet Minh weapons superiority over the French. This could only happen after the war had been
internationalised in 1950 and the Viet Minh had access to the ordnance depots of Communist China.

Meanwhile, as the community's economy was being organised for
war, the regional forces were expected to contribute to production in
the region when they were not fighting. For this purpose contemporary Viet Minh sources say that 'units established self sufficiency
committees in the political command structure and organised sections
of peasant soldiers.'[93] Thus, we have examples of units in Inter-Zone
5 which were involved in 'planting vegetables, raising chickens,
making hats, sandals, kit bags, and leather belts'.[94] Some sources also
talk of soldiers growing jute, tea, and plowing the land confiscated
from 'Vietnamese traitors'.[95] Then if a unit had to go on operations

> to resolve the problem of manoeuvering from one area to
> another area this unit changes over vegetable fields with that
> unit or reminds their combat mothers to look after their fields
> until they are harvested.[96]

Thus integrating the army and its operations with the society were
institutional arrangements within the unit to ensure production, and
'combat mothers' (*me chien si*) outside the unit to give a helping
hand. 'Combat mothers' were, moreover, a function of the army's
wider social as well as economic relationship with the community for
the official history says

[91]*LSQD*, p. 372.
[92]Tran Dai Nghia, 'Les Méthodes', p. 5.
[93]*CKCT*, Vol. 2, p. 254.
[94]Ibid., p. 257. *LSQD*, p. 312 says soldiers made their own *mu nan* (hat from
bamboo splints), eating bowl made from large sections of bamboo, and water bottles
made out of buffalo skins.
[95]Quan Doi Quoc Gia, *Tu Cung Tu Cap*, p. 9.
[96]*CKCT*, Vol. 2, p. 257.

Associations of combat mothers together with women's national salvation organisations assumed a large responsibility for mobilising and taking care of units, and looking after wounded and sick soldiers.[97]

By early 1949 when such careful nurturing of resources had become widespread in the army and the community, regional force companies well established in most areas, and numerous 'concentrated battalions' and even several 'main force regiments'[98] could now be counted on the Viet Minh's order of battle. As the army grew, so too did its economic functions. Bigger units now became responsible for 'large scale'[99] economic activity. Indeed, the economic enterprise of some big units was so large that they were authorised to issue bank notes.[100]

'Large scale, economic activity was generally carried out by Independent Regiments at an Inter-Provincial level when 'peasant units' were given the task of clearing land and other long term economic tasks.[101] Often, in major land clearing projects, irrigation projects, and raising livestock and poultry the army had to coordinate its activities with the local population. This need meant the formation of special propaganda teams to explain the army's role in general and that of the supply units in particular. It led to the formation of various army-community associations such as 'The Association for the Assistance of Local Units' that tended to strengthen the army's bonds with the society. In theory, it also meant that supply units mingling with the population could 'teach the people military skills as they cultivate the fields'.[102]

In areas close to the battle front Party publications emphasised the need for armed units at all levels to help protect and harvest the rice crop. For instance the journal *National Salvation* explained on 12 October 1949 how 'at Bac Giang, Bac Ninh, Phuc Yen, and most recently at Vinh Yen French rebels have destroyed our crops or sabotaged them by crushing our rice cultures in their water tanks'. Thus, along with local guerrillas and regular soldiers stationed in the region, 'cooperative teams of harvesters' consisting of multiple cells from families and community groups in the locality were to divide the crop into sections and be ready for a rapid harvest. Each village was further ordered to establish a special team of harvesters whose task it

[97]*LSQD*, p. 371.
[98]Ibid., p. 368.
[99]*CKCT*, Vol. 1, p. 257.
[100]Despeuch, *Le trafic*, p. 312.
[101]*CKCT*, Vol. 1, p. 257. *LSQD*, p. 312.
[102]*CKCT*, Vol. 2, p. 275. Quan Doi Quoc Gia, *Tu Cung Tu Cap*, pp. 6–8.

was 'to come to the aid of localities situated close to enemy positions that need to carry out a very rapid harvest, or those where the stage of the maturation of the cultures calls for a rapid intervention.' If harvesters were under extreme pressure they could cut the rice plant near the top, but they were never to let 'a grain of rice fall into enemy hands'. Army units were particularly responsible for early warning of French patrols, the supervision of transport for the harvest—buffalo carts and sampans—in some areas, and they were often sent to ambush French patrols to cover the working harvesters.[103] This was the meaning of the slogan 'produce as you fight' which was indeed the 'door bolt', as the Vietnamese expression has it, of the entire strategy of people's war.

For such social-military and economic interaction to be effective, however, the door bolt had to sit firmly in its political lock. Especially when Party sources raised disturbing examples where Resistance and Administration committees 'forced' the population to support the army, and where the army itself behaved 'arrogantly and in an authoritarian manner' such as in the matter of 'recruiting "labourers" by force'[104] the army's economic relationship with the society had to be reinforced through political work. On the other hand, the army was operating in a complex and variegated social environment and even with the best intentions it could sometimes fall a foul to local custom. As an instance, when armed units entered the Lao Kay area in early 1949 and began their usual 'bowl of rice for the resistance' style exhortations, all they met with was scorn. In the words of the training manual, *Self Sufficiency*, the reason for this was that the people were asking themselves, 'Is the army really so poor that every day it runs after a handful of rice?'[105] Smoothing out misunderstandings and teaching the army tolerance were also political tasks for the Party and government as they marshalled the resources to supply it.

In the plethora of army training courses being run all over the country, slogans like 'the people are the foundation, the father and mother of the army' were thus put forward by political officers. There were also drives to raise the cultural and social standards of the troops. One in March 1949 called for

> artists to enter the army to create (works) for soldiers and the people so that the whole people will be more tightly linked (*doan ket chat che*), will love the country and hate the enemy more, and will believe more in victory. Artists must also help in the task of internationalist propaganda and campaign in

[103]Ibid.
[104]Truong Chinh, *Selected Works*, p. 205.
[105]Quan Doi Gia, *Tu Cung Tu Cap*, p. 8.

particular areas . . . like recruiting, paying into resistance funds, proselytising the enemy, and mobilising the people in temporarily occupied regions. In armed units artists must help with political work.[106]

Here we have the early stages of what later became a systematic attempt to engage the 'total consciousness'[107] of each soldier. By having writers in units, by encouraging soldiers to keep diaries and write poems for both private and public consideration, the army was being merged into the collective consciousness of the nation. Thus, by 1949, as this limitless resource complemented all the others, there was no longer anything the French could do to prevent the rise of the main forces.

Rise of the Main Forces

By late 1949 the French had tried a number of strategies to stifle the expansion of the people's militia. Up to 1947, as we have seen, the plan was to achieve a rapid political solution with a series of lightning strikes. When this strategy seriously disrupted the Viet Minh, but nevertheless failed to achieve the desired solution, the Expeditionary Corps gradually turned, in 1948, towards a methodical combination of 'force and political means'.[108] This change in emphasis included the so called 'Bao Dai solution'—although even the French were calling Bao Dai's ministers 'puppets'[109]—and a half serious attempt to raise a non-communist Vietnamese National Army. Thirty three Vietnamese battalions had been raised by December 1948, but this only gave the Viet Minh another justification for the popular slogan 'the French take Vietnamese to fight Vietnamese'[110] because all of these battalions were officered by the French and incorporated into the French Expeditionary Corps which only totalled seventy battalions.[111] At the same time, French attempts to blockade Viet Minh zones and consolidate their position in the main rice growing deltas enjoyed limited success in some parts of the Mekong and Red River Deltas but generally failed to stop the expansion of the guer-

[106]*CKCT*, Vol. 2, p. 170.

[107]Koko, *Anatomy of a War*, p. 257.

[108]Tueliers, *La guerre*, p. 57.

[109]Gras, *Histoire*, p. 251. On the Bao Dai solution also see Irving, *The First*, p. 55ff., and Devillers, *Histoire*, Chapters 23–26. For a contemporary Viet Minh perspective see *CKCT*, Vol. 2, pp. 13–22, and for internal Party perspectives see *VKD*, pp. 167–169.

[110]*LSDC*, p. 562.

[111]Gras, *Histoire*, p. 250.

rilla war. Sometimes the main French effort was concentrated in the south and sometimes it was concentrated in the north. But by 1949 when the French concentrated their effort in the south not only did they find Viet Minh 'battalions' 'showing a combativeness hitherto unknown in Cochinchina',[112] they also found that 'as soon as the Expeditionary Corps concentrated its effort in Cochinchina, the Viet Minh went on the offensive in the north'.[113] By late 1949, although the war had reached a stalemate insofar as the French could not pin the Viet Minh down and the Viet Minh could not dislodge the French, the Viet Minh had still been able to develop the complex mechanism of a people's war on two levels as a result of its armed propaganda successes in the society and its careful nurturing of resources. The first level was in the field of guerrilla war and the second in the field of regular war. The ancient structure of Vietnamese armies and the strategic interactions they thrived on were beginning to reemerge under modern conditions.

At the first level the guerrilla war was now virtually unbounded. The village guerrillas and the regional forces were capable of extensive armed propaganda and guerrilla operations in the Viet Minh zones. Moreover, the basic force structure of the people's army had been consolidated to the point where Independent Companies, Special Action Units, and main force Regiments, were being fortified with such slogans as 'hold fast and win back the hearts of the people'. They were also being sent to establish 'combat villages' 'in places where armed propaganda units had already created bases.'[114] Such places were the rice growing areas around Saigon, Da Nang, Hue, Hai Phong, and Hanoi.

In the southern provinces around Saigon armed propaganda and guerrilla actions had created such broad bases by 1948 that some of the mobile Chi Doi's were being consolidated into Regiments. Around Bien Hoa in March and April, for example, some successful attacks on French surveillance towers with ladders and grenades coincided with a sufficient increase in local support for Chi Doi 10 to become Regiment 310.[115] Around Hue and the districts of Thua Thien, one Party history gives some indication of what was happening in 1948 and 1949 when it records that 'self-armed people surrounded and seized pro-French organisations, exterminated traitors,

---

[112]Ibid., p. 259.

[113]Ibid., p. 262.

[114]Ibid., p. 235; *LSQD*, p. 349, p. 353, p. 358; *VKD*, p. 151 mentions 'combat villages' as early as October 1947.

[115]Ban Chap Hanh, *Dong Nai*, p. 84 for method of attacking towers and 310 Regiment; pp. 78–87 for general discussion.

and educated the people to mend their ways and return to the masses'.[116] Meanwhile, in and around Hanoi which was theoretically a French stronghold, another recent Vietnamese study claims that Special Action Units often entered the city from August 1948 to set up weapons workshops and organise political cells, while Independent Companies of the 48th Regiment built bases in the surrounding villages. According to this source, 100 villages around Hanoi had Viet Minh bases, 15,600 people were 'organised', and 2,095 people had been 'formed into guerrilla units'[117] by late 1948.

In the other countries of Indochina, Cambodia and Laos, the guerrilla war was gradually developing. After the initial impulse for Viet Minh involvement in these countries had been the need to secure resistance supply lines from Thailand in 1946. Général Salan dated one of the earliest Khmer Issarak attacks from August of that year.[118] In 1947 and 1948 various sources note the expansion of Viet Minh armed propaganda and the creation of Viet Minh controlled organisations for the political-military mobilisation of the people in both Cambodia and Laos.[119] By 1949, as the Central Committee became increasingly aware that 'all of Indochina is one battle field',[120] the 'Cambodian Front' was opened under the direction of 'Son Ngoc Minh' and the Nam Bo Resistance and Administration Committee.[121] *Inner Life* also said in March that the Cambodian and Lao Liberation Armies had 'begun'[122] operations to establish bases in conjunction with the Viet Minh. These indigenous guerrilla armies in Cambodia and Laos were not large—there were perhaps 1,200 Khmer Issarak and 200 Lao Issarak[123]—and compared to the development of the

---

[116]*LSDC*, p. 577.

[117]Ban Nghien Cuu Lich Su Dang [Committee for the Historical Study of the Party], *Cuoc Khang Chien Chong Thuc Dan Phap va Can Thiep My o Hanoi* [The Resistance War Against the French Colonialists and the American Interventionists in Hanoi], Hanoi, 1980, pp. 63–66.

[118]Raoul Salan, *Mémoires: Fin d'un Empire: Le Viet Minh mon adversaire Octobre 1946-Octobre 1954*, Paris, 1971, p. 23.

[119]For example, Pierre Christian, 'Le Viet Minh au Cambodge', *Indochine Sud-Est Asiatique*, Fevrier-Mars 1952; Claude Guigues, 'Le Viet Minh au Laos', *Indochine Sud-Est Asiatique*, Novembre 1952; Gras, *Histoire*, p. 231; *LSDC*, p. 581.

[120]Quoted in *LSDC*, p. 581. See also *LSQD*, p. 254, pp. 258–259.

[121]*LSDC*, p. 568, pp. 581–582. To my knowledge neither Viet Minh nor recent Vietnamese official histories refer to the communist leader pseudonymously called Son Ngoc Minh although David Chandler has told me he, rather than Son Ngoc Thanh was the one at work on the 'Cambodian Front'. For more information on these figures see Ben Kiernan and Chanthou Boua eds., *Peasants and Politics in Kampuchea 1942–1981*, London: Zed Press, 1982, see index.

[122]*CKCT*, Vol. 2, p. 165.

[123]Gras, *Histoire*, pp. 232–233.

armed forces in Vietnam they were no more than a minor irritation to the French. However, both these countries retained their importance to the Viet Minh from a supply point of view and, as we will see in a moment, Laos began to assume some of the strategic importance it was to have after 1950 for the conduct of a regular war of movement.

As the guerrilla war expanded throughout Indochina, the main force units of the regular army retained a capacity to operate even though, after April 1948, they had largely been broken down into Independent Companies to help rebuild the regional forces. As these Companies worked with the regional forces in many places they could still be concentrated quickly for action if need be. Moreover, while the level of organisational development varied enormously from one region to another very many new main force battalions, twelve new main force regiments with supporting engineer and heavy weapons units, and even an embryonic division, had been formed from units with the most battle experience, the best weapons, and the best cadres between the second half of 1948 and late 1949.[124]

On 31 October 1949 *Truth* published an article which said

> Now, our armed and semi-armed forces have three categories: the main force units, the regional units, and people's guerrilla forces in the villages. Each category has a concrete responsibility. The main force units manoeuvre, fight big battles and train and lead the regional units in a coordinated struggle. Regional forces have the responsibility of protecting the region, leading the people's guerrilla units in the villages, armed propaganda, harassing and tiring the enemy, and advancing in cooperation with the main force units . . . The people's guerrilla units in the village protect the village, pay attention to strengthening the village, destroying and exterminating traitors and spies . . . and developing into regional forces to take the place of some of the regional forces that enter the main force.[125]

At the pinnacle of this military hierarchy in late 1949 was Regimental Group 308, which was the first embryonic division to be formed on 28 August 1949 in the Viet Bac. It was based on the prestigious Capital Regiment 308 which had been created during the battle for Hanoi in early 1947,[126] and was commanded by Vuong Thua Vu who had played a prominent training role in 1946 before being appointed to take charge of the defence of Hanoi. The rest of the Regimental Group was composed of several well tried battalions with a high

---

[124]*LSQD*, p. 368, p. 370.
[125]*CKCT*, Vol. 2, p. 258.
[126]*LSQD*, p. 369. Vuong Thua Vu, *Truong Thanh*, pp. 148–168.

proportion of soldiers from the ethnic minorities from Inter-Zones 3 and Viet Bac. The organisation of the Regimental Group, which Vuong Thua Vu says in his memoirs was by no means uniformly armed, dressed, or equipped—under the self sufficiency policy many individuals had home made uniforms or wore clothing taken from the bodies of French soldiers[127]—was as follows:

> Regiment 98; consisting of three infantry battalions (23, 29, 322), and an artillery battalion (Battalion 38 with one 120 millimetre mortar company and two artillery companies). Regiment 102; the old Capital Regiment with three infantry battalions (18, 54, 79), and an artillery battalion (Battalion 69 consisting of one 120 millimetre mortar company and two artillery companies.[128]

It seems unlikely that the strength of this Regimental Group could have exceeded about 10,000 men, although some sources say its strength was 15,000.[129] At any rate, the formation of Regimental Group 308 clearly reflected a significant increase in the Viet Minh's capacity to fight a regular war of movement and set piece battles.

As early as March 1948 Regiment 310 from Bien Hoa had inflicted the first of many staggering losses on the French when it annihilated a large French convoy on the road from Saigon to Dalat in a well planned multi-battalion ambush that killed forty nine people.[130] In the north the first major set piece assault on a French post took place between 20 and 25 July 1948, when some 3,000 troops organised into five or six main force battalions attacked at Phu Tong Toa. After opening the attack with an artillery bombardment that completely surprised the French, and leaving forty bodies on the objective, the assault was finally repulsed by the French garrison that was only 100 strong.[131] However, this was one of the Viet Minh's first set piece attacks on any scale, and in a similar attack eight months later on the Song Ky Cong post in the northwest on 16 March 1949 two main force battalions overran a post held by French regulars for the first time. This victory took three hours.[132] In all, between the last quarter of 1948 and early 1950 the official history says there were thirty

---

[127] Vuong Thua Vu, *Truong Thanh*, p. 162.

[128] Ibid., p. 168.

[129] Gras, *Histoire*, p. 297 says 'about 15,000'.

[130] Salan, *Le Viet Minh mon adversaire*, p. 137. Boyer de Latour, *Le Martyre*, pp. 89–99. There are slight discrepancies in the French accounts of the casualty list. The Vietnamese account of the ambush in *LSQD*, p. 342, says 150 were killed. For another Vietnamese view of the ambush see Ban Chap Hanh, *Dong Nai*, p. 80.

[131] Gras, *Histoire*, pp. 238–239.

[132] Ibid., p. 263.

campaigns in which groups of from three to five battalions to three regiments[133] manoeuvred through the countryside and concentrated for battles like those already mentioned.

However, it must always be remembered that because of the nature of the army's social and economic base this escalation in the regular war was structured by the interaction of regular campaigns with local guerrilla action. As Vo Nguyen Giap rationalised this interaction in 1961:

> if you do not have guerrilla war then you are unable to have a war of movement; but if you have guerrilla war and do not advance to a war of movement then not only will the strategic responsibility to destroy the enemy's main force be unrealised but you will not be able to maintain and develop the original guerrilla war.[134]

Thus, during the Le Loi campaign of November and December 1949, when Giap deployed what some sources say were as many as thirty main force battalions[135] for an offensive aimed at reestalblishing links between Inter-Zone 4 and the Viet Bac, different tactical combinations were used. As the official history says, 'at times the (regiments) were dispersed to fight a guerrilla war to tire the enemy along roads and rivers, and then concentrated to attack posts'.[136]

What this combination of tactical forms meant in social-military terms was that the maintenance of the main force and its operations was synonymous with the maintenance or creation of institutional links with the population in each area of operations. Especially when the Le Loi campaign spread over an area that extended from Lao Kay in the northwest border region through the Sam Neua salient in Laos and Bac Bo to the sea,[137] the need for tens of thousands of porters and as many tons of rice, was largely dependent on the army's capacity to mobilise local support. In general, the regional forces in each area would prepare the necessary support with a bout of armed propaganda. But in areas where the Viet Minh's political-military organisation was weak or non existent, as in the Ma river valley in northeastern Laos in late 1949, the regular units had to carry out their own armed propaganda. Whole battalions would often be sent into a

[133]*LSQD*, pp. 384–386.

[134]Vo Nguyen Giap, *Nhung Kinh Nghiem Lon cua Dang ve Lanh Dao Dau Tran Vu Trang va Xay Dung Luc Luong Vu Trang Cach Mang* (Major Experiences of the Party in Leading Armed Struggle and Building Revolutionary Armed Forces], Hanoi, 1961, p. 41, quoted in *LSDC*, p. 579.

[135]Gras, *Histoire*, p. 283.

[136]*LSQD*, p. 385.

[137]Gras, *Histoire*, pp. 283–285.

region to propagandise the population, set up rudimentary political organisations, and organise logistic support before the main battle force entered the area. Once in the area the battle force would make intensive use of local forces or personnel to gain intelligence, prepare the battle field, and muster local resources for the attack.[138] Such a combination of effort then does much to explain how, by late 1949, a growing number of French posts were being surprised by preparatory artillery bombardments and assaulted by waves of regular Viet Minh infantry, sometimes preceded by herds of charging buffalo.

But if the emergence of such battles unquestionably indicated what Général Gras has called the 'immense progress'[139] of the People's Army by late 1949 there is still something about the quality of the progress that should not be allowed to elude us. George Tanham has argued that even without Chinese aid after 1950 'line divisions would soon have been created'[140] in Vietnam as a natural extension of the indigenous mobilisation that had produced Regimental Group 308 by August 1949. This argument may be strengthened if it is added that from at least the Sixth Cadre Conference of the Central Committee in January 1949 the Viet Minh were sufficiently sure of their growing strength to press for 'preparations for the general counter offensive'[141] in the journals. For instance, in May and June 1949 several articles appeared in *Truth* explaining a Central Committee decision to push mobilisation forward on all fronts—military, economic, cultural, political—between then and the end of the year.[142] Yet, in some ways the new emphasis on the general counter offensive

[138]Later in the Second Indochina War the most elaborate preparation of operational areas was carried out up to a year before the assault force moved into it. For example, preparations for the Spring Offensive in 1975 were begun by September 1974 when logistics groups, sappers, and staff officers had moved into the Central Highlands to grow gardens of maize, sweet potatoes, and cassava for the next campaign season, set up supply dumps, and make a reconnaissance of the area. Foreign Languages Publishing House, *The Ho Chi Minh Trail*, Hanoi, 1982, pp. 171–173.

[139]Gras, *Histoire*, p. 299.

[140]George K. Tanham, *Communist Revolutionary Warfare: The Viet Minh in Indochina*, London, 1962, p. 41.

[141]*CKCT*, Vol. 2, p. 119. This source reflects internal Party deliberations published in *VKD*, pp. 279–280.

[142]The push towards a general counter offensive in the Party journals was also parallelled in internal Party documents for 1949, and a major statement on preparations for the offensive was made on 18 August 1949, around the time of the formation of Regimental Group 308. This statement, which mentions the need to 'concentrate main forces' but does not specially mention the Regimental Group, can be found in *VKD*, pp 327–335.

and the creation of a regimental group in 1949 was curiously premature.

Almost all of the successful regular manoeuvres and set piece battles had occurred in the northwestern highlands where the weather, terrain, and remoteness had kept the main force beyond the range of French air power. In the plains, the guerrilla war was certainly a constant strain on French resources, but the formation of large regular units was still out of the question. The fire power of regular Viet Minh units was still very inferior to that of French units, although an intimate knowledge of the terrain often permitted the Viet Minh to move in close to French positions and so neutralize the effects of their heavy weapons.[143]

For these reasons, therefore, I would argue that in terms of the virtual military stalemate that existed in Vietnam in 1949 the emphasis on the general counter offensive and the formation of Regimental Group 308 was to some extent artificial. However, when Viet Minh perceptions of the rapidly changing situation in China are taken into account the real sense of these developments is complete. By late 1947 we have seen that Truong Chinh raised the need to make propaganda out of the Viet Bac victory of that year 'inside the country' and 'outside the country'. We have also seen that artists were called into the ranks of the army to help make 'internationalist propaganda', and from early 1948, at a time when some Chinese personnel were already involved in supporting the Viet Minh,[144] there are many references in Party journals to the great impact that the imminent communist victory in China would have on the world revolution in general and the Vietnamese revolution in particular. Then, as the day approached in November 1949 when *Truth* published a five page article celebrating the birth of the People's Republic of China on 30 October, there were numerous other references to China which show that the Viet Minh clearly anticipated significant support from Mao Zedong. These references also strongly suggested that the creation of Regimental Group 308 was part of an elaborate armed propaganda operation designed to attract support from China and so strengthen internal unity.

In its account of the Sixth Cadre Conference of the Central Committee in January, when the concentration of regular units and the development of a war of movement was first given serious emphasis,[145] *Truth* stated that

---

[143]Despuech, *Le Trafic*, p. 144 makes this point.

[144]These people were in fact involved from no later than 1947, according to a private communication with David Marr.

[145]Published resolutions of the conference are in *VKD*, pp. 279–303. Also see Vuong Thua Vu, *Truong Thanh*, p. 149.

thanks to the glorious success of the Chinese Revolution and the resounding influence of this success on the democratic world movement in general, and on our resistance war in particular, we are very able to shorten the holding phase of our war. We must do everything to prepare for the general counter offensive and advance to the third phase.[146]

By August, in the same month as Regimental Group 308 was formed, the strategist Hong Nam then Published a twelve page article in *Inner Life* stressing the need for further development of both regional and main force units which said:

If the enemy wants to strengthen the Bac Bo battle field before the (Chinese) Liberation Army reaches the border we must keep our main force intact to take complete advantage of the opportunity and do everything to prepare for the general counter offensive . . . Skilled cadres must be deployed at province and district level in the border region with clear instructions for the army and the people to deal with the French rebels . . . and coordinate their actions with the Liberation Army when it advances to the border.[147]

Finally, after the People's Republic of China had been founded and Regimental Group 308 along with many other main force units prepared to embark on major campaigns like Le Loi and Le Hong Phong 1, *Truth* explained how feudalism was falling all over the world. The Chinese revolution was the greatest event in world history since the Russian revolution, Marxism-Leninism had been the secret to China's success just as it had been in Vietnam, and Vietnam was now linked up to the great arc of socialist countries that swept from East Germany, through Central Europe, the Soviet Union and China to the countries of Southeast Asia.[148] Now, as *Truth* said, 'thanks to the deeply determined struggle of the people of Indochina and the help of the Soviet Union, China, and the democratic countries in the whole world, the day of liberation for the people of Indochina is not far off'.[149]

The changing military emphasis of the Viet Minh in 1949 was related clearly to the changing situation in China. This need to link internal political-military developments in Vietnam with those in China does not, of course, detract from the remarkable indigenous development of the regional militia and the main force in 1948 and 1949, when the strength of consolidated armed units (as opposed to

[146]*CKCT*, Vol. 2, p. 119.
[147]Ibid., pp. 244–247.
[148]Ibid., pp. 293–298.
[149]Ibid., p. 295.

the millions of village guerrillas) was around 80,000 to 100,000.[150] Moreover, Regimental Group 308 was formed well before material aid began to arrive in Vietnam from China. But this is not necessarily to say that 'line divisions' would have been created anyway, or that if they were created they would have taken the same formidable shape we will see they did after aid came from China in the early 1950s. When the quality of the changes which the formation of Regimental Group 308 represents are considered we are simultaneously drawn into the Viet Minh's armed propaganda campaign inside the country and outside the country. In 1949 the formation of the Regimental Group was like the formation of a link between an independent international world order and the internal constitution of state power in Vietnam that were mutually reinforcing. The Viet Minh's big achievement in 1948 and 1949, therefore, was that the country was prepared to take advantage of the changed situation in China as the next chapter will show.

---

[150]*LSQD*, p. 308; *LSDC*, p. 573 says there were three million village querrillas by late 1949.

7
Independence in the Modern World, 1950–1954

The year 1950 began a new phase in the history of the People's Army. From December 1949 links with Communist China led to the diplomatic recognition of the Democratic Republic of Vietnam by the socialist world in January. Significant quantities of Chinese military aid that would break the stalemate in Indochina by the end of the year began arriving in April. By 1953 this aid contributed a great deal to the formation of six modern main force infantry divisions and a heavy weapons division by the Viet Minh. But when Chinese aid began arriving the Viet Minh at first had great difficulty domesticating it.

Western accounts overlook this difficulty. Fall and others have simply emphasised that with the receipt of Chinese aid Vietnam became a model satellite of China. However, conditions in Vietnam were so different from those in China that a slavish application of Chinese models was quite incompatible with the idea of victory. For example, we will see that Chinese battle field advice during the delta offensive in 1951 could encourage disaster and had to be rejected at Dien Bien Phu in 1954. But at a deeper institutional level there was also no possibility of victory if large regular divisions were simply built up and hurled into battle. Such an application could only lead to gross institutional distortion as it did in 1951 because of the society's incapacity to support such development. Political-military mobilisation at the social base always remained fundamental to the army's growth and strategic ability, and a low level of mobilisation could never be compensated for by infusions of Chinese aid.

The Party's problem after 1950 was thus one of how it could best balance the need for foreign aid with internal political-military development. Because Chinese aid was so important, Chinese models could not be overlooked. Besides, there were cultural similarities which made the Chinese model positively useful in some cases. But none of this changed the fundamental need for foreign aid to be integrated with Vietnamese capacities to use it.

Once initial errors in the application of Chinese aid had therefore been recognised, major changes in political-military administration occurred. From 1951 the state increasingly centralised its power as an open communist party reappeared, important tax reforms were enacted, the size of divisions was reduced, and land reform legislation was passed in December 1953. On such rationalised bases we will then see how the army was integrated more effectively with the society's capacity to support it at the same time as Chinese aid was vital to the last great efforts to defeat the French. The victories at Hoa Binh in 1952 and Dien Bien Phu in 1954 would indeed epitomise Vietnam's national struggle for unity and independence within a supportive international order.

International Recognition and Aid

After a Viet Minh military mission was sent to Beijing in December 1949 and Vo Nguyen Giap went on a mission to Nanjing soon afterwards, the Democratic Republic of Vietnam was recognised by China on January 18. The Soviet Union followed China's example on January 31, and numerous other socialist countries followed the Soviet Union in early February. Meanwhile, French recognition of the Bao Dai's 'State of Vietnam' on 2 February, soon followed by America and Britain, was an unconvincing reaction to the Viet Minh's diplomatic success. For eleven months the French government had failed to ratify the Elysée Agreement on 8 March 1949 with Bao Dai which had first granted independence to Vietnam, Cambodia, and Laos. Then, when the Agreement was ratified, Bao Dai's residual puppet status was left in no doubt as he was not even allowed to occupy the palace in Saigon, which the French High Commissioner retained as his symbol of power.[1]

---

[1]Most of these events are well known. For another discussion see Chen, *Vietnam and China*, pp. 232–235. The trip which Hoang Van Hoan, *Giot Nuoc*, p. 330 says Ho made to Moscow with Tran Dang Ninh around this time may well have had something to do with Soviet recognition, although this source is not precise about the date. Bao Dai had of course held out for a year to extract French assurances on the 'unity' and 'independence' of Vietnam which were never kept. On Bao Dai's palace problems and a general discussion of his decadence see Bodard, *La guerre d'Indochine*, Vol. 3, pp. 28–38. If he had wished Bao Dai could have occupied the old residence of the Governors General in Hanoi, the Puginier Palace, which Bodard, Vol. 3, p. 30

Predictably, the resistance journals viewed these developments as a vindication of the Party's internationalist line. *Truth* explained in February:

> For four years the Vietnamese people have struggled to gain their freedom and independence at the same time as they have also struggled to support world peace . . . The fact that the Soviet Union and the People's Democracies have recognised the Democratic Republic of Vietnam proves that the Vietnamese problem is clearly an international problem. While the imperialists are on the point of recognising the puppet Bao Dai and worrying about increasing their aid in money and weapons so that they can attack Vietnam, the Soviet Union and the People's Democracies recognise the Vietnamese Government and establish diplomatic relations . . . The diplomatic victories of the Vietnamese government . . . Strengthen the Vietnamese position in the international arena and make Vietnam's power stronger.[2]

Now, as the journals began to use the powerful metaphor of 'family' in their propaganda, it could be said that Vietnam had entered the 'great family' (*dai gia dinh*)[3] of world socialist nations. And within this family a sense of Vietnam's national identity could only be strengthened, as could the foundation for Vietnam's power to project it.

In early 1950 new main force units continued to be raised as the first general mobilisation order 'for no matter what Vietnamese'[4] was given on 15 April. This order was reinforced with a major propaganda drive stressing preparations for 'the general counter offensive',

---

describes as 'une sorte d'énorme pâtisserie en pierres, un tarabiscotage 1900'. However, Hanoi was too close to events, and so Bao Dai retired to Dalat where his sad court overlooked a lake.

[2]*CKCT*, Vol. 2, pp. 331–332.

[3]Ibid, p. 363. This metaphor is used in many contexts. For an example of another usage see Nguyen Chi Thanh, *Nhung Bai Chon Loc ve Quan Su* [Selected Military Writings], Hanoi: Quan Doi Nhan Dan, 1977, p. 22 which uses the term 'great revolutionary family' (*dia gia dinh cach mang*).

[4]*CKCT*, Vol. 2, p. 348. Of course there had been earlier mobilisation orders. As Fall points out in *The Viet Minh*, p. 75 a 'general mobilisation of both men and women over eighteen was decreed throughout the Republic on November 4, 1949'. *CKCT*, Vol. 2, pp. 348–351 also recognises this, but it points out that the April 1950 order envisaged the adoption of a 'concrete plan' for mobilisation in each region in which 'propaganda was still the essential condition'. Moreover, the mobilisation order now had to be executed in enemy occupied territory as well as the free zone and their were strict punishments for evasion. In other words, Chinese recognition was at the centre of the armed propaganda campaign to mobilise people in all areas in early 1950.

'the patriotic emulation movement',[5] and a continuation of the military campaigns begun in late 1949 which we saw in the last chapter were at least partly designed to link developments in Vietnam with those in China. The Le Loi campaign around Hoa Binh begun in November 1949 continued into the new year. From January to May Le Hong Phong 1 campaign saw some 15,000 men thrown into heavy combat around Lao Cai, Phu Tho, and Cao Bang. During this campaign the French received a 'real surprise'[6] when Viet Minh infantry captured their first major post at Dong Khe on 27 May.

By April the Viet Minh's internal political-military development was further reinforced when material support began to arrive from China. Around this time a military mission under General Lo Kuei-po was sent to work with Giap.[7] In May official Vietnamese sources tell of the Central Committee stressing the need for 'urgent repair of large roads in the Viet Bac Inter-Zone that enter (the region) from the border'. 'At the present time communications and liaison between our country and foreign countries, especially China, is most essential'.[8] Convoys carrying arms, munitions, and equipment then began to arrive in small quantities by various routes. One ran from Wenshan to Bac Giang and Bac Kan, and another ran from Chingshi towards Nuoc Hai and Trung Khanh Phu. The maritime route from Yulin on Hainan to the coast of Central Vietnam was also in use. And, as such aid came south, at least 20,000 Viet Minh troops went north to China for refitting, reorganisation, and training during the wet season from May to September.[9]

They crossed the border unarmed. They were then ferried in trucks to training camps around Wenshan, Long Chou, and Chingshi where they were organised along the lines of a Chinese infantry division. This meant that after units were fitted out with new uniforms, arms, and equipment, the size of the regiments was expanded from 2,000 to 3,500. Up to 40,000 rifles, 125 machine guns, 75 mortars, 3,000 cases of ammunition, and 870 tons of general stores were supplied to the Viet Minh by the Chinese during this period. At all echelons heavy

[5]*CKCT*, Vol. 2, p. 348.

[6]Gras, *Histoire*, p. 300.

[7]Ibid., p. 315. *LSQD*, p. 399 says material began to arrive in August. I follow Gras because there is no doubt the French were well informed on the opening of Chinese aid and Vietnamese sources also show that urgent measures were being taken to receive aid well before August. See Notes 9, 10, and 11 below.

[8]*LSQD*, p. 393. See also interview with Hoang Van Hoan in *Beijing Review*, November 23, 1979; Hoang Van Hoan, *Giot Nuoc*, p. 343–344.

[9]Gras, *Histoire*, pp. 315–316; Chen, *Vietnam and China*, pp. 262–263. Tanham, *Communist Revolutionary Warfare*, p. 67. These western accounts are generally supported by Hoang Van Hoan, *Giot Nuoc*, p. 343, p. 347.

weapons units, communications detachments, service units, and command groups were built into the new organisation. Special emphasis was also placed on promoting experience cadres from the ranks to command infantry platoons, companies, and battalions.[10]

Unfortunately, references in Vietnamese sources to these developments are oblique. While we have seen the Vietnamese literature acknowledges the importance of Chinese aid — this was after all the internationalist line — sensitivity to any claim of Chinese domination prevents it from giving the kind of detailed evidence to be found in the Western sources. Such references as those in the official history to 'studying the precious experiences of our brothers and sisters in the Chinese People's Liberation Army'[11] nevertheless make it clear that lessons from the training in China were widely spread throughout the army. In fact, by late 1950 a range of contemporary Chinese and Vietnamese sources show that a study campaign based on Vietnamese translations of the writings Mao, Zhu De, and Liu Shaoqi was undertaken, and, as Chen says, in time it 'was carried to almost every Viet Minh unit, civilian and military'.[12] Moreover, when the official history notes the stress that was placed on the standardisation of weapons from 1950[13] there can be no doubt that this reflects Chinese aid. A number of French writers like Jacques Despuech[14] show that the arming of the infantry regiments and heavy weapons units both in China and Vietnam with 82 millimetre mortars and maxim machine guns became standard. Also, by late 1950, the arming of Viet Minh units with bazookas and recoilless rifles, which were prized because they were 'as powerful as elephants',[15] became relatively commonplace.

---

[10]Gras, *Histoire*, p. 315. This information had its source in what Gras p. 314 calls the 'nombreux renseignements' which kept French intelligence well informed of Sino-Viet Minh cooperation from early 1950 at least. During 1950 such information then became common knowledge as documents like, French Embassy in the United States, 'Document Number 29', November 10, 1950, were circulated to support French requests for American aid. From here the information was incorporated into the literature by writers like Jacques Despuech and Bernard Fall.

[11]*LSQD*, p. 394.

[12]Chen, *Vietnam and China*, p. 240. The Vietnamese and Chinese sources referred to are listed in the notes on p. 240 by Chen.

[13]Ibid., p. 392.

[14]Despuech, *Trafic*, pp. 143–144. See also Gras, *Histoire*, for Deuxième Bureau estimates of the impact of Chinese aid.

[15]Nguyen Huy Tuong, *Tuyen Tap*, p. 174. It is clear that these bazookas and recoilless rifles were of American origin. However, it does not necessarily follow from this that those weapons supplied to the Viet Minh came from stocks which the Chinese army captured from the Americans in Korea as some French sources suggest. This may have

Less commonplace, but also highly prized for its power was the artillery supplied by China. As the introduction to one Vietnamese artillery manual of 1950 noted:

> At the present time we have neither the tanks nor the aircraft to destroy the solid defence works of the enemy . . . In order to fulfill the missions outlined by President Mao we must pay particular attention to arms of different categories and employ them in attacks on fortified positions. The Commander in Chief has said: 'No artillery, no victories'.[16]

Specialist Viet Minh artillery men were trained on gunnery ranges at Tsin-tsi and Long Chow in Kwangsi, and regimental training in infantry-artillery coordination distinguished pre and post 1950 training programs.[17] Often, as the above reference to 'arms of different categories' suggests, the Viet Minh tended to call heavy weapons from 12.7 machine guns to 75 millimetre canons 'artillery'. However, by 18 September 1950 when the 308th Division and the 209th and 179th Regiments were ready for operations in Vietnam after at least major elements of them had been rotated through China, the Viet Minh won their first artillery duel at Dong Khe.[18]

Oddly enough, the French did not view these developments with much seriousness at the time. For them the fear that the Chinese would launch a massive invasion of Tonkin clouded all their thinking until 1951 and virtually paralysed the decision making process. Domestic pressures in France exacerbated the problem. Even though, as many writers have shown, the generals in Indochina had increasing difficulty in obtaining directions, troops, and supplies from France, nothing was done to mobilise popular support in Vietnam for a genuine National Army, and the substantial shipments of American aid that began arriving in mid-1950 merely reinforced French weaknesses.[19] And in this context it is worth making a comparison

---

increasingly been the case after 1951, but especially in 1950 weapons of American origin would have come from old Kuomintang Army stores. Furthermore, the 82 mm mortars the Viet Minh were supplied with were made in China. The US Army used 81 mm mortars. The Chinese mortars could use US ammunition but not vice-versa. This was pointed out to me by Brigadier R.L. Burnard of Sydney.

[16]L'Etat Major des F.T.N.V., *Notes sur l'Artillerie Viet Minh, 9 Novembre 1950: Traduction d'une brochure Viet Minh reproduisant une étude chinoise sur l'emploi de l'artillerie*, Hanoi, 1951, p. 2. This manual was translated from a Chinese manual of 1948 and originally based on Russian doctrine.

[17]Fall, *The Viet Minh*, p. 78. On coordination in training see *LSQD*, p. 391.

[18]Bodard, *La Guerre*, Vol. 3. p. 106.

[19]Many sources deal with French difficulties in this period. See Roger Levy, *Regards sur l'Indochine*, Paris, 1952; Irving, *The First Indochina War*; Gras, *Histoire* for an

between the amount of Chinese aid to the Viet Minh and American aid to the French.

By late 1950 transport difficulties had kept Chinese aid to the Viet Minh down to what one well informed French source describes as 'very irregular' deliveries that did not exceed '500 tons a month'.[20] On the other hand, American sources show that after an American Military Assistance Advisory Group was set up in Saigon around the time the Korean war began in June 1950, a comprehensive program of technical and economic aid was in place. It initially included $132 million, large quantities of arms and munitions, naval vessels, aircraft, and military vehicles. By February 1954 when America was financing around 80% of the French war effort, the Director of the Policy Planning Staff of the American State Department was reporting that while the Viet Minh had survived on 'mere pick up stocks' between 1946 and 1950, American aid to the French was 'scores of times greater in tonnage' than Chinese aid to the Viet Minh between 1950 and 1954.[21] The reason why this aid could not then be directed towards the building of an independent National Vietnamese Army under Bao Dai as the Americans desired, was that the French would not allow it. In fact, the American plan to give aid direct to Bao Dai's army in March 1950 was frustrated when the French Commander, Général Carpentier, told a press conference that he would resign in twenty-four hours if this happened.[22]

Naturally, the Viet Minh were well aware of the mutual suspicion characterising the Franco-American relationship. On 19 March, in an article entitled 'Imperialist America Intervenes Directly in the Problem of Indochina' *Truth* began by tracing the alleged role of the Special Envoy, Jessup, in securing final recognition of the Bao Dai

---

introduction. For a very good American perception of French paralysis see George Herring, *America's Longest War: The United States in Vietnam, 1950–1957*, New York, 1979. Franchini, *Les guerres*, pp. 33–35 discusses the Pau Conference from June to November 1950, where the development of a National army was discussed by the French and Bao Dai supporters. However, no serious initiatives were taken as a result of the talks.

[20] Gras, *Histoire*, p. 285.

[21] Herring, *America's Longest War*, p. 16 for aid program in 1950. Memorandum by Guillion to Bowie, 24 February 1954, in Department of State Washington, *Foreign Relations of the United States*, 1951–1952, Vol. XVI, Washington: Government Printing Office, 1981, p. 419 for the Policy Planning Staff quotes from 1954. See also George McTurnan Kahin, *Intervention: How America Became Involved in Vietnam*, New York: Knopf, 1986, p. 45.

[22] *New York Times*, March 9, 1950. Although he does not refer to this incident the best analysis of American policy at this time in Dunn, 'American Policy and Vietnamese Nationalism', Chapters 5–6.

regime in the French Assembly on 2 February. It then broadened its propaganda attack by explaining

> The Americans are studying a list of items the French need to continue attacking Vietnam. At the same time as the American Ministry of Foreign Affairs is also studying ways of giving weapons directly to the puppet Bao Dai without sending them through the hands of the French. At the recent Bangkok Conference on the problem of Southeast Asia, and especially the problem of Indochina, Jessup announced to journalists: "Vietnam is able to sign a treaty directly with the United States". In this way the Americans continue to give weapons to the French on the one hand . . . but on the other hand America does not trust the French and wants to replace the French in Indochina . . .[23]

Therefore, while American aid largely failed to reach the National Army and Viet Minh writers were analysing the contradictions in the Franco-American position in 1950, it was not until 1952 when these contradictions had contributed to a major deterioration in the French military position that the French writers began to analyse the impact of Chinese aid on the Viet Minh.

By 1952 and 1953 the French writers were showing that by late 1950 the Viet Minh had a main battle force whose fire power was roughly equivalent to that of the French Expeditionary Corps, and in some ways superior. For example, Despuech was one of the first to show how in certain heavy weapons like bazookas, recoilless rifles, and mortars a Viet Minh battalion could outgun a French battalion. Fall later noted the existence of about forty Viet Minh battalions which were supposed to have this capacity, and in 1979 Gras wrote of a Viet Minh battle corps that 'almost' reached that of the French.[24] Although the French always retained total superiority in aircraft, armoured vehicles, naval vessels, and, with some qualifications, artillery, Chinese aid had unquestionably increased the fire power of the People's Army to the point where it presented the French with a most serious military problem by late 1950.

Nevertheless, in their attempt to highlight the gravity of the situation the early French writers overlooked much in connection with Chinese aid that shaped the history of the People's Army, and later

---

[23]*CKCT*, Vol. 2, p. 341. For more on American policy and the Jessup mission see Dunn, 'American policy and Vietnamese Nationalism' especially pp. 130–132.
[24]Despuech, *Le Trafic*, pp. 143–144; Claude Guigues, 'Panoplie Viet Minh', *Indochine Sud Est Asiatique*, No. 7, June 1952; Fall, *The Viet Minh*, p. 75; Bernard B. Fall, *Street Without Joy*, New York: Schocken, 1975, see notes on p. 56, p. 94; Gras, *Histoire*, p. 317.

writers have followed their example. Chinese aid had undoubtedly
created a marked shift in the power balance towards the Viet Minh
by late 1950, and the pre-1950 stalemate would soon be broken.
However, the literature obscures the fact that this great change also
caused great difficulties for the Viet Minh. As early as January 1949
when the prospect of Chinese aid was being discussed in Party circles,
Truong Chinh had already signalled a fundamental problem in his
criticism of cadres who 'had a tendency to rely in China and cannot
bear to make efforts themselves'.[25] There were tensions in the Party
over what the implications of Chinese aid might be, and these clearly
reflected the problem a relatively small national liberation movement
had in domesticating aid from a more powerful benefactor. Aid was
essential to gain independence, but reliance on aid could jeopardize
independence. Without some understanding of this fundamental
tension the basis on which the state built its power and the army built
its main battle force will always remain a mystery.

Problem of Chinese Aid

In institutional terms the problem of Chinese aid was that the rapid
formation of main force units to attract Chinese aid and meet the
high expectations generated by that in Vietnam could easily leave the
regional guerrilla forces relatively undeveloped. The main force
would then be cut off from its social base, and no matter what
quantities of Chinese aid were forthcoming they would soon become
ineffective. The strategist, Hong Nam, drawing on operational experience in Inter-Zone 4 and around the Lo River made this point in
Truth in early 1950, although he did not refer directly to Chinese aid:

> When speaking of campaigns and the activities of the main force
> the essential conditions for victory are the work of preparing the
> battle field, preparing the people's organisations, investigating
> the enemy's situation, and transport and resupply before the
> battle. Then during and after the battle, participating in the
> destruction of the enemy and clearing the battle field to develop
> the victory (is also essential).
>   But are the main force units able to carry out these tasks by
> themselves? If the main force has to shoulder the burden itself
> as it moves from place to place it is certainly unable to do these
> things. However, if there is coordination between the regular
> forces and a people's militia mobilised to carry out these tasks,
> not only will the strength of the regional forces (be mobilised),
> but all the strength, riches, initiative, and bravery of the people

[25]*CKCT*, Vol. 2, p. 121.

(will be mobilised) as well so that we will be able to strengthen
and multiply the results. . .[26]

No matter how much Chinese aid was forthcoming political-military
mobilisation at the social base was the first and most fundamental
requirement for building the army. Truong Chinh thus drew the
inevitable conclusion from this realisation in an article he wrote for
the *Communist Review* six months later:

> We have a number of countries helping us. But if we want
> victory before all else we must make our own efforts. Our own
> efforts are the first condition, foreign help is secondary. We
> must not depend on outside help . . . The work of building the
> forces pays attention to building the main force units at the same
> time as the regimental regional units, the militia and so on . . .
> To build the forces too slowly will not be good for the war
> effort, but to build the forces too quickly without a basis of
> support, equipment and essential cadres will be decidedly
> harmful.[27]

Yet it was one thing to recognise that victory could only come from
within, as Hong Nam and Truong Chinh clearly did, and quite
another to implement the kind of balanced institutional development
this recognition suggested. Balanced institutional development essentially meant a continuation of guerrilla strategies. But in 1950
there were strong reasons why the arrival of even relatively small
quantities of Chinese aid began to build up pressure for a general
counter offensive which meant regular war.

First, when the change to the general counter offensive (*tong phan
cong*) had been widely discussed in the Party in association with the
projected victory in China for over a year and the war had been going
for so long, it is not difficult to see why the Chinese victory and the
opening of aid led many cadres to believe automatically that the
move to the general counter offensive was imminent. Second, the
influence of events in Korea was strong. For internationalist reasons
the Party had been proclaiming its solidarity with the Korean people's struggle against imperialism since the outbreak of the Korean
War in June. Thus, in August, at a time when the Americans had
suffered staggering reversals that almost pushed them off the Korean
peninsula, *Truth* was saying: ' we must regard an advance of the
Korean people as an advance for us, and the suffering of the
Korean people as our suffering.'[28] So, although the general counter offensive
is not specifically mentioned in the journals in this context, there was

[26]Ibid, pp. 318–319.
[27]Ibid, pp. 400–401, p. 413.
[28]Ibid, p. 431.

still much in the Korean experience that would have suggested the time was ripe for such an offensive in Vietnam.

Certain tactical considerations reinforce the point. Chinese tactics in Korea and Chinese tactical advice to the Viet Minh stressed the massing of force on the enemy's weak point – some manuals say as much as seven or eight ninths of the assaulting force – [29] and destroying him in 'battles of destruction' rather than 'battles of dispersal'.[30] In other words, these were the human wave tactics on the Korean 'meat grinder'[31] model which would fit in perfectly with the ideology of the general counter offensive. Even though many in the Party could see that the development of the army required balanced strategies, great pressure was building up against them.

In July 1950 two long articles by Truong Chinh in the *Communist Review*[32] show just how big the problem of rationalising the use of Chinese aid still was. One of the first things the articles show is that there were at least three strands of thought on what the counter offensive might be. The kind of unrealistic optimism of one group of cadres and the damage it did to mobilisation comes out in the following comment:

> When they go to make propaganda on the general mobilisation or on preparing strongly for the general counter offensive, our cadres usually exaggerate the truth so that the masses will eagerly contribute to the resistance war . . . When the enemy attacks the plains in the Bac Bo (they say) this is because the enemy is preparing to withdraw to the coast. They say high flying planes will be sent from the Soviet Union and China etc . . . After the masses see that what the cadres have told them is not correct they became skeptical and discouraged.[33]

[29]Document Viet Minh Traduit et Diffusé par le Deuxième Bureau de L'Etat Major des F.T.N.V., *Réglement d'Infanterie Viet Minh: Le Bataillon et la compagnie d'infanterie dans l'attaque d'une position fortifiée, 26 Septembre 1953*, Hanoi, 1954, p. 7.

[30]See Note 57 below.

[31]Fall, *Street Without Joy*, p. 47.

[32]These articles appear in *CKCT*, Vol. 2, pp. 397–420 and were entitled 'Nhan Dinh Dung de Hanh Dong Dung: Hoanh Thanh Nhiem Vu Chuan Bi Manh Sang Tong Phan Cong' ['Realise Correctly to Act Correctly: Complete the Task of Preparing to Move Strongly towards the General Counter Offensive']; and 'Chung Ta Da Lam gi va Con Phai Lam gi de Chuyen Sang Giai Doan Moi' ['What Have We Done and What Is Still To Be Done to Move into the New Period']. In his discussion of the general counter offensive and the border campaign Duiker, *The Communist Road*, pp. 143–152 also discusses Vo Nguyen Giap, *Nhiem Vu Quan Su truoc Mat Chuyen Sang Tong Phan Cong* [The Military Task in Preparing for the General Counter Offensive], Hanoi, 1950. I have not been able to locate this document but from Duiker's discussion it essentially contains the same ideas as Truong Chinh's.

[33]*CKCT*, Vol. 2, pp. 404.

On the other hand, there were pessimistic cadres who thought that the only consequence of Chinese aid would be a dangerous increase in American aid to the French.[34] As Truong Chinh quickly dismissed this idea because it was based on fear of the United States and a lack of faith in the masses, his view of how the general counter offensive might evolve then occupied the middle ground.

Truong Chinh argued for more preparations and a gradual trans-formation of the military situation. In drawing a comparison between the mechanics of the 'General August Insurrection' in 1945 and the 'General Counter Offensive' Truong Chinh argued that they were 'intimately related'. But since the balance of forces in 1950 was very different from that in 1945 he emphasised that 'the word "*general*" (*tong*) must not be used in a mechanical way'[35] Moreover, recent reversals in the south had demonstrated that any idea of such offen-sive was foolhardy when the Vietnamese polity lent itself so easily to great regional variations in military development which could only be accentuated by Chinese aid.

As we have seen, successful French tactics meant that there had been no formation of embryonic regiments or divisions in the low lying south as there had been in the mountains of Viet Bac and parts of Trung Bo by late 1949. When the Southern Commander, Nguyen Binh, raised fifteen main force battalions rapidly from the regional forces in late 1949 this was part of a desperate move to reduce French pressure and gain access for the Viet Minh to rice growing areas. In the course of furious assault around Tra Vinh, Vinh Long, Bien Hoa, Thu Dau Mot, Thanh Son, Can Tho, Soc Trang, and Sa Dec between December 1949 and April 1950 Nguyen Binh inflicted 'serious losses'[36] on the French but this major offensive failed. From the French point of view this was because of the weakness of Viet Minh logistics – too often battles could not be pushed to the limit for want of munitions – and the open terrain which permitted the French to manoeuvre and employ their fire power to best advantage.[37] From the Central Committee's point of view in the north the problem was then articulated in terms of the gross imbalance between main force and regional force strength that had developed as a result of Nguyen

---

[34]Ibid.

[35]Ibid., p. 399.

[36]Gras, *Histoire*, p. 292.

[37]Ibid. On this phase of the war see also Boyer de Latour, *Le Martyre*, p. 114. This source claims Nguyen Binh was 'seriously wounded' in the offensive, but I have seen no other evidence for this. Bodard, *La guerre d'Indochine*, Vol. 2, pp. 361–365 offers another account of this phase of the war.

Binh's tactics. After Central Committee Member Le Duc Tho was sent south in April with 'new instructions', the Party journals began to emphasise that any southern strategy had to be based on 'a worker-peasant infrastructure' and wrote of 'realising people's war'.[38] This was in great contrast to the north where the slogan 'all for complete victory on the battle front'[39] seemed more apt.

But accentuating these differences between north and south by mid-1950 was the effect of Chinese and American aid to the protagonists in the war. When Chinese aid began arriving in the north, and, as the Viet Minh journals put it, the Americans began turning Cambodia and southern Vietnam into a Free World 'drill ground',[40] the major regional differences were only accentuated. The People's Army in Bac Bo with its difficult terrain and proximity to a secure rear area in China would get stronger, and the People's Army in Nam Bo with its relatively easy terrain and great distance from China would get weaker as American interests in the region deepened. And there is no doubt at all that the Central Committee could see this.

What to my knowledge has not come out in the literature on the Vietnam War is that in 1950 the Central Committee was already so sure the war against the French could only be won in the north, that it began preparing for the time when the French were defeated in the north and forced to re-group in the south. As Hong Hoa wrote in the resistance journal *Inner Life* in April:

> Nam Bo and Cambodia will very likely be the place (the French) will concentrate their army once they have run out of ways of holding Bac Bo under the pressure of our strong offensive. That the Americans are edging their way into Cambodia with the idea of taking over from the French is already obvious . . .
> Therefore, a second strategic responsibility in Nam Bo is to urgently establish a United People's Front with Cambodia to resist the international imperialists.[41]

To develop this front and make preparations for a protracted struggle with no end in sight in the south, the journals then devoted their attention to the question of developing guerrilla bases in the southern highlands around Tay Nguyen 'to create a foothold connecting the eastern Cambodian, southern Laotian, and Nam Bo battle fronts.'[42]

[38] *CKCT*, Vol. 2, pp. 353–358.

[39] *LSQD*, p. 398.

[40] *CKCT*, Vol. 2, p. 356.

[41] Ibid. The first responsibility was to overthrow the international imperialists on all fronts and destroy their schemes. The third responsibility was to reinforce the national front on the basis of worker peasant organisations already mentioned.

[42] *CKCT*, Vol. 2, p. 380.

In these preparations for events that were to divide the country, we therefore have one of the main reasons why Truong Chinh was arguing in July 1950 that 'you cannot decide to have a general counter offensive whenever you want and do it just like that'.[43] Rather, strategy had to be thought through:

> With respect to space; the general counter offensive is a general counter offensive on a principal front while secondary fronts restrain the enemy . . . With respect to time; the general counter offensive is a general offensive extending through an entire strategic period. That period is divided into many phases. In each phase open one or many big and small battles to reach the final goal of the resistance war: complete victory.[44]

But in this turgid prose we still have the central dilemma which the Party had to deal with once it became a recipient of Chinese aid. Despite the intricate formula, 'the general counter offensive is a general counter offensive . . .', Truong Chinh was still describing a protracted guerrilla war strategy. Put another way, even though he was plainly trying to minimise it, Truong Chinh was caught in the contradiction that adherence to Mao's model of a three stage guerrilla war culminating in the general counter offensive was necessary to gain Chinese aid, yet the regional nature of the People's Army worked against the use of Mao's model.

This contradiction could not then be contained as the momentum of events projected the problem of Chinese aid onto the battle field in an interrelated sequence of success and failure in late 1950 and early 1951. The success we are referring to was the destruction of 6,000 French troops along Colonial Route 4 on the Sino-Vietnamese border in October 1950. The failure was the loss of an equal number of Viet Minh troops in the general counter offensive on the Red River Delta in January 1951.

Success on the Border and Failure of the General Counter Offensive

While Truong Chinh was grappling with the Party line preparations were already underway for an offensive along Colonial Route 4 on the Sino-Vietnamese border. This offensive was to test 308 Division and Regiments 174 and 209 which were the first major formations to return from training in China.[45] In June 1950 and Viet Bac Inter-

---

[43]Ibid., p. 404.
[44]Ibid., p. 398.
[45]Phan Huy Thiep and Trinh Vuong Hong, 'Buoc Dau Tim Hieu Mot So Van De ve

Zone Committee had already been given responsibility for the general mobilisation of people and resources. In July some 200 specialist logistics cadres under Tran Dang Ninh were sent into the region to assist. Meanwhile, Chu Van Tan of Armed Propaganda Army fame in 1945 worked to spread the slogan 'all for complete victory on the battle front'.[46] However, the magnitude of the victory which the Viet Minh achieved as a result of these preparations was quite unexpected.

It would have been reasonable for the Viet Minh to think they could create some difficulties for the French by carrying out a border campaign in late 1950. French problems in the region were well publicised in the acrimonious public debate that followed the leaking of a secret strategic assessment which Général Revers had made for the French government in 1949. This assessment had recommended that the isolated string of border posts from Lao Cai to Lang Son should be evacuated to tighten the over-extended positions of the French Expeditionary Corps in Tonkin. Arguably, these posts served no useful military purpose, and they were certainly expensive to maintain.[47] By mid-1950, when the French began to notice increased guerrilla activity in the border area, each mission to re-supply the posts was a sizeable military operation in itself.[48] But, whatever the strategic and economic sense in evacuating the border posts, the Viet Minh could not possibly have anticipated the scale of the tactical blunder the French were about to make.

The French operational plan devised by 30 September was for the garrison at Cao Bang to withdraw to the east along Route 4, while another column moving from the east at That Khe would camouflage the move of the Cao Bang column, meet it half way, and then escort it back to That Khe. However, with the central fort at Dong Khe already occupied by the Viet Minh, poor planning, dissension between higher headquarters, and no idea that 308 Division plus two

---

Su Chi Dao Nghe Thuat Quan Su cua Dich Bien Gioi Thu Dong 1950' [An Initial Investigation of a Number of Questions Relating to the Party's Guidance of Military Art During the Border Campaign in the Autumn and Winter of 1950], *NCLS*, No. 2, 1980, p. 7. This source also mentions 304 Division. But as we will see it had been formed around Thanh Hoa Province in early 1950 and I have seen no evidence that its regiments had been trained in China by this time or had taken part in the border campaign. On the plans for the campaign also see Hoang Van Hoan, *Giot Nuoc*, pp. 349–351.

[46]Quoted in *LSQD*, p. 398.

[47]For an introduction to the acrimony and scandal surrounding the leak of the Revers report see Irving, *The First Indochina War*, Chapter 5.

[48]Bodard, *La guerre*, Vol. 3, pp. 73–79. Duiker, *The Communist Road*, p. 144.

regiments were in the area, disaster was almost assured.[49] With some 6,000 highly vulnerable French troops strung out along the isolated mountain passes the five Viet Minh regiments in the area were presented with an opportunity they had never expected. Within ten days both columns were annihilated in a series of deadly regimental attacks using automatic weapons and artillery, and the French suffered what Bernard Fall called their 'greatest colonial defeat since Montcalm had died at Quebec'.[50]

Dramatic defeat was followed by panic in the French camp. In the mistaken belief that an invincible Viet Minh force was now massing for an attack on the border post at Lang Son, French forces abandoned the garrison without firing a shot and left behind enough equipment and munitions for the Viet Minh to supply an entire division.[51] As Viet Bac broke out in red bunting to welcome the victorious soldiers of the border campaign, French families began preparing to evacuate Hanoi. Resistance Committees mushroomed in the mountains, and, in sympathy, a recrudescence of guerrilla war occurred in the delta. By late September 1950 the combattant Ngo Van Chieu, who had taken part in the border campaign, says that army political officers were telling the troops they would be 'in Hanoi for Tet', and by November he had no doubt that 'the general counter offensive had begun.'[52] That these ideas also had wide currency among the population is shown by Chieu's observation of a typical mass rally in the Viet Bac he came across as his regiment marched from the border area towards the delta in November:

> The propaganda sections were already in place and had installed an information room where a phonograph played military tunes. A propagandist on a box decorated by the red flag with the yellow star harangued the crowd and the young people. "The People's Army will be in Hanoi for Tet. This is the present the army will give President Ho for the new year".[53]

But as preparations for the counter offensive on the delta were reflected in the activities of this propaganda section, Giap, undoubtedly supported by key Party leaders including Truong Chinh,[54] was about to make his biggest blunder of the war.

---

[49]Bodard, *La guerre*, Vol. 3, pp. 96–377; Marc Dem, *Mourir pour Cao Bang*, Paris: Editions Albin Michel, Paris, 1978; Gras, *Histoire*, pp. 323–354; Duiker, *The Communist Road*, pp. 144–145.

[50]Fall, *Street Without Joy*, p. 33.

[51]Ibid.

[52]Ngo Van Chieu, *Journal d'un combattant*, pp. 128–129, pp. 140–141.

[53]Ibid., p. 141.

[54]Despite his earlier resistance to an uncritical acceptance of the virtue of the 'general

On the basis of a widespread rumour, Chen argued in 1969 that 'Giap dismissed Chinese advice to be cautious'[55] in his attacks on the delta in 1951. But there is mounting evidence that this was not the case. When Giap began his general counter offensive with a vengeance in mid-January 1951 he used the kind of massed human wave tactics the Chinese were concurrently using in Korea. Since it is well known that Chinese advisers accompanied Chinese aid to the Viet Minh it is not surprising that their advice reflected the practice of the Chinese Army in Korea. This line of reasoning is supported by the recent researches of Georges Boudarel who has demonstrated that Chinese advice to the Viet Minh from at least December 1952 revolved around the use of human wave tactics.[56] Furthermore, one document unearthed in the French military archives shows that by late 1950 Chinese advice revolved around human wave tactics, and 'battles of destruction' rather than 'battles of dispersal'.[57]

This document is a captured Vietnamese language copy of a regimental debriefing conducted by a Chinese officer immediately after the successful border campaign in mid-October. The aim of the debriefing was 'to point out several essential points on the spirit of Mao Zedong to complete your studies'.[58] It stressed that Chinese aid was one of the 'essential conditions' for victory, and in reference to the successful border campaign it said:

> with a single battle of destruction . . . Cao Bang, Dong Khe, That Khe, Lang Son, Na Sam, and Dong Da have fallen into our hands . . . If we have some more battles of destruction Hanoi will fall into our hands. During the three years of liberation war China applied the method of destroying the enemy's vital force which gave it total triumph.[59]

The officer did warn that victory around Hanoi would be more difficult than on the border, because the enemy would have learned

---

counter offensive' in the Party journals, Georges Boudarel argues on the basis of first hand knowledge the Truong Chinh vigorously supported the 'general counter-offensive' on the delta in 1951.

[55]Chen, *Vietnam and China*, p. 267, quoting O'Ballance, *The Indochina War*, pp. 141–142.

[56]Georges Boudarel, 'Comment Giap falli perdre la bataille de Dien Bien Phu', *Le Nouvel Observateur*, 8 Avril, 1983, pp. 90–98.

[57]SHAT, C. 94, D.4, 'Buoi Noi Chuyen cua Dong Chi XX tai Hoi Nghi Can Bo Trung Doan–Tieu Doan trong Bien Gioi' ['A Talk by Comrade XX at a Conference of Regimental and Battalion Cadres on the Border], November or December 1950. From the context of the document it is clear that Comrade XX was a Chinese adviser.

[58]Ibid.

[59]Ibid., pp. 8–9.

from his experience and would be in a stronger position in the Delta. But this understanding only made him recommend the concentration 'of *all* our means so that we can destroy the enemy'.[60] Hence, although such strategy had worked on the border where the French had placed themselves at a major disadvantage, it was clearly at variance with the dispersal of forces that had been the characteristic of successful Viet Minh strategy since the revival of the armed propaganda campaign in early 1948. It was also variance with the opinion of those who had been arguing for a gradual transformation of the military situation since mid-1950. As we have seen, this argument had been put forward so that an undue reliance on Chinese aid would not lead to an artificial build up of the main forces without the prior development of the regional ones. Apart from any impulsiveness on his part, Giap's decision to follow rather than dismiss Chinese advice therefore shows how the pressure of Chinese aid and advice, and the momentum of events after the unexpected border victory were about to propel the People's Army into a campaign for which it was not suited.

In taking the decision to launch a massive counter offensive on the delta, Giap exaggerated the strength Chinese aid had given him and over estimated the 'weakness and immobility of the French'.[61] In particular, he overlooked the transformation in the fighting capacity of the Expeditionary Corps after the arrival of Général De Lattre in December, while his own preparations for the campaign were hasty and his forces improvised. Both French and Vietnamese sources agree[62] that by January 1951 only Divisions 308 and 312 were ready for battle. The first of these divisions commanded by Vuong Thua Vu was based on regiments from around Hanoi, Vinh Yen, and Phuc Yen, and the second, commanded by Le Trong Tan, had been built up on regiments from Viet Bac. Division 304 under Hoang Minh Thao had been raised around Thanh Hoa, Phat Diem, and Ninh Binh from early 1950, but on the eve of the delta campaign in January 1951 it was still moving from Thanh Hoa towards the delta to be equipped with Chinese arms. As for the three other divisions that were to be raised during the war none was ready for battle by January 1951. 316 Division commanded by Le Quang Ba did not begin to form from units left over in the Viet Bac before February and March 1951.

---

[60]Ibid., p. 4. Emphasis added.

[61]Vuong Thua Vu, *Truong Thanh trong*, p. 288. Contemporary sources were also full of the 'complete immobility' of the French. See *CKCT*, Vol. 2, p. 487 for example.

[62]Corps Expéditionñaire d'Extrême Orient, Forces Terrestres Sud Vietnam, Etat Major, Deuxième Bureau, *Historique sommaire des grandes unites de l'armée regulière Viet Minh*, Saigon, 1954, (Mimeographed), pp. 1–45.

Similarly, 320 Division, based on regiments with long experience of guerrilla war in the delta region of Inter-Zone 3, did not begin to take shape under the command of Van Tien Dung until February. The final division, 351 Heavy Weapons Division commanded by Tran Dai Nghia and later by Vu Hien, was also embryonic in January. In fact, its engineer and artillery regiments did not really begin to function until around July 1951, and it was not until at least 1952 that they were fully equipped by the Chinese.

When the official history then confirms the haste with which these units were thrown together in the comment that 'at the beginning of 1951 *all* the regiments of the Army of National Defence on the Bac Bo Front were concentrated to build three infantry divisions',[63] we begin to understand in institutional terms why Giap's first attempt to break into the delta in mid-January around Vinh Yen failed. To support only five regiments operating in ideal terrain against an isolated enemy in the border campaign at least three months preparatory mobilisation of people and resources had taken place. Yet to support a multi-divisional attack on the delta where the French were operating on internal lines across a relatively compact and open piece of territory there is virtually no evidence of any mobilisation of mass organisations and regional forces, especially in the delta where a very high level of guerrilla action would have been necessary to prevent the French concentrating their fire power.[64] Giap simply massed what units he had around the delta, permitted the French to meet his attack most notably around Vinh Yen, and then, despite Chinese aid, lacked the fire power, the organisation, and the popular support to overcome his adversary.

After three days of extremely heavy fighting around the main position between Vinh Yen and the Tam Dao massif in mid-January, the assault waves of 308 and 312 Divisions were decimated by napalm (unloaded in Hai Phong by the Americans a few days before the battle) and concentrated artillery fire. Then on the 17th, with the French in a critical position and nothing between them and the road to Hanoi but the central French artillery position, the Viet Minh withdrew because their reserves of men and ammunition were exhausted.[65] From Vietnamese accounts such as those of Vuong Thua Vu and Ngo Van Chieu who took part in the battle, it appears that the use of napalm for the first time in Indochina against dense formations of attacking infantry had a considerable bearing on the

[63]*LSQD*, p. 432. Emphasis added.
[64]On this point see Gras, *Histoire*, p. 383.
[65]Ibid., pp. 375–383.

outcome.[66] But the official history gives the fundamental reason for failure when it concludes that 'the enemy was confounded, but we also did not have the forces prepared to develop the battle'.[67]

What this failure and the loss of 3,000 men killed and wounded at Vinh Yen, and a further 3,000 killed and wounded at Mao Khe in March and alongside the Day River in June[68] had brought into sharp focus was the gross distortion of the army in organisational terms. On 15 April, just after Giap's second failure to break into the Red River Delta around Mao Khe, expressions of the need for integrated institutional development reappeared in the Party press. In an article called 'Strategic Methods at the Present Time' Truong Chinh made it clear that integrating the army's level of organisation with the society's capacity to support it was the central problem.

> Naturally, we must build a force completely capable of meeting its strategic and tactical reponsibilities on the battle field. But, if you do not reckon on the people's (capacity) to shoulder the burden and the financial potential of the government, it is adventurous and dangerous to mobilise and concentrate forces that have no rice to eat and clothes to wear and no weapons to fight with. The number of people emancipated from production is far too high, the development of the economy is not sufficient to guarantee re-supply, the people do not have the strength to nourish the army.[69]

And on 7 June the Party journals published an article by the failed General Giap himself:

> At the present time a careful analysis of our forces (shows) that in both the main force and regional force units the advanced level of organisation is not commensurate with its needs and equipment potential.[70]

Chinese aid in itself could not propel the People's Army into the kind of offensive that would rapidly end the war. Indeed, as Giap's

---

[66]Vuong Thua Vu, *Truong Thanh trong*, p. 238; Ngo Van Chieu, *Journal d'un combattant*, pp. 154–155.

[67]*LSQD*, p. 433.

[68]Chen, *Vietnam and China*, p. 267 says '6,000 Viet Minh were killed' but a far more reliable source on this point is Gras, *Histoire*, p. 382, notes 1 and 2. This source uses General De Lattre's report to the French government of 23 January 1951 which gave Viet Minh casualties as '1,600 killed, 480 prisoners, and 6,000 wounded'. French casualties were in the order of 43 killed, 545 missing, 100 wounded. For an account of all these attacks on the delta see Fall, *Street Without Joy*, pp. 36–47.

[69]*CKCT*, Vol. 3, p. 25.

[70]Ibid., p. 67.

campaign had demonstrated, Chinese military aid and the associated commitment of the army to Chinese style battles for which it was not suited could have a very detrimental effect on the army's development.

Yet the nature of Vietnam's capacity for independent institutional development still precluded the Viet Minh from dispensing with Chinese aid. If only because China was Vietnam's most direct and powerful link to a supportive international order Chinese support could not possibly be terminated. Without heavy weapons and ammunition it was simply not possible to defeat major French military formations.

While Chinese aid was indispensible, it had to be used in such a way that it reinforced the army's development in Vietnamese society, rather than jeopardize it with insupportable levels of military organisation and inappropriate tactics. As Truong Chinh had argued, the need was for balanced institutional development so that the power of the People's Army would come from the people's willingness and capacity to support it. The integration, or, to use a word that sits more comfortably in Vietnamese literature, the *unity* (*thong nhat*) of the army with the community's capacity to support it was the only possible foundation for victory and independence. The most conspicuous change in the Viet Minh's attitude to Chinese support from early 1951 therefore reflected the reassertion of one of Vietnam's oldest political traditions.

From that time on, the resistance leadership placed increasing emphasis on the Chinese model. This, in history, had always had a dual function when Vietnamese kings were strong and independent. The model symbolised the power of the ruling dynasty in Vietnam through the support it simultaneously attracted from the Chinese court. Under modern conditions, the ICP consequently began to make a big demonstration of its adherence to Chinese models in 1951 in order to consolidate its power in Vietnamese society, and thereby pursue policies designed to ensure balanced military development. On this basis Chinese aid could be used to reinforce the political-military unity of the resistance, rather than to destroy it. And the first sign of this change after the battle of Vinh Yen was the reemergence of an open communist party to both legitimize and enforce the unity of the resistance.

The Great Unity

After five years of clandestine activity an open communist party, the Labour Party (*Dang Lao Dong*), reappeared at a special conference in February 1951. The following month the Viet Minh Front and the

Lien Viet or the League for the National Union of Vietnam, which had been created in 1946 to help focus the support of a wide range of political groups for the patriotic resistance war, were merged at a 'Congress of Unification'. The Viet Minh Front was officially replaced by the 'United National Front of Vietnam' (*Mat Tran Lien Hiep Quoc Dan Viet Nam*),[71] although the term 'Viet Minh' was so entrenched that its almost universal use continued until 1954. The Congress also included delegates from Laos and Cambodia, and the 'great unity' (*dai dong*)[72] of the resistance effort in Vietnam and all of Indochina was proclaimed. The Party's decision to make these changes may have been influenced by attempts Général De Lattre was making after his victory at Vinh Yen to increase Vietnamese participation in the French war effort.[73] But in view of the warm diplomatic exchanges between China and Vietnam at the time— Peking showered congratulations on the new Party and the new Party renewed pledges to study diligently the thoughts of Chairman Mao[74]—it is clear that both the Chinese and the Party saw the need for more disciplined direction of the war effort.

This does not mean, as Fall suggests, that Ho Chi Minh's Republic had now become a 'model satellite'.[75] Nor does it mean, as Chen sought to show, that the resistance slavishly followed Chinese models of civil and military administration.[76] There were many fields in which the Party did make use of Chinese models as it promised the Chinese it would in its international propaganda. But in the very subtle manoeuvres of the Sino–Vietnamese relationship it is of the greatest importance to understand that Ho Chi Minh's government was not a passive partner. The positive aspect of the Sino–Vietnamese relationship for the Lao Dong Party after February 1951 was the way it was able to use its imitations of the Chinese model to

---

[71]*LSDC*, pp. 616–631, especially p. 629. Chen, *Vietnam and China*, p. 241; Fall, *The Viet Minh*, p. 34. I follow popular usage and continue to refer to the 'Viet Minh' until 1954.

[72]*CKCT*, Vol. 3, p. 18. This concept of the 'great unity' (*dai dong*) is of course very old and suggests a utopian world as discussed in Chapter 2. Also see Woodside, *Community and Revolution*, p. 170. In 1951 we thus see how the Party was attempting to constitute the political unity necessary for successful resistance to French imperialism by linking it to a transcendental world order that was old and new.

[73]For a discussion see Franchini, *Les guerres*, Vol. 2, pp. 47–52.

[74]Chen, *Vietnam and China*, pp. 240–249 describes the diplomatic exchanges. But, as we will see, I do not accept the tone of Chen's discussion which suggest the Vietnamese blindly obeyed Chinese instructions.

[75]Fall, *The Viet Minh* p. 34.

[76]Chen, *Vietnam and China*, pp. 240–249.

strengthen its internal position, develop independent state power, and integrate the army into the society.

To illustrate this point we may take the first number of the official Party journal, *Nhan Dan*, *The People's Daily*, which was first published on 11 March.[77] At one level, this journal was published in imitation of the Chinese Communist Party's main journal, *Ren Min*, of the same name. At this level a closer and more intimate relationship with China was signified. But as soon as one reads the journal, it becomes clear that this signification was supposed to have an important impact, perhaps unknown to the Chinese, within the Vietnamese polity.

After employing familiar imagery to note that 'we are *one family* with President Ho standing at the head',[78] the journal went on to explain that before the national conference which gave birth to the Lao Dong Party there hung 'the portraits of the *predecessors* Marx, Engels, and Lenin, and the portraits of the Stalin and Mao Zedong. The spirit of these world leaders was always alive at the conference.'[79] Since predecessors or ancestors had always played such a vital role in the integration of family identity and unity in Vietnam what the Lao Dong Party was doing was straightforward. It was using the fathers of proletarian internationalism and its current international affiliations to establish a genealogy and thus its right to rule Vietnam. Now at the head of 'one family', in the 'great family' of world socialist nations, the Lao Dong Party and President Ho could justify the tighter Party control necessary to develop the strength of the army. The army was the force of the emerging Vietnamese nation, and so, as we will see, the use of the Chinese model was paradoxically a sign of the nation's growing independence.

In ancient times, one way Vietnamese kings signified and exercised their independence was through the institution of civil and military mandarinates on the Chinese model. More recently, the Viet Minh signified and exercised their growing independence after the battle for Vinh Yen in a similar way. In 1950 the army's general staff had been reorganised along the lines of the French model to accommodate the expansion that followed the opening of Chinese aid. However, the creation of a Political Bureau in 1951 signalled another change to the system of more numerous bureaus on the Chinese model.

When the reorganisation was complete in 1953, at least ten Chinese style bureaus had replaced the four French style bureaus with

[77]*CKCT*, Vol. 3, pp. 9–17.
[78]Ibid., p. 11, emphasis added.
[79]Ibid., p. 12, emphasis added. I have translated *tien boi* as 'predecessors'.

responsibility for personnel, intelligence, operations, and supply. The main divisions of responsibility in the new General Staff organisation were for politics, intelligence, operations, training, administration, main forces, popular forces, military affairs, communications and liaison, special artillery and engineer sections, and codes. Main supply and maintenance functions were also removed from the General Staff on the Chinese model and placed under separate direction.[80] And, as the staff functions were rationalised, a new breeze began to blow from the Political Bureau where Nguyen Chi Thanh, also a member of the Executive Committee of the Central Committee of the Party, was placed in charge.[81]

A perusal of his speeches and writings in the first half of 1951 shows that political-military ideology was unified at the highest levels of government and army. As part of the 'great revolutionary family'[82] the People's Army of Vietnam came under the leadership of the Lao Dong Party to carry out the revolution. Aid from friendly countries was 'very important', but it was necessary to remember that 'our revolution is a task originating within us'.[83] Many cadres had unfortunately forgotten this. They had also failed to pay sufficient attention to the government's policy of 'great unity', and failed to understand that 'our army is a people's army, born of the people, and raised by the people from the time it was weak and small as well as when it is prosperous'.[84] A rigorous campaign of criticism and auto-criticism was to be conducted 'to educate cadres and soldiers to the level of an enlightened class'.[85]

What this meant was a purge to place the army more firmly under the Party's control. Although elitism was never eradicated—ranks[86] and saluting were not abolished, and secondary school diplomas were required for command in the artillery—it was from around this time that many intellectuals, doctors, and cadres of bourgeois background either left the resistance and went home, or rallied to the Bao Dai

---

[80]Tanham, *Communist Revolutionary Warfare*, pp. 38–39.
[81]Nguyen Chi Thanh, *Nhung Bai Chon*, p. 10.
[82]Ibid., p. 22.
[83]Ibid.
[84]Ibid., p. 42.
[85]Ibid., pp. 17–18.
[86]There were four grades of Under Officer, one of Aspirant, six officer ranks from Second Lieutenant to Colonel, and three General ranks. These grades were signified by badges of rank which graduated from chevrons, to bars, to stars. There were also different hat badges to signify rank. Political officers had the same badges of rank but with red backing. In addition to badges of rank there were military medals, combatants medals, and resistance medals of first, second, and third class.

regime.[87] The usual reasons given for such departures or defections were the oppressive surveillance of the security police, the appointments of incompetent cadres to high positions, low pay, and the hard life of the resistance.[88] Also by late 1953, when there was at last some sign of a comprehensive implementation of the Party's land reform policy,[89] cadres of rich peasant or gentry background often found their careers broken when they were sent home for public denunciations. Grim tales of suffering and suicide often accompanied these denunciations.[90] But, while purges did serve to strengthen the Party's control, they were also part of a wider movement for reductions in the ranks so that more people could be freed for work in the fields.

As armed propaganda action was employed on a large scale to consolidate the army's regional forces and to mobilise political and economic support between 1951 and 1953, the main force divisions were reduced from 15,000 men per division to 9,000–10,000.[91] Some idea of the need for these reductions may be gathered from a few statistics. To keep one 75 millimetre artillery battalion of only four guns in operation it required five hundred porters excluding those

[87]For a class analysis of this phenomenon see Gareth Porter, 'Imperialism and Social Structure in Twentieth Century Vietnam', PhD, Cornell University, 1976, pp. 195–215. Porter's analysis is compelling but it still does not deal with the fact that the leadership of the revolution was made up of intellectuals who often came from similar backgrounds to the lesser intellectuals who left or defected.

[88]See Lucien Bodard, 'Interview d'un général Viet Minh', *Sud Est*, No. 16, Septembre 1950, for a typical explanation of one who defected to the French. The general was Nguyen Huy Thanh who defected around September 1950 after being with the Viet Minh since 1945 and reaching the position of Inspector General of Industry and Armament.

[89]For full discussions of the land question see Porter, 'Imperialism and Social Structure', pp. 195–215; and Christine Katherine White, 'Agrarian Reform and National Liberation in the Vietnamese Revolution, 1920–1957', PhD, Cornell University, 1981, especially Chapter 4.

[90]Georges Boudarel, who has read novels not available to me about the purges, has told me about the grim tales.

[91]Tanham, *Communist Revolutionary Warfare*, p. 42. Gras, *Histoire*, p. 494 says that in early 1953 the mobility of the divisions was increased by reducing their size to 9,600 men. 320 Division was the exception. Its strength remained at 12,000 which reflects the difference between its role which was to infiltrate the Red River Delta and stimulate guerrilla war and the other divisions which had to march for thousands of miles through the northwestern highlands and fight big battles. *LSQD* also discusses various stages of reorganisation. For example, p. 487 notes a reduction of eleven men and an increase of six rifles per infantry company in mid 1952 before the army began its major manoeuvres in the highlands. This meant a reduction of some 1,000 men in a division but greater fire power.

necessary to transport ammunition.[92] To keep an infantry division of 10,000 combatants in operation it is generally accepted that 40,000 to 50,000 porters were necessary.[93] If only the six divisions whose members were emancipated from work in the fields and the other 80,000 odd people emancipated in the main force regional regiments and independent battalions in 1952 are taken into account,[94] we then have some basis for calculating the expense of the war. The salary of a soldier was about three pounds of rice a day and rose on an ascending scale to fifty pounds for a general.[95] A crude calculation then reveals that aside from the salt, the medical supplies, and whatever else a soldier needed to survive, a population of around ten million had to produce well in excess of 164 million pounds of rice a year to keep the army marching.

These statistics suggest a major problem in military logistics. Yet they also bring something about the nature of the Sino-Vietnamese relationship and its effect on the emergence of an independent nation-state into focus. Only the availability of military supplies from China permitted the formation of the main force divisions that were necessary to defeat the French. Many Sino-Vietnamese conference were thus held from 1951 to regulate the flow of aid, and in October 1951 a rail link from China to the border near Lang Son was also completed to facilitate it.[96] However, we have seen that the relatively high level of military development which Chinese aid made possible could only be sustained by the state's ability to collect large quantities of rice and mobilise large numbers of work brigades within Vietnam itself. A most important effect of the well regulated Sino-Vietnamese relationship from 1951, therefore, was the centralisation and expansion of independent state control in Vietnam to support the kind of

---

[92]Tanham, *Communist Revolutionary Warfare*, p. 42.

[93]Ibid., pp. 70–71; Fall, *The Viet Minh*, p. 77.

[94]French sources like Teuliers, *La guerre*, pp. 77–78 summarise estimates of Viet Minh strength in July 1952 as 108,000 regulars, 53,000 regional forces, 115,000 local self defense forces, or a total of 276,000. By July 1953 the figures were 125,000 regulars, 75,000 regional forces, 150,000 local guerillas, or a total of 350,000. Nothing in Vietnamese sources like *LSQD* suggests these figures were an unreasonable reflection of reality. It should be noted, however, that the reluctance of Vietnamese sources to tabulate troop strengths reflects the porous boundaries in the force structure of the People's Army. In fact, at the social base French estimates probably underestimate the numbers of local guerrillas while the Viet Minh probably never knew how many they had because of constant fluctuations and changes in the situation.

[95]Fall, *The Viet Minh*, p. 75 quoting Democratic Republic of Vietnam Decrees No. 14/SL and 91/SL of 31 January, 20 May, and 22 May 1950.

[96]Gras, *Histoire*, pp. 445–446.

army Chinese aid made possible. This may be demonstrated with reference to economic affairs.

While the cooperatives, army labour units, and so on discussed in the last chapter continued to expand their operations, what was new in economic affairs after 1951 was the degree to which a centralized state superstructure using Chinese models became directly involved in commerce, taxation, and distribution of wealth in order to sustain the army. As one economics expert said in 1960: 'In 1951 and 1952 our commerce developed more than before because we had a clear commercial policy modelled after that of China'.[97] A state bank was opened in May 1951 under Nguyen Luong Bang,[98] and state controlled trade offices opened in border centers like Cao Bang and southern Chinese cities to deal with trade from China and the Soviet bloc. Supply offices to facilitate internal commerce in cloth, kerosene, medicines, explosives, typewriters, salt, and rice were also established in the major market towns of Cao Bang, Bac Ninh, Bac Giang, and Thanh Hoa.[99] But at the root of all these centers of commerce, at the source of the army's supply line, was the agricultural tax which the government moved to simplify and bring under much tighter central control from mid-1951.

This important agricultural tax has not been given the attention it merits in Western literature, because Western commentators have generally failed to confront a simple point. This is the reality that the development of the People's Army was a manifestation of an increasingly consolidated and independent nation-state whose existence the French and American goverments opposed. However, the rationalization of the agricultural tax in 1951 could not be a better example of how the Party's use of the Chinese model reinforced the national independence of Vietnam.

In June Pham Van Dong pointed out in *The People's Daily* that, although Vietnamese financial conditions were different from those in China, there were still many precious lessons which Vietnam could learn from Chinese experience. For example,

Following the Chinese experience the contributions of a hundred people (men, women, old, young) is enough to provide for two soldiers or cadres. To take this example and consider it, we see that if the standard provision for a soldier or a cadre averages two tonnes of rice a year (including expenses to feed and cloth

---

[97]W.S. Turley and J.M. Halpern eds., *The Training of Vietnamese communist Cadres in Laos*, Brussels, 1977, p. 38.
[98]*CKCT*, Vol. 3, p. 57.
[99]Turley, *The Training*, pp. 37–44; Clermont, 'L'Economie Viet Minh'.

him for work or fighting) then each person must contribute forty kilos of rice.[100]

In order to collect this rice, not just so the 'government' (*chinh phu*) could guarantee supplies for the front, but what now became known significantly as the 'central government' (*chinh phu trung uong*)[101] could guarantee supplies, Pham Van Dong emphasised the need 'to unify and simplify' the existing system of tax collection according to decree number 13/SL of 1 May 1951:

1. Abandon the various agricultural contributions to the national budget and regional treasuries like the land tax, paddy for workers wages, reserve paddy, paddy for mass education, paddy for the maintenance of regional units, paddy for the village treasury, paddy for building roads, etc . . .
2. Abandon the practice of buying paddy at a determined price.
3. Establish an agricultural tax collected in paddy on the income obtained in a normal year in the rice fields.

    The agricultural tax is paid by the person who benefits from the income. In addition to the main agricultural tax (the central government) will collect a percentage for the regional budget. Apart from these collections there are no others.[102]

In Pham Van Dong's view this system was practical because it avoided the muddle surrounding multiple contributions, and it would make more people eager to work and increase production because each paid according to his income. It was a progressive tax, and, as Vo Nhan Tri has pointed out, there is no foundation for Bernard Fall's claim that it was detrimental to small land holders.[103]

The point to be stressed here is that this system of taxation tended to strengthen the independent power of the central government. Although the tax registers on which the system depended were not nearly completed until after the armistice of 1954, more centralised control of the tax system did allow the government to supply the

---

[100]*CKCT*, Vol. 3, p. 52.

[101]Ibid., p. 54. The term 'state finances' (*tai chinh cua nha nuoc*) also appears in this article.

[102]Ibid., p. 55.

[103]Vo Nhan Tri, *Croissance économique de la République Démocratique du Vietnam*, Editions en Langues Etrangères, Hanoi, 1967, pp. 172–173 comments on Fall, *Le Viet Minh*, p. 250. Tri p. 173 explained that the tax had a 'double aspect': 'From the economic point of view it served to collect rice destined for the army and the population. From the political point of view it constituted an effective instrument of class struggle against the landed proprietors, and prelude to proper agrarian reform'.

army 'including' the regional forces. In his article Pham Van Dong thus envisaged that the new arrangement would reduce the burden on the regional committees, because they could hold up to twenty percent of the central collection for tasks 'directed by the centre' (*trung uong se giao*).[104]In other words, 'the centre' would have increasing control over the regional forces, which in turn reinforced its capacity to mobilise political and economic support for the main force at its social base. On an index of 100 for 1951, it has in fact been shown that tax receipts increased to 277 in 1952, 430 in 1953, but dropped to 326 in 1954, [105] while events on the battle field from around mid-1951 confirmed the trend.

At a strategic level greater revenues led to a greater integration of main and regional force actions in overlapping regular and irregular campaigns that would reinforce the original tendency towards the centralisation of state power. As the need for armed propaganda and irregular strategies were continuously emphasised from around mid-1951, [106] the effective mobilisation of people and resources for a high level of political-military development caused an increasing dispersal of French forces. The regular main force units could now draw the French out their stronghold in the plains by threatening the Thai Country and Laos in the northwestern highlands, because these countries maintained their political allegiance to the French until the end of the war. For example, when 312 Division began to menace Nghia Lo in the Thai Country in September 1951, the French had to reinforce that post from more secure occupied areas. [107] But this then reduced security in the occupied areas, especially in the Red River Delta where 320 Division was fast becoming the armed propaganda especialist responsible for a rising level of guerrilla activity there. Under the integrated pressure of such regular and irregular strategies the French would inevitably falter, and when they did at Hoa Binh in early 1952 they would highlight the greater unity that an increasingly centralised government had created between the army and the society since its failure at Vinh Yen one year before.

After his defeat of Giap's counter offensive on the delta, De Lattre decided to try to capitalise on it by occupying the town of Hoa Binh sixty kilometers southwest of Hanoi. It was anticipated that such an unexpected move outside the delta would disrupt resistance supply

---

[104]*CKCT*, Vol. 3, p. 56.

[105]Vo Nhan Tri, *Croissance économique*, p. 72. The drop in 1954 probably reflected the cessation of hostilities in June.

[106]For example, see Giap's articles on guerrilla war in ibid., pp. 102–109, pp. 142–146. Page 380 also discusses 'the coordination of guerrilla action and armed propaganda'.

[107]Fall, *Street Without Joy*, p. 47; Gras, *Histoire*, pp. 417–423.

lines between rice rich Thanh Hoa and the inhospitable mountain strongholds in the northwest. But as soon as the French occupied Hoa Binh, Giap brought his entire main battle force into action, enveloped the town, and brought great pressure to bear on its extended supply lines.[108] As the battle then developed, the interaction of Vietnam's regular and irregular forces could not have been revealed with greater clarity, nor could the political-military unity that underpinned it.

While the Chinese equipped Divisions 304, 308, and 312 fully supported by Chinese equipped artillery, engineer, and anti-aircraft units engaged the enemy around Hoa Binh on the Chinese 'meat grinder' model, Divisions 316 and 320 were ordered *into* the Red River Delta to lead the masses in guerrilla tactics which successfully disrupted French supply lines. Giap thus combined a Chinese style 'battle of destruction' with a Vietnamese style 'battle of dispersal'. Furthermore, very many regional force units, especially those in the west of the delta, and hundreds of thousands of porters in the region around Hoa Binh, including the politically suspect Muong and Catholic areas where the French had set up an 'Autonomous Zone',[109] were effectively mobilised. While reinforcements from various Inter-Zones were fed into the battle as required, adequate supplies of rice and ammunition were available to sustain 304, 308, and 312 Divisions for the extremely heavy three month campaign it took them to force a French withdrawal.[110] It should also be added that a sixth infantry division, 325 in Trung Bo, was added to the People's Army's order of battle around February as it facilitated the victory at Hoa Binh with independent regimental attacks around Hue, Dong Hoi, and Nam Dong.[111]

From the point of view of *The People's Daily*, on 15 March, this victory was correctly seen as a result of 'the association of Vietnamese experience with the military thought of Mao Zedong'. And the main implication of this association was the 'great unity' necessary to bolster the Vietnamese nation's fight for independence into the modern world:

[108]Fall, *Street Without Joy*, pp. 47–48; Gras, *Histoire*, pp. 424–427.

[109]This was part of their general attempt to divide and rule Vietnam after 1945. For a Vietnamese perspective see Ngo Tien Chat, 'Ve Nhung Cuoc Dau Tranh Vu Trang cua Nhan Dan Cac Dan Toc Tinh Hoa Binh trong Cuoc Khang Chien chong Phap (1945–1954)' [On the Armed Struggle of the Peoples of Hoa Binh Province in the Anti-French Resistance War (1945–1954)], *NCLS*, No. 109, April 1968, pp. 44–54.

[110]This analysis of the battle is based on *LSQD*, pp. 447–462; Salan, *Le Viet Minh mon adversaire*, pp. 271–272; R. Delpey, *Soldats de la boue: Glas et tocsin*, Vol. 3, Paris, 1952, pp. 83–89; Gras, *Histoire*, pp. 429–462.

[111]See Bernard Fall's classic account in *Street Without Joy*, pp. 455–458.

The battle for Hoa Binh teaches us to recognise clearly the
strength of the policy of great unity held by President Ho, the
Central Committee of the Party, and the government. The Army
has understood to policy of unity better than before and
correctly carried out this policy. Thanks to that it has helped a
lot in the task of unifying all the people, and developing strongly
the resistance war. Compatriots in temporarily occupied zones
and guerrilla zones have understood the policy and so warmly
participated in the resistance war. Compatriots in the Free Zone
have understood the policy and have contributed millions of
days of labour to serve the front and take care of the wounded.
Our Muong and Catholic compatriots have understood the
policy and so rushed to fight the enemy, defend the villages,
support the army and the government. The victory at Hoa Binh
is a victory for the policy of great unity.[112]

Much had crystallised in the battle for Hoa Binh a year after the
Lao Dong Party had come to life beneath the portraits of Marx and
Mao. By using international support and the Chinese model to
legitimise its position in the society, the Lao Dong Party had largely
solved the problem of Chinese aid by fostering balanced institutional
development. By early 1952 the Party had built the political and
economic foundations on which it could effectively integrate the
army's institutional development and combined regular and irregular
strategies with the society's capacity to support them. This was the
unity of army and society which led to the consolidation of an
increasingly independent central government and vice-versa. And it
was on this basis that the army and the society made the final
adjustments in political-military strategy that would bring about the
final defeat of the French.

Dien Bien Phu: A Stake in the Land

From mid-1952 there is no doubt that the Viet Minh were danger-
ously increasing their strategic mobility, while the French efforts
lapsed into 'stagnation'.[113] The French knew this at the time, for their
incessant sweeps of the Red River Delta in 1952 and 1953 failed
increasingly to prevent the base installations of the Expeditionary
Corps from being susceptible to infiltration from Giap's main force.[114]
From September 1952, Divisions 308, 312, and 316 had also moved
into the north western highlands to place pressure on the Thai
Country and Laos, while other units in the Red River Delta were

---

[112]*CKCT*, Vol. 3, pp. 222–223.
[113]Henri Navarre, *Agonie de l'Indochine, 1953–1956*, Paris: Plon, 1956, p. 26.
[114]Gras, *Histoire*, pp. 455–462; Franchini, *Les guerres*, Vol. 2, Chapter 3.

using armed propaganda to build up bases deep in the temporarily occupied zone. Especially in the two provinces of Thai Binh and Hung Yen kill the enemy emulation movements strongly developed the guerrilla war in close coordination with the political front.[115]

Consequently, the major highland air heads which the French established at Nghia Lo and Na San had to be reinforced from forces that could hardly be spared from the delta, and Nghia Lo still fell when 308 Division appeared out of the mountain mists without any warning on 17 October. Thus, although the French defeated waves of attacking Viet Minh infantry at Na San in December, the results of the 1952–1953 campaign in the north-west were significant for the People's Army.

Most of Son La province was liberated, which meant that the Viet Minh now had continuous political-military linkage between the Viet Bac region and Inter-Zone 3.[116] As this success greatly expanded the rear area from which people and resources could be mobilised for next campaign season, the last French combat Commander, Général Navarre, then gave the French government an accurate account of his predicament a few days after he took up his command in May 1953:

> The *dispersion* and *the immobility* of our forces only leaves the command with an *extremely reduced capacity for manoeuvre*. We do not have a Battle Corps to oppose the Viet Minh's Battle Corps. The general reserves are not articulated and are reduced to such a level that *all strategic manoeuvre of any amplitude is impossible* in the present state.[117]

It was against this backdrop that the so-called 'Navarre Plan' was conceived and implemented in ways that would affect the final arrangements which the People's Army had to make for the campaign season in 1953–1954.

The Navarre plan was not a plan 'for victory'[118] in a military sense, as the French and American presses were to popularise it.[119] As Navarre conceived his mission, it bore no relationship to the

---

[115]*CKCT*, Vol. 3, p. 363.

[116]Vien Su Hoc, *May Van De ve Chien Thang Lich Su Dien Bien Phu* [Some Questions on the Historical Victory at Dien Bien Phu], Hanoi: NXB Khoa Hoc Xa Hoi, 1985, pp. 132–133.

[117]Quoted in Navarre, *Agonie*, pp. 49–50. Emphasis in original.

[118]Ibid., p. 72.

[119]In Navarre's view, there was general consensus among French ministers in May 1953 about the need to find 'an honourable way out' of the 'Indochina impasse'. Ibid., p. 71. See also p. 3, p. 69, p. 72. This view is supported strongly by the *reductions* which the French government had already made in French troop strengths between the

'euphoria'[120] which enveloped Hanoi when Operation Castor was launched to occupy Dien Bien Phu on 20 November. Nor did it bear any relationship to the renewed hope in a military miracle that spread through the French and American governments around the same time. Navarre's plan was 'to create the military conditions for an honourable political solution'.[121] It was a plan to increase rapidly the size of Bao Dai's Vietnamese National Army to fifty three Light Infantry battalions by late 1953 and double that number in 1954, so that mobile French troops would be free to attack Viet Minh strong-holds. The initiative gained over a two year period would then be the basis for a negotiated settlement to the war.

The Viet Minh could be confident that this scheme had inherent problems. Navarre himself has highlighted 'the incapacity of the Vietnamese government to assure recruits',[122] and there is little doubt that Viet Minh's policy of propagandizing the 'suspended' distribution of communal land to 'peasants forced to be puppet soldiers' created difficulties for the French, because it encouraged Bao Dai's peasant recruits to return to the resistance.[123] Moreover, the Light Infantry Battalions raised in 1953 did not generally perform well in battle: French units often had to be deployed to save them or the regions they were phased in to pacify. There were even battles such as those in Nam Dinh in October where the Party journals could boast that village guerrilla units made whole companies of Bao Dai's infantry 'run like ducks'.[124]

Yet by mid-1953, the Navarre Plan posed a new threat to the resistance. The paranoia of the Public Security Services (*Cong An*), which reached new and dizzy heights around this time, is one indica-tion of the increased sense of threat. 'Spies' of various categories are said to have increased from two to five times, and 'bandits' twenty

---

defeat at Hoa Binh and Navarre's arrival in May 1953. Ibid., p. 26. For a good American analysis of the Navarre Plan see Dunn, 'Vietnamese Policy and Vietnamese Nationalism', pp. 196–210.

[120]Pierre Rocolle, *Porquoi Dien Bien Phu?*, Paris: Flammarion, 1986, p. 204.

[121]Navarre, *Agonie*, p. 72.

[122]Ibid., p. 140.

[123]Quotes in Christine White, 'Agrarian Reform and National Liberation in the Vietnamese Revolution, 1920–1957', PhD, Cornell University, January 1981, p. 185. This source also says that most of Bao Dai's recruits came from the Red River and Mekong deltas where landlordism was deeply entrenched, and that the Bao Dai government's sensitivity to the Viet Minh propaganda is reflected in the various agricultural decrees it made in June 1953, although these failed because of landlord opposition.

[124]*CKCT*, Vol. 4, p. 147.

times since 1952.[125] A major factor which this heightened anxiety may be seen to reflect, was that Navarre's plan required American equipment, and, as Navarre said, American equipment meant 'a more direct integration of American aid with strategic projections'.[126]

By March when the American Senate history says that Indochina was 'probably the top priority in foreign policy'[127] of the United States because the United States government felt the effects of the Korean War could be localised at that stage. From March 1953 high American officials like President Eisenhower, General O'Daniel, and Admiral Radford were thus goading the French by saying that they were far too defensive given their technological superiority, that they should take an aggressive initiative to win the war within two years.[128] As the Viet Minh journals could see, one of the main effects of the Korean armistice of July 1953 was that it left the Americans free to develop their intervention in Indochina.[129]

In Bac Bo and northern Trung Bo, where the balance of forces favoured the Viet Minh to an overwhelming extent, scope for such intervention would be relatively limited. Yet after seven years of war the Viet Minh had still not defeated the French who were now being equipped by the Americans for more aggressive action. Also in Nam Bo, and Cambodia, the situation was still quite manageable from the French point of view.[130] Despite a political crisis in Cambodia in which Prince Sihanouk emerged at the head of the government in 1952 the military threat to the French there was insignificant. It consisted of no more than about 1,000 Viet Minh troops and about 2,500 Khmer Issarak.[131] In Nam Bo the return to guerrilla tactics after the failure of Nguyen Binh's offensive in the first quarter of 1950 had led to the regeneration of the regional forces whose estimated strength of 40,000 to 50,000 was sufficient to hold down 100,000 badly needed French regular and auxiliary troops. But while this repre-

---

[125]Vien Su Hoc, *May Van De*, p. 133.

[126]Navarre, *Agonie*, p. 137.

[127]Congressional Research Service, Library of Congress, *The U.S. Government and the Vietnam War: Executive and Legislative Roles and Relationships, Part I, 1945–1961*, Washington, U.S. Government Printing Office, 1984, p. 123. The entire section beginning with the sub-title 'U.S. Increases Pressure on French', pp. 121–129 amply supports Vietnamese fears.

[128]Ibid.

[129]*CKCT*, Vol. 4, pp. 93–100, warns of U.S. intervention in Vietnam, Laos, and Cambodia.

[130]Navarre, *Agonie*, Chapter 3, especially p. 81.

[131]Gras, *Histoire*, pp. 467–469.

sented a significant demand on French resources, the six or seven main force battalions in Nam Bo had been effectively pushed into the Plain of Reeds, and from January 1952 after a final bombing outrage in Saigon that city was quiet for the rest of the war.[132] Therefore, after seven years of exhausting conflict, it was in a context of incomplete success and a renewed French threat doubled by American intervention, that the Party had to make renewed efforts to mobilise people and resources.

Christine White has made this point and shown us that the Party's land reform policy was being seriously debated in 1953. For many years the Party had largely restricted itself to the moderate policy of reducing rents and taxes. This was because of fears that a more radical emphasis on land reform would 'rupture' resistance unity as a result of 'the adverse reaction from the landlords'.[133] Nevertheless, while the first major decree on land reform was made in April[134] an essay recently published in Hanoi by Cao Van Luong does confirm what Christine White argued in 1981 was 'reasonably certain':[135] that both the Navarre Plan and the Korean Armistice of 27 July gave an important impetus to the land reform campaign.

To 'smash' the Navarre Plan and to 'push' the strategic offensive in the 1953-1954 campaign season, Cao Van Luong explains that the Party had 'to increase production strongly' and that this meant 'the question of peasants and land' was the 'door bolt'.[136] Of course, even though poor and landless peasant had become increasingly involved in the Resistance and Administration Committees and dominated the militia and police in most liberated areas by 1953, the scale of the task was such that 'land reform had barely begun'[137] before the armistice in mid-1954. Yet as the Party decided to push on with its preparations for land reform in late 1953, the propaganda effect of these preparations certainly helps to explain why hundreds of thousands of people were mobilised to support the 1953–1954 campaign. It also helps to

[132]Ibid., pp. 462–464. M.N., 'May Net Lon ve Phong Trao Cong Nhan Sai-Gon tu 1945 den 1954' [An Outline if the Workers Movement in Saigon from 1945 to 1954], NCLS, No. 95, February 1967, especially pp. 11–13.

[133]Quoted in White, 'Agrarian Reform', p. 195. These comments were made by cadres in late 1953.

[134]See Nhan Dan's report in CKCT, Vol. 4, 52–56.

[135]White, 'Agrarian Reform', p. 195.

[136]Cao Van Luong, 'Duong Loi Givong Cao Ngon Doc Lap Dan Toc va Chu Nghia Xa Hoi voi Chien Thang Dien Bien Phu' [Raising High the Flag of National Independence and Socialism and the Dien Bien Phu Victory], in Vien Su Hoc, May Van De, pp. 31–66. Quotes are on pp. 37–38.

[137]White, 'Agrarian Reform', p. 241. For information on poor peasants in militia etc see p. 176.

explain why thousands of soldiers would soon die at the culminating battle at Dien Bien Phu in the belief that they were fighting for their land.

In early October 1953, about six weeks before the French occupied Dien Bien Phu with vague notions about defending Laos as 316 Division marched in that direction,[138] a wave of political re-education swept through the ranks of the People's Army. The aim of the re-education was to enable

> the army to define a standpoint on the struggle that would serve the interests of the labouring people, and support the struggle of the peasants to realise the land reform policy of the Party and the Government with determination.[139]

Because the vast majority of the soldiers were from hungry peasant families the 'denounce sufferings' sessions were often harrowing:

> After each session of recounting suffering, no one could hold back their tears. Many sobbed, many felt extreme hatred and wanted to rush straight out to look for traitors, reactionaries, landlords and cruel local despots to punish them for their crimes . . .[140]

As the re-education campaign was then guided through the ranks by Nguyen Chi Thanh 'holding firmly to the Marxist military line of the Party'[141] in the Political Bureau, the Commander in Chief of the People's Army was one of the main speakers in the National Assembly Meeting of about 200 delegates which finally passed the land reform law on 4 December.

After Ho Chi Minh spoke to the slogan 'all for the front line, all for victory', Truong Chinh told the delegates with some degree of inaccuracy that 'the peasants make up almost 90% of the population

---

[138]Navarre, *Agonie*, pp. 188–200 sets out his reasons for occupying Dien Bien Phu. In a situation where he was obliged to defend Laos with inadequate forces, Navarre persuasively eliminates the choices available to him and gives a strong sense of how inexorable his decision was, especially when he never counted seriously on the possibility of Chinese aid, especially in artillery, for the Viet Minh. However, while his miscalculation was a fundamental error, he makes it clear that the occupation of a fortified camp at Dien Bien Phu was only a 'mediocre' solution to his strategic problem and therefore undertaken because it was the 'only possible' solution (p. 191). In other words, while Navarre had no strategic initiative the Viet Minh were forcing his weak hand. Barring some external intervention, disaster for the French at Dien Bien Phu or some other place was thus inevitable by late 1953.

[139]*CKCT*, Vol. 4, p. 126.

[140]Ibid., p. 128. I have followed the translation in White, 'Agrarian Reform', p. 183 but made a minor alteration.

[141]Nguyen Chi Thanh, *Nhung Bai Chon Loc*, p. 60.

but have less than 30% of the rice fields'.[142] At a time when indiscretions by French generals and journalists had begun to convince him that the French intended to hold Dien Bien Phu and were not merely manoeuvering to throw the People's Army off balance,[143] General Giap told the National Assembly that 'land reform was an important element in strengthening and developing the armed forces'.[144] By the 6th the Voice of Vietnam was spreading news of the land reform law all over the country along with a mobilisation order for the Winter campaign. Before long, people in villages where the reforms had actually begun were also urged to send news of these developments to relatives at the front, and delegations of selected villagers were even taken to the battle of Dien Bien Phu to give the troops the good news from home. Consequently, there may be some truth in Tran Do's claim that the first national hero of Dien Bien Phu, Phan Dinh Giot, whose body was shredded by machine gun fire when he threw it against the slit of a French bunker to facilitate an attack on the first day of the battle, had been inspired by news of land reform from his home village in Ha Tinh province.[145]

In any case, there is little question that the Party's satisfaction with the political standpoint reached in the army just before the battle for Dien Bien Phu was justified:

All soldiers and cadres saw clearly that our army was the child of the labouring people, that they were *"peasants dressed in uniforms"* fighting to overthrow imperialism and feudalism, gain independence for the people, fields for the peasants, and advance to socialism.[146]

[142]*CKCT*, Vol. 4, p. 175, p. 177. Truong Chinh's estimate of the number of landless peasants seems to have been exaggerated. Andrew Vickerman, *The Fate of the Peasantry: Premature 'Transition to Socialism' in the Democratic Republic of Vietnam*, Monograph Series number 28, Yale University Southeast Asia Studies, 1986, pp. 57–58 points out there are considerable limitations to the use of any data on rural questions in the period concerned. Population records and cadastral surveys could not generally be described as reliable. Bearing these limitations in mind, figures which Vickerman gives on p. 65 suggest that in 1953 while middle and poor peasants were 77.1% of the population they owned 50.3% of the land.

[143]For Giap's calculations on what the French were up to at Dien Bien Phu see Rocolle, *Pourquoi*, pp. 202–215. These calculations were important for if Giap had moved to invest Dien Bien Phu with his main force, and the French had evacuated the position in good time he would have been caught with his divisions in the highlands and their base areas in the lowlands exposed.

[144]*CKCT*, Vol. 4, p. 181.

[145]Rocolle, *Pourquoi*, p. 211 on the radio broadcasts. White, 'Agrarian Reform', p. 230 on letters and visits to the front. Tran Do, *Récits sur Dien Bien Phu*, Hanoi: Editions en Langues Etrangères, 1962, Chapter 7 on Phan Dinh Giot.

[146]*CKCT*, Vol. 4, p. 127, emphasis added.

Indeed, not only had the exploited Vietnamese peasantry been mobilised by the promise of a better life in a new world order, but its main force had also been dressed in uniforms of largely Chinese origin to ensure that they would take their place in it.

As Tran Do marched from Phu Tho towards Dien Bien Phu with his 'well equipped' 312 Division in late December 'the first successes of the agrarian reforms' were the main topics of conservation in the highland regions.[147] In the opening shots of the 1953–1954 campaign, 316 Divisions had already liberated Lai Chau on 20 November, the day the first French paratroopers landed at Dien Bien Phu about 170 kilometers to the south. Some 45% of the rice harvested in the region and 16,000 porters were then mobilised for the front, while complementary rice supplies and artillery and heavy mortar ammunition were trucked and portered about 700 kilometers south from the Chinese border through Lai Chau to Dien Bien Phu.[148] Meanwhile, as the guerrilla war was intensified in Nam Bo, as 325 Division with a regiment of 304 Division from around Thanh Hoa had marched into the central highlands, and as 308 Division marched into northern Laos in December to further divide French forces, mobilisation was intensified in the northern delta areas. Indeed, 5,000 of the 7,000 villages which the Viet Minh now controlled in the northern plains were being mobilised to send huge quantities of rice and hundreds of thousands of porters to support the front.[149]

Various supply lines from the Red River Delta and Thanh Hoa along the Ma river thus converged on Son La which was the nodal supply point to the east of Dien Bien Phu. With Pham Van Dong at the head of the Supply Commission, the 165 kilometre route due east from Son La to Dien Bien Phu was divided into three sections. The first was a 100 kilometre section to Tuan Giao, the second was a 47 kilometre section along an old colonial road that had to be rebuilt by

---

[147]Tran Do, *Récits*, pp. 7–8. Although he does not name the division he marched with, it must have been 312 because he says on p. 45 his division had the honour of making the first attack on 13 March and we know that was the 312 Division. That 312 Division marched from around Phu Tho on 24 December is stated in Vo Nguyen Giap, *Dien Bien Phu*, Hanoi: NXB Quan Doi Nhan Dan, 1979, p. 366. This source lists all the main manoeuvres of the Divisions in chronological order. See especially pp. 362–374.

[148]Vien Su Hoc, *May Van De*, pp. 108–115; Rocolle, *Pourquoi*, p. 212 on the Chinese contribution.

[149]Vien Su Hoc, *May Van De*, p. 97. The figure generally given in Vietnamese sources like this and *LSQD*, p. 559 in 260,000 porters. Many other sources deal with the deployments of the main force divisions and the general situation in the months leading up to Dien Bien Phu. For example, see Giap, *Dien Bien Phu*, pp. 362–369; *LSQD*, pp. 563–565; Tran Do, *Récits*; Navarre, *Agonie*; Gras, *Histoire*; Franchini, *Les guerres*, vol. 2.

engineer units and work brigades, and the third was a short but difficult 18 kilometre section under enemy observation to the rear store houses of the front line divisions.[150]

Along each of these sections, transshipment points and river crossings had to be established. These were manned by supply personnel who had to receive, sort, pack, and earmark huge quantities of general stores for specific units at the front. They were also manned by work brigades and engineer units that were necessary to repair the roads and bridges after the constant attempts of French fighter bombers to cut them. Furthermore, anti-aircraft units that were in action by December were also positioned along the supply routes from Lai Chau and Son La to create what the pilots of the French air command called the 'flak corridor'.[151] In some places the tree tops were tied together to create protective tunnels for the roads and the transport units that worked them. The main capacity of these units was provided by the 800 two and a half ton Molotova trucks that often moved in convoys of thirty to forty vehicles. But the use of hundreds of cars, thousands of rafts and sampans, thousands of mountain ponies, and tens of thousands of bicycles packed with rice sacks and ammunition was also indispensible.[152] As the regiments which would do most to break the back of the French garrison, the artillery regiments of 351 Heavy Division, could therefore begin the extremely arduous task of hauling their weapons into position in January, and as 304, 308, and 316 Divisions also moved to close the siege ring around Dien Bien Phu, we have some idea of one of the most stupendous logistics efforts in modern history. Moreover, we have some idea of how the roughly 37,000 combatants on the firing lines at Dien Bien Phu and the 10,000 replacements that were fed into the battle before it was over,[153] where the head of the 'human serpent'[154] that came up from the plains and wrapped its coils around the 12,000 strong French garrison by 13 March when the main battle began.

Yet if this great national effort to win the logistics battle was

---

[150]Vien Su Hoc, *May Van De*, pp. 174–176. Bernard Fall, *Hell in a Very Small Place*, Pall Mall Press, 1967, pp. 128–129 discusses the roads. This classic account of the battle was first published in Philadelphia by J.B. Lippincott in 1966.

[151]Fall, *Hell*, p. 131. Vien Su Hoc, *May Van De*, pp. 196–208 offers an essay by Hoang Van Khanh on the anti-aircraft defenses at Dien Bien Phu. *LSQD*, p. 558 on keeping the roads open.

[152]Nguyen An's essay on the transport system in Vien Su Hoc, *May Van De*, p. 174; Fall, *Hell*, p. 128 for Molotova trucks.

[153]Vien Su Hoc, *May Van De*, p. 94, p. 99.

[154]Tran Do, *Récits*, p. 13.

fundamental to the final victory, so too was the artillery battle that was won with an indispensible measure of international support from China. As opposed to the sixty guns of over 57 mm caliber in exposed pits with no alternate positions the French could call on in the first week of the battle, and the never more than forty they could call on after that, the Viet Minh were able to bring at least 200 guns of similar calibre into action from concealed positions. These included at least forty eight 105 mm field howitzers, forty eight 75 mm pack howitzers, and forty eight heavy 120 mm mortars which bombarded the French position with at least 200,000 rounds of artillery and heavy mortar ammunition during the battle. Very many 75 mm recoilless rifles and flak guns also helped to intensify the destructive effects of the Viet Minh's heavy armoury.[155] But while Vietnamese sources neither highlight this crucial international support from China,[156] nor the Chinese battle field advice that came with it, aspects of the battle epitomised Vietnam's struggle for national independence.

Georges Boudarel has demonstrated clearly that Giap would have lost the battle if he had not taken the independent decision to countermand the Chinese battle plan.[157] The Chinese plan for 'a rapid attack to achieve a rapid solution'[158] was virtually impossible to execute. In order to strike rapidly at the heart of the French position and destroy it from the inside out in two or three days of intense combat, the assaulting divisions would have to attack from the western side of the valley of Dien Bien Phu when their main supply lines came from the east. Also the artillery could not be positioned to support such an attack because of the nature of the terrain. Therefore, after strenuous efforts to position the artillery for an attack on the Chinese model had failed, Giap had a stormy debate with his Chinese advisers on January 25 and suspended the battle which the French legionnaires expected to begin that night.[159] From this point the battle was completely reoriented so that it would develop into a protracted seige designed to ensure victory. When, in accordance with the Vietnamese plan, the battle began, it came with an attack from the east on the outer French strong point known as Beatrice at 1700 hours on 13 March.

At this moment, Sergeant Kubiac of the 3rd Battalion of the 13th

[155]Ibid., p. 127; Navarre, *Agonie*, p. 218, p. 220.

[156]Giap, *Dien Bien Phu*, is a 392 page account of the battle which does not discuss Chinese aid.

[157]Georges Boudarel, 'Comment Giap a falli perdre la bataille de Dien Bien Phu', *Le Nouvel Observateur*, 8 April, 1983.

[158]Quoted in Ibid., p. 97.

[159]Ibid.

Foreign Legion Half Brigade described later how his position on Beatrice began to collapse immediately as 'shells rained down on us without stopping like a hail storm on a fall evening. Bunker after bunker, trench after trench, collapsed, burying under them men and weapons'.[160] Once 312 Division opened the infantry attack and took the position the same night, the Viet Minh had direct line of sight onto the airfield around which the French garrison was positioned the next day, and its effective closure after the 14th had a major bearing on the battle because it cut the garrison off from reliable air resupply and all means of evacuation. In fact, the first of the three phases into which Giap divided the battle[161] was already over and, as with this phase, it is clear that the rhythm of the last two was related to the availability of supplies and ammunition.

Once the army had 'collected'[162] itself and its supplies of ammunition, the second crucial phase of the battle began with an intense rolling artillery barrage on the central French positions at 1800 hours on 30 March. Within a few minutes the infantry of 312 and 316 Divisions sprang up from the miles of communication trenches that had been dug around the French positions and, as Bernard Fall put it, 'blasted its way through the mine fields and barbed wire so rapidly that the prearranged French defensive fires fell far beyond the Communist assault waves.'[163] However, while a number of French posts were submerged in the first hours of the attack, the most vicious fighting probably took place on 4–5 April when the assaulting divisions left 500 bodies sprawled over the breast works of just one French position (Huguette 6).[164]

By 6 April the battle went into a lull as the dazed survivors in the reduced French perimeter began their stock take, and the Vietnamese 312th Division alone had lost at least a regiment from its order of battle. Giap also makes it clear that various 'supply difficulties',[165] which undoubtedly included a shortage of artillery ammunition, again necessitated a period of relatively light attacks. By 1 May, however, enough artillery ammunition had arrived from China for over 100 field guns[166] to open the third phase of the battle with a thunderous bombardment at 1700 hours. Divisions 312, 316, and 308 then pounded the ravaged French garrison until it fell on the 7th.

---

[160]Quoted in Fall, *Hell*, p. 137.
[161]Giap, *Dien Bien Phu*, pp. 144–183.
[162]Ibid., p. 155.
[163]Fall, *Hell*, p. 196.
[164]Ibid., pp. 221–223.
[165]Giap, *Dien Bien Phu*, p. 177.
[166]Fall, *Hell*, p. 351.

In the protracted three phase siege of Dien Bien Phu, which killed 7,900 Vietnamese soldiers and wounded an estimated 15,000, it was the independence of the People's Army within a supportive international socialist context that yielded victory. Given the strength and tenacity of the French garrison at Dien Bien Phu the Chinese battle plan would have failed. Yet one of the main reasons why the Chinese plan would have failed was interrelated with one of the main reasons why the Vietnamese plan succeeded. If the artillery could not be positioned to support a rapid attack from the west, success in the protracted battle initiated from the east depended largely on the 200 guns and 200,000 rounds of artillery ammunition from China. Thus, along with the land reform law of 4 December, the stupendous logistics efforts, and the fifty five days of sustained Vietnamese infantry attacks, the Chinese guns and ammunition were necessary to destroy the French garrison.

Conclusion

The destruction of this garrison only represented a loss of 5% of the French Expeditionary Corps and, if the Army of the Associated States is included, 3.3% of the total 450,000 strong forces opposed to the Viet Minh.[167] Furthermore, while there is no evidence that after the victory at Dien Bien Phu, Giap's divisions were being reoriented for an attack on the delta, the situation there was more relaxed than it had been for some time. Traffic between Hai Phong and Hanoi flowed freely. For almost three more months there was fighting in some regions, most notably in central Vietnam where Mobile Group 100 was destroyed in a deadly multi-battalion ambush outside An Khe on 24 June. Nevertheless, when it came with the decision to abandon the southern zone of the Red River Delta on 23 June, the precursor to the entire French withdrawal from Indochina bore no relationship to an immediate threat.[168] It was just that after the fall of Dien Bien Phu on 7 May everyone knew the French had been defeated.

In far away Geneva, international negotiations began to deal with the Indochina question on 8 May. To reach the cease fire agreement on 20 July and to provide for the regrouping of French forces prior to their withdrawal from Indochina within two years, the DRV came under strong pressure from China and the Soviet Union as well as France to accept the partition of the country at the seventeenth

---

[167]Gras, *Histoire*, p. 569 gives a detailed breakdown of French figures.

[168]Ibid., pp. 570–573. The classic account of the destruction of Mobile Group 100 is contained in Fall, *Street Without Joy*.

parallel. However, acceptance by the DRV was undoubtedly conditioned by its belief that overwhelming domestic support and the strength of the People's Army would guarantee the Geneva Accords.

The French government had in fact emphasised the 'temporary' and 'provisional' nature of the partition, and agreed that the 'military demarcation line' should not 'in any way be interpreted as constituting a political or territorial boundary.'[169] The Final Declaration of the Geneva Accords also stated that re-unification elections 'shall be held in July 1956'.[170] In keeping with the legitimate power of the DRV, the provisions of the Geneva Accords which deal with Vietnam were clear and unambiguous in their assurances of the 'unity and territorial integrity'[171] of the nation.

Yet even though it was generally accepted that the DRV controlled 80% of the population and 75% of the country,[172] the war of national liberation was not over. Neither the United States government nor the French created State of Vietnam with its capital in Saigon adopted the Final Declaration. With strong American support the Saigon regime then sabotaged the elections in 1956. But as the war was revived in the south in 1957, deepening American intervention in support of the Saigon regime overlooked the reality that at Dien Bien Phu the People's Army had consolidated the legitimate national government of post-colonial Vietnam, while the division of the country had nothing to do with the strength of Vietnamese support for the Bao Dai regime. And if the immediate political gains of the DRV in 1954 were not commensurate with the great victory its army achieved at the battle of Dien Bien Phu, its legitimacy meant they would be.

Because of its origins the People's Army epitomised the nation in arms. In a situation where the Vietnamese people had no alternative but to fight for their independence, the army played a central role in constituting the power of the nation-state. The formation of the first guerrilla bases was a political as well as a military manifestation of the revolution already under way in the society. Once the DRV had therefore come into existence with overwhelming popular support and declared its independence in 1945, the regional and regular forces were pumped up out of the villages with armed propaganda to oppose the invasion of the French Expeditionary Corps. As the

---

[169]Contained in the 'Final Declaration of the Geneva Conference' in Robert F. Randle, *Geneva 1954: The Settlement of the Indochinese War*, Princeton University Press, 1969, p. 570, pp. 277–278, p. 283.

[170]Ibid., p. 571.

[171]Contained in the 'Declaration of the French Republic', 21 July 1954, in Randle, *Geneva*, p. 610.

[172]Kahin, *Intervention*, p. 53.

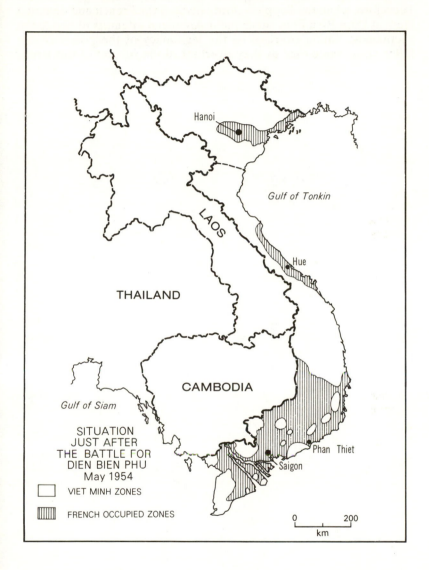

Hanoi

Gulf of Tonkin

LAOS

Hue

THAILAND

CAMBODIA

Gulf of Siam

SITUATION
JUST AFTER
THE BATTLE FOR
DIEN BIEN PHU
May 1954

Phan Thiet

Saigon

VIET MINH ZONES

FRENCH OCCUPIED ZONES

0   200
km

People's Army consolidated the unity of the nation within an international socialist context over the next seven years, it then consolidated and reflected the legitimate power of an independent government. Therefore, while the People's Army divided the French and defeated them at Dien Bien Phu, subsequent American attempts to divide the Vietnamese nation overlooked the legitimacy of the power of the DRV at the same time as they overlooked the subject of this book.

Epilogue

On April 10, 1956, ninety seven years after the first French units landed at Saigon, others paraded there for the last time. Many Vietnamese wearing French medals watched sadly as Paratroopers clad in camouflage uniforms, Foreign Legionnaires wearing white kepis, and bearded Moroccans in tan turbans carried their battle standards through the streets of the southern capital and boarded their ships.[1] The French imperial adventure had ended in Vietnam, even if its consequences had not.

True to the nature of almost 100 years of colonial rule the French left Vietnam a divided country. Yet Vietnamese of all political persuasions opposed this division. In 1954, Ho Chi Minh's government only accepted the Geneva partition under strong international pressure, and with clear assurances of reunification elections for which it knew it had the overwhelming support of the population. Although Bao Dai was by now a broken playboy living at Cannes, the delegation his State of Vietnam sent to Geneva was still so trenchantly opposed to partition that, like the American government, it refused to adopt the Final Declaration. In 1954 what divided Vietnamese was the kind of government that would rule the unified nation.

Within months of Geneva, however, the Americans were involved in consolidating the partition. In October 1954, Bao Dai's Premier, Ngo Dinh Diem, who seemed attractive to the Americans because he had not served the French, received a letter of unconditional support from President Eisenhower. In February 1955, Diem handed over the training of the Army of the Republic of Vietnam (ARVN) from

---

[1] Bernard B. Fall, *The Two Viet-Nams: A Political and Military Analysis*, New York: Prager, 1964, pp. 319–320.

267

the French to the Americans. ARVN would now be the responsibility of the U.S. Military Assistance Advisory Group under General (Iron Mike) O'Daniel, a master of assembly line techniques for turning out South Korean divisions.[2] As Diem then moved with full American support to eliminate the Binh Xuyen and the religious sects, extinguish all political opposition, and announce on 5 August 1955 that his government would have nothing to do with reunification elections, Bao Dai protested. He criticised Diem's police state and pleaded internationally that, as he worded it in his memoirs, 'relations between the two parts of Vietnam be normalised'.[3]

By the time Diem's Republic of Vietnam came into existence in October 1955, Bao Dai's ineffectual pleas from Cannes could do nothing to prevent his final rift with Diem nor the emergence of a second state in Vietnam. Yet from August 1945 when he abdicated and became the DRV's Supreme Advisor, Bao Dai, whose ancestor Gia Long established the unity of the country in 1802, never broke faith with the Viet Minh on this issue. The at least tenuous contacts which Saigon governments, including Diem's, continued to have with the DRV and the NLF in the late 1950s and 1960s had a precedent in the diplomacy of the last heir to the Nguyen court in Hue. One tends to believe Bao Dai when he claims in his memoirs that, if he had still been emperor when the south was divided and ruled by Diem's private armies in 1955, 'I would have abdicated for the second time.'[4]

Of course the Americans were hostile to Bao Dai at least partly because of his committment to Vietnamese unity, and later they feared that if they did not intervene his successors might have come to a negotiated settlement with the DRV. Yet Bao Dai was a patriot rather than a revolutionary nationalist. Unlike Ho Chi Minh he never had a mandate from 'the people'. The French conquest had caused a revolution as well as a disjunction in Vietnamese history when it destroyed the ancient institution of the monarchy, and brought 'the people' into view as a new political category. Marxist-Leninist internationalism then became the integrating ideology of 'the nation' because it located 'the people' in an international context which opposed colonialism. Marxist-Leninists like Ho Chi Minh were thus able to shape the force of the nation, while patriots like Bao Dai and Ngo Dinh Diem were broken by the West.

[2]Bao Dai, *Le Dragon d'Annam*, pp. 336–337. Fall, *The Two Viet-Nams*, pp. 318–326 offers a good introduction to the phasing out of French influence and the phasing in of American influence.

[3]Bao Dai, *Le Dragon d' Annam*, p. 343. The plea was made to the French, American, British, Indian, and Soviet governments. Also see, Fall, *The Two Viet-Nams*, pp. 254–259.

[4]Ibid., p. 343.

Bao Dai's army was not taken seriously by the French before 1953 and even then it and its successor, ARVN, were never treated by their benefactors as independent forces. On the other hand, revolutionary nationalist leaders in Vietnam understood from 1941 that a properly constituted army would have to depend on popular support. Such an army would have to reflect generally accepted political and social goals and be rooted in the society's capacity to support it. Because it was a political as well as a military force, the People's Army thus mobilised the nation and consolidated its independence at Dien Bien Phu. And if international support from China made a vital contribution to this victory, the Vietnamese need for this support, like the desire for unity, was something the Americans never understood for what it was.

The badge of the American Military Assistance Command Vietnam which came into existence in 1962 was a stylised Great Wall of China, pierced by a sword. This, in its way, was the emblem of America's 'loss of China' and also of the 'Korean trauma'. By 1955, when American advisers such as General O'Daniel had taken over ARVN's training, their experience of massed Chinese attacks down the Korean peninsula was still high in their minds. With massive infusions of aid they therefore began to structure ARVN with heavily armed, motorised divisions rather than the mobile combat groups the French training mission had formerly tried to implement. In other words, ARVN was designed to stop another advance of the monolithic power of communist China across the seventeenth parallel. The People's Army was not thought to be independent.

Unlike the People's Army which had been able to override inappropriate Chinese advice, however, ARVN never had the independence or the background to override inappropriate American advice. Many Saigon generals began their careers as sergeants in the French colonial army. The officer corps in general was urban in origin and, by the 1960s, many of it members had been trained in America. When American money also kept this urban officer corps subordinated to American ideas of how the war should be run,[5] it is not surprising that, unlike the People's Army and the People's Liberation Armed Forces (PLAF) of the 'National Front for the Liberation of the Southern Region' (NLF) with their plethora of mass organisations in the countryside, ARVN gave very low priority to the development of regional forces.

On the assumption that, as in Korea, they would have to combat a

[5]For more background on the ARVN's officer corps see Woodside, *Community and Revolution*, pp. 281–284; Kolko, *Anatomy of a War*, p. 205, while much can be gleaned from Chapters 19 and 20.

massive invasion from the north, the American advisers had constructed an ineffective army. Indeed, American strategy overlooked the forces for national unity that existed in the south under the 'National Front', as well as the support they soon received as People's Army units from the north outflanked ARVN divisions by coming along the Ho Chi Minh Trail.[6] Strategically as well as in every other way, ARVN was divided from the population.

By the early 1960s when Western observers were surprised at how little heavy equipment the People's Army had received from communist countries—it amounted to small numbers of obsolete Soviet armoured vehicles and medium artillery pieces[7]—ARVN's existence was tied to the lifeline of American aid. At a time when Giap's infantry had a high reputation in the French Army, and Bernard Fall was impressed in 1962 by the troops he saw dogtrotting around Hanoi with full field kits in the blazing sun,[8] ARVN was already corrupt.

Among many forms of corruption that would reach incredible proportions by 1975 the main ones might be stated. These were: misappropriation of funds, the sale of promotions or safe posts, kickbacks from contractors, the diversion of American supplied equipment to the black market, cheating on soldiers food and pay, and the creation of 'ghost soldiers' (*linh ma*) for which officers pocketed the payrolls.[9] Therefore, by the time of the battle for Binh Gia in December 1964, over two People's Army regiments plus local forces marked a new stage in the war when they destroyed a 2,000 strong ARVN force. ARVN was soon losing a battalion a week.

To maintain the regime that was totally dependent on American support, the American government now intensified its bombing of the north (to defeat the south), pushed ARVN into the background, and committed American ground troops whose strength peaked at 425,000 in mid-1967. Between 1965 and 1973, therefore, almost the only obstacle to the victory of the NLF was, as Woodside has aptly decribed it, the enormous firepower of the Americans 'employed in Macbeth-like progressions from one act of destruction to another'.[10] Then, when the economic and political costs of this grotesque performance could no longer be sustained by the American government, the American Army began to withdraw and embarked on a program of 'Vietnamisation'.

[6]William S. Turley, *The Second Indochina War: A Short Political and Military History, 1954–1975*, Boulder, Colorado, Westview Press, 1986, pp. 39–45 is probably the best introductory discussion.

[7]Bernard B. Fall, *Viet-Nam Witness 1953–66*, London: Pall Mall Press, 1966, p. 251.

[8]Ibid., 110.

[9]Kolko, *Anatomy of a War*, p. 253. Woodside, *Community and Revolution* p. 303.

[10]Woodside, *Community and Revolution*, p. 278.

But just as the seriousness with which the French began to take Bao Dai's army in 1953 was too late to prevent massive desertions once the Geneva Conference was announced, Vietnamisation never had a chance between 1973 and 1975. By this time the National Front forces had had their set backs, most notably in the Tet 1968 offensive and in the Phoenix Program. Moreover, in early 1975 the ARVN had an immense superiority in men and arms: a three to one advantage in troops, a three and a half to one advantage in artillery pieces, a two to one advantage in tanks and armoured vehicles, and total superiority in air.[11] Nevertheless, with an effective system of mass mobilisation in the countryside, and international support from socialist countries which provided an excellent anti-aircraft defence system and most of their heavy weapons, the revolutionary forces had the singular advantage over ARVN that they would fight.

On 11 March 1975, the Republic's President, Nguyen Van Thieu, precipitated the final crisis. After consultations with his astrologer and a mysterious Australian named Ted Serong, Thieu responded to mounting internal pressure and drastic cuts in American aid by ordering the evacuation of the southern highlands. As a result his realm was thrown into chaos. Once the evacuation began and the People's Army attacks around Ban Me Thuot led to indescribable panic between there and the coast, the fighting was virtually over as the revolutionary forces entered what Kolko has called the 'void'.[12] By dumping their heavy equipment and boarding hundreds of abandoned American trucks, the People's Army concentrated eighteen divisions around Saigon by late April. There was some fighting with the four ARVN divisions around Saigon, most notably with the 18th Division around Xuan Loc. But at 5 am on the 30th, the final evacuation of the American Embassy took place after days of hysteria and, at 10.45 am, the war ended when a T.54 tank crashed through the gates of the deer park containing President Thieu's Palace.

The thirty year war had ended with the failure of American attempts to divide and, if not rule, then dominate Vietnam. But as this failure only repeated the French failure to divide and rule, parallels between the French and American phases of the war can be drawn from beginning to end. In late 1945 French Army sources

---

[11]Kolko, *Anatomy of a War*, p. 523. Pentagon estimates were that the People's Army and PLAF had an estimated 185,000 combat troops, 107,000 support troops, and 45,000 guerillas. Against 1,400 ARVN artillery pieces People's Army/PLAF had 400, against 1,200 ARVN tanks and armoured vehicles People's Army/PLAF had 600, and against 1,400 ARVN aircraft People's Army/PLAF had virtually no air force.
[12]Ibid., p. 535.

were telling Paris of the 'universal' popular support for Ho Chi Minh's government. In 1955 the U.S. Central Intelligence Agency reported to Washington that if the elections agreed to at Geneva were held in 1956 Ho Chi Minh's government would 'almost certainly win'.[13] In spite of such well understood realities, the gradual escalation of Western forces from 1945 and from 1960 forms another parallel. So too does the reluctant acknowledgement by around 1952 and 1968 that further increases in Western troops would not have the desired effect. The recourse to Vietnamisation in 1953 and in 1973 and its failure in both cases has been mentioned. Finally, there was the ultimate betrayal of those who supported both the French and Americans: broken Bao Dai, and helpless Nguyen Van Thieu who, when he needed it most in 1975, did not enjoy the intervention of American air power that President Nixon promised.[14]

At the root of a great double-tragedy was the fact that successive French and American governments juggled an imperial lie. For thirty years Western powers wilfully ignored the national unity and independence which Ho Chi Minh's government first constituted in 1945. Meanwhile, the People's Army never stopped expanding under the pressure of French and American attacks. This was because the Army's ethos, organisation, and strategies integrated old political-military methods with the profound changes that had overcome them in the course of French colonialism. The People's Army was pumped up from a guerrilla platoon of thirty four people in 1944 to the fifth largest standing army in the world with over a million regular troops and three million trained reserves today, because it was the main force of the nation.

[13]Quoted in Ibid., p. 84. For the French report of 1945 see Introduction to Chapter 5 above.

[14]Tonnesson, *1946*, Epilogue offers another discussion of the American repetition of the French experience.

Appendix

The First Vietnamese Maoist Writings

Nguyen Duc Thuy's *Phuong Phap Khang Nhat cua Hong Quan Tau* [The Method of Anti-Japanese Resistance of the Chinese Red Army], Hanoi, January 1938, which I found in the Bibliothèque Nationale in Paris in 1981, is a significant book in the history of the Vietnamese revolution. It is a compilation of twenty one tracts by the major Chinese revolutionary strategists Mao Zedong, Zhou Enlai, Zhu De and others translated into Vietnamese, which sets Mao's idea of guerrilla war out in considerable detail. Along with Nguyen Van Tay's *Lam Sao Cho Tao Thang Nhat?* [What Can the Chinese Do to Defeat the Japanese?], My Tho, March 1938, which summarises various Chinese writings in Vietnamese, and which I also found at the Bibliothèque Nationale, it may be the first book to introduce Mao's ideas of guerilla war to the Vietnamese. (It is also known that Ho Chi Minh arrived in China in 1938 and began to send articles about Chinese methods to Vietnam under the name of P.C. Lin, and although it is unlikely that these reached Vietnam by January I have not been able to find them.) In any case, as argued in Chapter 2, the works by Nguyen Duc Thuy and Nguyen Van Tay, and perhaps others like them, had an impact on the ICP's decision to adopt a Maoist line in 1939.

The following passage is therefore a translation of the section in Nguyen Duc Thuy's compilation of Vietnamese translations, pp. 10–11, entitled 'Guerilla Strategy is the Main Strategy for a War of National Liberation' by Zhou Enlai. It has been selected because it is one which shows that the Vietnamese had a grasp of all Mao's basic ideas on guerilla war by 1938. Capitals and emphasis are in the Vietnamese text.

The essential problem in the Anti-Japanese Resistance is a political problem. Strategy and politics are intimately related to each other. . . . With respect to strategy we must use PROTRACTED WAR (*CHIEN TRANH LAU DAI*), with respect to (individual) campaigns we are in favour of

273

RAPID STRIKES (*DANH GIET THUC MAU LE*), and with respect to tactics we must use MOBILE WAR (*VAN DONG CHIEN*). Why is this so? It is because China has not invaded any country but is only protecting itself and the method of fighting for self protection must be supple to ensure victory. China is inferior to Japan in the military armaments industry therefore it is not able to fight one rash life or death battle with the enemy as soon as the war breaks out. *Our victory must depend on the participation of the masses in the resistance war.* All the people of China are the enemy of Japanese Imperialism, but we must mobilise the masses and organise the masses in time of war. When the war breaks out, perhaps China will be defeated for a short time, but the situation will naturally change day by day. The Chinese Army will have the support of the people, the Japanese Army will be hated by the people. That is the crucial thing which some people still do not understand. Although our method of fighting is mobile war, this does not mean we avoid clashes with the enemy. Our method of carrying out military action is to follow local circumstances, and not to have our actions dictated by the battle because if we do this we will be destroyed easily. We must use small numbers to defeat large numbers of the enemy so that the method of following local circumstances will be most advantageous. On campaigns we use rapid strikes because with them we will be able to diminish the enemy's advantage in modern weapons and cause his aircraft, tanks, and poisonous gasses to have no effect at all. We use the method of rapid strikes to attack so that the enemy has no opportunity to take precautions. We have very timely news of the enemy's actions, the enemy has very slow news (or our actions). We understand the situation clearly and therefore are able to use a more powerful force to defeat an inferior force. The method of using rapid strikes allows us to capture enemy weapons to build up our strength in weapons. After we have attacked the enemy on numerous occassions in this way the enemy will naturally not dare to scatter his forces anymore but will have to keep them concentrated, and in this way we will be able to blockade the enemy and besiege him. This means we have encircled the enemy strategically and caused him to waste his strength and become helpless. At the same time we mobilise and organise the masses around us in order to encircle the enemy, to harass and attack him, to break his lines of communication, and to cause him to lose his strength to defend himself. Gradually, we increase the enemy's difficulties. We attack and destroy his reinforcements so that in his front there will be no way to advance and in his rear there will be no reinforcements. To advance will mean death and to withdraw will be equally dangerous. If the enemy cannot move then he will surely tire, his food will be bad, and his sleep troubled, and as this continues over a protracted period his situation will become increasingly perilous. But the essential condition for this is the mobilisation of the masses. The reason why we call for the establishment of a democratic political foundation is that we want to be victorious over the Japanese. To achieve democracy is to allow the masses to participate in the Anti-Japanese War of Resistance.

Select Bibliography

Bibliographies

Désiré, Commandant Michel, *La Campagne d'Indochine 1945–1954*, 4 Vols., Ministère de la Defense, Etat Major de l'Armée-de Terre, Service Historique, Château de Vincennes, 1971, 1973, 1976, 1977.

Giok Po Oey, *A Checklist of the Vietnamese Holdings of the Wason Collection, Cornell Universitary Libraries, as of June 1971*, Ithaca, New York: Cornell University Southeast Asia Program Data Paper, 1971.

Rageau, Christiane, *Catalogue du Fonds Indochinois de la Bibliothèque Nationale (Vol. 1: Livres vietnamiens imprimés en quoc ngu 1922–1954)*, Paris, Bibliothèque Nationale, 1979.

Ruscio, Alain, *La première guerre d'Indochine (1945–1954), Bibliographie*, Paris: L'Harmattan, 1987.

Primary Sources

1. Archives and Other Sources of Documents

Archives Nationale de France, Section Outre-Mer, Rue Oudinot, Paris. Section, Indochine, Nouveau Fonds.

Le Service Historique de l'Armée de Terre, Château de Vincennes, Paris. Section, Etat Major Interarmées Forces Terrestres.

Bibliothèque Nationale, Paris. Les Fonds Indochinois.

Centre de Hautes Etudes Administratives sur L'Afrique et L'Asie modernes, Rue du Four, Paris. Red Series. This library contains some military reports by French officials during the Franco-Viet Minh War. Most helpful in the Red Series were the following:

Capitaine Le Flahec, *Quelque missions en pays Viet Minh (Souvenirs)*, no date, but deals with the phasing of French troops into northern Vietnam in 1946.

Colonel Charles Lacheroy, *Action Viet Minh et Communiste en Indochine ou une leçon de 'guerre révolutionaire"* 1954.

Commandant Levain, *L'Indochine pendant la deuxième guerre mondiale: Evolution politique*, 1948.

Commandamnt Simon, *Experiences d'action politico-militaire au Centre-Vietnam*, 1957.

Foureau, *Quelques aspects de l'action du Viet Minh sur les minorities du Haut Tonkin*, 1953.

Lieutenant Hanns, *Les forces armées du Viet Minh dans le Viet Nam du Nord*, 1950.

Savani, A., *Notes sur la secte Phat Giao Hoa Hao*, Saigon, 1951.

—— · *Sectes et Groupements Armées du Sud Viet Nam*, 1956.

Cornell University Library, Ithaca, New York. Through the purchase of microfilms I was able to gain access to a number of key works that would otherwise have been unavailable.

Menzies Library, Australian National University, Canberra. The Menzies Library has a useful collection of early French writings on Indochina, and it has a growing collection of recent publications from Hanoi.

2. Official Studies and Documents

Ban Chap Hanh Trung Uong Dang Cong San Viet Nam [Executive Board of the Central Committee of the Communist Party of Vietnam], *Van Kien Dang ve Khang Chien chong Thuc Dan Phap, Tap 1 (1945–1950)* [Party Documents on the Resistance War against the French Colonialists, Volume 1 (1945–1950)], Hanoi: NXB Su That, 1986.

Ban Chap Hanh Dang Bo Dang Cong San Viet Nam Tinh Dong Nai [Executive Board of the Party Branch of the Communist Party of Vietnam in Dong Nai Province], *Dong Nai: 30 Nam Chien Tranh Giai Phong So Thao* [Dong Nai: Draft History of the Thirty Years of Liberation War], Dong Nai Publishing House, 1986.

Ban Nghien Cuu Lich Su Dang [Board for the Historical Study of the Party], *Cuoc Khang Chien chong Thuc Dan Phap va Can Thiep My o Ha Noi* [The Resistance War Against the French Colonialists and the American Interventionists in Hanoi), Hanoi, 1980.

—— · *Lich Su Dang Cong San Viet Nam So Thao, 1920–1954* [Draft History of the Communist Party of Vietnam, 1920–1954], Vol. 1, Hanoi, 1981.

Ban Nghien Cuu Lich Su Quan Doi Thuoc Cuc Chinh Tri [Board for the Historical Study of the Army in the Political Department], *Lich Su Quan Doi Nhan Dan Viet Nam* [History of the People's Army of Vietnam], Hanoi: NXB Quan Doi Nhan Dan, 1974.

Commandement Française En Extreme Orient, Etat Major Interarmées Forces Terrestres, 'Le Viet Minh Utilisant des Japonais', Saigon, 1947. The late Général Salan kindly permitted to read a copy of this document from his personal papers.

Congressional Research Service, *The US Government and the Vietnam War: Executive and Legislative Roles and Relationships, Part I, 1945–1961*, Washington: US Government Printing Office, 1984.

Corps Expéditionnaire d'Extrême Orient, Forces Terrestres Sud Vietnam, Etat Major, 'Historique Sommaire des Grandes Unites de L'Armée Reguilière Viet Minh', Saigon, 1954 (Mimeographed).

Degras, Jane,*The Communist International, 1919–1943*, 3 Vols., New York and London. Oxford University Press,1956–1960.

Exposition Coloniale Internationale de Paris, Commissariat Générale, *Indochine Documents Officiels*, Paris, 1931.

Foreign Languages Publishing House, *The History of the August Revolution*, Hanoi, 1972.

Indochine Française, Section de l'Administration de la Justice, Exposition Coloniale Internationale, Paris, 1931, *La Justice en Indochine*, Hanoi, 1931.

Ngo Si Lien, *Dai Viet Su Ky Toan Thu*, [The complete Annals of Dai Viet], 3 Vols., translated by Cao Huy Giu, Hanoi: NXB Khoa Hoc Xa Hoi, 1972.

NXB Quan Doi Nhan Dan [People's Army Publishing House], *Van Kien Quan Su cua Dang, 1930–1945*, [Military Documents of the Party, 1930–1945], Hanoi, 1968.

NXB Su That [Truth Publishing House], *Cuoc Khang Chien Than Thanh cua Nhan Dan Viet Nam* [The Sacred Resistance War of the Vietnamese People], 4 Vols., Hanoi, 1958–1960. This source is a compilation of newspaper articles, mainly from *Su That* [Truth], *Sinh Hoat Noi Bo* [Inner Life], and *Nhan Dan* [The People], covering the period from 23 September 1945 to July 1954.

Thomas, Major, 'Report on the Deer Mission', in *Hearings before the Committee on Foreign Relations, United States Senate, Ninety Second Congress, Second Session on Causes, Origins, and Reasons of the Viet Nam War*, Washington, May 1972.

Tran Huy Lieu et al., *Tai Lieu Tham Khao Lich Su Cach Mang Can Dai Viet Nam* [Research Documents on the History of Vietnam's Modern Revolution], 12 Vols., Hanoi: Van Su Dia, 1955–1958.

Vien Su Hoc [Board for Historical Studies], *Tai Lieu Tham Khao Cach Mang Thang Tam (Tong Khoi Nghia o Hanoi va Cac Dia Phuong)* [Research Documents on the August Revolution (in the General Uprising in Hanoi and Other Regions], 2 Vols., Hanoi: NXB Su Hoc, 1960.

3. Vietnamese Military Manuals

Ban Bien Tap Bo Chinh Tri Khu Giai Phong Xuat Ban [Published by the Editorial Committee of the Political Department in the Liberated Zone], *Cong Tac Khang Nhat Hau Phuong: Van Dap* [Anti-Japanese Resistance Work in Rear Areas: Questions and Answers]. Viet Bac, 1945.

Muc Dich va Phuong Phap Huan Luyen [The Aims and Methods of Training], Viet Bac, 1945.

Document Viet Minh Traduit et Diffusé par le Deuxième Bureau de L'Etat

Major des Forces Terrastres Nord Vietnam, *Règlement d'Infantrie Viet Minh: Le Batallion et la Compagnie d'Infantrie dans l'attaque d'une Position Fortifée, 26 Septembre 1953*, Hanoi,1954.

Notes sur l'Artillerie Viet Minh, 9 Novembre 1950: Tradúction d'une brochure Viet Minh reproduisant une étude Chinoise sur l'emploi de l'Artillerie, Hanoi, 1954.

Phep Chien Dau o Nhung Noi Dia Hinh Dac Biet [The Method of Combat in Various Special Kinds of Terrain], no place (Viet Bac?), no date (1945?).

Lien Khu 3, [Inter-Zone 3], *Dich Van: Mot Niem Vu Chien Luoc* [Proselytising the Enemy: A Strategic Responsibility], 1950.

Quan Doi Quoc Gia Viet Nam [National Army of Vietnam], *Tu Cung Tu Cap* [Self Sufficiency], Lien Khu Viet Bac, 1949.

Reinert, M., *Manoeuvre Traduit en Quoc Ngu, (Extrait du décret du 25 Août 1915)*, Hanoi, 1916.

—— · *Service en Campagne, Traduit en Quoc Ngu, (Extrait du décret 2 Septembre 1913)*, Hanoi, 1916.

Tong Bo Viet Minh Xuat Ban [Published by the Central Committee of the Viet Minh), *Bac Son Khoi Nghia* [The Bac Son Uprising], fourth edition, 1945. This text may also be read as an account of the Bac Son uprising. However, because of the political and military lessons it draws and its generally didactic nature I have classified it as a military manual.

Viet Nam Doc Lap Dong Minh [Vietnam Independence League], *Chinh Tri Vien trong Quan Doi* [Political Cadres in the Army], Hanoi, 1945.

Viet Nam Giai Phong Quan [Vietnam Liberation Army], *Chien Thuat Co Ban* [Basic Tactics], Khu Giai Phong, September 1945.

—— · *Chuong Trinh Huan Luyen (Can Bo Quan Su-Tieu Doi Truong)* [A Training Program (Military Cadres-Squad Commanders)], Viet Bac, 1945.

—— · *Phan Tich Dong Tac Quan Su* [An Analysis of Military Work], Hanoi: Le Van Tan, September l945.

Vien Su Hoc [Historical Institute], *Binh Thu Yeu Luoc* [The Art ofWar], Hanoi, 1977.

4. Vietnamese Political and Military Writings

Dang Tri Dung, 'Les Mouvements Strategiques', in *Traduction de deux articles extraits de la publication Viet Minh intitulé: Quan Chinh Tap San*, Etat Major des F.T.N.V., Hanoi, 1950.

Ho Chi Minh, *Ve Dau Tranh Vu Trang va Luc Luong Vu Trang Nhan Dan* [On Armed Struggle and People's Armed Forces], Quan Doi Nhan Dan, 1970.

—— · *Ve Quan Su* [On the Military Question], Hanoi: Su That, 1975.

—— · *Tuyen Tap* [Collected Works], Vol. 1, Hanoi: Su That, 1980.

—— · *Duong Cach Mang* [The Road to Revolutioin], Canton, 1927, in *Tuyen Tap*, Vol. 1, Hanoi: Su That, 1980, pp.229–300.

Hoang Van Su, *Dong Duong Du Bi Chien Tranh* [Indochina Prepares for War], Hanoi, 1938.

Le Quang Hoa, *Quan Su Dia Phuong: Su Hinh Thanh va Phat Trien* [The

Regional Militia: Their Form and Development], Hanoi: Quan Doi Nhan Dan, 1978.

Nguyen Duc Thuy, *Phuong Phap Khang Nhat cua Hong Quan Tau* [The Method of Anti-Japanese Resistance of the Chinese Red Army], Hanoi, January 1938.

Nguyen Van Tay, *Lam sao cho Tau Thang Nhat* [How can the Chinese be Victorious over the Japanese], My Tho, February 1938.

Nguyen Chi Thanh, *Nhung Bai Chon Loc ve Quan Su* [Selected Military Writings], Hanoi: Quan Doi Nhan Dan, 1977.

Nguyen Vy, *Cai Hoa Nhat Ban* [The Japanese Peril], Hanoi, 1938.

——· *Ke Thu la Nhat Ban* [The Enemy is Japan], Hanoi, 1938.

Sieu Hai, *Hoa Chien Tranh voi Van De Phong Thu Dong Duong* [The Peril of War and the Problem of Defending Indochina], Vinh, 1938.

Tran Dai Nghia, 'Les méthodes de la production d'armement', in *Traduction de deux articles extraits de la publication Viet Minh intitulée: Quan Chinh Tap San*, Etat Major des F.T.N.V., Hanoi, 1950.

Tran Van Tra, *Nhung Chang Duong Lich Su cua B2, Thanh Dong, Ket Thuc Cuoc Chien Tranh 30 Nam* [The Stages on the Historical Path of B2, Brass Wall of the Country: The End of the Thirty Year War], Vol. 5, Ho Chi Minh City: Van Nghe, 1982.

Tri Binh,*Van De Thu Dong Duong* [The Problem of Defending Indochina], Saigon, 1939.

Truong Chinh, *Cach Mang Thang Tam* [The August Revolution], fifth edition Hanoi 1955. This work was originally published in Hanoi in September 1946.

——· *Khang Chien Nhat Dinh Thang Loi* [The Resistance Will Win], Bac Bo, September 1947.

——· *Selected Writings*, Hanoi: Foreign Languages Publishing House, 1977 contains English translations of both *The August Revolution* and *The Resistance Will Win*.

Van Dinh (Vo Nguyen Giap), *Con Duong Chinh: Van De Dan Toc Giai Phong o Dong Duong* [The Proper Path: The Question of National Liberation in Indochina], Hanoi, 1939.

Van Tien Dung, *Chien Tranh Nhan Dan Quoc Phong Toan Dan* [People's War: The Entire People Defend the Country], 2 Vols., Hanoi: Quan Doi Nhan Dan, 1978–1979.

Vo Nguyen Giap, *Muon Hieu Ro Tinh Hinh Quan Su o Tau* [Understanding Clearly the Military Situation in China], Hanoi: 1939.

——· *Nhung Khinh Nghiem Lon cua Dang ve Lanh Dao Dau Tranh Vu Trang va Xay Xung Luc Luong Vu Trang Cach Mang* [Major Experiences of the Party in Leading Armed Struggle and Building Revolutionary Armed Forces], Hanoi, 1961.

——· *Tu Nhan Dan ma Ra* [Born of the People], Hanoi, 1964.

——· *People's War, People's Army*, Hanoi: Foreign Languages Publishing House, 1961. This famous essay was first published in Vietnamese in 1959 on the occasion of the fifteenth anniversary of the People's Army.

——· *The Military Art of People's War: Selected Writings of General Vo Nguyen Giap*, edited with an introduction by Russell Stetler, New York and London: Monthly Review Press, 1970.

——· *Vi Tri Chien Luoc cua Chien Tranh Nhan Dan o Dia Phuong va cua Luc Luong Vu Trang Dia Phuong* [The Strategic Position of People's War in the Regions and of Regional Armed Forces], Hanoi: Quan Doi Nhan Dan, 1972.

——· *Ve Suc Manh Tong Hop cua Cach Mang Viet Nam* [On the United Strength of the Vietnamese Revolution], Hanoi: Su That, 1978.

——· *Dien Bien Phu* [i.e. the battle], Hanoi: Quan Doi Nhan Dan, 1979.

5. Memoirs and Biographies

Bao Dai, *Le Dragon d'Annam*, Paris: Plon, 1980.

Boyer de Latour, Pierre, *De l'Indochina à l'Algérie: Le Martyre de l'Armeé française*, Paris: Les Presses du Mail, 1962.

Bui Cong Trung, Van Tien Dung, Xuan Thuy, and others, *Len Duong Thang Loi* [Onwards to Victory], Hanoi: Van Hoc, 1960.

——· and others, *Nguoi Truoc Nga Nguoi Sau Tien* [The Front Rank Falls, the Rear Advances], Hanoi: Van Hoc, 1960.

Catroux, Général, *Deux actes du drame indochinois*, Paris: Plon, 1959.

Cao Van Luan, *Ben Giong Lich Su: Hoi Ky 1940–1965* [On the River of History: Memoirs 1940–1965], Glendale, California: Dai Nam, 1976.

Chu Van Tan, 'With Uncle Ho', *Vietnamese Studies*, No. 15, Hanoi, 1968.

——· *Reminiscences on the Army for National Salvation:* Memoirs of General Chu Van Tan, translated by Mai Elliot, Data Paper Number 97, Southeast Asia Program, Cornell University, September 1974. The original title is *Ky niem cuu quoc quan: hoy ky*, Hanoi: NXB Quan Doi Nhan Dan, in several editions.

Dang Kim Giang, 'Truong quan chinh trong nha tu Son La' [A Military-Political School in Son La Prison], in Bui Cong Trung et al., *Nguoi Truoc* (see above).

D'Argenlieu, Thierry, *Chronique d'Indochine 1945–1947*, Paris: Albin Michel, 1885.

Decoux, Amiral, *A la barre de l'Indochine*, Paris: Plon, 1949.

Ducoroy, Maurice, *Ma trahison en Indochine*, Paris: Editions Internationales, 1949.

Fenn, Charles, *Ho Chi Minh: A Biographical Introduction*, London, 1973.

Foreign Languages Publishing House, *In the Enemy's Net: Memoirs from the Revolution*, (contains memoirs of Nguyen Duy Trinh, Nguyen Tao, Truong Sinh and others), Hanoi, 1962.

——· *A Heroic People: Memoirs from the Revolution*, (contains memoirs of Nguyen Luong Bang, Vo Nguyen Giap, Hoang Quoc Viet and others), Hanoi. 1965.

——· *Our President Ho Chi Minh*, Hanoi, 1970.

Gaudron, Max, *Legionnaire au Nord-Tonkin*, Paris: Copernic, 1980.

Ha Thi Que, 'Rung Yen The' [The Yen The Forest], in Le Thiet Hung et al., *Rung Yen The*, Hanoi: NXB Quan Doi Nhan Dan, 1962.

Ho Nam, *Ky Niem Nghe An Bao Dong* [The Anniversary of the Nghe An Violence], no place, 1 August 1932. This hand written memoir is in the

Library of Congress in Washington.

Hoang Van Hoan, *Giot Nuoc trong Bien Ca: Hoi Ky Cach Mang* [A Drop of Water in the Ocean], Peking: NXB Tin Viet Nam, 1986.

Huyen, N. Khac, *Vision Accomplished? The Enigma of Ho Chi Minh*, New York, London: Collier Macmillan, 1971.

Huynh Van Nghe, 'Ra Mat Tran' [Off to the Battle Front), in Le Thiet Hung et al, *Rung Yen The* [The Yen The Forest], Hanoi: NXB Quan Doi Nhan Dan, 1962.

Lacouture, Jean, *Ho Chi Minh* Paris: Seuil, 1977.

Le Quang, Gerard, *Giap: Ou la guerre du peuple*, Paris: Denoel, 1973.

Le Quang Ba, 'Reminiscences of Underground Revolutionary Work', *Vietnamese Studies*, No. 15, Hanoi, 1968.

Leroy, Jean, *Un homme dans la rizière*, 1955.

Le Thiet Hung et al., *Rung Yen The* [The Yen the Forest], Hanoi: NXB Quan Doi Nhan Dan, 1962.

Le Tien Giang, *Cong Giao Khang Chien Nam Bo 1945–1954: Hoi Ky* [Catholic Resistance in Nam Bo 1945–1954: Memoirs], Saigon, 1972.

Le Thanh Nghi, et al., *Con Duong Cach Mang: Tap Hoi Ky Cach Mang ve Dong Chi Hoang Van Thu, Le Thanh Nghi, Nguyen Duy Trinh, Tran Do* [The Revolutionary Road: Revolutionary Memoirs of Comrades Hoang Van Thu, Le Thanh Nghi, Nguyen Duy Trinh, Tran Do], Hanoi: Thanh Nien, 1970.

Le Tung Son, *Nhat Ky Mot Chang Duong* [Diary: One Stretch of Road], Hanoi: Van Hoc, 1978.

Navarre, Henri, *Agonie de l'Indochine 1953–54*, Paris: Plon, 1956.

Ngo Van Chieu, *Journal d'un combattant Viet Minh, translated by Jacques Despuech*, Paris: Seuil, 1955.

Nguyen Tao, *Chung Toi Vuot Nguc* [We escape from Prison], Hanoi: Van Hoc, 1977.

Nhuong Tong, *Nguyen Thai Hoc 1902–1930*, Saigon: Tan Viet, 1949.

Patti, A., *Why Viet Nam? Prelude to America's Albatross*, University of California Press, 1980.

Phan Boi Chau, *Phan Boi Chau Nien Bieu* [Memoirs of Phan Boi Chau], Hanoi: Van Su Dia, 1957. See also 'Mémoires', Georges Boudarel, translator, *France-Asie*, 3/4 trim., 1968.

——. *Nguc Trung Thu* [Prison Diary], Saigon: Tan Viet, 1950.

Pham Kiet, *Tu Nui Rung Ba To* [From the Ba To Forests], Hanoi: Quan Doi Nhan Dan, 1977.

Sabattier, Général, *Le destin de l'Indochine: Souvenirs et documents 1941–1951*, Paris, 1952.

Sainteny, Jean, *Histoire d'un paix manquée*, Paris: Fayard, 1967.

Salan, Raoul, *Mémoires Fin d'un Empire: Le Viet Minh mon adversaire, Octobre 1946–Octobre 1954*, Paris, 1971.

Tran Do, 'Nhung Mau Truyen...Sung' [Some Anecdotes about . . . Guns], in Bui Cong Trung et al., *Len Duong Thang Loi* [Onwards to Victory], Hanoi: Van Hoc, 1960.

——. *Récits sur Dien Bien Phu*, Hanoi: Editions En Langues Etrangères, 1962.

Tran Huong Nam (ghi), *Khong Con Duong nao khac: Hoi Ky cua Ba*

Nguyen Thi Dinh [No Other Way: The Memoirs of Madam Nguyen Thi Dinh], Hanoi, 1968.

Tran Trong Kim, *Mot Con Gio Bui* [A Puff of Dust] Saigon: Vinh Son, 1969.

Tung Lam, *Cuoc Doi Cach Mang Cuong De* [The Revolutionary Life of Cuong De], Saigon: Ton That Le, 1957.

Vo Nguyen Giap, *Unforgettable Days*, Second Edition, Hanoi: Foreign Languages Publishing House, 1978.

Vuong Thua Vu, *Truong Thanh trong Chien Dau* [Coming of Age in War], Hanoi: NXB Quan Doi Nhan Dan, 1979.

All Other Books, Theses, Articles

1. Vietnamese Language Sources

Ban Tuyen Giao va Ty Thong Tin Van Hoa [Propaganda and Education Office and News Service], *Chien Thang Rach Gam-Xoai Mut (20–1–1785)* [The Rach Gam-Xoai Mut Victory] Tien Giang, 1977.

Bao Hung, *Nhat Nga Chien Tranh* [The Russo-Japanese War], Hanoi, 1927.

Bui Dinh Thanh, 'Dau Tranh Vu Trang trong Cach Mang Thang Tam' Armed Struggle in the August Revolution], *NCLS*, No. 17, August 1960.

Cao Van Luong, Pham Quang Toan, Quynh Cu, *Tim Hieu Phong Trao Dong Khoi o Mien Nam Viet Nam* [An Investigation into the Partial Uprisings in the Southern Area of Viet Nam], Hanoi: NXB Khoa Hoc Xa Hoi, 1981.

Chiem-Te, 'Cach Mang Thang Tam, Mot Bo Phan cua Cach Mang The Gioi [The August Revolution, A Part of the World Revolution], *NCLS*, No. 18, September 1960.

Chu Thien (Hoang Minh Giam) *Le Thai To* [i.e. the founder of the Le dynasty], Hanoi, 1940.

——· *Chinh Tri Ho Quy Ly* [The Politics of Ho Quy Ly], Hanoi, 1945.

Chu Thien, 'Ve Nhung Cuoc Nong Dan Khoi Nghia Trieu Nguyen' [On Righteous Peasant Uprisings against the Nguyen Dynasty], *NCLS*, 1960, No. 19.

Dang Huy Van, 'Cuoc Dau Tranh giua Phai "Chu Chien" va Nhung Phai "Chu Hoa" trong Cuoc Khang Chien Chong Phap o Cuoi The Ky XIX' [The Struggle Between the "War Faction" and the "Peace Factions" in the Resistance War Against the French at the End of the Nineteenth Century], *NCLS*, No. 94, 1962.

——· and Chuong Thau, *Nhung De Nghi Cai Cach cua Nguyen Truong To Cuoi They Ky XIX* [The Reformist Proposals of Nguyen Truong To at the End of the Nineteenth Century], Hanoi: Giao Duc, 1961.

Dang Kim Giang,'Truong Quan Chinh trong Nha Tu Son La' [A Military-Political School in Son La Prison] in Bui cong Trung et al., *Nguoi Truoc Nga Nguoi Sau Tien* [The Front Rank Falls the Rear Advances], Hanoi: Van Hoc, 1960.

Dang Ngoc Tot et al., *Suc Song cua Dan Viet Nam* [The Life Force of the Vietnamese People], Hanoi, 1944.

Dang Thuc Lieng, *Le Van Duyet* [i.e. the nineteenth century general], Hanoi, 1934.

Dao Dang Vy, *Nguyen Tri Phuong* [i.e. the nineteenth century general], Hanoi, 1974.

Dao Duy Anh, *Thuc Dan Lich Su* [A History of Colonialism], Hue, 1928.

——· *Viet Nam Van Hoa Su Cuong* [An Outline History of Vietnamese Culture], Hue, 1938.

Dao Trinh Nhat, *Viet Nam Tay Thuoc Su* [A History of Vietnam Under the French], Vol. 1, Cho Lon, 1937.

——· *Viet Su Giai Thoai* [Anecdotes from Vietnamese History], Hanoi, 1943.

——· *Phan Dinh Phung* [i.e. the nineteenth century mandarin and resistance leader], Saigon, 1957.

Diep Van Ky, *Su Cach Mang* [A History of Revolutions], Saigon, 1927.

Doan Van Phong, (dich), *Baden Powell Thi To Chu Nghia Huong Dao* [Baden Powell the Father of Boy Scouting], Hue, 1935.

Hai Trieu, *Chu Nghia Max-Xit Pho Thong* [Popularising Marxism], Hue, 1938.

Ho Hai, 'Moy Vai Y Kien ve Moi Quan He giua Nong Thon va Thanh Thi Nuoc Ta trong Thoi Ky 1939–1945' [A Few Ideas on the Relationship between the Countryside and the Cities in the Period 1939–1945], *NCLS*, No. 50, July 1963.

Ho Thanh, *Duoi Banh Xe Thiet Giap* [Under the Wheels of an Armoured Car] Hanoi: Tien Hoa, 1950.

Hoa Bang (Hoang Thuc Tram), *Quang Trung 1778–1792* [Quang Trung was the reign name of Nguyen Hue], Hanoi, 1944.

Hoang Cao Khai, *Viet Nam Nhan Dan Than Giam* [Some Great figures in Vietnamese History], parallel French and Vietnamese texts, Hanoi, 1915.

Hoang Du, *Tom Tat Sach Tu Ban Luan* [A Summary of Capital, i.e.—the work by Karl Marx], Saigon, 1937.

Hoang Minh, *Tim Hieu ve To Tien Ta Danh Giac* [An Investigation into the Wars of Our Ancestors], Hanoi: NXB Quan Doi Nhan Dan, 1977.

Hoang Nhat Tan, *Xo Viet Nghe-Tinh* [The Nghe-Tinh Soviets], Hanoi, 1962.

Hoang Quang Khanh, Le Hong, Hoang Ngoc La, *Can Cu Dia Viet Bac trong Cuoc Cach Mang Thang 8–1945* [The Viet Bac Base Area in the August 1945 Revolution], NXB Viet Bac, 1976.

Hoang Van Dao, *Viet Nam Quoc Dan Dang, Lich Su Dau Tranh Can Dai, 1927–1954* [The Vietnamese Nationalist Party, A History of its Modern Struggle, 1927–1954], Saigon: Nguyen Hoa Hiep, 1965.

Hoang Xuan Han, *La Son Phu Tu* [i.e. the eighteenth century figure who supported the Tay Son], Paris: Minh Tan, 1952.

Hoai Tan, *Chien Cong Oanh Liet cua Dong Bao Nam Bo* [The Glorious Resistance of our Compatriots in Nam Bo], Hanoi, November 1945.

——· *Trung Bo Khang Chien* [The Resistance War in Trung Bo], Hanoi, 1946.

Hoc Tu, *Nhung Ngay Dau cua Mat Tran Nam Bo* [The First Days of the Battle of the Nam Bo Front], Hanoi, 1945.

Hoi Van Hoa Cuu Quoc Viet Nam [Viet Nam National Salvation Cultural

Organisation], *Quyen va Bon Phan Lam Dan* [The Rights and Duties of a Citizen], Hanoi, 1945.

——· *Hien Phap la gi?* [What is a Constitution?], Hanoi, 1945.

Hong Ky,*Cach Mang Vo San* [The Proletarian Revolution], Saigon, 1937.

Kim Thach, *Quoc Te Cong San De Tam trong Cuoc Trung-Nhat Chien Tranh*, [The Third International in the Sino-Japanese War], Hanoi, 1937.

Lam Chinh Thien va Hai Bang, *Phong Than Vu Thuat* [The Art of Self Defence], Hanoi, 1941.

Le Dong va Nguyen Huy, *Nhut Hoa Chien Tranh va Su Hoat Dong cua To Chuc ve Gian Diep Nhut* [The Sino-Japanese War and the Activities of the Japanese Spy Network], Saigon, 1927.

Le Manh Trinh, *Cuoc Van Dong Cuu Quoc cua Viet Kieu o Thai Lan* [The National Salvation Activities of the Vietnamese Community in Thailand], Hanoi, 1961.

Le Quoc Su, 'Kheo Ket Hop Cac Hinh Thuc Dau Tranh Chinh Tri va Vu Trang trong Cach Mang Thang Tam' [The Skilful Combination of Political and Military Forms of Struggle in the August Revolution], *NCLS*, No. 50, May 1963.

Le Thi, 'May van de Phuong Phap Luan cua Tac Pham "Duong Kach Menh" cua Ho Chu Tich' [On Some Methodological Issues of the "The Road to Revolution" by President Ho], *Triet Hoc* 1, No. 28, March 1980.

Le Van Nho, *Ve Linh Mo va May Thay Sang Phap Quoc* [On Recruiting Soldiers and Some Dignatories Going to France], Saigon, 1917.

Luong Duc Thiep, *Xa Hoi Viet Nam* [Vietnamese Society], Saigon: Hoa Tien, 1971. This book was originally published in Hanoi in 1944.

Mai Khac Ung et al, *Di Tich Cach Mang Viet Nam, 1930–1945* [Vestiges of The Vietnamese Revolution, 1930–1945], Hanoi, 1976.

M.N., 'May Net Lon ve Phong Trao Cong Nhan Sai-Gon tu 1945 den 1954' [An Outline of the Workers Movement in Saigon from 1945 to 1954], *NCLS*, no, 95, February 1967.

Nam Cao, *Nam Anh Hang Thit* [Five in a Butcher's Shop], Hanoi: Hoi Van Hoa Cuu Quoc Viet Nam, 1945.

Nghiem Ke To, *Viet Nam Mau Lua* [Vietnam Blood and Fire], Saigon: Mai Linh, 1954.

Nghien Cuu Lich Su Quan Su [Researches into Military History], *NCLS*, No. 17, July 1985, devotes its entire space to this subject. Deals mainly with the period 1965–1975.

Ngo Tien Canh, *Mot Chuong Trinh Tiep Te* [A Program of Resupply], Hanoi, 1945.

Ngo Tien Chat, 'Ve Nhung Cuoc Dau Tranh Vu Trang cua Nhan Dan Cac Dan Toc Tinh Hoa Binh trong Cuoc Khang Chien Chong Phap (1945–1954)' [On the Armed Struggle of the Peoples of in Hoa Binh Province in the Anti-French Resistance War (1945–1954)], *NCLS*, No. 109, April 1968.

Ngo Van Trien, *Lich Su Nam Tien cua Dan Toc Ta* [A History of the Southern Advance of Our People], Hanoi, 1929.

Nguyen Binh Khiem, *Sam Ky* [Prophesies], Hanoi, 1945.

Nguyen Cong Binh, 'Ban ve Tinh Chat Cuoc Cach Mang Thang Tam' [On the Nature of the August Revolution], *NCLS*, No. 17, August 1960.

------· 'Khoi Dau va Ket Thuc cua Cach Mang Thang Tam' [The Beginning and End of the August Revolution], *NCLS*, No. 51, June 1963.

Nguyen Hoai, 'Ve Cong Tac Binh Van trong Thoi Ky Khang Chien chong Phap, 1945–1954' [About the Work of Proselytizing (Enemy) Soldiers in the Period of the Resistance War Against the French], *NCLS*, No. 97, April 1967.

Nguyen Hong, *Sam Vang Trung-Nhat* [The Sino-Japanese Conflict], Hanoi, 1938.

Nguyen Hu Dang va Nguyen Dinh Thi, *Mot Nen Van Hoa Moi* [A Foundation for New Culture], Hanoi, June 1945.

Nguyen Huu Hop, 'Buoc Dau Tim Hieu ve Co Cau cua Giai Cap Cong Nhan Viet Nam Thoi Ky Khang Chien Chong Phap (1945–1954)' [An Initial Investigation into the Structure of the Vietnamese Working Class in the Period of the Anti-French Resistance War (1945–1954)], *NCLS*, No. 3, May-June 1979.

Nguyen Huu Tao, *Robert Baden Powell Kim Chi Nam Huynh-Truong Huong Dao* (Robert Baden Powell, Pathfinder of the Boy Scouting Brotherhood), Hanoi, 1942.

Nguyen Huy Tuong, *Tuyen Tap* [Collected Works], Hanoi: Tac Pham Moi, 1978.

Nguyen Khanh Toan, *Van De Dan Toc trong Cach Mang Vo San* [The National Question in the Proletarian Revolution], Hanoi: Su That, 1962.

Nguyen Lan , *Nguyen Truong To* [i.e. the nineteenth century reformer], Hanoi, July 1942. Second edition.

Nguyen Luong Bich va Pham Ngoc Phung, *Tim Hieu Thien Tai Quan Su cua Nguyen Hue* [An Investigation of the Military Genius of Nguyen Hue], Hanoi: Quan Doi Nhan Dan, 1971.

Nguyen Manh Bong va Mai Dang De, *Nhat Hoa Xung Dot Thuc Luc* [A Factual Record of the Sino-Japanese War], Hanoi, 1959.

Nguyen Nghia, 'Cong Cuoc Hop Nhat Cac To Chuc Cong San Dau Tien o Viet Nam va Vai Tro cua Dong Chi Nguyen Ai Quoc' [The Unification of the First Communist Organisations in Vietnam and the Role of Comrade Nguyen Ai Quoc], *NCLS*, No. 59, February, 1965.

Nguyen Quang Ngoc va Phan Dai Doan, 'Can Cu Dia Buoi Dau cua Cuoc Khoi Nghia Tay Son' [The First Base of the Righteous Tay Son Uprising], *NCLS*, No. 1, January/February, 1979.

Nguyen Te My, *Ly Thuong Kiet* [i.e. the eleventh century general], Hanoi, 1944.

Nguyen The Anh, *Viet Nam duoi Thoi Phap Do Ho* [Vietnam Under French Domination], Saigon: Lua Thieng, 1970.

Nguyen Thuong Huyen, *Cach Menh* [Revolution], Saigon?, 1925.

Nguyen Trong Con, 'Vai Net ve Phong Trao Diet Giac Dot o Viet Nam trong 5 Nam Dau Khang Chien Chong Phap (1945–50)' [A Few Lines on the Movement to Wipe Out Illiteracy in Vietnam in the First 5 Years of the Resistance War against the French (1945–1950)], *NCLS*, No. 3, May-June 1979.

Nguyen Tuong Phuong, *Luoc Khao Binh Che Viet Nam qua Cac Thoi Dai* [A

Short Examination of Vietnam's Military System over the Centuries], Hanoi, 1950.

Nguyen Van An va Trinh Nhu Luan, *Giai Phong va Doc Lap* [Freedom and Independence], Hanoi, 1945.

Nguyen Van Mai, *Phong Trao Thanh Nien Tien Phong* [The Advance Youth Guard Movement], Saigon, 1947.

NXB Quan Doi Nhan Dan [The People's Army Publishing House], *Anh Hung Luc Luong Nhan Dan* [Heroes of the People's Forces], 4 Vols., Hanoi, 1979–1982.

Pham Van Son, *Che Do Phap Thuoc tai Viet Nam* [The French Colonial Regime in Vietnam], Saigon, 1972.

——· *Viet Su Tan Bien* [A Modern History of Vietnam], 7 Vols., Saigon, 1968–1972.

Pham Xuan Nam, 'Ve Nhung Nguyen Nhan Phat Sinh Cuoc Chien Tranh The Gioi Thu Hai (Xet theo nhan dinh cua nhung nguoi cong san Viet Nam luc do)' [On the Causes of the Outbreak of the Second World War (As Understood by Vietnamese Communists at theTime)], *NCLS*, No. 5, September-October, 1979.

Phan Boi Chau, *Viet Nam Vong Quoc Su* [A History of the Loss of the Country Viet Nam], translated by Chu Thien and Chuong Than, Hanoi: Van Su Dia, 1957. For another *quoc ngu* edition with a copy of the original Chinese language text see *Dai Hoc Van Khoa* [Journal of the Faculty of Letters], 1959–1960 edition, Saigon 1961.

——· *Trung Quang Tam Su* [The Secret History of Trung Quang], translated by Nguyen Van Bach, Hanoi: Van Hoc, 1971.

Phan Huy Le, 'Chien Thang Ngoc Hoi Dong Da Ngay Tet Ky Dau tuc ngay 30–1–1759]', *NCLS*, No. 154, January/February, 1974.

Phan Huy Le va Phan Dai Doan, *Khoi Nghia Lam Son* [The Righteous Lam Son Uprising], Hanoi: Khoa Hoc Xa Hoi, 1977.

Phan Huy Thiep va Trinh Vuong Hong, 'Buoc Dau Tim Hieu mot so Van De ve Su Chi Dao Nghe Thuat Quan Su cua Dang trong Chien Dich Bien Gioi Thu Dong 1950' [An Initial Investigation of a number of Questions about the Party's Guidance of Military Affairs in the Border Campaign in the Autumn and Winter of 1950], *NCLS*, No. 2, 1980.

Phan Khoang, *Viet Su Xu: Cuoc Nam Tien cua Dan Toc Viet Nam* [The Southern Advance of the Vietnamese People], Saigon, no date (1960?).

——· *Viet Nam Phap Thuoc Su* [A History of Vietnam under the French], Saigon, 1961.

Phan Ngoc Lien, 'Tim Hieu ve Cong Tac Van Dong Giao Duc Quan Chung cua Ho Chu Tich trong Thoi Gian Nguoi o Pac Bo' [An Investigation of President Ho's Mass Mobilisation and Education Work in the Period he was at Pac Bo], *NCLS*, No. 14, 1975.

Phan Quang, 'Khoi Nghia Le Duy Luong' [Le Duy Luong's Righteous Uprising] *NCLS*, No. 5, 1985.

Phan Tran Chuc, *Le Hoan*, Hanoi, 1935.

Phan Van Hum, *Bien Chung Phap Pho Thong* [A popular Exposition of The Dialectic], Chop Lon, 1936.

Tam Vu, 'Chu Nghia Quoc Te Vo San, Mot trong Nhung Dong Luc Tinh

Than cua Cach Mang Viet Nam tu sau Chien Tranh The Gioi Lan Thu
Nhat den Thang 8–1945' [Proletarian Internationalism, One of the Spiritual Forces of the Vietnamese Revolution from after the First World War
to August 1945], *NCLS*, No. 82, March-April 1979.

To Minh Trung, 'Kheo Ket Hop Cac Hinh Thuc Dau Tranh Chinh Tri va Vu
Trang trong Cach Mang Thang Tam' [The Skilfull Combination of Political
and Military Forms of Struggle in the August Revolution], *NCLS*, No.
153, August 1963.

Tran Giang, 'Cuoc Khoi Nghia Nam Ky' [The Nam Ky Uprising]. *NCLS*,
No. 5, September-October 1979.

Tran Huu Do, *De Quoc Chu Nghia* [Imperialism], Saigon, 1937.

Tran Huu Ta, 'Doc Hoi Ky Cach Mang, Nghi ve Ve Dep cua Nguoi Chien Si
Cong San Viet Nam' [Reading Revolutionary Memoirs and Thinking of
the Beautiful Appearance of Vietnamese Communist Militants], *Tap Chi
Van Hoc*, 2, 1977.

Tran Huy Lieu, translator, Luong Khai Sieu, *Guong Phuc Quoc* [A Mirror
for Restoring the Country], Saigon, 1928.

——· *Nghia Lo Khoi Nghia* [The Nghia Lo Uprising], Hanoi: Hoi Van Hoa
Cuu Quoc,l 1946.

——· 'Tuoc An Kiem cua Hoang De Bao Dai' (Dispossessing Emperor Bao
Dai of the Seal and Sword), *NCLS*, No. 18, September 1960.

——· *Lich Su Tam Muoi Nam chong Phap* [A History of Eighty Years
Struggle Against the French], 3 Vols., Hanoi: Van Su Dia, 1957–61.

Tran Luc, *May Kinh Nghiem Trung Quoc ma Chung Ta Nen Hoc* [Some
Chinese Experiences that We Must Study], Hanoi: NXB Su That, 1958.

Tran Tan Quoc, *Saigon, September 45*, Saigon: Viet Thanh, 1947.

Tran Trong Kim, *Viet Nam Su Luoc* [A Short History of Viet Nam], 2 Vols.,
Saigon, 1971 reprint of the first 1928 edition.

Tran Van Giau, *Giai Cap Cong Nhan Viet Nam* [The Vietnamese Working
Class], 3 Vols., Hanoi: Vien Su Hoc, 1962–1963.

——· *Su Phat Trien cua Tu Tuong o Viet Nam tu The Ky XIX den Cach Mang
Thang Tam* [The Development of Ideas in Vietnam from the Nineteenth
Century to the August Revolution], 3 Vols., Hanoi: Khoa Hoc Xa Hoi,
1973 and 1975. To my knowledge the third volume has not yet been
published.

Tran Van Mai, *Ai Gay Nen Toi?* [Who Committed This Crime], Saigon,
1956.

Tran Van Thao, *Thanh Nien Chien Si Cong Giao* [Catholic Youth Militants],
Hai Phong, 1940.

Trung Chinh, 'Thu Tim Xem Ho Chu Tich Tiep Thu Chu Nghia Le Nin va
Truyen Ba vao Viet Nam nhu the nao' [How did President Ho Receive
Leninism and Propagate it in Vietnam), *NCLS*, No. 132, May/June 1976.

Truong Chinh, 'Mot so Van De ve Cach Mang Thang Tam' [A Number of
Questions about the August Revolution], *Hoc Tap*, No. 92, September,
1963.

Van Hoc, *Hop Tuyen Tho Van Yeu Nuoc Nua Sau The Key XIX (1858–1900)*
[Collected Patriotic Poetry of the Second Half of the Nineteenth Century
(1858–1900)], Hanoi: NXB Van Hoc, 1970.

────· *Hop Tuyen Tho Van Yeu Nuoc va Cach Mang Dau The Ky XX (1900–1930)* [Collected Patriotic and Revolutionary Poetry at the Beginning of the Twentieth Century], Hanoi: NXB Van Hoc, 1972.

Van Tao et al., *Lich Su Cach Mang Thang Tam* [History of the August Revolution], Hanoi: Su Hoc, 1960.

────· 'Mot Vai Nhan Dinh ve Qua Trinh Phat Trien cua Luc Luong Vu Trang Cach Mang Viet Nam, Vai Tro va Tinh Chat cua No trong Giai Doan Gianh Chinh Quyen Cach Mang' [Some Observations on the Process of Developing the Armed Forces of the Vietnamese Revolution, their Role and Character in the Period of Seizing Revolutionary Power], *NCLS*, No. 93, December 1966.

Vien Su Hoc, *May Van De ve Chien Thang Lich Su Dien Bien Phu* [Some Questions about the Historical Victory at Dien Bien Phu] Hanoi: NXB Khoa Hoc Xa Hoi, 1985.

Viet Nam Dan Chu Cong Hoa [The Democratic Republic of Vietnam], *Tong Tuyen Cu Ngay 6–1–1945* [The General Election of 6–1–1945], Hanoi, 1945.

────· *Van Quoc Ngu* [Learning the National Language], Hanoi: Bo Quoc Gia Giao Duc, 1945.

Vu Tho, 'Tu *Duong Cach Menh* den *Luan Cuong Chinh Tri cua Dang Cong San Dong Duong*' [From *The Road to Revolution* to the *Political Theses of the Indochinese Communist Party*], *NCLS*, No. 72, March 1975.

Vuong Kha Lam (Huynh Thi Bao Hoa), *Chiem Thanh Luoc Khao* [An Outline History of Champa], Hanoi, 1936

2. Western Language Sources

Adelman, Jonathan R., *Revolution Armies and War*, Boulder, Colorado: Lynne Rienner, 1985.

Anderson, Benedict, *Imagined Communities: Reflections on the Origins and Spread of Nationalism*, London: Verso, 1983.

Anonymous, 'La Défense de l'Indochine', *Revue des Deux Mondes*, XXXII, Mars-Avril, 1906.

Anonymous, 'Jeunes Armées', *Sud-Est*, No. 7, Juillet, 1949.

Arendt, Hannah, *On Revolution*, New York: The Viking Press, 1963.

Axelrad, Edouard, 'Nguyen Binh', *Indochine Sud Est Asiatique*, No. 7, Juin, 1952.

Battye, N.A., 'The Military, Government, and Society in Siam, 1886–1910: Politics and Military Reform During the Reign of King Chulalongkorn', PhD, Cornell Universitys, 1974.

Bauchar, René, *Rafales sur l'Indochine*, Paris, 1946.

Baugher, Peter Frederic, 'The Contradictions of Colonialism: The French Experience in Indochina, 1860–1940', PhD, University of Wisconsin-Madison, 1980.

Baulmont, Lieutenant, 'Les Troupes du Dai Viet Quoc', *Revue Indochinoise*, Octobre, 1905.

——· 'Nos Premières Troupes Indigènes en Indochine', *Revue Indochinoise*, 1905.

——· 'La Prise de Tourane (Septembre 1858–7–8 Mai 1859–15 Septembre 1859), *Revue Indochinoise*, 1904. pp. 691–704, 1905, pp. 13–29.

Bernal, Martin, *Chinese Socialism to 1907*, Cornell University Press, 1976.

——· 'The Nghe-Tinh Soviet Movement', *Past and Present*, No. 92, August 1981.

Bernard, P., *Le problème économique indochinois*, Paris: Nouvelles Editions Latines, 1934.

Bissing, James Albert, 'The Admirals' Government: A History of the Naval Colony that was French Indochina', PhD, New York University, 1972.

Bodard, Lucien, 'Interview d'un général Viet Minh', *Sud-Est*, No. 16, Septembre 1950.

——· *La guerre d'Indochine* 5 Vols., Paris: Gallimard, 1963, 1965, 1967.

Boissière, Jules, *L'Indochine avec les française*, Paris: Plon, 1900.

Bonifacy, A.L.M., 'La Révolte de Nong Van Van', *Revue Indochinoise*, Juillet 1914.

Boudarel, Georges, 'Essai sur la pensée militaire vietnamiene', in Jean Chesneaux et al., *Tradition et révolution au Vietnam*, Paris: Editions Anthropos, 1971.

——· *Giap*, Paris, 1977.

——· et al., *La bureaucratie au Vietnam*, Paris: L'Harmattan , 1983.

——· 'Comment Giap a failli perdre la bataille de Dien Bien Phu', *Le Nouvel Observateur*, 8 Avril 1983.

Bower Bell, J., *The Myth of the Guerrilla*, New York, 1971.

Boyer de Latour, Pierre, *De l'Indochine à l'Algérie: Le Martyre de l'Armée française*, Paris: Les Presses du Mail, 1962.

Brocheux, P., 'L'Implantation du Mouvement Communist en Indochine Française: Le Cas du Nghe-Tinh 1930–1931', *Revue Historique et Contemporaine*, XXIV, 1977.

Buttinger, Joseph, *Vietnam: A Political History*, New York and Washington: Praeger, 1972.

Cadière L., et Pelliot, P., 'Le Mur de Dong Hoi: Etude sur l'Etablissement des Nguyen en Cochinchine, *BEFEO*, Vol. 6, 1906.

——· 'Les éléphants royaux', *Bulletin des Amis du Vieux Hue*, 1922.

Cady, J.T., *The Roots of French Imperialism in Eastern Asia*, Ithaca, 1954.

Chack, Paul, *Hoang Tham Pirate*, Paris, 1933.

Chaigneau, Michel Duc, *Souvenirs de Hue*, Paris, 1867.

Chen, King, *Vietnam and China 1938–1954*, Princeton University Press, 1969.

Chesneaux, Jean, *The Vietnamese Nation: Contribution to a History*, translated by Malcolm Salmon, Sydney, 1960 from *Contribution à l'histoire de la Nation Vietnamienne*, Paris: Editions Sociales, 1955.

——· et al., *Tradition et révolution au Vietnam*, éditions anthropos, 1971.

——· *Peasant Revolts in China, 1840–1949*, London, 1973.

Christian, Pierre, 'Le Viet Minh en Cambodge', *Indochine Sud-Est Asiatiqie*, Fevrier/Mars, 1952.

——· 'Son Ngoc Thanh', *Indochine Sud-Est Asiatique*, Octobre, 1952.

Cipolla, Carlo M., *Guns and Sails in the Early Phase of European Expansion, 1400–1700*, London, 1965.

Clausewitz, C. Von, *Vom Kriege*, Bonn: Ferd. Dümmlers Verlag, 1973; also the Michael Howard and Peter Paret translation, *On War*, Princeton University Press, 1984.

Cleremont, André, 'L'Economie Viet Minh', *Indochine Sud-Est Asiatique*, Juin/Juillet, 1953.

Cook, Megan, *The Constitutionalist Party in Cochinchina: The Years of Decline, 1930–1942*, Monash Papers on Southeast Asia, Number Six, Monash University, 1977.

Cooke, Nola, 'Proteges and Protectors: Relations Between The Protectorate Government and The Government of Annam, 1897–1925', M.A. thesis, University of Sydney, 1980.

Coughlin, M., 'Vietnam in China's Shadow', *JSEAH*, Vol. 8, No. 2, 1967.

Dan Hong et al., *The Ho Chi Minh Trail*, Hanoi, Foreign Languages Publishing House, 1982.

Daufès, E., *La Garde Indigène d'Indochine de sa création à nos jours*, 2 Vols., Avignon, 1933 and 1934.

De La Bissachère, *Etat actuel du Tunkin, de la Cochinchine, et des royaumes de Cambodge, Laos, et Lac-Tho*, 2 Vols., Paris: Galignani, 1812.

Dechaseaux, E., 'Notes sur les anciens Don Dien annamites dans la Basse Cochinchine', *Excursions et Reconnaissances*, XIV, 1889.

Delpey, R., *Soldats de la boue*, 4 Vols., Paris, 1949, 1951, 1952, 1953, 1954.

Dennis, Peter, *Troubled days of peace: Mountbatten and South East Asia command, 1945–46*, Manchester University Press, 1987.

Despuech, Jacques, *Le Trafic des piastres*, Paris: Deux-Rives, 1953.

Destroyat, Leonce, *La France dans l'Indo-Chine*, Paris: Librairie Ch. Delagrave, 1886.

Devéria, G., *Histoire des relations de la Chine avec l'Annam-Vietnam du XIVème au XIXème siècle*, Paris, 1880.

Devillers, Phillippe, *Histoire du Viet Nam de 1940 à 1952*, Paris : Seuil, 1952.

Devillers, Phillippe et Lacouture, Jean, *Viet Nam de la guerre francaise à la guerre américaine*, Paris: Seuil, 1969.

Duiker, William, 'The Revolutionary Youth League: Cradle of Communism in Vietnam', *China Quarterly*, July/September, 1972.

——·'The Red Soviets of Nghe-Tinh: An Early Communist Rebellion in Vietnam', *JSEAS*, IV, 2, September, 1973.

——· *The Rise of Nationalism in Vietnam 1900–1906*, Cornell University Press, 1976.

——· *The Communist Road to Power in Vietnam*, Boulder, Colorado: Westview Press, 1981.

——· *China and Vietnam: The Roots of Conflict*, Indochina Research Monograph, Institute of East Asian Studies, University of California, Berkeley, 1986.

Dumoutier, G., 'L'astrologie considerée plus spécialement dans ses applications à l'art militaire', *Revue Indochinoise*, 1914.

Dunn, William B., 'American Policy and Vietnamese Nationalism: 1950–1954', University of Chicago PhD, 1960.

Durrwell, Georges, 'Les colonies militaires dans la Basse-Cochinchine', *Bulletin de la Société des Etudes Indochinoises*, 1898.

Eastman, Lloyd E., *Throne and Mandarins*, Harvard University Press, 1967.

Elvin, Mark, *The Pattern of the Chinese Past*, Stanford University Press, 1975.

Engels, F., *The Peasant War in Germany*, New York, 1926.

——· *Engels as Military Critic*, Manchester University Press, 1959.

——· *Anti-Duhring*, in Tucker, Robert, ed., *The Marx-Engels Reader*, New York: Norton, 1972.

E-Tu Zen Sun and De Francis, J., *Chinese Social History: Translations of Selected Studies*, Washington, 1956.

Fall, Bernard B., *The Viet Minh Regime: Government and Admistration in the Democratic Republic of Vietnam*, Data Paper Number 14, Southeast Asia Program, Cornell University, April 1954.

——· 'Local Administration under the Viet Minh', *Pacific Affairs*, Number 1, 1954.

——· 'The Political-Religious Sects of Vietnam', *Pacific Affairs*, September 1955.

——· *Le Viet Minh, 1945–1950*, Paris, 1960.

——· *Street Without Joy*, Harrisburg: Stackpole Press, 1961.

——· *Viet-Nam Witness 1953–66*, London: Pall Mall Press, 1966.

——· *Hell in a Very Small Place*, Philadelphia: J.B. Lippincott, 1966.

——· *The Two Vietnams: A Political and Military Analysis*, London, 1967.

——· *Last Reflections on a War*, New York, 1967.

Félixine, Lucien, *L'Indochine livrée aux bourreaux*, Paris: Nouvelles Editions Latines, 1959.

Figuères, Leo, *Je reviens du Vietnam libre*, Paris, 1950.

Fonde, Général J.J., *Traitez à tout prix . . .Leclerc et le Viet-Nam*, Paris: Lafont, 1971.

——· 'Giap et le maquis de Cho Ra (Mars 1945–Mars 1946)', *Revue Historique des Armées*, No. 2, 1976.

Foreign Languages Publishing House, *Our Military Traditions: Vietnamese Studies*, No. 55, Edited by Nguyen Khac Vien, Hanoi, no date.

Fourniau, Charles, 'Les traditions de la lutte nationale au Vietnam: L'insurrection des lettrés, in Jean Chesneaux, et al., *Tradition et révolution au Vietnam*, Editions Anthropos, 1971.

Franchini, Philippe, *Les Guerres d'Indochine*, 2 Vols., Paris: Editions Pygmalion, 1980.

Gallieni, Général, *Gallieni au Tonkin (1892–1896)*, Paris: Editions Berger-Levrault, 1948.

Garstin, Crosbie, *The Dragon and the Lotus*, London, 1928.

Ginsburgs, George, 'Local Government and Administration in North Vietnam, 1945–1954', *China Quarterly*, No. 10, April/June, 1962.

Girardet, Raoul, *L'idée coloniale en France de 1871 à 1962*, Paris: La Table Ronde, 1972.

Gosselin, Charles, *L'Empire d'Annam*, Paris: Perrin, 1904.

Gourou, P., *Les Paysans de Delta Tonkinois: Etude de geographie humaine*, Paris, 1936.

Gras, Général Yves, *Histoire de la guerre d'Indochine*, Paris: Plon, 1979.

Griffith, Samuel B., translator, *The Art of War (Sun Tzu)*, Oxford: Clarendon Press, 1962, with an introduction by Griffith.

Guigues, Claude, 'Panoplie Viet Minh', *Indochine Sud-Est Asiatique*, No. 7, Juin, 1952.

——· 'Le Viet Minh au Laos', *Indochine Sud-Est Asiatique*, Novembre 1952.

Hammer, E., *The Struggle for Indochina*, Stanford University Press, 1954.

Harrison, James Pinckney, *The Endless War: Fifty Years of Struggle in Vietnam*, London: Macmillan, 1982.

Hémery, Daniel, *Révolutionnaires vietnamiens et pouvoir colonial en Indochine*, Paris: François Maspero, 1975.

Herring, George, *America's Longest War: The United States and Vietnam 1950–1975*, New York: John Wiley, 1979.

Hoang Minh Thao, *The Victorious Tay Nguyen Campaign*, Hanoi: Foreign Languages Publishing House, 1979.

Hoang Van Chi, *From Colonialism to Communism: A Case History of North Vietnam*, New York, Praeger, 1954.

Hodgkin, Thomas, *Vietnam: The Revolutionary Path*, London: Macmillan, 1981.

Honey, P.J., translator, *Voyage to Tonkin in the Year At Hoi (1876)*, School of Oriental and African Studies, University of London, 1982. The work was originally written in Vietnamese by P.J.B. Truong Vinh Ky and published in 1881 under the title *Chuyen di Bac ki.*

Hue-Tam Ho Tai, *Millenarianism and Peasant Politics in Vietnam*, Cambridge, Mass.: Harvard East Asian Series, No. 99, 1983.

Hulse, James, W., *The Forming of the Communist International*, Stanford University Press, 1964.

Huynh Kim Khanh, 'The Vietnamese August Revolution Reinterpreted', *Journal of Asian Studies*, 30, 4, August, 1971.

——· *Vietnamese Communism, 1925–1945*, Cornell University Press, 1982.

Irving, R.E.M., *The First Indochina War*, London, 1975.

Isoart, Paul, *Le phénomène national vietnamien*, Paris: Librairie Générale de Droit et de Jurisprudence, 1976.

Kahin, George McTurnan, *Intervention: How America Became Involved in Vietnam*, New York: Knopf, 1986.

Kierman, Frank A., and Fairbank, John F., *Chinese Ways in Warfare*, Harvard University Press, 1974.

Kiernan, Ben, and Boua, Chanthou, *Peasants and Politics in Kampuchea*, London: Zed Press, 1982.

Kiernan, V.G., *Marxism and Imperialism*, London, 1974.

Kolko, Gabriel, *Vietnam: Anatomy of a War, 1940–1975*, London and Sydney, Allen and Unwin, 1985.

Langlet, Philippe, 'Point de vue sur Nguyen Truong To et le réformisme vietnamien au milieu du XIX ème siècle', *Etudes Interdisciplinaires sur le Viet-nam*, Saigon,Vol. 1, 1974, pp. 179–195.

Laqueur, Walter, *Guerrilla*, Boston, 1976.

Lawson, Eugene K., *The Sino-Vietnamese Conflict*, New York: Praeger Special Studies, 1984.

Le, Nicolle Dominique, *Les missions étrangères et la pénetration française au Viet-Nam*, Paris: Mouton, 1975.

Lebas, J., 'Le Mouvement de Jeuness en Indochine', *L'Indochine*, 2, No. 57, Mai 1951.

Lenin, V.I., *Selected Works*, 5 Vols., Moscow: Foreign Languages Publishing House, 1967.

—— *Leninist Strategy and Tactics*, Moscow: Novosti Press, 1970.

Le Thanh Khoi, *Le Vietnam: Histoire et Civilisation*, Paris: Editions de Minuit, 1955.

—— *Histoire du Vietnam des origines à 1858*, Paris: Sudestasie, 1981.

Levy, Roger, *Regards sur l'Indochine*, Paris, 1952.

Lewis, Norman, *A Dragon Apparent*, London: Jonathan Cape, 1951.

Lin Piao, 'Long Live The Victory of People's War', *Peking Review*' September 2, 1965.

Loewald, Uyen, *Child of Vietnam*, Melbourne: Hyland House, 1987.

Mao Tse Tung, *China's New Democracy*, Sydney, August, 1955.

—— *Selected Military Writings*, Peking: Foreign Languages Press, 1965.

Mao Tse Tung and Che Guevara, *Guerrilla Warfare*, London, 1965.

Marr, David G., *Vietnamese Anticolonialism*, University of California, Berkeley, Los Angeles, London, 1971.

—— 'World War Two and the Vietnamese Revolution' in Alfred W. McCoy, editor, *Southeast Asia Under Japanese Occupation*, Monograph Series No. 22, Yale University, 1980.

—— *Vietnamese Tradition on Trial 1920–1945*, University of California, Berkeley, Los Angeles, London, 1981.

Martin, Francoise, *Heures tragiques au Tonkin*, Paris, 1948.

Marx, Karl., *The Eighteenth Brumaire of Louis Bonaparte* and *The Civil War in France*, both in Tucker, Robert, editor, *The Marx-Engels Reader*, New York: Norton, 1972.

Marx, Karl and Engels F., *On Colonialism*, Moscow, no date (1950s?).

Maybon, Charles, *Histoire Moderne des pays d'Annam 1592–1820*, Paris: Plon, 1920.

McAleavy, Henry, *Black Flags in Vietnam*, London: Allen and Unwin, 1968.

McAlister, Jr., John T., 'The Origins of the Vietnamese Revolution', PhD, Yale University, 1966, published as *Vietnam: The Origins of Revolution*, New York: Alfred A. Knopf, 1969.

—— 'Mountain Minorities and the Viet Minh: A Key to the Indochina War', in Peter Kunstadter, editor, *Southeast Asian Tribes, Minorities, and Nations*, 2 Vols., Princeton University Press, 1967.

McAlister, Jr., John T. and Paul Mus, *The Vietnamese and Their Revolution*, New York: Harper and Row, 1970.

McKenzie, Kermit, *Comintern and World Revolution*, New York, 1964.

Meyer, Alfred G., *Leninism*, Harvard, 1957.

Mus, Paul, *Le Vietnam chez lui*, Paris: Centre d'études politiques étrangères, 1946.

—— 'The role of the Village in Vietnamese Politics', *Pacific Affairs*, September 1949.

—— *Vietnam: sociologie d'une guerre*, Paris: Seuil, 1952.

Ness, Gayl D., 'Western Imperialist Armies in Asia', *Comparative Studies in Society and History*, 19, 1977.

Ngo Vinh Long, *Before the Revolution: The Vietnamese Peasants under the French*, Cambridge: MIT Press, 1973.

Nguyen Khac Vien, *Tradition and Revolution in Vietnam*, Berkeley: Indochina Resource Centre, 1975.

—— *The Long Resistance, 1858–1975*, Hanoi: Foreign Languages Publishing House, 1975.

—— editor, *Vietnamese Studies, Number 55, Our Military Traditions*, Hanoi, no date.

Nguyen The Anh, 'Traditionalisme et réformisme à la cour de Hue dans la seconde moitié du XIX ème siècle', in Pierre Brocheux, *Histoire de l'Asie du Sud-Est: Révoltes, réformes, révolutions*, Presses Universitaires de Lille, 1981.

—— *The Withering Days of the Nguyen Dynasty*, Research Notes and Discussions No. 7, Institute of Southeast Asian Studies, Singapore, 1978.

O'Ballance, Edgar, *The Indochina War*, London, 1964.

Osborne, Milton, 'Rule and Response: Interaction in Cambodia and Cochinchina (1859–1905)', PhD, Cornell University, 1968.

—— 'Continuity and Motivation in the Vietnamese Revolution', *Pacific Affairs*, Spring, 1974.

Pagniez, Yvonne, *Le Viet Minh et la Guerre Psychologique*, Paris, 1955.

Pérez, P. Lorenzo, 'Les Espagnols dans l'empire d'Annam', *Bulletin de la Société des Etudes Indochinoises*, Tome XV, No. 3/4, 1940.

Pham Quynh, 'Pham Quynh', *Sud-Est*, No. 13, Juin 1950.

Phan Thanh Son, 'Le mouvement ouvrier de 1920 à 1920', in Jean Chesneaux, et al., *Tradition et révolution au Vietnam*, Páris: éditions anthropos, 1971.

Phung Van Dan, 'La Formation Territoriale du Vietnam', *Revue du Sud-Est Asiatique*, 1963.

Pike, Douglas, *The Vietcong: The Organisations and Techniques of the National Liberation Front*, Cambridge, Mass., 1966.

—— *History of Vietnamese Communism, 1925–1976*, Stanford, 1976.

—— *PAVN: People's Army of Vietnam*, Novato: Presido Press, 1986.

Popkin, Samuel L., *The Rational Peasant: The Political Economy of Rural Society in Vietnam*, University of California Press, 1978.

Porter, Gareth, 'Imperialism and Social Structures in Twentieth Century Vietnam', PhD, Cornell University, 1976.

Randle, Robert F., *Geneva 1954: The Settlement of the Indochinese War*, Princeton University Press, 1969.

Reznikov, A., *Lenin and Revolution in the East*, Moscow, 1969.

Roberts, Stephen A., *History of French Colonial Policy, 1870–1925*, 2 Vols., London, 1929.

Rocolle, Pierre, *Porquoi Dien Bien Phu?*, Paris: Flammarion, 1968.

Rosie, George, *The British in Vietnam: How the Twenty Five Year War Began*, London: Panther, 1970.

Rouyer, Capitaine, *Histoire militaire et politique de l'Annam et du Tonkin depuis 1799*, Paris: Lavauzelle, 1906.

Ruscio, A., *Les communistes française et la guerre d'indochine (1944–1945)*, Paris: L'Harmattan, 1985.

—— *Dien Bien Phu: La fin d'une illusion*, Paris: L'Harmattan, 1986.

Sampson, Cedric Allen, 'Nationalism and Communism in Vietnam 1925–1931', PhD, University of California, Los Angeles, 1975.

Savani, A.M., *Visage et images du Sud Vietnam*, Saigon, 1955.

Schreiner, A., *Les institutions annamites en Basse Cochinchine avant la conquête francqise*, Saigon, 3 Vol., 1901.

Scott, James C., *The Moral Economy of the Peasant: Rebellion and Subsistence in Southeast Asia*, Yale University Press, 1978.

Spence, Jonathan D., *The Gate of Heavenly Peace: The Chinese and Their Revolution 1895–1980*, Penguin, 1982.

Smith, Ralph, B., 'Politics and Society in Vietnam During the Early Nguyen Period, 1802–1862', *Journal of the Royal Asiatic Society*, 1974, pp. 153–169.

—— 'The Japanese Period in Indochina and the Coup of 9 March 1945', *JSEAH*, 9, 2, September 1978.

—— *An International History of the Vietnam War*, New York: St. Martin's Press, Vol. 1, 1983.

Taboulet, G., *La geste française en Indochine*, 2 Vols., Paris: A. Maisonneuve, 1955 and 1956.

Tai Quang Trung, *Collective Leadership and Factionalism*, Institute of Southeast Asian Studies, Singapore 1985.

Tanham, George K., *Communist Revolutionary Warfare: The Viet Minh in Indochina*, London, 1962.

Taylor, Keith Weller, *The Birth of Vietnam*, University of California Press, 1983.

Teuliers, André, *La guerre de Viet Nam 1947–1975*, Paris: Lavauzelle, Paris, 1979.

Thayer, Carlyle, 'The Origins of the National Front for the Liberation of South Vietnam', Australian National University PhD, 1977.

Thomazi, A., *La Conquête de l'Indochine*, Paris: Payot, 1934.

Tonnesson, Stein, *1946: le déclenchement de la guerre d'Indochine*, Paris: L'Harmattan, 1987.

Trager, F., *Marxism in Southeast Asia*, Stanford University Press, 1959.

Tran Cong Tan, et al., *The One Eyed Elephant and the Elephant Genie*, Hanoi: Foreign Languages Publishing House, 1959.

Trotsky, Leon, *The History of the Russian Revolution*, London, Pluto Press, 1977.

Truong Buu Lam, *Patterns of Vietnamese Response to Foreign Intervention, 1858–1900*, Southeast Asia Studies, Yale University Monograph Series 11, 1967.

Truong Chinh, *Selected Works*, Hanoi: Foreign Languages Publishing House, 1977.

Tuck, Patrick, J.N., *French Catholic Missionaries and the Politics of Imperialism in Vietnam, 1857–1914: A Documentary Survey*, Liverpool University Press, 1987.

Turley, William S., 'Army, Party, and Society in the Democratic Republic of

Vietnam: Civil and Military Relations in a Mass Mobilization System', PhD, University of Washington, 1972.

——· ed., *Vietnamese Communism in Comparative Perspective*, Boulder, Colorado: Westview Press, 1980.

——· *The Second Indochina War: A Short Political and Military History, 1954–1975*, Boulder, Colorado: Westview Press, 1986.

——· 'The Vietnamese Army', in Jonathan R. Adelman, editor, *Communist Armies in Politics*, Boulder, Colorado, Westview Press, 1982.

Turley, William S. and Halpern, J.M., editors, *The Training of Vietnamese Cadres in Laos*, Brussels, 1977.

Turner, R.F., *Vietnamese Communism: Its Origins and Development*, Stanford University Press, 1975.

Ungar, Esta Serne, 'Vietnamese Leadership and Order: Dai Viet Under the Le Dynasty', Cornell University PhD, 1983.

Valentine, Daniel Bart, 'The British Facilitation of the French Re-Entry into Vietnam', PhD, University of California, Los Angeles, 1971.

Van Tien Dung, *Our Great Spring Victory*, Translated by John Spragens Jr., New York and London: Monthly Review Press, 1977.

Vella, W., editor, *Aspects of Vietnamese History*, University of Hawaii, 1973.

Vickerman, Andrew, *The Fate of the Peasantry: Premature 'Transition to Socialism' in the Democratic Republic of Vietnam*, Monograph Series Number 28, Yale University Southeast Asia Studies, Yale Center for International and Area Studies, 1986.

Vo Nguyen Giap, *Unforgettable Days*, Hanoi: Foreign-Languages Publishing House, 1978.

Vo Nhan Tri, *Croissance economique de la république démocratique du Viet Nam*, Hanoi: Editions en Langues Etrangères, 1967.

Vu Chieu Ngu, 'Political and Social Change in Vietnam Between 1940 and 1945', PhD, University of Wisconsin-Madison, 1984.

Vu Quoc Thong, *La décentralisation administrative au Viet Nam*, Hanoi: Presses Universites du Viet Nam, 1952.

Wales, H.Q.G., *Ancient South-East Asian Warfare*, London, 1952.

Werner, Jayne Susan, 'The Cao Dai: The Politics of a Vietnamese Syncretic Religious Movement', PhD, Cornell University, 1976.

——· *Peasant Politics and Religious Sectarianism: Peasant and Priest in the Cao Dai in Vietnam*, Monograph Series No. 23, Yale University, Southeast Asia Studies, 1981.

White, Christine P., translator, Truong Chinh and Vo Nguyen Giap, *The Peasant Question*, Data paper No. 14, Southeast Asia Program, Cornell University, January 1974.

——· 'Agrarian Reform and National Liberation in the Vietnamese Revolution, 1920–1957', PhD, Cornell University, January 1981.

Whitmore, J.K., 'The Development of Le Government in Fifteenth Century Vietnam', PhD, Cornell University, 1968.

Whitson, William, *The Chinese High Command*, London, 1973.

Woodside, A.B., 'Early Ming Expansion (1400–1427): China's Abortive Conquest of Vietnam', *Papers on China*, XVIII, East Asia Research Center, Harvard University, 1963.

—— *Vietnam and the Chinese Model*, Harvard University Press, 1971.
—— *Community and Revolution in Modern Vietnam*, Boston: Houghton and Mifflin, 1976.
Yoshiharu Tsuboi, *L'Empire Vietnamien face à la France et à la Chine*, Paris: L'Harmattan, 1987.

Index

Administration, 8, 11; Chinese models for, 14; in nineteenth century, 15–16; resistance administration, 193–196; related to strategy, 196; decentralisation of, 196; major changes in, 223; see French colonialism; see Viet Minh

Algeria, 47

Allesandri, Général Marcel, 112

American: revolution, 58; support for Viet Minh, 131; atomic bombing of Japan, 133; intervention anticipated, 198; plans to support Bao Dai frustrated, 228; State Department, 228; defeats in Korea, 231; goading of French, 255; efforts to divide Vietnam, 266, 267–268; attitude to Bao Dai, 268; Military Assistance Command Vietnam, 269; 'loss of China', 269; Army, 270; bombing, 270; experience parallels that of French, 271–272; see Military aid

Ammunition, 118, 121, 225, 251; portered from Chinese border, 259; resupplies for Dien Bien Phu, 262; expended at Dien Bien Phu, 263; see Military aid (from China)

Anderson, Ben, 5

Anti-aircraft units, 251, 260

Anti-French Resistance War, 145, 205

Anti-Japanese Resistance War, 112–113, 117, 127–129

Anti-War Movement in France, 198

Armed demonstrations, 137

Armed propaganda, 8, 11, 75, 92–95, 104–05, 112–120, 126–132, 158, 161, 164, 172, 196–205, 213–214, 215, 217–219, 221, 246, 250, 253; definition of, 92–95; 'Flash effect' of, 116, 139, 140; and seizure of power in August, 133–143; pumps up government, 148–149, 264

Army for National Salvation (AFNS), 86–87, 92, 99, 101, 117, 121, 123

Army of National Defence, 162; development in north in 1946, 164–165, 173–180; attacks conservative opposition, 171; complex nature of, 172; feeding of, 174; size of in 1946, 175; recruitment of old colonial soldiers, 175–176; French